UNIX®
SYSTEM
ADMINISTRATOR'S

INTERACTIVE WORKBOOK

JOE KAPLENK

Prentice Hall PTR
Upper Saddle River, NJ 07458
http://www.phptr.com

D1534559

ISBN 0-13-081308-7

90000

9 780130 813084

Editorial/production Supervision: *Kathleen M. Caren*
Acquisitions editor: *Mark L. Taub*
Development editor: *Ralph E. Moore*
Marketing manager: *Dan Rush*
Manufacturing manager: *Alexis R. Heyd*t
Editorial assistant: *Audri Anna Bazlen*
Cover design director: *Jerry Votta*
Cover Designer: *Anthony Gemmelaro*
Art director: *Gail Cocker-Bogusz*
Series design: *Meryl Poweski*
Web site project manager: *Yvette Raven*

 © 1999 Prentice Hall PTR
Prentice-Hall, Inc.
A Simon & Schuster Company
Upper Saddle River, New Jersey 07458

Prentice Hall books are widely used by corporations and government agencies for training, marketing, and resale. The publisher offers discounts on this book when ordered in bulk quantities.
For more information, contact: Corporate Sales Department, Phone: 800-382-3419;
FAX: 201-236-7141; email: corpsales@prenhall.com
Or write: Corp. Sales Dept., Prentice Hall PTR, 1 Lake Street, Upper Saddle River, NJ 07458

Printed in the United States of America
10   9   8   7   6   5   4   3   2   1

ISBN 0-13-081308-7

Prentice-Hall International (UK) Limited, *London*
Prentice-Hall of Australia Pty. Limited, *Sydney*
Prentice-Hall Canada Inc., *Toronto*
Prentice-Hall Hispanoamericana, S.A., *Mexico*
Prentice-Hall of India Private Limited, *New Delhi*
Prentice-Hall of Japan, Inc., *Tokyo*
Simon & Schuster Asia Pte. Ltd., *Singapore*
Editora Prentice-Hall do Brasil, Ltda., *Rio de Janeiro*

DEDICATION

This book is dedicated to my parents,
Joe and Elizabeth Kaplenk, both of whom have passed away.
It is through them that I have gained my often
unique perspective and approach to life.

It is also dedicated to the many students that have
endured a number of versions of my workbook in order to
come up with the approach I have used here.

CONTENTS

FROM THE EDITOR

Prentice Hall's Interactive Workbooks are designed to get you up and running fast, with just the information you need, when you need it.

We are certain that you will find our unique approach to learning simple and straightforward. Every chapter of every Interactive Workbook begins with a list of clearly defined Learning Objectives. A series of labs make up the heart of each chapter. Each lab is designed to teach you specific skills in the form of exercises. You perform these exercises at your computer and answer pointed questions about what you observe. Your answers will lead to further discussion and exploration. Each lab then ends with multiple-choice Self-Review Questions, to reinforce what you've learned. Finally, we have included Test Your Thinking projects at the end of each chapter. These projects challenge you to synthesize all of the skills you've acquired in the chapter.

Our goal is to make learning engaging, and to make you a more productive learner.

And you are not alone. Each book is integrated with its own "Companion Website." The website is a place where you can find more detailed information about the concepts discussed in the Workbook, additional Self-Review Questions to further refine your understanding of the material, and perhaps most importantly, where you can find a community of other Interactive Workbook users working to acquire the same set of skills that you are.

All of the Companion Websites for our Interactive Workbooks can be found at `http://www.phptr.com/phptrinteractive`.

Mark L. Taub
Editor-in-Chief
Prentice Hall PTR Interactive

ABOUT THE AUTHOR

 Everyone has a story to tell. Some tell it in person, some in pictures and some in words. Every person is an individual. Every story is different and every situation is unique. So the number of stories is infinite.

EDUCATION

The author, Joe Kaplenk, graduated with a Physics degree from the University of Utah. He also studied Mathematics, Chemistry, Biology, and Journalism on an undergraduate and graduate level. His first writing experience was in college, where he served as the Science Editor and Reporter for the Daily Utah Chronicle. He has also attended undergraduate college at Orange County Community College in Middletown, NY where he majored in Physical Science. This was followed by a Mathematics major at Rensselaer Polytechnic Institute in Troy, NY. He has also studied Computer Science classes at the University of Illinois at Chicago, College of Dupage, Joliet Junior College, and a number of non-credit seminars. His first experience with computers was in 1967 with an IBM mainframe that did not even have a disk or tape drive and the operating system was loaded from punch cards. He is actively involved in the computer world through Usenet and his e-mail. He can be found hanging around the net-abuse, Solaris, Linux, and skating newsgroups.

WORK EXPERIENCE

Joe's experience includes working in Physics and Computer Science for Argonne National Labs, Fermi National Accelerator Lab, the University of Illinois at Chicago Physics Dept., Motorola, Loyola University Chicago, R.R. Donnelley, and Comdisco. He currently works for IBM Global Services as a UNIX System Administrator. He has been working with UNIX since 1980.

TEACHING EXPERIENCE

Joe has been teaching part-time at the College of Dupage in Glen Ellyn, Illinois for over 13 years. His experience includes teaching classes in Introduction to Computers, Program Logic and Design, Pascal, FORTRAN, Basic, Introduction to UNIX, and Advanced UNIX. He has been teaching Advanced UNIX for six years.

This current book is based on his experience in teaching those classes and is the outcome of his constant search for a good textbook to teach UNIX Administration. Because he could not find a good text, he wrote his own and has been using an earlier version of this text for several years now.

OUTSIDE LIFE

Joe's enjoys spending time with his wife Ramona and daughter Anisa, likes to visit museums, enjoys skating, and the outdoors.

Joe has achieved some notoriety in the skating world. He has been an active ice, roller, and inline skater. He served as the first chair of the United States Figure Skating Association (USFSA) Adult Skaters Advisory Committee from 1992 to 1995 and as the chair of the Adult Nationals Task Force. He was actively involved in getting the first adult figure skating national championships started in 1995. At the age of 48, his first year of competition in roller skating, he went to the Junior Olympics in Sacramento, CA, where he placed 11th in figures. He was also a charter member of the International Inline Skating Association. He has studied skating under some of the top skating coaches in the Chicago area.

Joe enjoys country music. He plays guitar, keyboard, and has written many songs, some of which have been rated as "very good" by other professional song writers. His voice instructor in Nashville, Renee Grant Williams, has been the instructor for many top country and pop singers.

INTRODUCTION

 The only way to really learn administration is to get your feet wet and your hands burnt.

—Joe

It is difficult to learn UNIX or any computer operating system without being an administrator. I have not yet found a book that can satisfactorily teach UNIX in an academic or commercial training environment. That is the reason for this book.

Being a UNIX administrator is something that is learned by hands-on experience and by fixing problems. Some of the assignments and programs in this book will not work properly. Most of this is intentional. Some errors are accidental. It is up to the student to find any problems and fix them. The only way to really learn is get your feet wet and your hands burnt. However, if you really think something is an error, please let me know.

This text emphasizes generic UNIX as much as possible. Much effort has been made at helping you to think like a UNIX administrator. So some exercises will be entirely academic and not something that you can directly apply to your work. Other exercises will be directly applicable to your work or future work. There will be some exercises that will be run in Solaris, and there will be others that run in Linux. Whenever differences between running UNIX on the various versions are known, they will be pointed out. Every attempt will be made to run on other versions of UNIX. If there are some versions that need a variant of what is in this text, please let me know and I will consider including it in the next version of this text.

LINUX, a fully-functional freeware version of UNIX, gives the student the ability to administer a UNIX system in a relatively inexpensive manner. Linux can be installed in many environments and can coexist on the same PC as DOS/Windows/NT. By merely doing a dual or multiple boot, the student can run each of the operating systems at separate times. In one of the Appendixes in this book, you will see how to set up a dual/multiple boot environment.

In a commercial or industrial training environment, PCs or UNIX systems can be dedicated to training. After a class is finished, the system can be wiped out and rebuilt. These classes are usually limited to a week or less in duration.

In an academic environment, the student is generally limited to doing assignments on the UNIX system. There, an attempt is being made to emulate acting as an administrator. This is because colleges do not have the resources to dedicate a PC to UNIX for a term and cannot dedicate a UNIX system to a single user. This would be necessary for a student to really have control of the learning process and control of the system. So, because many—dare I say most—students have their own PCs, it should not be difficult to have the students run all of their assignments off their own PCs. They can have total control of the box and of what they do. Some colleges could and do require this as a prerequisite for some classes.

Besides running Linux off the hard disk. There are ways to run it off a CD-ROM. Yggdrasil LINUX, 1995 and earlier version, can be run entirely off the CD-ROM and files can be saved or executed off of diskette and from RAM. This allows you to get around some of the restrictions present in an academic environment. Appendix C discusses how you can do this. Assignments have been designed or modified with this in mind. Further discussion of these issues are in the pages that follow for the student and for the instructor.

Much emphasis is placed on using the **man** pages and other online help. The **man** pages are a very important tool for students and administrators. This book tries to include information you can't find online or in the required textbooks. It also tries to avoid duplicating information that would be in your texts.

Good luck, and I hope you have an excellent learning experience.

—Joe

Notes to the Student

The main focus of education is the student. However, there are many kinds of students and perhaps just as many ways of learning.

—*Joe*

Each chapter is this interactive workbook is divided into a number of sections. Each chapter section is designed to stand alone as much as possible. There are answers and hints that are available for the looking. Much emphasis has been placed on using standard UNIX tools such as man and help. I have tried to avoid rewriting the man pages, but assume you have access to them.

There is some duplication from one section to another in order to emphasize the concepts learned up to that point. This is an attempt to repeat something from a different angle that might be harder to learn or may have given a number of people problems.

If you are learning UNIX on your own, it is essential that you have a system that you can totally control. In the traditional UNIX corporate or education environment, it is difficult to find a box that it is totally free.

A version of UNIX, called Linux, allows you to do such a thing. It runs on your PC and does not affect the current software on your disk. You will see in one of the chapters in the Appendix how you can use Linux to share your PC and disks with other operating systems. You can even run Linux totally off a CD-ROM if necessary.

If you are in an academic environment with an instructor, you usually cannot have system administrative access to a UNIX system. There are too many concerns about security in such an environment. So usually you have access to a UNIX box as a regular user only. Fortunately, UNIX is a very open environment. Things are not hidden unless it is absolutely essential. So you can look at most of the system files and even copy them and edit them as a regular user. You just can't modify the critical system files in their original location, or copy your modified files back. Therefore, there is also an emphasis in this text to you looking at files, modifying them, and then seeing if the changes would give the desired effect if they were implemented.

If you are in a commercial training environment, this is perhaps the best possibility for learning administration. You generally have a system that is totally under your control. At worst, you will be sharing the box with one or two others. When you start the class, the system will usually have been totally rebuilt from scratch. This is like have a blank canvas ready to be painted on. So now you can change the system, install software, remove software, make mistakes, and so forth, and all without having to worry about the long-term effects.

Still, learning administration is very much as self-directed activity. It requires persistence, courage, and sometimes a bit of abandon to try new ideas and see the effects.

This book is broken down into various topics that try to highlight certain aspects of administration. There is no way that all the topics needed can be covered in detail. So emphasis is placed on developing a way of thinking that can be used as a basis to develop your skills.

As a result, each chapter is divided into the following sections:

- Chapter Objectives.
- Introduction to the chapter, with general discussion.
- Labs related to the chapter topic. This is broken down into sections, as explained next.
- Test Your Thinking, which are projects that are designed to have you utilize all of the skills you should have learned in the chapter. Answers to these projects are available on this book's Companion Web Site, located at http://www.phptr.com/phptrinteractive/.

Each Lab is then divided into five parts, as follows:

- Lab Objectives
- Lab Introduction (with examples)
- Exercises
- Exercise Answers (with discussion)
- Self-Review Questions

You are encouraged to submit questions, answers, and any ideas that you may have to the contacts listed at the Companion Web Site.

NOTES TO THE INSTRUCTOR

 The challenge for the instructor is to teach in the quickest and most effective way. Different teachers have different approaches, but each must work within constraints that are often outside of their control.

—Joe

This book has been written for the teacher that is often faced with constraints that are placed by budget, security, time, or politics. Teaching system administration is not one of those traditional topics that come immediately to mind when we think of an academic environment. Yet there are many colleges, community colleges, technical institutes, corporate, and commercial training environments where system administration is a very important part of the curriculum.

There are a number of different training environments in which you may be involved. But they fall into two basic categories, with variations in each:

- An academic credit course—This usually runs for a full term, is assigned credit, and the student is given a grade.
- A commercial, corporate, or non-credit college training program—This is short-term, usually several days to a week, and does not involve college credit or grades and the student's attention is wholly focused on the class.

Each one of these approaches has their own particular concerns.

AN ACADEMIC CREDIT ENVIRONMENT

This is a college, university, or community college where the class is set up so that college credit is granted to students taking the class. These classes typically run for a full term or more. Their environment usually has PCs set up to access a network. Only the fortunate ones will actually have dedicated UNIX boxes. The PCs are typically Microsoft Windows-based PCs. Many times they don't have a hard drive at all, but boot entirely off the network. However, as Windows software has become more demanding, the PCs often do have disk drives.

The concerns in such an environment focus around two issues: Computer Integrity and Network Integrity.

COMPUTER INTEGRITY

In such an environment, there are many concerns about security. Students often download software with viruses—sometimes accidentally, sometimes otherwise. Such PCs often get other software accidentally or intentionally loaded onto them. Therefore anything, such as a live full-blown UNIX operating system on a PC that the students can fully administer, gives nightmares to the administrators of the network and PCs. Even doing a dual boot system still leaves the PC open to abuse.

Some of the solutions include:

- Running Linux off a CD-ROM, as is possible with Yggrasil Linux.
- Having two hard drives on a system and making one write-protected via hardware configuration or jumpers and the other writable and easy to rebuild via the network and a boot disk.
- Having a separate computer lab for UNIX. This is often difficult to achieve and may not make the most use of the available systems. In many cases, the PCs are used for Windows applications and classroom space is sometimes at a premium. However, if the school is upgrading their 486, or even 386, PCs to new Pentiums, they can find new life as Linux boxes because Linux can run very happily with a single user on a 386 box. A 486 in this case would be a luxury. There are also a number of vendors, such as Sun and SCO, that make UNIX versions that happily run on a 486 PC with 16 MB of memory.

NETWORK INTEGRITY

There is a concern that if a student can have root access on such a system, they can perhaps compromise the network. This is because the root user in UNIX has access to many network tools that are not present on the Windows PC. A student may accidentally or intentionally do something that can bring down the network.

There are a number of solutions to the network security problem. The classroom or user area where UNIX is being run can be easily isolated from the rest of the network. A router blocks TCP/IP traffic—except traffic that meets certain criteria. It can block indiscriminate packets from getting through and damaging the network integrity.

An even better way of isolating the network would be to use a firewall, which would protect the campus network's integrity even further. A firewall does add additional processing over what a router would do, so performance needs should be looked at also. Fortunately, UNIX and particularly Linux, provide router and firewall capabilities either with the operating system or just a click away on the Internet. Another option would be to totally isolate the network used to teach system administration from the rest of the campus network.

Thus, putting together a system that can be administered in an academic environment may require many special steps. However, the concerns outlined here may not be an important enough issue in some academic situations, so your mileage may vary.

A SHORT-TERM NON-CREDIT TRAINING ENVIRONMENT

Putting together a UNIX training environment for a commercial or short-term non-credit academic program is a lot simpler. These are classes that usually run for several days to a week. The systems are dedicated to the current training process. Students either have a system that is all theirs or they share it with one or two other students. The boxes are usually reloaded with software whenever a new class is started. Thus, system integrity is not a major concern. Also, network integrity is not as much of an issue, because each classroom can be totally isolated from the others if needed.

Because the focus is on UNIX, any UNIX servers can be put totally on that network or can have a separate access point or network interface card to other more central servers that may be needed. This way everyone else can be isolated from that network. The students need not see any other networks. If the classroom is needed for a different type of class afterwards, cables can be easily moved in a wiring closet to put the classroom on a new network. This method of teaching UNIX is a lot simpler to manage because of its dedicated function of doing one thing at a time.

FURTHER DISCUSSION FOR THE INSTRUCTOR

 You will note in the student's discussion area that each chapter is broken down into sections. In addition, all questions and projects have the answers readily available. This text is designed to supplement whatever other training materials you may be using. Therefore, you should choose those materials with this in mind. Visit the Web companion to this book, at `http://www.phptr.com/phptrinteractive`, for further areas of discussion that might help make your teaching easier. Some of the exercises can be done by a regular user, while others require root access. Whenever possible, exercises are designed to be done by a regular user. This is book is not an exhaustive treatment of UNIX, but is designed to get a student's mental juices flowing. Any comments, ideas, or suggestions would be greatly appreciated.

ACKNOWLEDGMENTS

Many thanks go to Ralph Moore, the development editor, who has been very helpful in reviewing the text for technical, grammatical, spelling, and various other issues. He has been very instrumental in helping develop the format you see in this book.

I'd like to thank Jeff Gitlin, the technical reviewer, for keeping me honest.

I'd also like to thank my wife, Ramona, for her patience and her assistance in reviewing much of the text for grammatical errors.

Many thanks go to the College of Dupage in Glen Ellyn, IL, for their assistance in allowing me to develop the previous versions of the workbook. They have allowed me the flexibility to explore new methods of teaching UNIX administration. This is a topic that is hard to teach in an academic environment.

Finally, thanks go to Mark Taub, the managing editor at Prentice-Hall, for giving me the opportunity to write this book and guiding me through the many steps necessary to get this book to print.

ABOUT THE WEB COMPANION

This book has a companion Web site, located at:

```
http://www.phptr.com/phptrinteractive/
```

The Web companion is designed to provide an interactive online environment that will enhance your learning experience. You'll find answers to the Test Your Thinking projects from the book, additional Self-Review Questions to challenge your understanding of chapter discussions, a virtual study lounge in which to mingle with other Interactive Workbook students, and an Author's Corner, where I will provide you with discussion that I think will be of interest to you.

Visit the Web site periodically to share and discuss your answers.

CHAPTER 1

SYSTEM SECURITY

The system administrator needs to be very concerned about system security. But it is something which few people are willing to rush into, and does not endear the system administrator to his or her fellow workers.

—Joe

M aintaining a secure system is a key system administration responsibility. Fixing security problems can be time-consuming and frustrating, primarily because many of these problems are caused not by malicious users, but by buggy software. The labs in this chapter are designed to introduce you to common security problems, and to get you thinking about your system from the standpoint of system security.

EXERCISES FOR THE MASSES

Hands-on experience is the best way of learning UNIX. These exercises are designed for the normal user id. They are not comprehensive, but are designed to give you a feel for what it takes to be a UNIX system administrator.

The learning process is dependent on learning from your mistakes and figuring out how to fix whatever happens as a result. This is the primary role of the teacher. In the absence of the teacher, the student needs to be able to figure out the answers. There are many ways to answer a question. Some are equally good; some are better than others. —Joe

L A B   1.1

USER'S LOGIN

LAB OBJECTIVES

After this Lab, you will be able to:

✓ Analyze Your ID

✓ Fix Your .profile

.PROFILE

One important file to look at in reference to security information is your `.profile` file. If you are running the Bourne Shell or the Korn Shell (otherwise known as ksh), you will have a file in your home directory known as .profile. This file contains the system environment setup informa-tion. For DOS aficionados, it is similar to the CONFIG.SYS and AUTOEXEC.BAT files on your PC. However, the .profile file only con-tains information about the current user, and does not have any system setup parameters. If you are running the csh, the related files are the .cshrc and the .login.

Look in the man pages for the following:
ls, profile, ksh, sh, csh, login, cshrc, chmod

ACCESS PERMISSIONS

Another place to look for security information is in the access permissions of your home directory. While you may already be familiar with the access permissions on files, there are some things that can be analyzed from a security standpoint.

■ *FOR EXAMPLE:*

The ls -ld command yields information related to your system's secu-rity access. A typical result from this command might be:

    drwxr - xr - - 1 sam users 70 Jan 29 17:13 dir1

For now, let's concentrate on the grouping drwxr - xr - -

The d in this case stands for the directory. A dash ("-") in this position represents a file. The remaining letters, then, are subdivided into three groups of three letters each, as follows:

- The first group of three stands for the permissions of the owner. In this example, you see rwx.
- The second group of three represents the permissions of the group attached to the file. In this example, you see r - x.
- The third group of three represents the permissions of oth-ers. In this example, you see r - -.

In each group of three, the following rules are used:

- The first letter stands for the read permissions, represented by r.

- The second letter stands for the write access permissions, represented by w.
- The third letter stands for execute permissions, in the case of a file, or access permissions in the case of a directory. This is represented by an x.

Note that a dash, "–", means the attribute is turned off.

So, this example is analyzed as follows:

rwx	This means that the owner has read, write, and access permissions to the directory.
r – x	This means that the group can read and access the directory, but cannot write to it.
r – –	This means that others have read, but not write or access permissions to the directory.

Look in Appendix B for the following:
access permissions

SETUSERID BITS

It is possible to run a program so the system thinks it is being run by someone else; this is due to a feature called setuserid. With the setuserid bits enabled, you can set the attributes of a file so that every time a program is executed, it runs with the same permissions as the owner and/or group of the file. You can also execute a file so the system thinks you are a member of the group that is attached to the file. Whenever you execute the passwd command, you are actually running a file with the setuserid bit enabled.

Before your security warning lights start flashing, be aware that only the owner of a file or root can give these rights to a file. No one can obtain these rights on their own, even if they are in the same group. In earlier UNIX studies, you may have seen that there are actually four fields for permission rights. Besides the three mentioned earlier, there is also one to the left that is actually between the bits for the directory and the owner. If you use the chmod command and enter chmod 4755, you will make a file executable by everyone with the same rights as the owner.

■ *FOR EXAMPLE:*

Let's apply this to one of our earlier samples. If you enter the command:

    chmod 4755 prog2

which can also be represented in a symbolic chmod as:

    chmod u+s prog2

and then enter ls -1, you see output similar to the following:

    -rwsr - xr - x 1 sam users 70 Jan 29 17:13 prog2

This means that the program will execute with the same rights as the owner sam. If you saw the following:

    -rwxr - sr - x 1 sam users 70 Jan 29 17:13 prog2

it would mean that the program executes with the same permissions as the group users. To change the rights of a file so that it has setgroupid enable, use the command:

    chmod 2755 prog2

or

    chmod g+s prog2

UMASK

The umask command is used to set the access rights of a file when you create it. We all start out with some default setting for umask. Often, this is built into the shell. It can then be modified by your profile or the system profile. In Solaris x86, this is set in /etc/profile, which is executed as umask 022.

■ *FOR EXAMPLE:*

Let's start out with umask set to 000. In this case, a file that you create will have the following rights when you do an ls -1:

    -rw-rw-rw-   1 myid staff   0 Jun 17 19:10 myfile

When you think of it in terms of an octal representation (you should review this in your earlier UNIX texts if you are not clear), you will see that the rights are represented as 666. If you have a umask of 022, then you can do the following arithmetic:

666   (The attributes of the above file)

<u>022</u>   (The umask setting)

644   (Generated by subtracting the first line from the second line)

Though the attributes are actually octal values, normal decimal arithmetic works in this case. (Note that any negative numbers that result from subtraction are treated as zeros, i.e., 2 - 6 is 0.) Now, when you create a new file, it will be read as follows when you enter ls -l:

```
-rw-r—r--   1 myid staff          0 Jun 17 19:10 myfile
```

Note: the umask command cannot be used to change the attributes of files that already exist; it only affects new files that are created. You also cannot create attributes with a number higher than 666.

When a new file is created, it is generally never created with the execute bit enabled. This prevents you from automatically executing files that you do not wish to execute. In order to execute a file, you must change the rights with the chmod *command, or execute the command by prefacing it with the name of the shell (i.e., to execute the file myfile, shown previously, in the Korn shell, use:* ksh myfile*). However, a directory can automatically be created with the x or access bit set.*

Look in the technical reference pages for the following:
chmod, umask, setuid

The first Exercise in this Lab deals with access permissions, and this information should be used to work through that Exercise. Subsequent exercises in this chapter detail other security issues that concern UNIX administrators.

LAB 1.1 EXERCISES

1.1.1 ANALYZE YOUR ID

Login with your normal, not root user id.

Next, type the following commands from your home directory:

```
mkdir  secur1 (if it doesn't already exist)
cd secur1
mkdir secur1.1a.d
touch secur1.1a.txt
ls -ld secur1.1a.d
ls -l secur1.1a.txt
```

a) What does each of these commands do?

_____

_____

b) What kind of results do you get? Make note of the actual results.

_____

_____

c) Explain the meaning of each column of information that resulted.

_____

_____

Look in the man pages for the command:
umask

Now enter the following commands in the `secur1` directory:

```
umask 077
```

```
cd $HOME/secur1
mkdir secur1.1e.d
touch secur1.1e.txt
ls -ld secur1.1e.d
ls -l secur1.1e.txt
```

d) Explain the meaning of these changes.

_____

_____

1.1.2 FIX YOUR .PROFILE

This program modifies your `.profile` so that each time you login, your home directory is modified to prevent unauthorized access.

Modify your `.profile` file to add the following lines:

```
chmod 700 .
umask 077
```

a) What is the result of these commands?

_____

_____

b) Could someone still write to your home directory, as root, or as another user?

_____

_____

c) What kind of results do you get when you log in?

_____

_____

d) Do you see anything on your screen?

_____

_____

e) Verify your answers by redoing the steps in the previous exercise. Do you get the same results?

_____

_____

LAB 1.1 EXERCISE ANSWERS

This section gives you some suggested answers to the questions in Lab 1.1, with discussion related to those answers. Your answers may vary, but the most important thing is whether or not your answer works. Use this discussion to analyze differences between your answers and those presented here.

If you have alternative answers to the questions in this Exercise, you are encouraged to post your answers and discuss them at the companion Web site for this book, located at:

```
http://www.phptr.com/phptrinteractive
```

1.1.1 ANSWERS

Type the following commands from your home directory:

```
mkdir  secur1 (if it doesn't already exist)
cd secur1
mkdir secur1.1a.d
touch secur1.1a.txt
ls -ld secur1.1a.d
ls -l secur1.1a.txt
```

a) What does each of these commands do?

Answer: These commands are explained as follows:

`mkdir secur1` `(if it doesn't already exist)`	Makes a subdirectory under your home directory
`cd secur1`	Changes your current directory to secur1
`mkdir secur1.1a.d`	Makes a subdirectory under your current directory
`touch secur1.1a.txt`	Creates an empty file in your current directory
`ls -ld secur1.1.d`	Lists the access rights of the directory
`ls -l secur1.1.txt`	Shows the access rights of the file

b) What kind of results do you get?

Answer: You should see something similar to the following:

```
drwxrwxr-x 2 jsmith users1024 Mar  4 21:59 secur1.1a.d
-rw - rw - r-- 1 jsmith users0 Mar  4 21:59 secur1.1a.txt
```

If you don't see the same thing, don't worry. You can determine what the results should be by typing the command `umask`. You will see this answer if your `umask` command returns `002`. –

You might try experimenting with different `umask` commands and viewing the results. Note that the `umask` command only changes the rights of any directory or file you create in the future. You might try `umask -S`, which gives a symbolic listing of the rights you give to files and directories. You will see the following:

```
    umask -S
    u=rwx,g=rwx,o=rwx
```

This represents a numeric `umask` of 000. These are the rights that will be given to a file when you create it. (Note that the x attribute is automatically set only for directories, not files.) It can also be used to set rights with symbolic options. By doing the following steps, you can see the change in your `umask` values:

```
    $ umask -S o-r
    $ umask
    026
```

Any files that result will look like this:

```
    -rw-r-----   1 myid staff     0 Jun 17 19:53 myfile
```

If you use the numeric representation, it shows or takes away rights to a file or directory, whereas the symbolic notation shows rights that will be given to a file or directory when you create it.

c) Explain the meaning of each column of information that resulted.

Answer: The discussion that follows offers more in-depth analysis of the results.

Let's take a closer look at the results of entering the `ls -ld` command in a sample home directory:

```
drwxr-xr-- 1 jsmith users 70 Jan 29 17:13 prog1
```

Once again, these results will be different on your machine, depending on the various factors explained previously in this chapter. However, the structure of your results should be similar. Let's focus first on the first grouping of information:

```
drwxr - xr - -
```

From the previous discussion, recall what the letters d, r, w, and x stand for. Also recall that a dash ("-") means that the attribute is turned off.

With this information, here is what this particular grouping means, broken down:

d	Means that this is the directory
rwx	Means that the owner can read, write, and access the directory or execute the file
r - x	Means that the group can read and access the directory, but does not have write access
r - -	Means that everyone has read access to the file or directory, but not write access, or execute access to a file, or access rights in the case of a directory

For a better understanding of this example, let's analyze this as three separate users trying to access the directory. The following capabilities would apply for these users:

- **The owner of the file.** The owner can do anything to the file, including execute it, read it, and modify it.
- **A member of the group that is attached to the file, but is not the owner.** This user:
  - *can* change into that directory
  - *can* modify any files that the user has rights to modify

- *can* execute any files that either the user or group rights allow the user to execute
- *can* change to any subdirectories to which the user has access
- *can* make any changes to the contents of files or sub-directories that the user has rights to do
- *cannot* create or delete any files
- *cannot* change the attributes of a file
- **A user that is neither the owner nor a member of the group.** This user:
  - *cannot* read the contents of the directory
  - *cannot* execute any files in the directory
  - *cannot* read the contents of any files in the directory
  - *cannot* look at the attributes of the files in the directory
  - *cannot* change to any subdirectories in this directory, no matter what the rights or ownership attributes are
  - *can only* read the attributes of the directory

This leaves the following remaining information in the results:

```
1 sam users 70 Jan 29 17:13 prog1
```

This can be broken down as follows:

1	Number of links to the file or directory (remember, in UNIX you can have multiple links to a file)
Sam	Owner of the file
Users	Group ownership of the file
70	Size of the file in bytes
Jan 29	Date of creation or modification
17:13	Time of creation
Prog1	Name of the file

Now, enter the following commands in the `secur1` directory:

```
umask 077
cd $HOME/secur1
mkdir secur1.1e.d
touch secur1.1e.txt
```

```
ls -ld secur1.1e.d
ls -l secur1.1e.txt
```

d) Explain the meaning of the changes.

Answer:The meaning of these changes are explained as follows:

`umask 077`	Creates a default umask of 077
`cd $HOME/secur1`	Working directory is changed to secur1
`mkdir secur1.1e.d`	Creates a directory secur1.1e.d under your secur1 directory
`touch secur1.1e.txt`	Creates a file called secur1.1e.txt in your directory secur1 (this is an empty file, but has the default attributes for any file that you create)
`ls -ld secur1.1e.d`	This returns the following results:

`drwx------   2 myid staff   512 Jun 17 20:14 secur1.1e.d`

`ls -l secur1.1e.txt`   This returns the following results:

`-rw-------   1myid  staff   0 Jun 17 20:13 secur1.1e.txt`

The umask of 077 will prevent any rights from being set for anyone but the owner. The owner will not have any rights affected. (See the Lab discussion on umask for more detail.)

1.1.2 ANSWERS

Modify your `.profile` to add the following lines:

```
chmod 700  .
umask 077
```

If you are logged in, go to your home directory. Otherwise, login.

a) What is the result of these commands?

Answer: These commands do two things:

chmod 700 . This changes the access rights of your current directory to be readable, writable, and accessible only by the owner and root. In this case, adding it to your .profile causes the access rights on your home directory to be changed to be readable, writable, and accessible only by you and root.

umask 077 This makes the default umask 077 so that any files or directories that you create after you log in will be readable, writable, and accessible only by you.

Both changes are applied every time you log in.

b) Could someone still write to your home directory, as root, or as another user?

Answer: Only root could then write to your home directory. Another user could not write to your home directory.

c) What kind of results do you get when you log in?

Answer: The access rights for your home directory are reset to 700, so that no one else can access it.

d) Do you see anything on your screen?

Answer: You should not see anything different on your screen.

e) Verify your answers by redoing the steps in the previous Exercise 1.1.1.

Answer: Redo the preceding Exercise and verify that everything is correct. You should have the same results as when you entered chmod *and* umask.

LAB 1.1 SELF-REVIEW QUESTIONS

In order to test your progress, you should be able to answer the following questions.

The command cd / ; ls -la was executed. The partial results follow. Use this information to answer the first five questions that follow.

```
Total 5808
drwxr-xr-x      29 root      root    1024   Jun 16 20:39    .
d r w x r w x r w x 18 root    bin     688    Mar 02 13:34.
drwxr-xr-x      29 root      root 1024   Jun 16 20:39   ..
```

```
d r w x r w r w x    18  root      bin   688   Mar 02 14:34 ..
- - - - - - - - - -   1  root      auth    0   Mar 15 9:38 .lastlogin
- r w - r - - r - -   1  bin       sys   521   Jun 04 1992 .login
- r w - r w - r w x   1  root      root 1386   Feb 12 16:00 .profile
d w r x r w x r w t   2  sys       sys   608   Mar 15 17:40 tmp
d r w x r w x r w x  20  jjones    auth  464   Feb 10 14:14 usr
- r w s r - x r - x  10  root      root  200   Feb 20  15:14 myksh
d r w x r w x r w x  18  root      bin   688   Mar 02 13:34 mydir
```

1) Anyone can write to the `mydir` root directory.
   a) _____True
   b) _____False

2) When was the last time root logged in?
   a) _____Mar 15
   b) _____Jun 04
   c) _____Jun 16Mar 02
   d) _____Feb 20
   e) _____Feb 12

3) The access rights on the tmp directory are a security problem and should be set to 700.
   a) _____True
   b) _____False

4) The access rights on `.profile` are set correctly.
   a) _____True
   b) _____False

5) One of the programs listed is a security problem. Which program or directory, when executed, can be modified by anyone? This file can have text embedded that can be used to run programs that can then be used to break into the system, and can give anyone access, will give anyone access to the system as root.

a) _____. `lastlogin`
b) _____. `login`
c) _____. `profile`
d) _____. (The dot directory)
e) _____. `myksh`

Use what you have learned in this Lab to answer the following questions:

6) Modifying the `umask` will changes the access rights of all files in a directory.
a) _____True
b) _____False

7) A permissions of 664 on a file means that a file has which of the following attributes?
a) _____. `- r - - r - - r - -`
b) _____ `- r - x  r - x  r - x`
c) _____ `-rw - rw - r - -`
d) _____ `-r - - r - - r w -`
e) _____None of the above

8) When you normally create a file, it has the permissions rights 664. Now, suppose you add a `umask` of 027123. When you create a new file, what access rights would you have?
a) _____ `-r- - rw - rwx`
b) _____ `-rwxrw - r - -`
c) _____ `-rw - r - -  r- - - -`
d) _____ `-r - - r - - r - -`
e) _____None of the above

9) Execute the command `ls -1` and see the following results:
```
-rwsrw - r - -  1 bjones others 4567  Mar 02  13:20
```

This result means that the program will execute with the rights of which of the following?
a) _____your loginid
b) _____the group to which you belong
c) _____the loginid bjones
d) _____the others group
e) _____root

Quiz answers appear in Appendix A, Section 1.1.

L A B   1.2

SEARCHING FOR FILES AS A REGULAR USER

 A good administrator is like a good detective. Oftentimes, one needs to be able to look for information and solve problems with a minimum of clues. One may need to dig in the muck to find the missing pieces and solve the puzzle. Like a good detective, one works behind the scenes. However, few reach the fame of a Sherlock Holmes.

LAB OBJECTIVES

After this Lab, you will be able to:

✓ Understand the find Command

✓ Check if Any Files Have Been Changed Under Your id.

✓ Fix Your .profile

✓ Check files Under Your id for Changes

FIND

The find command is one of the those tools that can be indispensable to an administrator. With its many options and capabilities, it allows us to look for such information as permissions, access rights, and modifications dates, and send this information directly to a program.

The first argument to the find command is a starting-point directory where the search begins. Because the UNIX filesystem is a tree structure, we can visualize a structure that gets increasingly complex as we go down the tree, but increasingly simple as we go up the tree. Look at the structure in Figure 1.1 to get the idea.

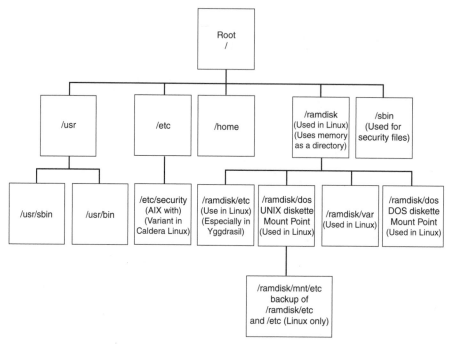

Figure 1.1 ■ The UNIX File System Structure

When you are in the top directory, a search covers 14 (count 'em, 14) directories when you start from only the top directory. If you go down to the bottom row, you only search one of those directories. Starting from the top covers more territory, but takes longer. Starting lower down in the tree covers less territory, but is quicker. So the more you know about what you are trying to find out, the quicker your search. Take a look at Chapter 7, "Filesystems and Disks," for more on UNIX's directory structure.

LAB 1.2 EXERCISES

1.2.1 UNDERSTAND THE *FIND* COMMAND

See the command reference pages in Appendix B for the following:
`find, diff, touch`

Specify the `find` command with the starting point by entering the following command:

        find /usr -print | more

a) What do you see on the screen?

_____

_____

We use the `more` *command because otherwise the display scrolls too quickly. To exit from the* `more` *display, just type* `q` *then press the* `enter` *key.*

Now, suppose you want to find all the files that have been modified more than four days ago. You start with the `find` command and give it an option for modification time, which is a "+" followed by the number that represents the number of days. In this case, use the following option:

        -mtime +4

With more current versions of UNIX, particularly the POSIX compatible versions, the $-print$ *option is understood. In this case, it is not necessary to specify the* $-print$. *This is particularly true of Linux 2.x and Solaris 2.6, which are referenced throughout this text. Older versions of UNIX will not display output on the screen unless you use the* $-print$ *option. In all versions of UNIX,* $-print$ *is not necessary and is often redundant if you pipe the results to another command. This is also true when you use the* $-exec$ *command, which is discussed later in this Lab.*

By putting the command and options together, you can create the following command:

```
find -print /usr -mtime +4
```

b) Try this command. What kind of results do you get?

_____

_____

The next useful option is the $-exec$ option. The $-exec$ is followed by the name of a command. It looks like the following:

```
-exec command {} \;
```

This option directs the output of the $find$ command into the command you're executing. In this case, use the {}, sometimes called braces or squiggly brackets. Specify the end of the command with \; (a backslash followed by a semicolon). So, you see the $find$ option as:

```
find /usr -print -mtime +4 -exec ls -l {} \;
```

This command executes $find$ so that it will generate a long listing of all files modified more than four days ago under /usr and in all its subdirectories. This says that any results from executing the command should be sent to the command, followed by the $-exec$ option, which in this case is the $ls -l$ command.

Try the following command:

```
find /usr -print -mtime +4 -exec ls -l {} \;
```

c) What kind of results do you get?

_____

_____

 If you are in a classroom environment, see your regular textbook, or see this text's exercises for: partitions, disk layouts

It is important to realize that the UNIX file system structure traverses multiple drives, so when you look at a structure starting at root, you could be looking at many drives. It is not possible to only look at a directory to see what partition it is on. Many UNIX commands can be restricted to only the drive on which the filesystem in question is located.

Suppose you only want to find all files that have been changed on the /usr partition. By using the option –mount, you can restrict access to only the partition that you choose. Try the following command:

```
find /usr -mount -mtime +4 -exec ls -l {} \;
```

d) What kind of results do you get? Discuss the meaning of these results.

_____

_____

1.2.2 MODIFY YOUR .PROFILE TO CHECK FILES UNDER YOUR ID FOR CHANGES

Log in with your normal id (user id).

Add the find command to change your .profile to locate all the files under your home directory. Send each of the results to a separate file. You will end up with three separate output files, one for each command.

Look in the man pages for the following:
`find`

What are the commands necessary to find all the files that have been modified within the last:

a) day?

_____

_____

b) week?

_____

_____

c) 30 days?

_____

_____

d) Look at the output files. What kind of results do you see?

_____

_____

1.2.3 SETTING UP YOUR SECURITY TESTING ENVIRONMENT

CHANGES IN ACCESS RIGHTS OF FILES

In this Exercise, you will enter a program that checks files under your id. It checks to see if any files have had their access rights changed. It does so by creating a list of files that have access rights for users other than the owner.

Log in with your normal id (user id).

If you haven't already done so, create a bin and security directory from your home directory as follows:

```
mkdir bin security
```

a) What is the full pathname of each of the preceding directories?

_____

_____

Enter the following command in the Bourne or Korn Shell:

```
echo $PATH
```

b) What kind of results do you get?

_____

_____

In the Bourne or Korn shell, change your `.profile` to include your new `bin` directory in your search by adding a line at the end of the file with the following entry:

```
PATH=$PATH:$HOME/bin; export PATH
```

c) What does this line do?

_____

_____

Execute the following:

```
.  $HOME/.profile (this is period space $HOME)
```

d) What does this line do?

_____

_____

Enter the following command in the Bourne or Korn Shell:

```
echo $PATH
```

e) What kind of results do you get?

_____

_____

If you do not see the bin directory in your search path, then you need to redo this Exercise.

1.2.4 CHECK FILES UNDER YOUR ID FOR CHANGES

Enter the following program into the computer. Call it `prog1.2.4` and put it in your `bin` directory. Make it executable by modifying the file permissions. (Note: You may need to modify this program for your particular flavor of UNIX.)

```
#!/bin/sh
#
cd $HOME
if test -f security/file_list
then
     cp security/file_list security/base_list
else
     touch security/file_list security/base_list security/diff_list
fi
chmod 700 security
chmod 600 security/file_list security/base_list  security/diff_list
find . -perm -077 -ls >  security/file_list
diff security/file_list security/base_list > security/diff_list
```

a) What does this program do? Explain in detail.

_____

_____

b) What kind of output would you expect the first time the program runs successfully?

_____

_____

c) Which file would you look at to see the files that have changes?

_____

_____

Once you have successfully executed `prog1.2.4` and created a `diff_file`, go ahead and execute it again.

d) What kind of results do you get?

_____

_____

e) What happens if the `security` directory does not exist? Rename the `security` directory, then try it out and see.

_____

_____

f) If this is the first time you are running the command and there is no security directory, what change could be made to your program so it does not get the preceding error and still end up with the same results? Don't change the logic. You could use this to automate the previous process on a new system with the fewest amount of manual steps.

You may, however, get an error if you add the preceding line to your program to create a directory and the directory already exists.

g) What additional code can you add to your program to prevent an error message if the directory already exists?

LAB 1.2 EXERCISE ANSWERS

This section gives you some suggested answers to the questions in Lab 1.2, as well as discussion related to those answers. Your answers may vary, but the most important thing is whether or not your answer works. Use this discussion to analyze differences between your answers and those presented here.

If you have alternative answers to the questions in this Exercise, you are encouraged to post your answers and discuss them at the companion Web site for this book, located at:

`http://www.phptr.com/phptrinteractive`

1.2.1 ANSWERS

Specify the `find` command with the starting point as follows:

```
find /usr -print | more
```

This instructs to start looking in the /usr directory and traverse down the directory tree, looking in all the subdirectories underneath /usr/lib. You may know from experience that this can cover a lot of files. Next, we discuss ways to restrict the search.

a) What do you see on the screen?

Answer: You should see something similar to the following:

```
$ find -print /usr | more
/usr
/usr/X11R6
/usr/X11R6/bin
/usr/X11R6/bin/fvwm
/usr/X11R6/bin/fvwm2
```

... and so forth.

Now, suppose you want to find all the files that have been modified more than four days ago. You start with the find command and give it an option for modification time, which is a "-", followed by the number of days. In this case, use the following option:

```
-mtime +4
```

This is an abbreviation for modification time. Then, choose either an option that specifies a time frame with which to look for modifications, or one that searches for files that have been modified later than a certain time.

If you specify a hyphen ("-") followed by a number of days, the command will look for files that have been modified within that number of days. So mtime -4 *means look for files that have been modified within the last four days.*

Putting the command and options together, you can create the following command:

```
find /usr -print -mtime +4
```

b) Try this command. What kind of results do you get?

> *Answer: You should see something similar to the following:*
> ```
> $ find /usr -mtime +4 | more
> /usr
> /usr/X11R6
> /usr/X11R6/bin
> /usr/X11R6/bin/fvwm
> ```
> *... and so forth.*

With this command, you get a listing of all files under the /usr directory that have been modified more than four days ago. With some versions of UNIX, you must specify the -print option in order to display the results; with other versions of UNIX, such as LINUX, this is not necessary. In that case, use:

```
find /usr -mtime +4
```

Try the following command:

```
find /usr -print -mtime +4 -exec ls -l {} \;
```

c) What kind of results do you get?

> *Answer: The results would be something like:*
> ```
> $ find /usr -mtime +4 -exec ls -l {} \; | more
> total 28
> drwxr-xr-x   7 root    root    1024 Nov  5  1997 X11R6
> drwxr-xr-x   3 root    root    8192 Dec 17 22:00 bin
> drwxr-xr-x   2 root    root    1024 Dec 17 11:39 dict
> drwxr-xr-x   2 root    root    1024 Dec 17 9:00 local/bin
> ```
> *... and so forth.*

Try the following command:

```
find /usr -mount -mtime +4 -exec ls -l {} \;
```

d) What kind of results do you get? Discuss the meaning of these results.

> *Answer: You should see something like the following:*
> ```
> find /usr -mount -mtime +4 -exec ls -l {} \;
> total 28
> ```

```
drwxr-xr-x   7 root       root       1024 Nov  5  1997 X11R6
drwxr-xr-x   3 root       root       8192 Dec 17 22:00 bin
drwxr-xr-x   2 root       root       1024 Dec 17 11:39 dict
```

... and so forth.

When you do the `mount` command, you will see several partitions mounted. You might see / , /usr, and /usr/local. If you do a simple `find` command starting at root, you will get files in all the mounted directories under root. By adding the `-mount` or `-xdev` option to the `find` command, only the files that are in the root partition will show up. The files in the /usr and /usr/local directories will be ignored if they are in a separate partition. Note that in the previous Exercise, the local/bin directory showed up, but now it doesn't. This is because in this example system, /usr/local is a separate partition.

This command checks the /usr partition for all files that have been modified more than four days ago and returns a listing of only those qualifying files, similar to the result of the preceding question.

You can perform this task by specifying one of two options: −xdev, which is an older option, or the more current `-mount`, as you have here.

Note that in some versions of UNIX, the `-print` option in the previous command will instruct twice as many lines to be printed out. Half of the lines are from the `-exec ls {} \;` command, and the other half will be from the `-print` option.

1.2.2 ANSWERS

Log in with your normal id (user id).
Add the `find` command to change your `.profile` to locate all the files under your home directory. Send each of the results to a separate file.

If you are logged in, go to your home directory. Otherwise, login. Use your editor to add the following entries to your `.profile`. The output file names can be whatever you feel is meaningful.

What are the commands necessary to find all the files that have been modified within the last:

a) day?

Answer: The command is as follows:
```
find $HOME -mtime -1 > files.day
```

b) week?

Answer: The command is as follows:
```
find $HOME -mtime -7 > files.wk
```

c) 30 days?

Answer: The command is as follows:
```
find $HOME -mtime -30 > files.mon
```

d) Look at the output files. What kind of results do you see?

Answer: You should see a listing of all the files that have been changed within the last day, week, or 30 days.

Note that all files listed in `files.day` will also appear in `files.wk`. The files in `files.day` and `files.wk` will also be part of `files.mon`.

1.2.3 ANSWERS

CHANGES IN ACCESS RIGHTS OF FILES

Login with your normal id (user id).
If you haven't already done so, create a bin and security directory from your home directory as follows:
```
mkdir bin security
```

The biggest problem you will encounter is not being in the correct directory, so be sure to determine where you are. Check this with the command `pwd`. You can change to the proper directory by typing the command `cd`, which takes you to your home directory. The bin and security directories are used in future exercises.

a) What is the full pathname of each of the preceding directories?

*Answer: If your home directory is **/home/myhome**, then the directories would be as follows:*

```
/home/myhome/bin
/home/myhome/security
```
Enter the following command in the Bourne or Korn Shell:
```
echo $PATH
```

b)   What kind of results do you get?

Answer: You should see a search path similar to the following:
```
PATH=/usr/local/bin:/bin:/usr/bin:/usr/X11R6/bin:/
usr/bin/mh:.
```

If there is a difference between this answer and what you get, it is due to the values set up on your system. Every manufacturer sets up the defaults a little differently.

You should always see the string ":." at the end of the path in this Exercise, because the dot directory (your current directory) should always be the last directory in your search. This prevents someone from putting a Trojan horse (a program pretending to be something else, capable of grabbing your password) in your search path. This is particularly harmful if you have root access to your system. If you type su, it can execute the bogus program and not the real one.

In the Bourne or Korn shell, change your `.profile` to include your new bin directory in your search by adding a line at the end of the file with the following entry:
```
PATH=$PATH:$HOME/bin; export PATH
```

c)   What does this line do?

Answer: PATH is the environment variable that is the search path used to locate executable files. The $PATH specifies that you must first put the current search path at the beginning of any new search path. The $HOME/bin that follows says that after you look in the original search path, you should look in the $HOME/bin, which is the bin directory underneath your home directory. The bin directory is the directory that you just created, or that was already there.

The security directory is not in the search path because it only includes the results of executing whatever program you did in the bin directory.

Execute the following:
```
.   $HOME/.profile (this is period space $HOME)
```

Be sure to execute the command as <u>period</u> <u>space</u> and then the command. Otherwise, your environment won't change.

d) What does this line do?

Answer: *This executes the $HOME/.profile file in your current Korn or Bourne environment.*

Any values that are set in your .profile are set in your environment. Once you log out and log in again, these values are automatically set by the new profile. However, you really don't want to test any changes you make to your .profile by logging out and logging in again. If your .profile is set improperly, you might not be able to log in again.

If you just execute the .profile by itself, it creates a shell, which is a child of the current process. This then sets, within the child, whichever environment variables that your .profile sets. However, once this program is finished, the login shell knows nothing about the setting. This is a great way of testing out whether you have properly created the shell program, but eventually you want to put those values into your environment.

If you type a period by itself, then a space followed by .profile, it puts whatever environment variables are set into your current shell process. This is what the .profile does normally when you login.

Enter the following command in the Bourne or Korn Shell:
```
echo $PATH
```

a) What kind of results do you get?

Answer: *Assuming your home directory is /home/myhome, you should see a search path similar to the following:*
```
PATH=/usr/local/bin:/bin:/usr/bin:/usr/X11R6/bin:/
usr/bin/mh:.:/home/myhome/bin
```
If you do not see the bin directory in your search path, then you need to redo this Exercise.

1.2.4 ANSWERS

Enter the following program into the computer; call it prog1.2.4 and put it in your bin directory. Make it executable by modifying the file permissions.

(Note: You may need to modify this program for your particular flavor of UNIX.)

```
#!/bin/sh
# This file will test for any changes to the access rights to
# your files or directories
cd $HOME
# Go to your home directory. This way you dont start off on the
wrong foot
if test -f security/file_list# If your security file list exists
copy it to starting list
then
     cp security/file_list security/base_list
else
      # create the file by touching it
     touch security/file_list security/base_list security/diff_list
fi
# the following steps will change the access rights on the
# security files
# the following entry will make the security directory accessible
# to you. The mode must be 700.
chmod 700 security
# The following entry will make the files readable only by you
chmod 600 security/file_list security/base_list security/diff_list
# Now look to see if any files have the wrong access rights starting
at your
# home directory. Save a long listing of those files to another file
find . -perm -077 -ls >  security/file_list
# Check to see what files have changed
# the filediff security/file_list security/base_list > security/
diff_list
```

First, make sure you create a bin directory. If you don't, just use the command from your home directory:

```
mkdir bin
```

Next, make sure that you have a security directory. If you don't, use the command from your home directory:

```
mkdir security
```

If you are not in your home directory, type the command:

```
cd
```

This gets you back to your home directory. The next step is to create the working directories for this Exercise:

```
mkdir $HOME/bin $HOME/security
```

If they already exist, you will get an error message.

One of the "Test Your Thinking" projects at the end of this chapter helps you develop a way of automating this whole process and handling errors automatically.

a) What does this program do? Explain in detail.

Answer: The comments in the listing explain this. Note that we have added the `diff` *command. This command displays the differences between two files. In this case, it displays each line that is different in one file than in the other. Consider the following example:*

```
diff file1 file2 > file.diff
```

The file named `file.diff` *contains only the differences between the two files.*

b) What kind of output would you expect the first time the program runs successfully?

Answer: If the program runs successfully, you will see nothing on the screen. This is keeping with the UNIX philosophy that no news is good news. However, you can examine the output files to determine what the results are.

c) Which file would you look at to see the files that have changes?

Answer: Because the results are being put in the security/diff_list, you should look in there. You then need to be able to interpret the output of the **diff** *command. The first time you run the program, you should see a listing of all files that are readable, writable, and executable by everyone in your group and by everyone. By using the cat file, you will see the following:*

```
$ cat diff_list
1,5d0
< 140327 128 -rwxrwxrwx  1 myid staff 120972 Nov  4  1997 ./libAu-
toAdmin.so
< 70175    1 drwxrwxrwx  2 myid staff   512 Jun 14 23:26 ./nav4.05
< 17585    1 drwxrwxrwx 11 myid staff   512 Jun 14 23:27 . /netscape
<    79    1 drwxrwxrwx  2 myid staff   512 Jun 17 20:05 ./security
/outfile
< 17615    1 drwxrwxrwx  3 myid staff   512 Jun 17 20:14 ./secur1
$
```

Once you have successfully executed prog1.2.4 and created a diff_file, go ahead and execute it again.

d) What kind of results do you get?

LAB 1.2

Answer: The second time you execute this program, the diff_file should be empty. This is because the first time you execute the program, the base_list file that is used for comparison from the previous run is empty. The other file, file_list, contains all files that meet the test criteria. There will be something in the diff_file. The second time you execute the program, the base_list file will contain a list of files that meet the criteria. The other file, file_list, should contain the same list of files. As a result, the diff_file will be empty, much like 2 - 2 = 0 in simple mathematics. In this case, $diff$ acts like a subtraction procedure.

e) What happens if the $security$ directory does not exist? Rename the security directory, then try it out and see.

Answer: You will get a number of errors because the program cannot access any of the files in the security directory.

A good program can handle any such errors, and is able to test for the directories to see if they exist. If they don't exist, your program should make them. (See the "Test Your Thinking" section at the end of this chapter.) You should see the following (or similar) errors in Linux and other OSs:

```
touch: security/file_list: No such file or directory
touch: security/base_list: No such file or directory
touch: security/diff_list: No such file or directory
chmod: security: No such file or directory
chmod: security/file_list: No such file or directory
chmod: security/base_list: No such file or directory
chmod: security/diff_list: No such file or directory
/home/myhome/bin/prog1.2.4: security/file_list: No such file or directory
/home/myhome/bin/prog1.2.4: security/diff_list: No such file or directory
```

f) If this is the first time you are running the command and there is no security directory, what change could you make to your program to avoid the preceding error, and still end up with the same results? Don't change the logic. You could use this to automate the previous process on a new system with the fewest amount of manual steps.

Answer: Add the following line to the beginning of the program before you reference the security directory:

```
mkdir $HOME/security
```

This will automatically make the security directory.

You may, however, get an error if you add the preceding line to your program in order to create a directory, and the directory already exists.

g) What additional code can you add to your program to prevent an error message if the directory already exists?

Answer: By adding the following lines of code, you will avoid an error message:

```
if test ! -d $HOME/security
then
     mkdir $HOME/security
fi
```

This is useful if you want to prevent error messages when you try to create directories that already exist. If you want to test whether or not the files already exist, simply use the following command:

```
if test -f  whatever_command
then
     some_other_command
fi
```

LAB 1.2 SELF-REVIEW QUESTIONS

In order to test your progress, you should be able to answer the following questions. You may want to refresh your knowledge of the commands used here by referring to the man pages, Appendix B of this book, or your textbook for more detail.

1) The `find` command can be used to get information about files and directories. Which of the following pieces of information can it find?
   a) _____File ownership
   b) _____The last time a file was accessed
   c) _____Files bigger than a certain size
   d) _____Files that have setuserid set
   e) _____All of the above

2) Which of the following does the command `find .  -print` (find followed by a dot) locate?
   a) _____All files under the root directory
   b) _____A directory called dot
   c) _____All files in your parent directory
   d) _____Files and directories in your current directory and all subdirectories
   e) _____Files called dot

3) The command `echo $HOME` gives the path of your home directory.
    a) _____True
    b) _____False

4) Which of the following does the command `find $HOME -print` locate?
    a) _____All files and directories under the root directory
    b) _____A directory called home
    c) _____All files and subdirectories your home directory and all sub-directories under it
    d) _____Files and directories in your current directory and all subdirectories under it
    e) _____Your home directory

LAB
1.2

5) Which of the following does the command `find $HOME -print -perm 755` locate?
    a) _____All files in your current directory created in the month 7/55
    b) _____A directory called perm
    c) _____All files and directories in your home directory and all subdirectories whose permissions exactly match 755
    d) _____Files and directories in your current directory and all subdirectories whose permissions exactly match 755
    e) _____Your home directory

6) Which of the following does the command `find / -mount -user root -print` locate?
    a) _____All files and directories in your current directory called root
    b) _____A directory called /
    c) _____All files and directories under the root directory and all mounted partitions under it
    d) _____Only files and directories on the root partition owned by root
    e) _____All files and directories that are mounted and owned by root and in the group user

7) If you type in the command `echo $PATH` and get the results:
`.:/usr/local/bin:/bin:/usr/bin:/home/myid/bin`

This is perfectly legitimate and has no security concerns.
    a) _____True
    b) _____False

8) Which of the following does the command `find /home -mtime - 7 -user myid   -print` locate?

a) _____All files in your current directory owned by the user myid

b) _____A directory called /home and owned by the user myid

c) _____All files under the /home directory that have been modified in less than seven days ago and owned by the userid myid

d) _____Only files under the /home directory that are owned by the user myid and that were modified exactly seven days ago

e) _____All files under the /home partition that are owned by the user myid and were modified more than seven days ago

9) What result would you expect from the following command?
`find /etc -type d -print`

a) _____A list of all files in your home directory

b) _____A list of all files in the /etc directory

c) _____Files that have security violations

d) _____All directories under the /etc directory

e) _____None of the above

10) What are the results of the following command?
`find / -xdev  -type l -print` (use the lower case L)

a) _____All files under the xdev directory

b) _____All devices under the root directory

c) _____A long listing of files on the root partition

d) _____All symbolic links under the root partition

e) _____All symbolic links on the whole system

11) What are the results of the following command?
`find $HOME -type f  -mtime +40 -print`

a) _____All files under the home directory

b) _____All files and directories under the home directory

c) _____All files under root that have been changed within the last 40 days

d) _____All files under the home directory that have been modified within the last 40 days.

e) _____All files under the home directory that have been modified in greater than 40 days

Quiz answers appear in Appendix A, Section 1.2.

LAB EXERCISES FOR THE GREAT AND SUPER USER

Every administrator worth his or her salt has made mistakes with the operating system or some software piece on it. If you don't make mistakes, you haven't really tried. Root and Superusers can damage a system, but they can also restore the system. The important thing is to learn from your mistakes. It is also important to safely test new ideas before trying them out.   —*Joe*

LAB 1.2

This section includes exercises that will attempt to give you more of an impression for the system itself, as opposed to individual security. Some exercises can be done by anyone, some can be done only by root, and some will work differently depending on who you are.

LAB 1.3

ANALYZE A SYSTEM'S SECURITY ACCESS

LAB OBJECTIVES

After this Lab, you will be able to:

✓ Understand find Under Root Versus Regular User IDs
✓ Find All Files That Have setuid bit Set

In the previous exercises, you learned how to use the find command as a regular user. UNIX restricts only a portion of the system to root only. Even if you can't execute a command or access a directory, you can generally learn that it exists and reveal its permissions. Some additional ways that you might use the find command include:

- To look for file ownership rights that allow anyone to read, write, and/or execute the files
- To look for system files with the setuid bit set
- To analyze the difference between what a regular user sees and what the Superuser sees

This does not differ much from what we did previously. However, one point of this Lab is to help you understand the differences between running the command as root and running the command as a regular user. That is why those exercises are in this section. Some parts can be run as your regular userid, but to get the full flavor, you must also run them as root.

Do a UNIX man page for `diff`; *in Linux, you can use* `diff  - -help`

Decide on which options are useful.

LAB 1.3 EXERCISES

1.3.1 UNDERSTAND FIND UNDER ROOT VERSUS REGULAR USER IDS

You should login with your regular, not root, userid.

This exercise will help you to understand the differences between running a command as a regular user and as root.

Use the `find` command to locate all directories in the root partition with permissions that allow them to be readable, writable, and accessible to you and are owned by you. (You should check only for files on the root partition; ignore files on other partitions, such as /usr. Use the appropriate option discussed in the previous Lab, not the root filesystem.)

a) What is the command line you used?

_____

_____

b) What kind of errors and screen display did you get?

_____

_____

c) Now use the `find` command as a `root` to find all directories that are readable, writable, and accessible by your regular login id in the root partition, not the root filesystem. What is the command line?

_____

_____

d) What kind of errors and screen display did you get?

_____

_____

e) Explain the difference between the preceding two results.

_____

_____

f) Why do you get an error on some directories as a regular user, but no error as root?

_____

_____

g) How would you modify the command so a regular user would not get an error message, but could still run the command on the same directory?

_____

_____

h) Rerun the commands in Questions (a) and (c) in this Exercise as a regular user and as root, and put each of the results into a separate file. Then use the `diff` command to produce a third file that contains only the differences between the two files.

_____

_____

1.3.2 FIND ALL FILES THAT HAVE SETUID BIT SET

The -perm flag to the find command is used to help you locate files that have a certain permissions flag set. The setuid flag is actually displayed as an s in the x field when you do an ls -l.

The perm option with either + or - before the permissions value may not work on some versions of UNIX. In Solaris, -perm +4000 is considered invalid, but it works in Linux.

Use the find command as a regular user to locate only files under /usr that have the setuid bit enabled. Ignore any partitions mounted underneath /usr by choosing the proper option.

a) What is the command line you used?

_____

_____

b) What kind of errors and screen display did you get?

_____

_____

Use the find command as root to locate only files under /usr that have the setuid bit enabled. Ignore any partitions mounted underneath /usr by choosing the proper option.

c) What is the command line you used?

_____

_____

d) What kind of errors and screen display did you get?

_____

_____

e) Explain the difference between the answers to Questions (b) and (d) of this Exercise.

_____

_____

f) How would you modify the command so that a regular user would not get an error message, but could still run the command on the same directory?

_____

_____

Rerun Questions (a) and (c) from this Exercise as a regular user and as root, and put each of the results into a separate file. Use a single command line with the `diff` command to produce a third file that contains only the differences between the two files.

g) What are the steps you used?

_____

_____

h) What kind of results do you get?

_____

_____

LAB 1.3 EXERCISE ANSWERS

This section gives you some suggested answers to the questions in Lab 1.1, with discussion related to those answers. Answers may vary, but the most important thing is whether your answer works. Use this discussion to analyze differences between your answers and those presented here.

If you have alternative answers to the questions in this Exercise, you are encouraged to post your answers and discuss them at the companion Web site for this book, located at:

LAB 1.3

```
http://www.phptr.com/phptrinteractive
```

1.3.1 ANSWERS

You should log in with your regular, not root, userid.
Use the `find` command to locate all directories that are owned by and readable, writable, and accessible by your regular user id in the root partition. (You should check only for files on the root partition; ignore files on other partitions, such as `/usr`. Use the appropriate option discussed in the previous Lab.)

a) What is the command line you used?

Answer: Use the following command and assume your id is called **myid**. *You can use the find command with the appropriate options as follows:*
```
find / -mount -user myid  -type d -perm 700
```

In this command, the following options are employed:

- Start at the root directory
- `-mount`—Look only on the mounted filesystem (in this case, root) for any files meeting the proper criteria. This is essential for using the `find` command to back up by mounted filesystems. The option `xdev` works just as well.
- `-user myid`—Look for files owned by the user myid
- `-type d`—Look only for directories that meet the criteria.
- `-perm 700`—Look only for files that meet the criteria of being readable, writable, and accessible only by the owner

b) What kind of errors and screen display do you get?

Answer:*You should get a screen display and errors similar to the following:*

```
$ find / -mount -user myid -type d -perm 700
find: /etc/X11/xdm/authdir: Permission denied
find: /etc/uucp: Permission denied
find: /var/log/corefiles: Permission denied
find: /var/spool/at: Permission denied
find: /var/spool/cron: Permission denied
/home/myid
find: /usr/doc/ppp-2.2.0f/scripts/keepalive: Permission denied
$
```

If you do not get identical results to what you see here, try to analyze whether the differences are due to system differences, command differences, or user error.

c) Now use the `find` command as a `root` to locate all directories that are owned by and readable, writable, and accessible only by your regular login id in the root partition, not the root filesystem. What is the command line?

Answer: *Use the following command and assume your id is called* `myid`:
```
find / -mount -user myid -type d -perm 700
```

d) What kind of errors and screen display do you get?

Answer:*You should get no errors. Your screen should look like the following:*
```
#  find / -mount -user myid -type d -perm 70
#
```

e) Explain the difference between the preceding two results.

Answer: *Running the command as root results in output that includes all the files that answer the question. There should be no errors when running the command as root because permissions are not enforced for root.*
Running the command as a regular user results in output that gives errors on those directories to which a regular user does not have access.

Any errors would generally be due to:

- System problems
- User errors
- Directories for which all the permissions and access have been disabled

f) Why do you get an error on some directories as a regular user, but no error as root?

Answer: Because there are some directories to which regular users do not have access. When you try to access them, you get an error. This is determined by the x flag that is shown when you do a long listing of files and directories.

g) How could you modify the command so that a regular user would not see an error message, but could still run the command to search every-thing else?

Answer: The details on this question are left as a project in the "Test Your Thinking" sec-tion at the end of this chapter.

**LAB
1.3**

h) Rerun Questions (a) and (c) in this Exercise as a regular user and as root, and put each of the results into a separate file. Then use the `diff` command to produce a third file that only contains the differ-ences between the two files.

Answer: Run the following command as a regular user:

```
find /usr -mount -user myid -type d -perm 70 > output.user
```

Now, run the following as root:

```
find /usr -mount -user myid -type d -perm 70 > output.root
```

Now use the **diff** command to see the difference, as follows:

```
diff output.user output.root > output.diff
```

To view the file, type either of the following:

```
pg output.diff
```

or

```
more output.diff
```

1.3.2 ANSWERS

The -perm flag to the find command is used to help you locate files that have a certain permissions flag set. The setuid flag is actually displayed as an **s** in the x field when you do an ls -l.

Use the find command as a regular user to locate only files under /usr that have the setuid bit enabled. Ignore any partitions mounted underneath /usr by choosing the proper option.

a) What is the command line you used?

Answer: Either of the following programs work:

```
find /usr -xdev -type f -perm -4000
find /usr -mount -type f -perm -4000
```

The meanings of the above are:

- Start at the /usr directory
- -mount—Look only in the partition where /usr is located
- -type f—Look only for files
- -perm -4000—Look only for files that have the setuid bit enabled

b) What kind of errors and screen display did you get?

Answer: You should see something similar to the following:
```
$ find /usr -mount -type f -perm -4000
find: cannot read dir /usr/lost+found: Permission denied
find: cannot read dir /usr/aset: Permission denied
/usr/lib/lp/bin/netpr
/usr/lib/fs/ufs/quota
/usr/lib/fs/ufs/ufsdump
/usr/lib/fs/ufs/ufsrestore
/usr/lib/exrecover
... and so forth
```

When running this command as a regular user, you will get errors on directories to which you have no access. If you get no errors, you should choose a directory that has directories to which you might not have access. Try / etc or /var/adm. If you still have no errors, then start from /. If this doesn't work, then you probably have a security problem, so you then need to research how the directories should be set.

Use the `find` command as root to find only files under `/usr` that have the setuid bit enabled. Ignore any partitions mounted underneath `/usr` by choosing the proper option.

c) What is the command line you used?

Answer: Use the same program that you used in Question (a) of this Exercise.

d) What kind of errors and screen display do you get?

Answer: You should get no errors on the screen. You should get results similar to the following:

```
# find /usr -mount -type f -perm -4000
/usr/lib/lp/bin/netpr
/usr/lib/fs/ufs/quota
/usr/lib/fs/ufs/ufsdump
/usr/lib/fs/ufs/ufsrestore
/usr/lib/exrecover
/usr/lib/pt_chmod
```

... and so forth.

e) Explain the difference between the answers to Questions (b) and (d) of this Exercise.

Answer: You will notice that, when you run the program as a regular user, you will get errors due to the fact that you cannot access certain directories as a regular user.

f) How would you modify the command so that a regular user would not get an error message, but could still run the command on the same directory?

Answer: Look at the answer to questions in Exercise 1.3.1.

Rerun Questions a and c in this Exercise as a regular user and as root, and put each of the results into a separate file. Use a single command line with the `diff` command to produce a file that only contains the differences between the two files.

g) What are the steps you used?

Answer: Run the following command as a regular user:

```
find /usr -mount -type f -perm -4000  > output.user
```

Now, run the following as root:

```
find /usr -mount -type f -perm -4000 > output.root
```

Use the `diff` command to see the difference, as follows:

```
diff output.user output.root > output.diff
```

To look at the file, type either of the following:

```
pg output.diff
```

or

```
more output.diff
```

h)   What kind of results do you get?

Answer: You should get results similar to the following:

```
find: cannot read dir /usr/lost+found: Permission denied
find: cannot read dir /usr/aset: Permission denied
```

... and so forth.

This is due to the fact that you do not have access to certain directories. If you did not get any errors, you should create some directories and use `chown` and `chgrp` so that the directories are not accessible by your regular userid and will return these errors. You should also examine your system to make sure that the security is not compromised. In order to do this, you need to find a system with the same OS and try these Exercises there.

EXERCISE 1.3 SELF-REVIEW QUESTIONS

In order to test your progress, you should be able to answer the following questions.

1) The command `find /usr -mount -type f -perm -4000` will find which of the following?
   a) _____All files in your current directory
   b) _____A directory called /usr
   c) _____All files under the /usr directory that have the setuid bit set to execute as a user that owns each of the files
   d) _____All files under the /usr directory that have the setgid bit set to execute as a member of the group that owns each of the files
   e) _____All files under the /usr partition that have the setgid bit set exactly to 4000 and to execute as a member of the group that owns each of the files

2) The command `find /usr -mount -user myid -type f -perm -4000` will find which of the following?
   a) _____All files in your current directory
   b) _____A directory called /usr owned by myid
   c) _____All files under the /usr partition owned by myid that have the setuid bit set to execute with the same rights as myid
   d) _____All files under the /usr directory owned by myid that have the setgid bit set to execute as a member of the group that myid is in
   e) _____All files under the /usr partition owned by myid that have the setgid bit set to execute as a member of the group that myid is in

3) The command `find /usr -type f -perm /4000` will find which of the following?
   a) _____All files in your current directory
   b) _____A directory called /usr with access rights 4000
   c) _____All files under the /usr directory with access rights exactly 4000
   d) _____All files under the /usr with setuid bit set to the file owner
   e) _____All files under the /usr partition with setgid set to the group of the owner

Quiz answers appear in Appendix A, Section 1.13.

LAB 1.3

C H A P T E R   1

TEST YOUR THINKING

 The projects in this section are meant to have you utilize all of the skills that you have acquired throughout this chapter. The answers to these projects can be found at the companion Web site to this book, located at:

`http://www.phptr.com/phptrinteractive`

Visit the Web site periodically to share and discuss your answers.

1) For this project, determine what kind of security concerns you would have if you saw the following results for files and directories:

    ```
    -rwxrwxrwx
    -rwxr-xr-x
    rwx --- ---
    ```

2) Write a program that checks security rights under your home directory if you are a regular user, or under /etc and your home directory if you are root. This program will check for security breaches. You will use the **find** command with the appropriate options. Use the following criteria:

    a) The program should check every half-hour for possible security breaches.

    b) The program should also execute every time root or the user logs in.

3) Write a program that can be run by a non-root user that lists files, under a user's home directory, that have been changed since the user's last login. Send the results to the owner by e-mail.

4) Take Exercise 1.3.2 and modify the program so that a regular user can execute it from any directory and get no permission errors. The user will still get some valid information.

CHAPTER 2

THE BOURNE SHELL USER

In the computer world, things are not always what they seem. Oftentimes the inner workings are hidden from us and beyond our control. Many people in the computer industry have made what we see simpler and easier to work with. But sometimes in the haste to simplify the view, they have also simplified our abilities and introduced new instabilities.

—Joe

In the early days of computers, the interface was simple. You punched some cards and ran them through a punch card reader. The user interface was a matter of load, push some buttons, and grab some printer output. While there were often manual steps necessary to achieve each function, they were primarily oriented toward the mechanical control of whatever input or output device was being used at the moment.

It became obvious that a simpler, more visual way of accessing the computer was needed. This is where the computer shell came from. An egg shell protects the innards of the egg from damage and isolates it from the outside. So does a computer shell. It disguises many computer operations and simplifies our lives.

One of the earliest UNIX shells was the Bourne Shell. It lacked some of the more advanced features of the later shells, but had the advantage of using only a small amount of memory. In those days, 64K of memory was a lot. To use more memory or a bigger program, you had to swap pages of disk space or memory in and out. So keeping the shell small was critical.

The shell is considered a command line interpreter. This means that the computer executes the program one command at a time and is interactive, so there is no need for a separate compiler. Even if you write a complete program in the UNIX shell, it still executes this way.

The bash is a public domain version of the Bourne Shell. Abbreviated from Bourne Again Shell, bash has some features not found in the Bourne Shell which will be discussed in this chapter. Chapters 3 and 4 discuss other UNIX shells, Korn and C.

This text assumes that you have used UNIX, and are familiar with the UNIX shell. While some of the material may be a repetition of what you learned earlier, we are now going to look at the shell from an administrator's perspective.

Look in the man pages for the following:

```
sh, bash, profile, ksh, tset
```

a) Explain the results you get. What does each line do?

_____

_____

Make a directory to use as your working directory for the next series of exercises. Enter the following command:

```
mkdir sh1 (if it doesn't already exist)
```

Now, save the original `.profile` by entering the following command:

```
cp .profile .profile.org
```

You have just made a backup copy of your `profile` that you can use to recover and a working copy that you copied to your `sh1` directory.

```
cd sh1
```

Be sure you know what your current environment variables settings are set to. You can save the list of the environment variables by entering the command:

```
set > my.env
```

You can view this file with the command:

```
more my.env
```

The `set` command, without any options, prints all set environment variables, both local and exported. This includes variables set to null.

Your environment is the computer space in which you have to work. Your environment includes variables that have been set by the operating system and values that have been set by your id. It includes values set when you log in, programs you have run, your current directory path, and anything that you need to be aware of when writing shell programs or debugging system or user problems. These are typically represented by a variable. They can be local variables, exported variables, or null values.

b) Viewing the file `my.env`, what are the variables that you recognize, what are they set to, and why are they important?

_____

_____

View your current search path by typing:

`echo $PATH`

c) What are your results?

_____

_____

Use your favorite editor to create a new file called `mynewprofile`. It should contain the following lines:

```
# This file is mynewprofile created for the
# Bourne Shell exercise
PATH=$PATH:$HOME/bin
export PATH
```

 Note that if you already have a bin directory under your home directory that is in your search path, you should use another directory name. Try the name `newbin` for your search directory instead.

Now you will want to test out your `newprofile`. In order to do that, you need to first test it out as a separate shell program that does not affect your current environment. Then you will want to execute it so that it makes changes to some of your current environment variables.

Now run the following program:

```
sh mynewprofile
```

d) What kind of results do you get?

Enter the following command:

```
echo $PATH
```

e) What is the value of $PATH?

f) Is there any difference between the answers to Questions (e) and (c) in this Exercise?

Running the sh command with an option can often reveal more information about the program as it is running than it you would normally get. A particularly useful option is the -x option, which produces a trace of the program while it executes. It shows the command lines and values to which they are set. This is very helpful in debugging a shell program.

Try executing the sh command with the -x option by entering the following:

```
sh -x mynewprofile
```

g) What do you see on the screen?

h) What is the difference between the results for Questions (d) and (g) in this Exercise?

_____

_____

Another useful option is the −n *option, which analyzes the Bourne Shell program for any syntax errors without actually running the program. This option works with all the shells. It allows you to get a much quicker analysis of any errors in your program than you might get by simply executing the program.*

Check your search path now by entering the following:

```
echo $PATH
```

i) Has your search path value changed?

_____

_____

j) What is the impact of this change on your environment?

_____

_____

A good way to put your new values into your current environment is to use the dot command, which executes a shell program. Any changes to the user's environment will be put into the current environment, and will not be passed on to a new shell. It also does not create a child shell program.

Look in the man pages to see how the following command relates to the dot command:

```
exec
```

Try out the following command:

```
. mynewprofile (That is, dot space mynewprofile)
```

k) What do you see on your screen?

_____

_____

Now execute the following command:

```
echo $PATH
```

l) Compare this with the results from Question (f). What do you see that looks different?

_____

_____

m) What is the impact of this command on your environment?

_____

_____

Now repeat the dot command again.

Try out the following command again:

```
. mynewprofile
```

Then type the following:

```
echo $PATH
```

n) What has happened, and what is the impact on your environment?

_____

_____

If you are satisfied that the two program lines from `mynewprofile` are working okay, you can add them to your `.profile`. Do this by entering:

```
cp ../.profile .profile.new
(you should still be in the sh1 subdirectory)
```

Now, edit the `.profile.new` file and add the following two lines from `mynewprofile`:

```
PATH=$PATH:$HOME/bin
export PATH
```

Test it in the following sequence:

```
sh .profile.new
```

If that works, then try:

```
. .profile.new (dot space .profile.new)
```

Remember that after changing your environment files, you should never log out and log in again without first being sure that the changed files work. It should give the proper results and no errors. This is true for all UNIX shells.

Test it out the new file as described earlier. If it is okay, then do the following:

```
cp .profile.new ../.profile
(note the use of the dot dot directories)
```

Now log out and log in again.

Next, type the command:

```
echo $PATH
```

o) What kind of results do you see?

_____

_____

If the results are not what you expected, then you need to step back through this Exercise and figure out what happened.

If the results are what you expected, then congratulations! Now you can get to some serious editing of the .profile file.

2.1.2 ADD FEATURES TO YOUR NEW .PROFILE

This section shows you how to modify your shell environment so that you have additional functionality. It should simplify some actions that you often perform.

You should have the file `mynewprofile` in the `sh1` subdirectory from Exercise 2.1.1. If not, go back and create the necessary files and directories. Next, enter the following command:

```
cd $HOME/sh1
```

Edit the `mynewprofile` file and add the following lines to those already there. Your new file should look like the following:

```
# this file is mynewprofile created for the
# Bourne Shell exercise
PATH=/usr/bin:/usr/ucb:/etc:.
PATH=$PATH:$HOME/bin
export PATH
PS1="`uname -n`-\!>" # use the back single quote
export PS1
echo "Enter terminal type:\c"; read myterm
if [ $myterm != "" ]
then
 TERM=$myterm
 export TERM
 tset
fi
```

Go back to the file that you created earlier in the `sh1` directory, called `my.env` and look for the terminal type set there. A good way to do this is to use the following command:

```
grep TERM my.env
```

a) What terminal type do you find?

_____

_____

Keep this terminal value in mind for the next few questions.

Next, you should test out your program using the testing techniques you learned in Exercise 2.1.1.

b) What is the meaning of each of the lines in the preceding program?

_____

_____

Look in the man pages or your text to see how exec relates to the dot command

When you are done, you should execute the following command:

```
. mynewprofile (dot space mynewprofile)
```

Use the value of the terminal type you found in Question (a) to answer the terminal type prompt.

c) What do you see on the screen?

_____

_____

Time to try some experimentation. Go ahead and re-execute the program in Question (b) of this Exercise. When you are prompted for the terminal type, enter the following terminal name:

```
xyz
```

Next, when you get the command line prompt, enter the following command:

```
vi newprofile
```

d) What do you see on the screen?

_____

_____

If you have never used vi before, you can get out of it by entering the sequence escape key - colon key - q!. This is a sure exit from the vi program. It does not matter if you are in the command or input mode for vi.

e) What do you think happened?

_____

_____

Once you are satisfied that `mynewprofile` works, copy it to the `.profile` in your home directory, just as you did in Exercise 2.1.1.

Now, log out and log in again. When you log in, use the terminal type you found in the answer to Question (a) of this Exercise.

Enter the following commands:

```
cd sh1
set > mynew.env
```

Now compare the two files `my.env` and `mynew.env`.

f) What is the difference between the two files?

_____

_____

g) What caused the difference between the two files?

_____

_____

h) What command would you use to compare the two files and produce a single output?

_____

_____

Examine the following two commands that we have discussed in this Lab:

```
sh mynewprofile
. mynewprofile (dot space mynewprofile)
```

i) Based on what you have learned from this Lab, what is the difference between using these two commands?

_____

_____

Remember that after changing your environment files, you should never log out and log in again without first being sure that the changed files work. It should give the proper results and no errors. This is true for all UNIX shells.

Finish up this Exercise by copying back the original `.profile` file that you saved in the beginning. Again, do this with the following commands:

```
cd       # to get back to home
cp .profile.org .profile
exit
```

Once you are out of the system, connect back to it and log in again. You should now see your original environment. You may want to copy some of the features of `mynewprofile` to your `.profile` if you like. Just be sure to test it before using it.

LAB 2.1 EXERCISE ANSWERS

This section gives you some suggested answers to the questions in Lab 2.1, with discussion related to those answers. Your answers may vary, but the most important thing is whether your answer works. Use this discussion to analyze differences between your answers and those presented here.

If you have alternative answers to the questions in this Exercise, you are encouraged to post your answers and discuss them at the companion Web site for this book, located at:

```
http://www.phptr.com/phptrinteractive
```

2.1.1 ANSWERS

Log in with your normal login id.
Type the following command:
```
more .profile
```

a) Explain the results you get. What does each line do?

Answer: Your results will vary from different versions of UNIX and from different manufacturers. Your .profile might look something like this:
```
stty istrip
umask 022
PATH=$PATH:/home/myid/bin
export PATH
PS1="`uname -n`-\!>"
LPDEST=mylp
export PS1 LPDEST
mesg n
```

These lines are described as follows:

```
stty istrip
```

This line says to add the `stty` characteristic `istrip` to the environment. This characteristic says to strip any 8-bit ASCII characters to 7 bits. This is designed to prevent problems in handling 8-bit characters in software that cannot handle it. ASCII code is what is used by your terminals, whereas the computer only knows about bits. Thus, the ASCII code acts as a translator.

```
PATH=$PATH:/home/myid/bin
```

This allows you to keep whichever path is set by the system, and just append your own directories to be searched at the end. This is similar to what you may see in the DOS search path.

```
PS1="`uname -n`-\!>"
```

The variable PS1 is the command line prompt. This particular variable gives a prompt that includes a hostname and the number of the command in the history list. The command line looks like the following:

```
myhost-274>ls
```

The following `.profile` entry sets the default printer destination:

```
LPDEST=mylp
```

Next, the following makes the variables global so they can be passed down to any child processes or shells that you might execute from this point on:

```
export PS1 LPDEST
```

Finally, the following says not to send messages to the screen.

```
mesg n
```

This prevents you from being interrupted by messages when you are working at your computer. If you want to be interrupted, just use `mesg n`.

You should have now created a file that contains variables that are part of your shell environment.

b) Viewing the file my.env, what are the critical variables that you might recognize, what are they set to, and why are they important?

Answer: You should get a listing of the characteristics of your environment at that time. The simplified results of running this in Solaris x86 with explanations, are as follows:

HOME=/export/home/myid	Your home directory
LOGNAME=myid	The name used for your current login or to which you did a setuserid
MAIL=/var/mail/myid	Your mail directory
MAILCHECK=600	Check your mail every ten minutes
PATH=/usr/bin:/usr/ucb:/etc:.	Your Search Path
PS1=myid@myhost:/home/myid/sh1	Your command line prompt
PWD=/export/home/myid	Your current working directory (PWD stands for Print Working Directory)
SHELL=/bin/ksh	You current shell
TERM=ansi	Your terminal type
TZ=US/Central	Your time zone
_=/usr/bin/sh	Last command executed

View your current search path by typing:
```
echo $PATH
```

c) What are your results?

*Answer: Your answer should look something like the following. If it is different, don't be concerned, because every system is different. Try to understand what it means. This is consistent with what you got from the **set** command for the **$PATH** variable and what you saw in the **my.env** file.*
```
PATH=/usr/bin:/usr/ucb:/etc:.
```
Use your favorite editor to create a new file called mynewprofile. It should contain the following lines:
```
# This file is mynewprofile created for the
# Bourne Shell exercise
PATH=$PATH:$HOME/bin
export PATH
```
Now run the following program:
```
sh mynewprofile
```

d) What kind of results do you get?

Answer: You should not see anything on the screen from the program, and you should get your $PS1 prompt back. If you do see something, look at your program and make sure there are no errors.

Now enter the following command:

```
echo $PATH
```

e) What is the value of **$PATH**?

Answer: You should see the following path:
```
PATH=/usr/bin:/usr/ucb:/etc:.
```

f) Is there any difference between the answers to Questions (e) and (c) in this Exercise?

Answer: There should be no difference. Once the shell is executed, the environment is returned to the earlier settings.

Try executing the **sh** command with the **-x** option by entering the following:

```
sh -x mynewprofile
```

g) What do you see on the screen?

Answer: You should see the following:
```
+ PATH=/usr/bin:/usr/ucb:/etc:.:/home/myid/bin
+ export PATH
```

h) What is the difference between the results for Questions (d) and (g) in this Exercise?

*Answer: The **sh mynewprofile** executes without any results on the screen. The only way to get something on the screen is to use output statements, or to have an error occur. The **sh -x mynewprofiile** executes and gives a listing of the program as it executes. It also displays things such as variable values, results of decisions, values for input and output, as well as errors. If you followed the tip and used **sh -n mynewprofile,** you would have the program analyzed for syntax errors, but it would not actually be executed.*

Check your search path now by entering the following:

```
echo $PATH
```

i) Has your search path value changed?

Answer: There should be no difference in your search path.
```
PATH=/usr/bin:/usr/ucb:/etc:.
```

j)   What is the impact on your environment of this change?

Answer: There is no impact.

Try out the following command:

```
. mynewprofile (That is dot space mynewprofile)
```

k)   What do you see on your screen?

Answer: You should see nothing on your screen and you should get your prompt back.

If you see something, then you need to examine your program for errors.

Next, execute the following command:

```
echo $PATH
```

l)   Compare this with the results from Question (f). What do you see that looks different?

*Answer: You should see that your **bin** directory has been added to your search path, as follows:*

```
PATH=/usr/bin:/usr/ucb:/etc:.:/home/myid/bin
```

m)   What is the impact of this command on your environment?

*Answer: The operating system will now search the directory **/home/myid/bin** for commands to be executed.*

*The directory **/home/myid/bin** is appended to end of the search path. This means that your current directory is no longer the last directory searched. As far as security is concerned, this is not a problem here. However, if you were to do the following, your **bin** directory would be the first one searched:*
```
PATH=/home/myid/bin:$PATH
```

This could be an ideal place for someone to hide a Trojan horse, or some program that is named the same as a system command, but can violate security. When you execute a command, this is the first place the system looks.

Now repeat the dot command again.
Try out the following command again:

```
. mynewprofile (That is dot space mynewprofile)
```

Then type the following:

```
echo $PATH
```

n) What has happened, and what is the impact on your environment?

Answer: You will see the following results:

```
PATH=/usr/bin:/usr/ucb:/etc:.:/home/myid/bin:/home/myid/bin
```

*The directory **/home/myid/bin** will be searched twice.*

One impact is that if you execute a command, the system searches the /home/myid/bin directory twice. Fortunately, this is not a problem as it is in DOS, where your search PATH is ignored after it reaches a certain number of characters. However, the longer the search path, the more time it takes to go through all the directories in searching for a command. So, when you set up your search path, and performance is a big issue, you should order the directories so that the most-used directories are hit first. It is easy in some environments to really get carried away and have a legacy of directories that no longer exist, and yet are still searched.

You should have now created and tested your new .profile as described in the Exercise section. Then you logged out and logged in again.

o) What kind of results do you see?

*Answer: You should not see any errors, and any screen messages should be the same as you would normally get. If you type **echo $PATH**, you will see the new search path as described previously.*

If the results are not what you expected, then you need to step back through this Exercise and figure out what happened.

2.1.2 ANSWERS

Go back to the file that you created earlier in the **sh1** directory called **my.env** and look for the terminal type set there. A good way to do this is to use the following command:

```
grep TERM my.env
```

a) What terminal type do you find?

Answer: You should see something like the following display:

```
TERM=ansi
```

So in this case the terminal type is ansi. ANSI stands for the American National Standards Institute, and they produce standards for many things from bicycle helmets to computer software.

Keep this terminal value in mind for the next few questions.
Next, you should test out your program using the testing techniques you learned in Exercise 2.1.1.

b) What is the meaning of each of the lines in this program?

Answer: The answers are given on each of the following lines as comments:

```
# this file is mynewprofile created for the
# Bourne Shell exercise
PATH=/usr/bin:/usr/ucb:/etc:. # The original path
PATH=$PATH:$HOME/bin# Search path for commands
export PATH# export it to future shells
PS1="`uname -n`-\!>" # use the back single quote
     # Set the prompt to hostname - command #
export PS1# export the value to future shells
# The following module will ask to set the terminal
   type
echo "Enter terminal type:\c"; read myterm
if [ $myterm != "" ]# If myterm is not a return
then
TERM=$myterm# set TERM to value typed in
export TERM
tset        # initialize the terminal
fi
```

When you are done, you should execute the command:

```
. mynewprofile (dot space mynewprofile)
```

Use the value of the terminal type you found in Question (a) to answer the terminal type prompt.

c) What do you see on the screen?

Answer: You are prompted to enter the terminal type, which you should enter just as you found it in Question (a).

Time to try some experimentation. Go ahead and re-execute the program in Question (b) of this Exercise. When you are prompted for the terminal type, enter the following terminal name:

```
xyz
```

Next, when you get the command line prompt, enter the following command:

```
vi profile
```

d) What do you see on the screen?

Answer: You should see something similar to the following:

```
I don't know what kind of terminal you are on - all I
  have is 'xyz'.
[Using open mode]
"profile" 54 lines, 831 characters
#ident "@(#)profile 1.17 95/03/28 SMI" /* SVr4.0 1.3
  */
```

This means you have entered the line editor mode. The line editors in UNIX date from the very beginning. Some of the UNIX line editors are ed, ex, and edit.

e) What do you think happened?

Answer: Because the system could not find a valid terminal type called xyz, it gave a message and then went into line editor mode.

You should note that sometimes when do this, it will go into vi and just give garbage. As an extra exercise, try using ibm3164 as your terminal type.

Once you are satisfied that `mynewprofile` works, copy it to the **.profile** in your home directory, just as you did in Exercise 2.1.1.
Now log out and log in again. When you log in, use the terminal type you found in the answer to Question (a) of this Exercise.
Enter the following commands:

```
cd sh1
set > mynew.env
```

Now, compare the two files `my.env` and `mynew.env`.

f) What is the difference between the two files?

Answer: You will see some differences such as a different search path, a different prompt, and a few other variables, including `myterm`, which was created by the new .profile when you logged in.

g) What caused the difference between the two files?

Answer: The differences occurred because the two .profiles may have different directories in their search path, a different prompt was set up, and other things will be different.

h) What command would you use to compare the two files and produce a single output?

Answer:You should use the following command:
```
diff my.env mynew.env | more
```

This command does a line-by-line comparison and shows you the differences between the two files. It is then piped into `more` because the output will generally be more than a page in size on the screen.

Examine the following two commands that we have discussed in this Lab:
```
sh mynewprofile
. mynewprofile (dot space mynewprofile)
```

i) Based on what you have learned from this Lab, what is the difference between using these two commands?

Answer:The following points should be considered:

- The `sh` command creates a new shell when it executes. These values are only good in the new shell. Any changes or new values in the environment are lost when the program is finished running.
- The `dot` command executes the program within the current shell. It overlays any memory, variables, or other environmental features from the parent process. Any changes or new values in the environment remain when the program is finished running. The command is similar to the `exec` command, which you should look up if you are not already familiar with it. You may realize that this is similar to the way in which DOS/Windows executes programs. All values in DOS remain in the environment when a program is done executing.

LAB 2.1 SELF-REVIEW QUESTIONS

In order to test your progress, you should be able to answer the following questions. Note that one answer may be valid in one version of UNIX and another answer may be valid in another version. It is important that you understand why you received such an error message.

1) You go into vi to edit a *text* file and you get garbage or a weird screen display. Which of the following is the most likely cause?

   a) _____You are editing a binary file
   b) _____The TERM variable is set incorrectly
   c) _____You don't have the proper file permissions
   d) _____The file is in use by someone
   e) _____The file is read only

2) Which of the following search paths will execute **$HOME/bin/ksh** before **/bin/ksh** (assuming there are no files linked between **/bin** and **/usr/bin**)?

   a) _____PATH=/usr/bin:/bin:$HOME/bin:
   b) _____PATH=.:/usr/bin:/bin:$HOME/bin
   c) _____PATH=$HOME/bin:/usr/bin:/bin:
   d) _____PATH=.:/bin:$HOME/bin:.:/usr/bin
   e) _____None of the above

3) Which of the following is the first file executed to set the login environment variables for all users in the Bourne Shell?

   a) _____.profile
   b) _____/etc/profile
   c) _____.cshrc
   d) _____.kshrc
   e) _____None of the above

4) Which of the following is the second file executed to set the login environment variables for a regular user in the Bourne Shell?

   a) _____.profile
   b) _____/etc/profile
   c) _____.cshrc
   d) _____.kshrc
   e) _____None of the above

5) Which of the following is the command and option for executing a Bourne Shell so that the variable substitutions and command executions are shown?

a) _____sh -a
b) _____sh -k
c) _____sh -n
d) _____sh -x
e) _____None of the above

6) Which of the following is the command and option for just parsing and looking for syntax errors, but not executing a Bourne Shell program?

a) _____sh -a
b) _____sh -k
c) _____sh -n
d) _____sh -x
e) _____None of the above

Quiz answers appear in Appendix A, Section 2.1.

L A B   2.2

THE USER AND SYSTEM ENVIRONMENT

We are all victims of our environment. We are molded and shaped by that around us. The environment puts restrictions on us. Yet it also makes life easier in many ways. So too does a user's environment on the computer affect and restrict us. We can change our environment there to make life easier or to make it more difficult.   —Joe

---

LAB OBJECTIVES

After this Lab, you will be able to:

✓ Further Customize Your Environment

In the previous Lab, you saw how to modify the user `.profile` to modify the environment and simplify some things that the user does. Often-times, users get carried away in making changes to their environments via the `.profile` (or any of the other setup files). It is important to distinguish whether or not to change a variable, and where to put it.

Never modify your environment until you understand the changes. In particular, never rename a UNIX command via the .profile or any other setup file. You are only asking for disaster, particularly if a UNIX batch program expects something to work one way and it actually works another.

USER ENVIRONMENT VARIABLES

Look in the man pages to see how this discussion on variables relates to:

`profile` *and* `/etc/profile`

Most user environmental values are set by the `/etc/profile` file first and then by the `.profile` file in the users' home directory. The values set by `/etc/profile` include many of the same things set by the user's `.profile`. However, the user's `.profile` can override most things that are set in the `/etc/profile`.

Most of the restrictions placed on a user relating to system use cannot be overridden.

Look in the man pages for the command:

`ulimit`

Some environmental values, such as maximum file size set by ulimit, cannot be increased in value, but can be decreased. Other values, such as priority, cannot be given a lower number, but can be given a higher number. Then there are values that cannot be changed at all, such as characteristics of files and directories that you don't own.

A good rule to help you remember in setting environment values is that, as a regular user, you can almost never make things run better for you. You can only make things run slower, take less space, use less resources and generally make things more difficult for you to run your program. Of course, root can usually change most values to go either better or worse, faster or slower, and so forth.

■ FOR EXAMPLE:

Let's examine some of the key login environment values that can be set.

Be aware that not all shells and all versions of UNIX handle the environment in the same way. In some cases, a value will change when you run the `su` command; other times, it may not.

- **LOGNAME, USER, USERNAME**—These are the id names that you logged in with or are currently working from. These values may change if you do a setuserid from your login name. If you run the command `su - newuserid`, when you go to `newuserid` it will generally change all those values.
- **TERM**—This is the value of your current terminal type. It is used by the full-screen editors to set your terminal characteristics for editing. If this value is set improperly, your screen will look like garbage when you go into the editor. This does not affect your command line screen, though. The most commonly-used setting is one of the DEC vt100 series of terminals, even when connecting with telnet from a PC. This family of terminals includes the vt100, vt220, vt320, and various other flavors of DEC vt terminals.
- **ulimit**—This is not actually a variable, but rather a command that is usually found in the files that setup your environment when you first login. Most commonly, this command is used to set restrictions on the maximum size of a file a user can create. You can also control the maximum CPU time the user has, and many other things. Once this is set by root or the system, the user can only increase, not lessen, his/her restrictions.
- **TZ**—This is the value used for the current time zone a user is in. The system default is often set in the `/etc/profile` file. But any user can change the value to his/her local time zone. This enables UNIX users to be spread across multiple time zones. Your time zone variable might look like:

      TZ=US/Central or
      TZ=CST6CDT

  The second form says that you are in the Central Time Zone and that you observe daylight savings time. You are also in time zone number 6, which is the sixth time zone from Greenwich Mean Time (GMT). GMT is used as the international time reference point. This is the same as what you may have seen in DOS.

- **PATH**—This is the search sequence used by UNIX to search for commands. It looks at the first directory listed and then continues on to the end of the list. This works just like the DOS path statement. The list would look something like this:

```
PATH=/usr/local/bin:/bin:/usr/bin:/home/myhome/bin:.
```

Note that if you are root, you should never have the ".", dot directory, in your search path. Doing so allows someone to place a Trojan horse program in your current directory. This program can masquerade as a system command, while it is in reality a program used to gain access to your system. Just leave it out of your search path.

- **PS1**—This variable is the command line prompt. The default prompt for a normal user is $, whereas the default prompt for root is #. The variations of this variable often-times include the following items:
  - The user's login name
  - The system name where the user is currently logged in. This is important because sometimes you may have several windows open on your screen, with each one pointing to a different system. You want to be sure you are accessing the right system when you execute the shutdown command. This helps to keep you honest.
  - Your current directory or directory path. Red Hat Linux likes to use just the directory name, but that can become confusing if you have several directories of the same name. The other option is to give the full path name, which sometimes fills up a whole line. This can lead to confusion because, when you are looking for something to be put on the prompt's line, it is actually wrapped over to the next line. Here is where short directory names are important. You should note that in some versions of the Bourne or Korn Shell, the value of the directory in PS1 is not reevaluated when you execute a command. Also, this may vary within the same manufacturer. Due to becoming POSIX compatible, some combinations of commands will work in Solaris 2.5.1 and not Solaris 2.6, and vice versa.

LAB 2.2

- Some kind of additional prompt indicating whether you are root or user
- Another prompt may indicate what kind of shell you are running and whether it is the Bourne Shell, Korn Shell, or bash shell.
  Of these items, only the current directory or directory path changes as the user moves from one directory to another. Of course, if your userid is changed, then other values change also. So PS1 might look like:
  ```
  myname@myhost:/home/myname/sh1
  ```
- **MAIL**—This points to the location of your mail folder where mail is stored when you receive it. It is possible to override this variable when you check your mail in order to look at mail from several ids. However, unless you are in root or have modified the rights to the mail file, you won't be able to look at someone else's file if it has a different userid number.

Use the UNIX man pages to find out more about the variables:

LOGNAME USER USERNAME TERM ulimit TZ PATH PS1 MAIL

Most of these are documented in the man pages for sh and ksh.

LAB 2.2 EXERCISES

2.2.1 FURTHER CUSTOMIZE YOUR ENVIRONMENT

This Exercise will help you understand what happens when you change your environment variables and items that are referenced by the environment variables.

Create the following program, called `prog221.sh`, and place it in your `sh1` directory.

```
#!/bin/sh
# this program is called prog221.sh and is
# used to test changing the value of the mail
```

```
# variable
cd $HOME/sh1
MYMAIL=$MAIL# This saves the mail file value
touch mymailfile
chmod 000 mymailfile
MAIL=./mymailfile
mail -f $MAIL# Read the mail from a local file
MAIL=$MYMAIL# reset the mail variable
```

a) What kind of results do you get when you execute `prog221.sh`?

_____

_____

b) Why did you get those results? Be specific—which line was the main cause of the messages you got?

_____

_____

c) You should now modify that line so that the error message does not occur. What do you need to do?

_____

_____

d) Now you should execute the program `prog221.sh` again. What kind of results do you get?

_____

_____

LAB 2.2 EXERCISE ANSWERS

This section gives you some suggested answers to the questions in Lab 2.2, with discussion related to those answers. Your answers may vary, but the most important thing is whether your answer works. Use this discussion to analyze differences between your answers and those presented here.

If you have alternative answers to the questions in this Exercise, you are encouraged to post your answers and discuss them at the companion Web site for this book, located at:

```
http://www.phptr.com/phptrinteractive
```

2.2.1 ANSWERS

This Exercise will help you understand what happens when you change your environment variables. Create the following program, called `prog221.sh`, and place it in your sh1 directory.

```
#!/bin/sh
# this program is called prog221.sh and is
# used to test changing the value of the mail
# variable
cd $HOME/sh1
MYMAIL=$MAIL# This saves the mail file value
touch mymailfile
chmod 000 mymailfile
MAIL=./mymailfile
mail -f $MAIL# Read the mail from a local file
MAIL=$MYMAIL# reset the mail variable
prog221.sh
```

a) What kind of results do you get when you execute `prog221.sh`?

Answer: Results vary and are discussed as follows. You should see the following results:

In Solaris x86, you will see:

```
mail: Invalid permissions on ./mymailfile
```

In Linux, you will see:

```
./mymailfile: Permission denied
```

b) Why did you get those kind of results? Be specific—which line was the main cause of the messages you got?

Answer: You get that message because the access rights on the mail file are set to 000. This means that no one can do anything with the file, not even the owner.

c) You should now modify that line so that the error message does not occur. What do you need to do?

Answer: You should modify that file so that the owner can access the file. If you just change the line that is giving a problem to the following, this should take care of it:
```
chmod 700 mymailfile
```

d) Now you should execute the program `prog221.sh` again. What kind of results do you get?

Answer: You should get a message similar to the following, depending on your system:

In Solaris x86, you will see:
```
No mail.
```

In Linux, you will see something similar to:
```
Mail version 5.5-kw 5/30/95. Type ? for help.
"./mymailfile": 0 messages
&
```

In this particular case, Linux entered the mail program and did not leave it. That is not a problem. Just enter the letter q to quit.

LAB 2.2 SELF-REVIEW QUESTIONS

In order to test your progress, you should be able to answer the following questions. Note that one answer may be valid in one version of UNIX and another answer may be valid in another version. It is important that you understand why you got such an error message.

1) You go into vi to edit a *text* file and you get garbage or a weird screen display. Which of the following is the most likely cause?
   a) _____You are editing a binary file
   b) _____The TERM variable is set wrong
   c) _____You don't have the proper file permissions
   d) _____The file is in use by someone
   e) _____The file is read only

2) Which of the following search paths will execute `$HOME/bin/ksh` before `/bin/ksh` (assuming there are no files linked between `/bin` and `/usr/bin`)?
   a) _____PATH=/usr/bin:/bin:$HOME/bin:
   b) _____PATH=.:/usr/bin:/bin:$HOME/bin
   c) _____PATH=$HOME/bin:/usr/bin:/bin:
   d) _____PATH=.:/bin:$HOME/bin:.:/usr/bin
   e) _____None of the above

3) Which of the following is the first file that is executed to set the login environment variables for all users in the Bourne Shell?
   a) _____.profile
   b) _____/etc/profile
   c) _____.cshrc
   d) _____.kshrc
   e) _____None of the above

4) Which of the following is the second file that is executed to set the login environment variables for a regular user in the Bourne Shell?
   a) _____.profile
   b) _____/etc/profile
   c) _____.cshrc
   d) _____.kshrc
   e) _____None of the above

5) Which of the following is the command and option for executing a Bourne Shell so that the variable substitutions and command executions are shown?

   a) _____sh -a
   b) _____sh -k
   c) _____sh -n
   d) _____sh -x
   e) _____None of the above

6) Which of the following is the command and option for just parsing and looking for syntax errors, but not executing a Bourne Shell program?

   a) _____sh -a
   b) _____sh -k
   c) _____sh -n
   d) _____sh -x
   e) _____None of the above

Quiz answers appear in Appendix A, Section 2.1.

C H A P T E R   2

TEST YOUR THINKING

The projects in this section are meant to have you utilize all of the skills that you have acquired throughout this chapter. The answers to these projects can be found at the companion Web site to this book, located at:

`http://www.phptrrenhall.com`

Visit the Web site periodically to share and discuss your answers.

1) Log in as a regular user. Write a program that will set all your environment variables. You can determine what they are by typing:
   ```
   set
   ```

   You can save the results and put them in a file, and then modify the file so that those values are set manually when you execute this file. A great way to understand your environment values are is to study the file. Save this program, because you can execute it whenever you need to reset your environment. Just use the "." dot command to execute the file.

2) Log in as root. Repeat Project 1.

If you don't have root access, you can still create a file that sets some of the root environment. You can determine much of the root environment by looking at `/etc/profile` *and noting the values that are set for the root user. You might also ask your instructor, if you have one, to provide the environment settings. You could also ask a nice, friendly system administrator if he/she could provide a copy.*

3) Write a program that compares the two programs that resulted from the previous two projects in this section. You might use the command:
   ```
   diff
   ```

Analyze this program to understand the differences in the environment between logging in as a regular user and logging in as root.

4)   Write a program that determines whether you are running the program as a regular user or root, and then set the environment accordingly. Use the programs you created in Projects I and 2 to set the proper environments.

If you don't have root access, you can still change some of your environment variables so that your program thinks you are root, even if you aren't. You could start a new shell by executing sh *if you are concerned about affecting your current environment. When you are done, you can just type the command* exit. *See the previous bit of Advice as well.*

5)   Now it's time to be a detective and check out the regular user's environment. Take Project I and determine which environmental settings are set up by:

a) /etc/profile

b) .profile

c) Bourne Shell

d) Other sources

6)   Continuing on as a detective, you need to look at root's environment. Take Project I and determine which environmental settings are set up by:

a) /etc/profile

b) .profile

c) Bourne Shell

d) Other sources

7) Go through the exercises in this chapter and redo them in the Bourne Shell, except this time, leave out the `export` command. You used this in places such as:

a) export PATH

b) export PS1

c) what happened to "c"?

d) Other exported variables

Then you should:

e) Determine which commands depend on those variables being set.

f) Execute them without the variables being set.

g) Export the values.

h) Determine what the differences are. Be aware that some variables do not need to be exported, whereas others do.

8) You have learned about some of the options to **sh** in this chapter. Some of those include **-x** and **-n**. Look up the following options for the Bourne Shell. Explain what effects they have on executing a shell program. Consider the option as it is used in the following:

```
sh -option myprogram
```

The options to be considered are as follows:

a) -e

b) -i

c) -v

d) Look at other options that might be useful

CHAPTER 3

THE KORN SHELL USER

 The computer world moves very quickly. What was standard yesterday is often obsolete today. Yet some things continue in their usefulness and importance. They just may get some pinstripes and a corner office, or perhaps a new engine, paint job, and racing stripes.   *-Joe*

CHAPTER OBJECTIVES

In this Chapter, you will learn:

Exercises for the Masses

The Bourne Shell is the first popular shell in UNIX. It gives a lot of power to the user and has the capabilities of an interactive programming language, such as BASIC. Early on, there were more things that people wanted to do that the Bourne Shell couldn't do, and which required a C program to execute. So additional shells were created. They include the Korn Shell(ksh), C Shell(csh), Bourne Again Shell (bash), tcsh, and other variants.

This is one of the legacies of UNIX. In its early days, UNIX source code was given away for cost, primarily to universities and research institutions. The only requirement was that any improvements be returned to AT&T Bell Labs to be added to UNIX, and then included in future improvements to be given away. UNIX no longer continues the legacy of giving away code. However, Linux has carried on this tradition, and as a result, improvements continue at a rapid pace in Linux. Because of this, UNIX benefits and new shells get produced.

Look in the man pages for the following:

`ksh, kshrc`

EXERCISES FOR THE MASSES

The Korn Shell gives us more power than the Bourne Shell. This chapter explores some of the additional capabilities of this shell.

After completing this chapter, you should go back and do the Bourne Shell exercises, except use the Korn Shell to execute them. Note the differences. Many of the differences are left as an exercise for you.

The differences between shells are subtle. The differences between versions of the same shell from various manufacturers is sometimes just as subtle. If something doesn't work, it may be due to of some of these differences. Sometimes things just don't work according to the book. To fix these types of situations, you need to have patience and experiment.

L A B   3.1

MORE ON THE .PROFILE

LAB OBJECTIVES

After this Lab, you will be able to:

✓ Review Your .profile

✓ Learn About Your .kshrc

.PROFILE

You have seen how the .profile was used in the previous chapter. This chapter looks at additional ways to set up your environment if you are using the Korn Shell.

If you are currently logging in with the Bourne Shell, you need to change your default login. It was not a problem in the Bourne Shell chapter to log in with the Korn Shell. This is because the Korn Shell runs all of the Bourne Shell programs with basically the same results. But the reverse is not true. If you are not root, you need to either run the chsh program (look it up, because it is not available on all versions of UNIX), or contact your system administrator and ask to have your shell changed. If worst comes to worst, you can just type ksh from your Bourne Shell, or, on the last line of your .profile, place the command ksh to execute the Korn Shell.

.KSHRC

The Korn Shell allows you to use an additional file to set your environment. That file is commonly called the `.kshrc`. This file is executed when you log in to the Korn Shell and have the following variable set:

```
ENV=.kshrc
```

where `.kshrc` is the name of the Korn Shell program that sets your login environment. It does not have to be called `.kshrc`, although this is standard procedure. If you are running the Korn Shell, this will be executed. If you log in with the Bourne Shell, it will be ignored. The file pointed at by ENV also executes every time you go to a new Korn Shell program or shell, whereas the `.profile` is only executed once.

Two powerful features of the Korn Shell, C Shell, and other variants of the Bourne Shell are their abilities to create `aliases` *and* `functions` *for commands. However, you must be very careful when using them. It is very easy to create an alias or function for a system command. People fall into the trap of using the same name as the original command. It might be nice to create an alias for* `rm` *called* `rm -i`*, which will then force you to be prompted every time you want to remove something. However, if you have a shell script that runs automatically from* `cron`*, the program sits there and hangs while it waits for a prompt which it will never get, because it does not run from a terminal. It is better to create an alias called* `myrm` *for* `rm` *called* `rm -i`*, and learn to use that. You might also want to decide whether using aliases will complicate things for yourself and other users. Many aliases can be written as short programs with unique names and put in* `/usr/local/bin` *where they can be accessed by everyone and everyone knows their origin.*

Look up the following Korn Shell commands in the man pages and your text:

alias, function, `rm`

LAB 3.1 EXERCISES

3.1.1 REVIEW YOUR .PROFILE

If you didn't do the labs in the Bourne Shell chapter, you must create the following file, called `mynewprofile`, which was created in that chapter.

 As mentioned in the Bourne Shell chapter, and reemphasized here, never log out and log in again without thoroughly testing any changes to your `.profile`, *or any files that change your environment.*

```
# this file is mynewprofile
# It was originally created for the
# Bourne Shell exercise, but is now
# Being used in the Korn Shell Chapter
PATH=/usr/bin:/usr/ucb:/etc:.
PATH=$PATH:$HOME/bin
export PATH
mesg y
PS1="`uname -n`-\!>"   # use the back single quote
export PS1
echo "Enter terminal type:\c"; read myterm
if [ $myterm != "" ]
then
        TERM=$myterm
        export TERM
        tset
fi
```

a) Test this file as a regular user as described in the Bourne Shell chapter and fix any errors. What do you see on the screen when you execute the program?

_____

_____

You can use this file for your `.profile`, but be sure to save your original file. You can just enter the following from your home directory:

```
cp .profile .profile.orig
```

This saves the file. See Chapter 2 on the Bourne Shell if you want more detail.

3.1.2 LEARN ABOUT YOUR .KSHRC

 In the Korn Shell, you can use the `set -o vi` *command to find the history of your commands. Once you do that, hit the* `Escape` *key or* `^[` *(control left-square-bracket on some terminals). Then use the* `j` *or* `k` *keys to move up or down in the history list. You can then edit each command and reenter it.*

Log in with your regular, not root, login id. (Be sure you are in the Korn Shell before completing the rest of this Exercise.) Determine if you have a `.kshrc` *by typing the following command in your home directory:*

```
ls .kshrc
```

b) What kind of results do you get?

_____

_____

If you have a `.kshrc`, type this command in your home directory:

```
more .kshrc
```

c) Explain any results you get. What does each line do?

_____

_____

Make a directory that you can use as your working directory for the next series of questions in this Exercise. Enter the following command:

```
mkdir  ksh1 (if it doesn't already exist)
```

If you have a `.kshrc` file, save the original file by entering the following command:

```
cp .kshrc .kshrc.org
cp .kshrc ksh1/.kshrc.org
cd ksh1
```

Create a file called `myksh.env` by executing the following:

```
set > myksh.env
```

Now, enter the following command:

```
more myksh.env
```

> **d)** What do you see?

_____

_____

Create a file called `mykshrc` that will be used as your new `.kshrc`. Create it as follows.

Note that you may have to change some values and directory paths to match your system. Your mileage may vary! Not for professionals only! Try this at home!

```
# This is .kshrc file the is used to set the
# Korn Shell environment once you have logged in.
stty erase '^h' kill '^x'
stty intr '^c' quit '^u'
umask 077
# environment variables:
CDPATH=.:$HOME:$HOME/ksh1
EDITOR=/usr/bin/vi
HISTSIZE=200
PS1='${PWD})  '
SHELL=/usr/bin/ksh
```

```
# Korn shell specific settings:
set -o allexport
set -o monitor
set -o trackall
set -o vi
# Define some aliases:
alias bye='tput clear;exit'
alias h='fc -l '
#define functions:
function expr {
            integer result
            let result="$*"
            echo $result
}
```

e) What is the meaning of each line in the `mykshrc` program you created?

_____

_____

Test this just like you tested the programs in the Bourne Shell chapter by executing the following command:

```
ksh mykshrc
. mykshrc   (dot space mykshrc)
```

Be sure to fix any problems and make any changes to match your system. Use
the methods your learned in earlier chapters to figure out the differences.

f) How does this change your environment?

_____

_____

g) What would you say are the significant differences between the "before" and "after" environments? (This is really a subjective decision on your part and could vary depending on your results.)

_____

_____

Once you are satisfied that this file is correct, enter the following:

```
cp mykshrc    .kshrc
```

Test this out again by typing:

```
ksh .kshrc
. .kshrc     (dot space dot kshrc)
```

h) What do you see on your screen?

_____

_____

In your `.profile,` enter the string:

```
ENV=$HOME/.kshrc; export ENV.
```

Log out, log in again, and make any further changes. Be sure that ENV is set in your `.profile,` as explained previously.

i) What do you see when you log in that is different?

_____

_____

Get a copy of your new environment and review it by executing the command:

```
set > mynewksh.env
more mynewksh.env
```

j) What do you see that is different? Again, use the previous techniques for determining the differences.

_____

_____

k) Why do you need to have the ENV variable set in the .profile?

_____

_____

l) Test out the expr function you just created. How did you test the
expr function?

_____

_____

m) What did you notice that was different about your $PS1 variable?
Think or look back to what it was before the .kshrc was created
when you just executed the .profile file.

_____

_____

n) What do you think caused the differences?

_____

_____

In this Exercise, you have created the following files:

- .profile (the new one)
- myksh.env
- hrc
- ewksh.env

Review them to make sure you understand what they mean for the user environment. Be sure you have any and all original files backed up. If you think you will have problems with other applications you are using, just copy your new files to a backup copy and then put back the original files. Then just logout and login again. The next time you need the new files, you can just copy them back in.

LAB 3.1 EXERCISE ANSWERS

This section gives you some suggested answers to the questions in Lab 3.1, with discussion related to those answers. Your answers may vary, but the most important thing is whether your answer works. Use this discussion to analyze differences between your answers and those presented here.

If you have alternative answers to the questions in this Exercise, you are encouraged to post your answers and discuss them at the companion Web site for this book, located at:

```
http://www.phptr.com/phptrinteractive
```

3.1.1 ANSWERS

For Exercise 3.1.1, you first created the `mynewprofile` file that was initially created in Chapter 2, "The Borne Shell."

a)   Test this file as a regular user as described in the Bourne Shell chapter and fix any errors. What do you see on the screen when you execute the program?

   Answer: You should see the following on your screen:
```
1$ . mynewprofile
Enter terminal type:vt100
myserver-203>
```

Note the following:

   • The terminal type that was entered is vt100. This is a standard terminal emulation. Your system may use other terminal emulations, or it may use X-Windows.

- The prompt has been changed.
- The number "203" that appears in the command line prompt is the number of the command in the history list.
- The uname command may not work on some versions of UNIX or Linux, so you may get an error. You can just replace it with the command hostname or some other command that gives you the name of your server.

3.1.2 ANSWERS

For this exercise, you logged in as a regular user and tried to determine if you have a .kshrc file.

a) What kind of results do you get?

Answer: If you have a .kshrc, you will see something like:
```
1$ ls .kshrc
.kshrc
$
```

If you don't have a .kshrc file, you should see something similar to:

```
.kshrc: No such file or directory
```

Don't be concerned if you don't have it, because you will be creating it.

For the next question, you were asked to enter the command more .kshrc in your home directory.

b) Explain any results you get. What does each line do?

Answer: Consider the following example of a portion of the .kshrc file:
```
# This is .kshrc file the is used to set the
# Korn Shell environment once you have logged in.
stty erase '^h' kill '^x'
stty intr '^c' quit '^u'
umask 077
```

When you execute this file, you will not see anything on the screen. An explanation of the lines are given in later Exercises.

For the next few questions, you made a directory to be used as a working directory. If you have a .kshrc file, you saved it in preparation for creating a new one, which you also did. Finally, you executed the command `myksh.env`.

c) What do you see?

Answer: You should see a file similar to the `.profile` *file. In fact, any of the commands that you have in the* `.profile` *can be put into the* `.kshrc`. *The difference is that the* `.kshrc` *is executed every time a new ksh program or shell is created or executed, whereas* `.profile` *is only executed when you login.*

d) What is the meaning of each line in the `mykshrc` program you created?

Answer: See the comments in the following program:

```
# This is .kshrc file the is used to set the
# Korn Shell environment once you have logged in.
stty erase '^h' kill '^x'#set    erase    and    line
  kill
stty intr '^c' quit '^u'#set interrupt and quit
  chars
umask 077#set file creation mask
# environment variables:
CDPATH=.:$HOME:$HOME/ksh1# directory list for cd
EDITOR=/usr/bin/vi#editor for history list
HISTSIZE=200#size of history list
PS1='${PWD}) '#primary   prompt   -   Note   the   single
  quotes prevent an immediate value substitution for
  the variable
SHELL=/usr/bin/ksh#use Korn subshells
# Korn shell specific settings:
set -o allexport#export all variables
set -o monitor#monitor backgroup jobs
set -o trackall# create full pathname aliases
set -o vi# be able to edit past history commands.
# Define some aliases:
alias bye='tput clear;exit'#clear    screen    and
  log out
alias h='fc -l  '# display history list
#define functions:
function expr {# replacement for expr
integer result# local integer variable
let result="$*"# do arithmetic
echo $result# output result
}
```

**LAB
3.1**

Next, you tested this program and fixed any problems that occurred.

e) How did this change your environment? Use the methods you learned in earlier chapters to figure out the differences.

Answer: Using methods you learned in earlier chapters and discussions, do the following:

```
cd $HOME/ksh1
set > mynewksh.env
diff myksh.env  mynewksh.env > myksh.env.diff
more ksh.env.diff
```

A sample result that was run on Solaris x86 follows:

```
 myserver-245>  diff myksh.env mynewksh.env
1c1,3
< ERRNO=13
---
> CDPATH=.:/export/home/myid/export/home/myid/ksh1
> EDITOR=/usr/bin/vi
> ERRNO=22
2a5
> HISTSIZE=200
21c24
---
26,28c29,31
< RANDOM=10642
< SECONDS=565
< SHELL=/bin/ksh
---
> RANDOM=21183
> SECONDS=595
> SHELL=/usr/bin/ksh
myserver-245>
```

f) What would you say are the significant differences between the "before" and "after" environment? (This is really a subjective decision on your part and could vary depending on your results.)

Answer: In the example, the differences that would be significant, though not earth-shattering, are outlined in the following table.

Before	After	Comment
	`CDPATH=.:/home/myid:/home/myid/ksh1`	The search path for the cd command
Not set	`EDITOR=/usr/bin/vi`	Your default editor
Not set	`HISTSIZE=200`	The number of commands in the history file
`SHELL=/bin/ksh`	`SHELL=/usr/bin/ksh`	Your default for the Korn Shell. This is usually the same program. Often, the two programs, or even the two directories they are in, will be linked.
`RANDOM=10642`	`RANDOM=21183`	Shell-generated numbers that will almost always be different
`SECONDS=565`	`SECONDS=595`	Shell-generated numbers that will almost always be different. It is the number of seconds you have been logged in.

There are other differences that don't show up when you type the set command, including the aliases. Aliases are not part of the Bourne Shell, but are shorthand commands that include other commands. They are like short batch programs and are often used in place of short programs.

Some of the aliases that will not show up, and are not set in your Bourne Shell or Korn Shell `.profile` or `.kshrc` include:

```
myserver-261>alias
autoload='typeset -fu'
command='command '
functions='typeset -f'
history='fc -l'
integer='typeset -i'
local=typeset
nohup='nohup '
r='fc -e -'
stop='kill -STOP'
suspend='kill -STOP $$'
myserver-262>
```

The third difference was the use of a function. A function in the Korn Shell works just like a function you would use in a programming language. It is a piece of code that returns a single value. Computer functions work in UNIX the same way the `sine` function does in math—returning one value.

Take a look at the `expr` function:

```
function expr {          # replacement for expr
integer result          # local integer variable
let result="$*"          # do arithmetic
echo $result             # output result
}
```

Next, you should have created the file, verified that it was correct, saved it and tested it again, but this time using the dot command.

g) What do you see on your screen?

Answer: Your command line prompt $PS1 will have changed. That should be all you see, unless your .profile and .kshrc have some additional settings. You should have seen it change as follows:

```
myserver-288>  . .kshrc
/home/mydir)
```

You have executed the program so that any changes are put into your current environment.

The next part of the exercise required that you set the ENV variable in your
.profile then log out and log in again.

h) What do you see when you log in that is different?

   *Answer: The command line prompt **$PS1** is different, as explained previously.*
Next, you were asked to get a copy of your new environment.

i) What do you see that is different? Again, use the previous techniques to
determine the differences.

   *Answer: You should see the same differences you saw previously when you executed
the program manually, without logging out and in again. If you don't, then you need to
reexamine your files and the steps you took to make sure that things are the same.*

j) Why do you need to have the ENV variable set in the *.profile*?

   *Answer: The Korn Shell looks for the value of the ENV variable to determine what to
execute every time a Korn Shell program is executed. Note that the file name does not
have to be *.kshrc*. It can be anything you want it to be.*

k) Test the expr function that was just created by the .kshrc file. How
did you test out the expr function?

   *Answer: The new **expr** function works like this:*

```
expr a + b
```

   In this function, a and b are two numeric values. So you can test it as follows:

```
/home/mydir)   expr 3 + 4
7
/home/mydir)
```

   Alternatively, you can try:

```
/home/mydir) result=expr 3 + 4
/home/mydir) echo $result
7
/home/mydir)
```

l) What did you notice that was different about your $PS1 variable?
Think back to what it was before the .kshrc was created when you
just executed the .profile file.

   Answer: Your command line prompt has changed, as seen previously.

m) What do you think caused the differences?

Answer: The `.kshrc` *has a different definition for the* $PS1 *than the* `.profile`.

LAB 3.1 SELF-REVIEW QUESTIONS

In order to test your progress, you should be able to answer the following questions. Note that one answer may be valid in one version of UNIX and another answer may be valid in another version. It is important that you understand why you get any error messages.

1) Which of the following is the first file executed to set the user's environment variables for all users in the Korn Shell?

   a) _____.profile
   b) _____/etc/profile
   c) _____.cshrc
   d) _____.kshrc
   e) _____None of the above

2) Which of the following is the second file executed to set the user's environment variables for a regular user in the Korn Shell?

   a) _____.profile
   b) _____/etc/profile
   c) _____.cshrc
   d) _____.kshrc
   e) _____None of the above

3) In the `.profile` in a user's home directory, the following variable is set:

```
ENV=.kshrc
```

   The file `.kshrc` contains the following entries:

```
mybin=/home/myid/bin
mydir=/home/myid/mydir
THIRD_DIR=/home/myid/etc
```

Starting with the initial login, which of the following is the third file executed to set the user's environment variables for a regular user in the Korn Shell?

a) _____$HOME/.profile
b) _____/etc/profile
c) _____/home/myid/etc
d) _____$HOME/.kshrc
e) _____$mybin

4) Which of the following is the command and option for executing a Korn Shell so that the variable substitutions and command executions are shown?

a) _____ksh -a
b) _____ksh -k
c) _____ksh -n
d) _____ksh -x
e) _____None of the above

5) Which of the following is the command and option for just parsing and looking for syntax errors, but not executing a Korn Shell program?

a) _____ksh -a
b) _____ksh -k
c) _____ksh -n
d) _____ksh -x
e) _____None of the above

You have logged in with the id myid. Use the following commands (referred to by lower-case roman numerals) to answer the next three questions (you might want to review the ~ command):

i) cd
ii) cd $HOME
iii) cd ~myid
iv) cd ~

6) Which of these commands will get you to your home directory? Choose the best combination:

a) _____i
b) _____i, iii
c) _____i, ii, iii, iv
d) _____ii, iii
e) _____None of the above

7) Which of these commands would get you to your regular login id,
   `myid`, and home directory, even if you changed your id to root?

   a) _____i

   b) _____iv

   c) _____ii

   d) _____iii

   e) _____None of the above

8) If you change your home directory variable to `/home/yourid`, which
   commands would still get you to your home directory?

   a) _____i

   b) _____i, iii

   c) _____i, ii, iii

   d) _____iii

   e) _____None of the above

EXERCISES FOR THE GREAT AND SUPER USER

The next Lab is designed to be executed by someone with root or superuser access rights. While some exercises may be done with a normal id, there will be some aspects that won't be seen until done as root or superuser.

In the Bourne, Korn, and bash Shells, it is possible to reduce the process of setting the user's environment to a single file that is executed at login. This reduces the need to customize each and every users' login. However, the root user should avoid putting in features that are really personal preferences. Particularly dangerous are aliases for standard UNIX commands.

L A B   3.2

THE /ETC/PROFILE FILE

LAB OBJECTIVES

After this series of Exercises, you will be able to:

✓ Better Understand the /etc/profile File

/ETC/PROFILE

The login environment for all users in the Bourne, Korn, and Bourne Again Shell (bash) is set first by the /etc/profile file. The profile file located in the /etc directory is executed by all users when logging in. After this, the user will execute the .profile in his/her home directory. As you will see in later chapters, there are similar files for the C shell.

Because /etc/profile files vary greatly from UNIX version to UNIX version, you should go back to Lab 2.2 and review the variables discussed there. Understanding those variables are key to understanding how to properly setup a user.

Look in the man pages to see how the following commands or files relate to /etc/profile:

profile

LAB 3.2 EXERCISES

3.2.1 BETTER UNDERSTAND THE /ETC/PROFILE FILE

In this Exercise, you should focus on a single variable that affects all users and does not do any harm if set improperly. That variable is PS1. As described in Lab 2.2, this variable will give a prompt to the user. This prompt can include information to help the user navigate around to various systems, and to know the user's location at all times.

As you've seen before, not all UNIX variables work the same in all UNIX environments, even when using the same shell. So consider this when doing the exercises. PS1 is particularly fussy.

This Exercise will experiment with various settings of PS1. While PS1 can be modified as a normal user, the full Exercises will require you to use root access.

Log in with your normal login id.

Type the commands:

```
OLDPS1=$PS1(This saves the current $PS1)
echo $OLDPS1 (This verifies the value of the variable)
```

a) What kind of results did you get?

_____

_____

Now enter the following commands:

```
ksh (This protects your old environment)
PS1=`echo "Hello there $PS1"` (This creates a new
prompt)
```

b) What kind of results do you get?

_____

_____

The following will help you look at and understand your current `.profile`.

First, you need to become root, so enter the following:

```
su -
```

c) How did your `PS1` prompt change?

_____

_____

If you are sharing your system with more than one user, be sure to work it out so that each of you gets a chance to modify /etc/profile. The best way is for only one person at a time to do this Exercise, with perhaps everyone else watching.

In case there are problems with your editing or execution, you should first backup `/etc/profile` **to** `/etc/profile.bak` (If the file `/etc/profile.bak` exists, choose another backup file name.) Use the following command:

```
cp /etc/profile /etc/profile.bak
```

Now, copy `/etc/profile` to a file to be edited and tested by the command:

```
cp /etc/profile /tmp/profile
```

Use your favorite editor to edit `/tmp/profile` and add the following lines to the end:

```
if test $LOGNAME = root
then
        PS1="$LOGNAME"'@'`uname -n`':$PWD# '
else
        PS1="$LOGNAME"'@'`uname -n`':$PWD$ '
fi
export PS1
```

You must test out your changes to make sure there are no errors. The following command will only check for syntax errors, and does not execute the program. Do this by entering:

```
ksh -n  /tmp/profile
```

> **d)** After backing up and testing `/etc/profile`, what kind of results do you get?

_____

_____

Be sure that any errors are fixed before the next stage.

Now, just copy `/tmp/profile` to `/etc/profile` by entering:

```
cp /tmp/profile /etc/profile
```

 Remember, you did a backup of `/etc/profile`*. In this particular case, an error is not fatal.*

Now change your userid to a new root shell by entering the following:

```
su -
```

    e) How did your `PS1` prompt change?

_____

_____

 With some versions of UNIX, $PS1$ will not give the proper directory listing when running as root and with the above changes to `/etc/profile`. This may be blamed on the implementation of the Bourne Shell. This occurs in Solaris x86 2.6, and Red Hat Linux 5.0, as well as some others. Solaris uses the Bourne Shell as the default for root, not the Korn Shell. In Linux, however, the value for $PS1$ has been defined in `/etc/bashrc`. In order for this Exercise to work properly, you need to comment out the value for $PS1$ in this file. If you run this Exercise by doing a setuserid to a regular user, it will work okay and will give the intended results.

Now change to a regular user—we'll call it `myid`—by entering the following:

```
su - myid
```

    f) How did your `PS1` prompt change?

_____

_____

You can examine the `PS1` by entering the following:

```
echo $PS1
```

    g) What value for `$PS1` did you see?

_____

_____

Keep typing the `exit` command or `ctrl-d` until you get back to the following prompt:

```
hello there $
```

Now reset the `PS1` value by entering:

```
PS1=$OLDPS1
```

h) What happened to your `PS1` prompt?

_____

_____

*If you did not see the original prompt, then you need to retrace your
steps, or start over again by logging out if you want to figure out what you
did wrong.*

LAB 3.2 EXERCISE ANSWERS

This section gives you some suggested answers to the questions in Lab 3.2, with discussion related to those answers.
Your answers may vary, but the most important thing is
whether your answer works. Use this discussion to analyze differences between your answers and those presented here.

If you have alternative answers to the questions in this Exercise, you are encouraged to post your answers and discuss
them at the companion Web site for this book, located at:

```
http://www.phptr.com/phptrinteractive
```

3.2.1 ANSWERS

Type the commands:

```
OLDPS1=$PS1     (This saves the current $PS1)
echo $OLDPS1 (This verifies the value of the variable)
```

a) What kind of results do you get?

Answer: *You should see something similar to the following as your prompt:*

```
$
```

Note that this assumes your default login prompt has not been changed in /etc/profile or in the .profile.

Enter the following commands:

```
ksh (This protects your old environment)
PS1=`echo "Hello there $PS1"` (This creates a new
prompt)
```

b) What kind of results do you get?

Answer: *Your prompt changes to something like:*

```
Hello there $
```

The following will help you look at and understand your current .profile. First, you need to become root, so enter the following:

```
su -
```

c) How does your PS1 prompt change?

Answer: *Your default prompt should change to:*

```
#
```

d) After backing up and testing /etc/profile, what kind of results do you get?

Answer: *You should just get your prompt back. If there are any errors, the message will depend on the types of errors.*

Be sure that any errors are fixed before the next stage.

You will need to treat /etc/profile as a regular shell program. Any errors that result should be treated as shell programming errors. Your most common errors will be typing errors, so review your typing closely. As you change directories, your directory path should also change. If your directory prompt does not change when you change directories, you may need to look for typing errors. Be sure you are in the Korn Shell, and that the part of the PS1 variable that gives the directory will work in your shell. Try to isolate the parts of PS1 and debug it as you would a normal program.

Now, copy `/tmp/profile` to `/etc/profile` by entering the following:

`cp /tmp/profile /etc/profile`

Next, change your userid to a new root shell by entering the following:

`su -`

e) How does your `PS1` prompt change?

Answer: This command sets your environment as though you just logged in. Your prompt should change to something like this:

`root@myserver:/#`

Now change to a regular user, and call it `myid`, by entering the following:

`su - myid`

f) How does your `PS1` prompt change?

Answer: You should now see:

`myid@myserver:/home/myhome$`

The command line prompt has changed because your `PS1` variable has changed.

You can examine the `PS1` by entering the following:

`echo $PS1`

g) What value for `$PS1` do you see?

Answer: Answers will vary, as follows.

In Solaris x86, you will see:

`PS1='myid@mohawk:/home/myhome$ '`

In Linux you, you will see

`PS1=myid@myserver:/home/myhome$`

Keep typing the `exit` command or `ctrl-d` until you get back to the following prompt:

`hello there $PS1`

Now, reset the `PS1` value by entering:

`PS1=$OLDPS1`

h) What happened to your PS1 prompt?

Answer: You should be back to the original prompt, which by default is as follows:

```
$
```

LAB 3.2 SELF-REVIEW QUESTIONS

In order to test your progress, you should be able to answer the following questions. Note that one answer may be valid in one version of UNIX and another answer may be valid in another version. It is important that you understand why you got such an error message.

Consider the following conditions when answering the questions in this section:

You are logged in as the id myid with group mygroup.

Your /etc/profile has the following entry:

```
if test $LOGNAME = root
then
        PS1="$LOGNAME"'@'`uname -n`':$PWD# '
        /bin:/usr/bin:/usr/ucb:/home/myhome/bin
else
        PS1="$LOGNAME"'@'`uname -n`':$PWD$ '
        /bin:/usr/bin:/usr/ucb:/home/myhome/bin:.
fi
export PS1
```

You have a file called `myfile` in your home directory. This is the only file on your system with that name.

1) Suppose you log in with your normal login id. If you execute the command **myfile**, it will execute properly.
   a) _____True
   b) _____False

2) Now change directories to your directory called `sh1`. When you execute the command `myfile`, it will execute properly.
   a) _____True
   b) _____False

3) Now login as root. If you execute the command `myfile`, which is in your regular user home directory, it will execute properly.
   a) _____True
   b) _____False

4) Still as root, change directories to the `/usr/ucb` directory. Now when you execute the command `myfile`, it will execute properly.
   a) _____True
   b) _____False

5) Still as root, your command line prompt is as follows:

   `myid@myserver:/home/myhome$`
   a) _____True
   b) _____False

6) As a regular user, you change directories to `/home/myid/bin`. To which of the following will your command line prompt change?
   a) _____root@myserver:/home/myid$
   b) _____myid@myserver:/#
   c) _____myserver@myid:/home/myid/bin$
   d) _____myid@myserver:/home/myid/bin$
   e) _____myid@myserver:/home/myid/bin#

7) Now do:

   `chown root myprog; exit; myprog`

If you get an error message, which is the most likely message you will receive:

a) _____sh: myprog: cannot execute

b) _____sh: myprog: not found

c) _____sh: myprog: cannot open

d) _____sh: myprog: permission denied

e) _____no error message

Quiz answers appear in Appendix A, Section 13.12.

CHAPTER 3

TEST YOUR THINKING

The projects in this section are meant to have you utilize all of the skills that you have acquired throughout this chapter. They are similar to the exercises in the Bourne Shell chapter, but are designed to help you understand the differences between the two shells. The answers to these projects can be found at the companion Web site to this book, located at:

`http://www.phptr.com/phptrinteractive`

Visit the Web site periodically to share and discuss your answers.

1) Log in as a regular user in the Korn Shell. Write a program that will set all your environment variables. You should set all that show up when you type:

```
set
```

Save this program, because you can execute it whenever you need to reset your environment.

2) Log in as root in the Korn Shell. Write a program that will set all your environment variables. You should set all that show up when you type:

```
set
```

Save this program, because you can execute it whenever you need to reset your environment.

If you don't have root access, you can still create a file that sets some of the root environment. You can determine much of the root environment by looking at `/etc/profile`. *You might also ask your instructor, if you have one, to provide the environment settings. Another alternative is to find a nice, friendly system administrator and ask if he or she could provide a copy.*

3) Write a program that compares the two programs that resulted from Projects I and 2 in this section. You might use the command:

```
diff
```

Analyze this program to understand the difference between logging in as a regular user and logging in as root.

4) Write a program that determines whether you are running the program as a regular user or root, and then sets the environment accordingly. Use the programs you created in Projects I and 2 in this section to set the proper environments.

 If you don't have root access, you can still change some of your environment variables so that your program thinks you are root, even if you aren't. You could start a new shell by executing ksh *if you are concerned about affecting your current environment. When you are done, you can just type the command* exit *. See also the advice in Project 2.*

5) Now it's time to be a detective and check out the regular user's environment. Take Project I and determine which environmental settings are set up by:

   a) /etc/profile

   b) .profile

   c) Bourne Shell

   d) Other sources

6) Continuing on as a detective, you need to look at root's environment. Take Project I and determine which environmental settings are set up by:

   a) /etc/profile

   b) .profile

   c) Bourne Shell

   d) Other sources

7) Work through the Exercises in this chapter again, except this time, leave out the `export` command. You used this in places such as:

a) export PATH

b) export PS1

c) Other exported variables

Then you should:

a) Determine which commands depend on those variables that are being set.

b) Execute them without the variables being set.

c) Export the values.

d) Determine what the differences are. Be aware that some variables do not need to be exported, whereas others do.

8) You have learned about some of the options to the ksh `sh` in this chapter. Some of them include **-x** and **-n**. Look up the following options for the Korn Shell. Explain what effects they have on executing a shell program. Consider the option as it is used in the following:

```
ksh -option myprogram
```

The options to be considered are as follows:

a) -e

b) -i

c) -v

d) Look at other options that might be useful

9) Look at the projects in Chapter 2. They are similar to the projects in this chapter. Take the similar projects and determine the differences between running the projects in the Bourne Shell and the Korn Shell.

CHAPTER 4

THE C SHELL USER

Oftentimes great ideas spawn other great ideas. It is human nature to grab the ball and run with it. So in the computer field, we have taken the user interface and built upon it. In so doing, we have given it more power to accomplish those things that we need to do. Very often, we have taken what we are familiar with and changed it to suit our needs. —Joe

CHAPTER OBJECTIVES

In this Chapter, you will learn about:

Exercises for the Masses

The C Shell has developed a strong following among programmers, particularly UNIX database programmers. Administrators and system developers, however, tend to prefer the Korn Shell. There are many reasons for this, but perhaps the strongest arguments for the C Shell are that there is much code written into it, and it gives users the power to do what they want to do.

C Shells include the command history capability. This creates a command history list to recall commands you have recently executed. The command can then be executed again, or modified and then executed, or even copied and saved into a file for future use.

The second major feature of the C Shell is job control. This allows a user more control of jobs, which is very important in some UNIX environments, where jobs can run for several hours and multiple processes must be monitored at the same time.

The third major feature of the C Shell is that it is similar to its cousin, the C programming language. Thus, if you know C, learning the C Shell will be easier.

One word of caution: while the C Shell is very similar to the C programming language, there are many subtle differences. The C Shell does not have the variety of types you see in a programming language, and some things just don't work the same. As always, the best advice is to practice and test a concept before you implement it, to make sure you understand what it is doing. In an administrative environment, this can be considered even more critical, because subtle differences can lead to major catastrophes.

EXERCISES FOR THE MASSES

There are endless religious arguments over the merits of the various shells. Database programmers seem to prefer the C Shell, probably because of its similarity to C. System developers and administrators tend to prefer the Korn Shell because it is considered more straightforward. Also, much of our administrative legacy comes from AT&T, which was primarily a Korn Shell shop.

As always, use whatever you feel most comfortable with—whatever gets the job done and is most consistent with your environment. While it is often admirable to try to satisfy both sides of the shell argument (or, through lack of knowledge, use both the C and Korn Shell simultaneously), it can lead to endless headaches. Much of the environment does not carry over when going from the C Shell to Korn Shell or the Korn Shell back to the C Shell.

A rule of thumb as an administrator is that you should never mix shells. If you do, then you need to thoroughly test your processes to make sure that everything is executing the way it should, and that the proper envi-

ronment is set. If you have problems with programs in such an situation, this should be the first place you check. They also show up in the most hidden locations.

Look in the man pages or your UNIX text to see if you can find the following:

```
csh  .login  .cshrc  /etc/cshrc,  tee,
back single  quotes(grave accent)
```

The C Shell gives us power that we did not have with the Bourne Shell. It is very much like the C language, but as mentioned previously, it has features that are unique to it alone. This chapter addresses some of those features, but focuses on those things that an administrator should be aware of. We'll look at some of the differences between the three shells we have discussed so far and learn how to avoid some of the problems.

After completing this chapter, you should go back and review the Bourne and Korn Shell Exercises and see how you might achieve some of the same things in the C Shell. Note any differences. Many of the differences are left as an exercise for you.

The three most important things to consider when learning a new shell are: experiment, experiment, and experiment. Ask yourself, "what if?"

L A B   4.1

THE .LOGIN FILE

LAB OBJECTIVES

After this Lab, you will be able to:

✓ Modify your .login File

.LOGIN

The .login file is the file that sets your environment when you first log in to UNIX in the C Shell. It functions the same way as the .profile file in the Bourne and Korn Shell. The C Shell also includes the .cshrc file (discussed further in the next Lab). The .cshrc file is executed whenever a csh program is executed, whereas the .login file is only executed once with each login.

In this chapter, you need to run your programs in the C Shell. In order to fully run these programs, you need to have your default login changed to the C Shell; however, you will start out with the Bourne or Korn Shell.

You can change your default login shell by using one of the following methods:

- Use the chsh command on some versions of UNIX (look this up in the man pages).
- If you have root access, edit the /etc/password file to change your default shell. Note, however, that some versions of UNIX, such as AIX, require that you use the built-in programs to change a user's attributes. That is because those values are actually stored in a database that is located elsewhere, and is easily accessible only through the menus.

- If you don't have root access, see if you can have the system administrator change your default shell, or ask your instructor about getting this done.
- If this is not possible, just type csh and do what you can to complete the exercises. You will then need to do a little more detective work in order to get the correct answers.

Two powerful features of the Korn Shell, C Shell, and other variants of the Bourne Shell are the ability to create aliases *and* functions *for commands. However, you need to be very careful in their use. It is very easy to create an alias or function for a system command. However, people fall into the trap of using the same name as the original command. It might be nice to create an alias called* rm *that is actually* rm -i, *which will then force you to be prompted every time you want to remove something. However, if you have a shell script that runs automatically from* cron *and uses* rm, *the program will sit there and hang while it waits for a keyboard response. It will never get a keyboard response because it does not run from a terminal. It is better to create an alias called something like* myrm *for* rm, *which is actually* rm -i, *and learn to use that. (Note: it is possible to program around this problem, but that is beyond the scope of this book. Just keep it simple.)*

Look up the following C Shell commands in the man pages and your text:

    alias, function, rm

LAB 4.1 EXERCISES

4.1.1 MODIFY YOUR .LOGIN FILE

You should first find out how to change your default login shell to the C Shell. If you have the chsh command, you will see later how to use it. Otherwise, do a little research ahead of time.

a) What did you find out?

_____

_____

Check to see if you currently have a .login file by using the following command:

```
cd $HOME
more .login
```

b) What do these commands do?

_____

_____

c) What is the meaning of the output from the commands executed in Question (b)?

_____

_____

Enter the C Shell from the Bourne or Korn Shell by entering the following command:

```
csh
```

d) What do you notice that is different on your screen?

_____

_____

Next, you must make a subdirectory in which to put your chapter Exercises. Do the following:

```
cd
mkdir csh1
```

If you have a .login file, do the following:

```
cp .login .login.bak
cd csh1
```

This saves the file. See Chapter 2, "The Bourne Shell," if you want more details.

Create a file that has your login characteristics by executing the following commands:

```
                set > mylogin.env
printenv >> mylogin.env
more mylogin.env
```

e) What kind of results do you get?

_____

_____

As mentioned in earlier chapters, and reemphasized here, never log out and log in again without thoroughly testing any changes to your .login or any files that change your environment.

Create a file called `mylogin` as follows, making appropriate changes. Comment each line as to what the line does. Comment or change those lines that don't work:

```
#   mylogin file
# This is for the .login file in the C Shell
stty intr '^c' erase '^h' kill '^x' quit '^u' echoe
umask 027
# Set environment variables;
setenv TERM ansi
setenv TZ PST8PDT
# set other variables;
set prompt = "$LOGNAME \!) "
# Display and record log-in times:
echo "Your  previous  login-in  time  was:  `cat
  .login_time`"
echo "Your current  login-in time is: `date | tee
  .login_time`"
```

f) What does each line of the `.login` file do?

_____

_____

Test your program with the following:

```
csh   mylogin
```

g) What kind of results do you get?

_____

_____

h) What kind of errors do you get? Explain what happened.

_____

_____

Once you are happy with this, do the following:

```
source mylogin
```

The `source` command works the same as the `dot` or `exec` command in the Bourne and Korn Shell. When "source some-command" is executed, it runs in the same space as the parent process that calls it. All values that are created by the program are part of the parent process.

Fix any problems or issues you might have had with the program.

i) What did you have to change?

_____

_____

j) What kind of results do you get from the source command?

_____

_____

Once you are satisfied that the file is correct, do the following:

```
cp mylogin .login
```

When you create a `.profile` *file in the Korn and Bourne Shell, it must have* `r` *and* `x` *file attributes, whereas in the C Shell, the* `.login` *file only needs the* `r` *attributes.*

You now need to change your default login shell to the C Shell. Follow the steps listed in this Lab's introduction, or use the `chsh` command as follows:

```
myid 34) chsh
Changing shell for myid.
Password:
New shell [/bin/bash]: /bin/csh
Shell changed.
myid 35)
```

k) If you can run it, what kind of changes do you see on the screen?

_____

_____

Now just log out and log in again. Be sure that your default shell is now changed to the C Shell (see the previous tips if you are not clear about this).

l) If you are unable to get into the C Shell, what do you think are the reasons?

_____

_____

m) If you get into the C Shell, do you see any errors on the screen? What are they, and how do you fix them?

_____

_____

Go ahead and fix any errors you found in question (l).

Create a file that has your new login characteristics by executing the following commands:

```
cd csh1
set > mynewlogin.env
printenv  >> mynewlogin.env
more mynewlogin.env
```

n) What kind of results do you get?

_____

_____

Run the following command:

```
diff mylogin.env mynewlogin.env > mylogin.diff
```

o) What are the differences that show up in the diff file you just created?

_____

_____

p) What is the meaning of each of the differences?

_____

_____

After doing this Exercise, you should have created the following files:

- `mylogin.env`
- `.login`
- `mynewlogin.env`
- `mylogin.diff`

After your login is tested, you should change your default shell back to the `ksh` by using the command `chsh`. If you used a different method, just reverse that process to get back to your original shell.

You should review the files listed and make sure you understand what they mean for the user environment. It is important for an administrator to be able to have some control over a user's environment. Be sure you have any and all original files backed up.

It is possible that your new environment will cause problems with your current programs. If you think this is causing problems with other applications you are using, copy your new files to a backup copy. Then put back the very original files (those created before doing any exercises; review the previous exercises if you don't remember which ones they are). Then log out and log in again. The next time you need the new files, you can copy them back in. You can always add features one by one from the new files until you find the ones that are causing problems.

LAB 4.1 EXERCISE ANSWERS

This section gives you some suggested answers to the questions in Lab 4.1, with discussion related to those answers. Your answers may vary, but the most important thing is whether or not your answer works. Use this discussion to analyze differences between your answers and those presented here.

If you have alternative answers to the questions in this Exercise, you are encouraged to post your answers and discuss them at the companion Web site for this book, located at:

`http://www.phptr.com/phptrinteractive`

4.1.1 ANSWERS

You should first find out how to change your default login shell to the C Shell. If you have the `chsh` command, you will see later how to use it. Otherwise, do a little research ahead of time.

a) What did you find out?

Answer: *In Solaris x86, the command* `passwd` `-e` *will work if you are root. However, you can also use the* `su` *command to log in with the C Shell (as follows) to test your C Shell:*

```
myid@myserver:/export/home/myid$ su - myid -c "/bin/
   csh"
Password:
Sun Microsystems Inc.   SunOS 5.6      Generic August
   1997
myserver%
```

In Linux, you can change your login with the `chsh` *command.*

```
myid 34) chsh
Changing shell for myid.
Password:
New shell [/bin/bash]: /bin/csh
Shell changed.
myid 35)
```

Check to see if you currently have a `.login` file by using the following command:

```
cd $HOME
more .login
```

b) What do these commands do?

Answer: `cd` `$HOME` *changes your current directory to your home directory. You can verify this with the command* `pwd.` *Then,* `more` `.login` *displays the* `.login` *file a screenful at a time, if there is such a file. If there is no such file, you should see the following:*

```
$ more .login
.login: No such file or directory
$
```

c)   What is the meaning of the output from the commands executed in Question (b)?

Answer: Results will vary depending on the system on which you are working. The default environment setup file for your shell is always copied over. Often, sample environment files, such as `.login`, *are copied in to your home directory when the id is created. Sometimes they have names such as* `sample.login, user.login,` *or* `.sample.login`. *Sometimes they just remain in the* `/etc/skel` *directory, as in Solaris, and are copied over only for the shell for which your id was first set up. You need to do some research on your system to find out precisely where they are located. The best place to start is the man pages.*

Enter the C Shell from the Bourne or Korn Shell by entering the following command:

```
csh
```

d)   What do you notice that is different on your screen?

Answer: Your command prompt should have changed. It should do something similar to the following, which you would see in Solaris x86:

```
myid@myserver:/home/myid$ csh
myserver%
```

Your results may be different, depending on how your default C Shell environment was set up.

Next, you made a subdirectory in which to put your chapter exercises, and you created a file that has your login characteristics.

e)   What kind of results do you get?

Answer: You should see something similar to the following:

```
myserver% more mylogin.env
argv    ()
cwd     /export/home/myid
history 32
home    /export/home/myid
path    (/bin /usr/bin /usr/ucb /etc .)
prompt  mohawk%
shell   /bin/csh
status  0
term    ansi
user    myid
```

LAB 4.1

```
_=/usr/bin/csh
HZ=100
LC_MONETARY=en_US
LC_TIME=en_US
PATH=/bin:/usr/bin:/usr/ucb:/etc:.
LOGNAME=myid
MAIL=/var/mail/myid
LC_MESSAGES=C
LC_CTYPE=en_US
SHELL=/bin/ksh
HOME=/export/home/myid
LC_COLLATE=en_US
LC_NUMERIC=en_US
TERM=ansi
PWD=/export/home/myid
TZ=US/Central
USER=myid
myserver%
```

You then created a file called `mylogin`.

f) What does each line of the `.login` file do?

Answer: Each line is explained in the following table:

Note that some of the lines below end in \. This is a shorthand in UNIX that says to take a command line in UNIX and continue it to the next line. So the first two lines below are actually `stty intr '^c'` *erase* `'^h'` *and so forth.*

stty intr '^c'\	Set your terminal characteristics such that an interrupt character is Control-c
	The erase character is Control-h
	The kill character is Control-x
	The quit character is Control-u

	Erase any characters that are back-spaced over by Control-h
umask 027	Set your umask (as in previous chapters) to 027. The umask controls the file access rights on files or directories you create. umask prevents access to files or directories to users who are not the owner or a member of the group assigned to the file.
setenv TERM ansi	Set your terminal type to ansi. ANSI is a standard terminal definition that is an extension of the DEC vt100. ANSI is the American National Standards Institute.
setenv TZ PST8PDT??	Set the time zone to follow both Pacific Standard and Pacific Daylight Savings time, depending on the time of the year. This time zone is the eighth time zone from Greenwich Mean Time in England, which is the international standard. Note that sometimes this is shown as PS8PDT, which is the more current format.
set prompt = "$LOGNAME \!) "	Set your prompt to be the value of your $LOGNAME, followed by the number used by the history command, and then the). The ! is expanded to the number in the history file of the current command.
echo "Your previous login-in time was: `cat .login_time`"	Read the .login_time file to find when your last login was. The command `cat .login_time` will execute the command inside the back single quotes. In this case, the .login_time contains the time of your last log in.

echo "Your current login-in time is: `date | tee .login_time`"

Reset the value in the .login_time file to the current log in time. The tee command will put the time and date of your current login into the .login_time file.

Test your program with the following:

```
csh   mylogin
```

g)   What kind of results do you get?

Answer: You should get results similar to the following:

```
myserver% csh mylogin
cat: cannot open .login_time
Your previous login-in time was:
Your current  login-in time is: Mon Apr  6 12:02:42 PDT
1998
myserver%
```

h)   What kind of errors do you get? Explain what happened.

Answer: If you don't have a file `.login_time`, *you should have gotten an error message on the line:*

```
cat: cannot open .login_time
```

This is because the file `.login_time` does not yet exist.

Once you are happy with this, do:

```
source mylogin
```
Fix any problems or issues you might have had with the program.

i)   What did you have to change?

Answer: You may have had to change your time zone.

If you are in the Central Time Zone, it would be CST6CDT. (You may also see CS6CDT, which is a more current form of the Time Zone variable.)

j) What kind of results do you get from the source command?

Answer:You should have seen the following results:

```
myserver% source mylogin
Your previous login-in time was: Mon Apr  6 12:02:42 PDT
1998
Your current  login-in time is: Mon Apr  6 12:36:51 PDT
1998
myid 17)
```

What happened is that `mylogin` read the file `.login_time` and reported the date that is stored there. This is actually the result of the last time that `mylogin` was executed, because you haven't yet logged out and back in again to reset the value.

Next, you copied this file to your home directory and changed your default login shell to the C Shell.

k) If you can run it, what kind of changes do you see on the screen?

Answer:You should not see any changes.

This is because the shell change does not take effect until after you log out and log back in again.

Now log out and log in again. Be sure that your default shell is now changed to the C Shell (see the previous tips if you are not clear about this).

l) If you are unable to get into the C Shell, what do you think are the reasons?

Answer:You need to verify that your login shell has in fact changed.

Do the following:

```
    grep myid /etc/passwd    (where myid is your login id)
```

You should see a line similar to the following:

```
myid:x:1001:1001::/home/myid:/bin/csh
```

The last entry on the line tells you what your default login shell is. There may be other reasons that you may need to research, such as a missing or defective /bin/csh shell. (If you have no shell listed, that is ok. Your system will just run the default shell.)

m) If you get into the C Shell, do you see any errors on the screen? What are they, and how would you fix them?

Answer: Once you log in to the login id with the C Shell, you should see the following on the screen in Solaris x86 (others will be similar):

```
SunOS 5.6
login: myid
Password:
Last login: Mon Apr  6 15:04:39 from skates
Sun Microsystems Inc.   SunOS 5.6    Generic August 1997
You have new mail.
cat: cannot open .login_time
Your previous login-in time was:
Your current  login-in time is: Mon Apr  6 13:09:59 PDT
1998
myid 1)
```

You then created a file that has your new login characteristics.

n) What kind of results do you get?

Answer: Depending on how your system is set up, you should get results similar to the following:

```
argv      ()
cwd       /export/home/myid/csh1
history 32
home      /export/home/myid
path      (/bin /usr/bin /usr/ucb /etc .)
prompt    myid !)
shell     /bin/csh
status    0
term      ansi
user      myid
HOME=/export/home/myid
```

```
PATH=/bin:/usr/bin:/usr/ucb:/etc:.
LOGNAME=myid
HZ=100
TERM=ansi
TZ=PS8PDT
SHELL=/bin/csh
MAIL=/var/mail/myid
LC_COLLATE=en_US
LC_CTYPE=en_US
LC_MESSAGES=C
LC_MONETARY=en_US
LC_NUMERIC=en_US
LC_TIME=en_US
PWD=/export/home/myid/csh1
USER=myid
myid 9)
myid 9)
```

After running the following command:

```
diff mylogin.env mynewlogin.env > mylogin.diff
```

o)   What are the differences that show up in the `diff` file you just created?

Answer: You should see the following results:

```
2c2
< cwd    /export/home/myid
---
> cwd    /export/home/myid/csh1
6c6
< prompt          myserver%
---
> prompt          myid !)
11,14c11
< _=/usr/bin/csh
< HZ=100
< LC_MONETARY=en_US
< LC_TIME=en_US
```

```
---
> HOME=/export/home/myid
16a14,17
> HZ=100
> TERM=ansi
> TZ=PS8PDT
> SHELL=/bin/csh
18,21d18
< LC_MESSAGES=C
< LC_CTYPE=en_US
< SHELL=/bin/ksh
< HOME=/export/home/myid
22a20,22
> LC_CTYPE=en_US
> LC_MESSAGES=C
> LC_MONETARY=en_US
24,26c24,25
< TERM=ansi
< PWD=/export/home/myid
< TZ=US/Central
---
> LC_TIME=en_US
> PWD=/export/home/myid/csh1
myid 13)
```

When you look at this output, you will see lines that begin with numbers and letters, or the symbols < and >. These are explained as follows:

- 2c2 gives an editor command that can be used to change the first file into the second file
- < indicates lines in the first file
- > indicates lines in the second file

p) What is the meaning of each of the differences?

Answer: The meanings are as follows:

`mylogin.env`	`mynewlogin.env`	Description
`cwd /export/ home/myid`	`cwd export/ home/myid/csh1`	Current working directory
`prompt myser- ver%`	`prompt myid !)`	New command line prompt
`TZ=PS8PDT`	`TZ=US/Central`	Time zone variable
`PWD=/export/ home/myid`	`PWD=/export/ home/myid/csh1`	Current working directory

Notice that these variables have changed. They are changed by your new `.login` file. You should go back to the original files and determine why there are differences.

LAB 4.1 SELF-REVIEW QUESTIONS

In order to test your progress, you should be able to answer the following questions. Note that one answer may be valid in one version of UNIX and another answer may be valid in another version. It is important that you understand why you got such an error message.

Use the following file as your new `.login` file, called `mylogin2`, for the questions that follow:

```
#    mylogin2 file
# This is for the .login file in the C shell
stty intr '^c' erase '^h' kill '^x' quit '^u' echoe
umask 700
# Set environment variables;
setenv TERM unknown
setenv TZ PS7CDT
# set other variables;
set prompt = "$LOGON \!) "
# Display and record log-in times:
echo "Your previous login-in time was:  `cat
  .login+time`"
echo "Your current  login-in time is: `date | tee
  .login_time`"
```

Go into vi to edit a text file called `junk` by doing the following:

```
mohawk# vi junk
```

```
I don't know what kind of terminal you are on - all I
  have is 'unknown'.
[Using open mode]
"junk" [New file]
```

1) What is the most probable reason for the error message? (You must distinguish between error messages and informational messages.)

a) _____The terminal type is not set

b) _____The TERM variable is set wrong

c) _____You don't have the proper file permissions

d) _____The file doesn't exist

e) _____The umask is set incorrectly

2) One of the error message you get when testing the .login program is:

```
LOGON: Undefined variable
```

What do you think is the reason for this?

a) _____Your terminal type is not set

b) _____There is no search path defined

c) _____The $LOGON variable is not known to the system

d) _____The umask is wrong

e) _____You are logging in with someone else's id

3) Another error message you will get is the following:

```
myserver# echo "Your previous login-in time was: `cat
.login+time`"
cat: cannot open .login+time
Your previous login-in time was:
myserver# Your current  login-in time is: Tue Apr 14
00:01:40 CDT 1998
myserver#
```

What would you say is the reason for this error message?

a) _____You logged in with someone else's id

b) _____There is no file .login+time

c) _____You are logging in from the wrong time zone

d) _____Your .login file is not executable

e) _____None of the above

4) To best fix the error in Question 3 so that it follows the intent of the program, which of the following you would do?

   a) _____Delete `.login+time`

   b) _____Fix the time zone

   c) _____Fix the typing error in the .login file above where it checks for the name `.login+time`

   d) _____Delete the `echo` statements

   e) _____None of the above

5) You go into `vi` and get the following message:

```
myid19)) vi /tmp/junk
"/var/tmp/Ex0000000403" Permission denied
```

   What is the most likely cause?

   a) _____Your term type is set incorrectly

   b) _____You need to own `/var/tmp`

   c) _____The file is in use

   d) _____The `umask 700` does not allow you to edit any files, even the ones you own

   e) _____`/var/tmp` doesn't exist

Quiz answers appear in Appendix A, Section 4.1.

L A B   4.2

LAB
4.2

THE .CSHRC FILE

LAB OBJECTIVES

After this Lab, you will be able to:

✓ Learn About Your `.cshrc`

This lab will discuss the `.cshrc` file. This file is executed whenever you execute a command in the C Shell. It is similar to the `.kshrc` file. However, unlike the `.kshrc` file, the `.cshrc` file in your home directory is always executed whenever you execute a C Shell command. When you first log in, the `.cshrc` file is also executed. It is then followed by executing the `.login` file in your home directory. Whatever values are set by your `.cshrc` file can be modified from the `.login` file.

LAB 4.2 EXERCISES

4.2.1 LEARN ABOUT YOUR .CSHRC

Log in with your regular, not root, login id. (Be sure to start out in the Korn Shell before doing the rest of the Exercise. You will be changing into the C Shell.)

Determine if you have a .cshrc by typing the following command in your home directory:

```
ls .cshrc
```

a) What kind of results do you get?

_____

_____

If you have a .cshrc, type the following command in your home directory:

```
more .cshrc
```

b) Explain any results you get. What does each line do?

_____

_____

Make a directory that you can use as your working directory for the next series of Exercises. Enter the following command:

```
mkdir  csh1 (if it doesn't already exist)
```

If you have a .cshrc file, you should save the original file by entering the following command:

```
cp .cshrc .cshrc.org
cd csh1
```

Now go into the C Shell by entering the command:

```
csh
```

Create a file called mycsh.env by executing the following:

```
set > mycsh.env
printenv >> mycsh.env
more mycsh.env
```

c) What kind of results do you get?

_____

_____

During and after creating the following file, be sure to verify that all commands are valid and that all directories exist. Be sure that the environment variables are appropriate for your system.

**LAB
4.2**

Create a file called `mycshrc` file as follows:

```
# This file is mycshrc
# which is to be used for.cshrc
# Set local variables
set history = 20
set ignoreeof
set noclobber
set prompt = "$LOGNAME \!)) "
set cdpath = (.  ~  ~/bin  ~/etc  ~/csh1)
# Define aliases:
alias mycd 'cd \!*;dirs;ls'
alias myls "ls -CF"
alias pwd  'echo $cwd'
alias myrm  "rm -i"
```

d) Explain the meaning of each line in the file.

_____

_____

e) Be sure to fix any problems and make any changes to match your system. What kind of problems do you need to fix?

_____

_____

Once you are satisfied that this file is correct, test this program by executing the following command:

```
csh mycshrc
```

f) What kind of results do you get?

_____

_____

g) What kind of errors do you get? Explain what happened.

_____

_____

If this works, do the following:

```
source mycshrc
```

h) What kind of results do you get? Fix any problems or issues that you might have with the preceding program. What do you have to change?

_____

_____

Once you are satisfied that this file is correct, do the following:

```
cp mycshrc $HOME/.cshrc
```

If `chsh` is available on your system, use it to change your default shell as:

```
myid 34) chsh
Changing shell for myid.
Password:
New shell [/bin/bash]: /bin/csh
Shell changed.
myid 35)
```

i) What kind of results do you get?

_____

_____

Now log out and log in again. Be sure that your default shell is now changed to the C Shell (see the above tips if you are not clear about this).

j) How do you verify that you are in the C Shell?

_____

_____

k) If you do not immediately get into the C Shell when you log in, what do you think are the reasons?

_____

_____

l) If you get into the C Shell, do you see any errors on the screen? How would you fix them?

_____

_____

Fix any errors that you found in question (j), and then enter the following command:

```
set  >  mynewcsh.env
printenv >> mynewcsh.env
more mynewcsh.env
```

m) What kind of results did you get?

_____

_____

Run the following command:

```
diff mycsh.env mynewcsh.env > mycsh.diff
more mycsh.diff
```

n) What kind of differences did you notice in the `diff` file you just created?

_____

_____

After your login is tested, change your default shell back to the `ksh` by using the command `chsh`.

o) What would you say are some of the differences between the following commands?
```
csh .login
source .login
```

_____

_____

In this series of Exercises, you should have created the following files:

- `mycsh.env`
- `.cshrc`
- `mynewcsh.env`

LAB 4.2 EXERCISE ANSWERS

This section gives you some suggested answers to the questions in Lab 4.2, with discussion related to those answers. Your answers may vary, but the most important thing is whether or not your answer works. Use this discussion to analyze differences between your answers and those presented here.

If you have alternative answers to the questions in this Exercise, you are encouraged to post your answers and discuss them at the companion Web site for this book, located at:

`http://www.phptr.com/phptrinteractive`

**LAB
4.2**

4.2.1 ANSWERS

Log in with your regular, not root, login id using the C Shell and determine if you have a `.cshrc` by typing the following command in your home directory:

```
ls .cshrc
```

a) What kind of results do you get?

Answer: If you have no such file, you will get the following results:

```
[myid@wheels]$ ls .cshrc
ls: .cshrc: No such file or directory
[myid@wheels]$
```

Otherwise, you will get the following:

```
[myid@wheels]$ ls .cshrc
.cshrc
[myid@wheels]$
```

If you have a .cshrc, type this command in your home directory:

```
more .cshrc
```

b) Explain any results you get. What does each line do?

Answer: You must research some of the items on your own system. See the descriptions in other parts of these Exercises for details on some of them.

Next, you made a directory to use as your working directory for the next series of exercises, saved the original .cshrc file, and switched to the C Shell. Finally, you created the `mycsh.env` file.

c) What kind of results did you get?

Answer: The results are as follows:

```
myid 10) cat mycsh.env
argv    ()
cwd     /export/home/myid/csh1
history 32
home    /export/home/myid
path    (/bin /usr/bin /usr/ucb /etc .)
prompt  myid !)
shell   /bin/csh
```

```
status    0
term      ansi
user      myid
HOME=/export/home/myid
PATH=/bin:/usr/bin:/usr/ucb:/etc:.
LOGNAME=myid
HZ=100
TERM=ansi
TZ=PS8PDT
SHELL=/bin/csh
MAIL=/var/mail/myid
LC_COLLATE=en_US
LC_CTYPE=en_US
LC_MESSAGES=C
LC_MONETARY=en_US
LC_NUMERIC=en_US
LC_TIME=en_US
PWD=/export/home/myid/csh1
USER=myid
myid 11)
```

In this Lab we are discussing the meaning of the various values that are displayed at this point. You might also research the meaning of the values on your own.

d) Explain the meaning of each line in the `mycshrc` file you created for this Exercise.

Answer: The lines are explained as follows:

set history = 20	Set the size of the history list
set ignoreeof	Ignore any `eof` characters, which by default is Control-D
set noclobber	Prevents you from overwriting an existing file
set prompt = "$LOGNAME \!)) "	This is your new prompt

set cdpath = (. ~ ~/bin ~/etc ~/csh1)	Use this parameter to search for any subdirectories when you do a `cd subdirectory`. It will look in all the directories for subdirectories with that name. You will usually want to start with your current directory and look for subdirectories there.
alias mycd 'cd \!*;dirs;ls'	`mycd` is an alias for cd, change directory; `dirs` will then give your relationship to your home directory and do an `ls` listing of your directory.
alias myls "ls -CF"	The command `myls` will actually execute `ls -CF`.
alias pwd 'echo $cwd'	`pwd` will actually echo the value of `cwd` (change working directory).
alias myrm "rm -i"	The command `myrm` will execute the command `rm -i`, which will prompt you as to whether you really want to delete the file or not.

e) Be sure to fix any problems and make any changes to match your system. What kind of problems do you need to fix?

Answer: These are system-dependent.

Your system may have a default set of values used for the C Shell. Some of the problems you may encounter include batch or system programs that actually have special meanings for some of the aliases identified previously. You might have a system definition that uses `myrm`. You might also have typos that could cause you problems.

Once you are satisfied that this file is correct, test the program by executing the following command:

```
csh mycshrc
```

f) What kind of results do you get?

> *Answer: You should just get your $PS1 command line prompt returned.*

If you had any errors, they would have been displayed here. Because a new shell is created and then destroyed, your current environment is unaffected.

g) What kind of errors do you get? Explain what happened.

> *Answer: If everything was OK, you should get no errors. Otherwise, you will need to debug and fix them.*

If this works, do the following:

```
source mycshrc
```

h) What kind of results do you get?

> *Answer: If you fixed any errors from the last step, you should get no errors. Instead, the results should be as follows:*

```
myserver% source mycshrc
myserver 9))
```

Notice how the prompt has changed.

Next, you changed your default login shell.

i) What kind of results do you get?

> *Answer: You should have no immediate changes on your screen or environment. It will change once you log out and log in again.*

Now log out and log in again. Be sure that your default shell is now changed to the C Shell (see the above tips if you are not clear about this).

j) After logging out and back in again, how do you verify that you are in the C Shell?

> *Answer: You can verify that you are in the C Shell by typing `set`. You will see a line like the following:*

```
shell    /bin/csh
```

If you use the `printenv` command, you will see a line like the following:

```
SHELL=/bin/csh
```

k) If you do not immediately get into the C Shell when you log in, what do you think are the reasons?

Answer: The most likely reason would be that your login shell was not changed in the /etc/passwd file. You can find out what your default login shell is by doing the following:

```
grep myid /etc/passwd      (where myid is your loginid)
```

l) If you get into the C Shell, do you see any errors on the screen? How would you fix them?

Answer: Your answers are dependent on your system. Talk to your instructor, if you have one, or your administrator to see if there are some special requirements or settings for your system.

Fix any errors that you found in Question (j); then enter the following command:

```
set > mynewcsh.env
printenv >> mynewcsh.env
more mynewcsh.env
```

m) What kind of results do you get?

Answer: You should get something similar to the following results:

```
argv     ()
cdpath   (. /export/home/myid /export/home/myid/bin /
export/home/myid
/etc /export/home/myid/csh1)
cwd      /export/home/myid/csh1
history 20
home     /export/home/myid
ignoreeof
noclobber
path     (/usr/bin .)
prompt   myid !))
shell    /bin/csh
status   0
term     ansi
user     myid
HOME=/export/home/myid
PATH=/usr/bin:
```

```
LOGNAME=myid
HZ=100
TERM=ansi
TZ=US/Central
SHELL=/bin/csh
MAIL=/var/mail/myid
LC_COLLATE=en_US
LC_CTYPE=en_US
LC_MESSAGES=C
LC_MONETARY=en_US
LC_NUMERIC=en_US
LC_TIME=en_US
PWD=/export/home/myid/csh1
USER=myid
myid 13))
```

Run the following command:

```
diff mycsh.env mynewcsh.env > mycsh.diff
more mycsh.diff
```

n) What kind of differences did you notice in the `diff` file you just created?

Answer:You should review the `diff` command to understand its meaning.

You saw a similar exercise in Lab 4.1.1. The process shows the differences
between the two files. It will also show you what changes you need to
make in order to make the two files match. Your results should be similar
to the following:

```
1a2
> cdpath          (. /export/home/myid /export/home/myid/
bin /export/home/
myid/etc /export/home/myid/csh1)
2a4
> history         20
4,5c6,9
< path   (/usr/bin /usr/ucb /etc .)
< prompt          myserver%
---
```

```
> ignoreeof
> noclobber
> path   (/usr/bin .)
> prompt        myid !))
10,14c14,15
< _=/usr/bin/csh
< HZ=100
< LC_MONETARY=en_US
< LC_TIME=en_US
< PATH=/usr/bin:/usr/ucb:/etc:.
---
> HOME=/export/home/myid
> PATH=/usr/bin:
15a17,20
> HZ=100
> TERM=ansi
> TZ=US/Central
> SHELL=/bin/csh
17,20d21
< LC_MESSAGES=C
< LC_CTYPE=en_US
< SHELL=/bin/ksh
< HOME=/export/home/myid
21a23,25
> LC_CTYPE=en_US
> LC_MESSAGES=C
> LC_MONETARY=en_US
23c27
< TERM=ansi
--- ---
> LC_TIME=en_US
25d28
< TZ=US/Central
myid 10))
```

The actual differences are as follows:

mycsh.env

cdpath   (. /export/home/myid /export/home/myid/bin /export/home/ myid/etc / export/home/myid/csh1)

path (/usr/bin /usr/ucb /etc)

prompt   myserver%

PATH=/usr/bin:/usr/ucb:/etc:.

SHELL=/bin/ksh

mynewcsh.env

history   20

path (/usr/bin .)

prompt   myid !))

ignoreeof

noclobber

PATH=/usr/bin:

SHELL=/bin/csh

After your login is tested, change your default shell back to the `ksh` by using the command `chsh`.

o) What would you say are some of the differences between the following commands?

```
csh .login
source .login
```

Answer: The `csh` command creates a new shell, or in more technical terms, it creates a child process. This process can inherit much of its parent's environment (i.e., genetic, such as good looks, great UNIX skills). But the parent process is not affected by what the child does (we should be so lucky!). When the child process dies, the parent process keeps running and is unaffected by what the child process does, except for any system changes.

However, the source command executes whatever command is being executed within the original process' environment. Whatever the second process does will intimately affect the first process (kind of like being married). When the second process stops running, the changes it makes to the first process remain.

LAB 4.2 SELF-REVIEW QUESTIONS

In order to test your progress, you should be able to answer the following questions. Note that one answer may be valid in one version of UNIX and another answer may be valid in another version. It is important that you understand why you got such an error message.

One important piece of information about the C Shell is that, when you log in, the C Shell is executed first. Use the following file as your new .login file, called mylogin3:

```
#    mylogin3 file
# This is for the .login file in the C shell
stty sane
umask 777
set history = 50
# Set environment variables;
echo "This is the .login file"
setenv TERM TERM
# set other variables;
set prompt = "LOGIN \!) "
```

Use the following file as your new .cshrc file:

```
# This file is cshrc2
# which is to be used for.cshrc
echo "This is the .cshrc file"
set history = 20
set ignoreeof
set noclobber
set prompt = "C shell \!)) "
set path = ( /bin /usr/bin /etc /usr/ucb /usr/local/
   bin .)
```

1) When you first login to the C Shell using these files as your .login and .cshrc files, which of the following prompts do you get?

    a) _____LOGIN 1)

    b) _____C shell 1))

    c) _____csh))

    d) _____\!))

    e) _____myid@myserver:/home/myid/bin $

After doing Question (1), type the following:

```
csh
```

2) What kind of prompt do you get?
    a) _____LOGIN 1)
    b) _____C shell 1))
    c) _____csh))
    d) _____\!))
    e) _____myid@myserver:/home/myid/bin $

Another error message you will get is the following:

```
csh: No entry for terminal type "TERM"
csh: using dumb terminal settings.
LOGIN 1)
```

3) What would you say is the reason for this error message?
    a) _____The .login file is not executable
    b) _____The .cshrc file does not have any terminal settings
    c) _____The .login file does not have a valid terminal type setting
    d) _____Your .login file is not executable
    e) _____None of the above

4) After first logging in, the history list size is which of the following?
    a) _____10
    b) _____20
    c) _____30
    d) _____40
    e) _____50

5) After entering the following command:

```
csh
```

which of the following is the history list size?
    a) _____10
    b) _____20
    c) _____30
    d) _____40
    e) _____50

Quiz answers appear in Appendix A, Section 4.2.

**LAB
4.2**

LAB EXERCISES FOR THE GREAT AND SUPER USER

Many manufacturers have moved away from the C Shell for administrative-type functions. SUN, which had been one of the big advocates of Berkeley UNIX and the C Shell, now runs root from the Bourne Shell. In fact, it is not easy to change the administrator's default shell to the Korn or C Shells.

After completing this chapter, you should go back and review the Bourne and Korn Shell administrative-type exercises, and see how you might achieve some of the same things in the C Shell. Note any differences. Many of the differences are left as an exercise for you.

L A B   4.3

THE C SHELL AND ROOT

> ## LAB OBJECTIVES
>
> After this Lab, you will be able to:
>
> ✓ Create a Generic User /etc/login File

As you saw in the previous exercises, the .login and .cshrc files set your environment when you first log in to UNIX in the C Shell. They work in a similar fashion to the .profile file in the Bourne Shell. However, there is no standard /etc/login, /etc/cshrc, or other file that functions like the /etc/profile in the Bourne Shell. Several manufacturers have tried implementing variants of the/etc/profile to be used for the C Shell, but there is no clear consensus among them as to a standard.

You can always implement something similar to the /etc/profile on your system such that, whenever a user logs in, it calls your standard C Shell program /etc/login first, then executes the .cshrc, and then executes the .login. The user can remove that entry from the file unless you take away their rights to .login also. But then you are also taking away much of the users' control of their environments. There are also some variants of the C Shell that have a standard user file. This is an issue on which you might do some research.

Be sure you understand the methods of changing your default shell by reviewing the previous exercises in this chapter. Also, review the previous warnings about creating aliases.

LAB 4.3 EXERCISES

4.3.1 CREATING A GENERIC /ETC/LOGIN FILE

In this Exercise, you will create a generic `login` file that will be executed by all users when they go into the `csh`.

LAB 4.3

Log in as a regular user. To become a superuser, enter the following command:

```
su -
```

Verify that you do not have a `/etc/login` file. Then go to the directory where you created the `.login` file in the previous exercises and do the following:

```
cp .login /etc/login
```

Your `/etc/login` file should look like the following:

```
#   /etc/login file
# This is for the generic login file in the C Shell
stty intr '^c' erase '^h' kill '^x' quit '^u' echoe
umask 022
# Set environment variables;
setenv TERM ansi
setenv TZ PS8PDT
# set other variables;
set prompt = "$LOGNAME \!) "
# Display and record log-in times:
echo  "Your  previous  login-in  time  was:  `cat
   .login_time`"
echo "Your current  login-in time is: `date | tee
   .login_time`"
```

You need to verify whether you have a `/etc/cshrc` file. If you don't, then copy the `.cshrc` as follows:

```
cp .cshrc /etc/cshrc
```

Your `/etc/cshrc` file should now look like the following:

```
# /etc/cshrc
# which is to be used for a generic .cshrc file
# Set local variables
set history = 20
set ignoreeof
set noclobber
set prompt = "$LOGNAME \!)) "
set time = 10
# set wordlist variables:
set cdpath = (.  ~  ~/Letters  ~/Vendors  ~/Clients)
set mail  = (/usr/mail/$LOGNAME 3600 /etc/motd
# Define aliases:
alias mycd 'cd \!*;dirs;ls'
alias myls "ls -CF"
alias pwd  'echo $cwd'
alias myrm  "rm -i"   # use the small letter I
```

**LAB
4.3**

Now create a new .login file in your regular, non-root, login directory. It should look like the following:

```
# My new .login file
# This file will call the generic /etc/login file
source /etc/login
# After here the user can insert any personal settings
```

Now you can create your new .cshrc file, as follows:

```
# My new .cshrc file
# This file will call the generic /etc/cshrc file
source /etc/cshrc
# After here the user can insert any personal settings
```

Be sure that you own the .login and .cshrc files as your regular, non-root id, and that you have read/write access to them. You can do this as follows:

```
cd /home/myid    (where myid is your regular login id)
ls -l .login .cshrc
```

a) What kind of results do you get?

_____

_____

If you don't get the proper results, change the files appropriately, then log out and log in again as your regular login id.

Next, input the following:

```
cd csh1
set > mynextlogin.env
printenv  >> mynextlogin.env
more mynextlogin.env
```

b) What kind of results do you get?

_____

_____

Run the following command:

```
diff mynewlogin.env mynextlogin.env > mynextlogin.diff
```

c) What are the differences that show up in the `diff` file you just created?

_____

_____

d) What is the meaning of each of the differences?

_____

_____

LAB 4.3 EXERCISE ANSWERS

This section gives you some suggested answers to the questions in Lab 4.3, with discussion related to those answers. Your answers may vary, but the most important thing is whether or not your answer works. Use this discussion to analyze differences between your answers and those presented here.

If you have alternative answers to the questions in this Exercise, you are encouraged to post your answers and discuss them at the companion Web site for this book, located at:

LAB 4.3

    http://www.phptr.com/phptrinteractive

4.3.1 ANSWERS

For this Exercise, you verified that you do not have the /etc/login file. If you do, then you backed it up before doing this Exercise.
You then copied the .login file used in Lab 4.3.1 to the /etc/login file.
If you did not have a /etc/cshrc file, then you copied the .cshrc that you created in Lab 4.2.1.
Finally, you created a new .login file in your regular, non-root, login directory, and a new .cshrc file.
To verify that you own the files as your regular, non-root, id, and that you have read/write access to the files, you did the following:

    cd /home/myid(where myid is your regular login id)
    ls -l .login .cshrc

a)   What kind of results do you get?

   Answer: If the file exists, you will see the file attributes from ls -l. *In Red Hat Linux, you would see:*

```
[myid@myserver]$ ls -la .login .cshrc
-rw-rw-r--    1 myid myid      331 Apr  8 20:47 .cshrc
-rw-rw-r--    1 myid myid      393 Apr  8 20:46 .login
[myid@myserver]$
```

   If the file doesn't exist, you will get something similar to the following:

```
[myid@myserver]$ ls -l .login .cshrc
ls:.login : No such file or directory
ls:.cshrc : No such file or directory
[myid@myserver]$
```

If you don't get the proper results, change the files appropriately, then log out and log in again as your regular login id.

Next, do the following:

```
cd csh1
set > mynextlogin.env
printenv >> mynextlogin.env
more mynextlogin.env
```

b) What kind of results do you get?

Answer: The results should be as follows:

```
myid 10) more mynextlogin.env
argv     ()
cdpath  (. /export/home/myid /export/home/myid/bin /
export/home/myid
/etc /export/home/myid/csh1)
cwd      /export/home/myid/csh1
history 20
home     /export/home/myid
ignoreeof
noclobber
path     (/bin /usr/bin /etc /usr/ucb /usr/local/bin .)
prompt  myid !)
shell    /bin/csh
status  0
term     ansi
user     myid
HOME=/export/home/myid
PATH=/bin:/usr/bin:/etc:/usr/ucb:/usr/local/bin:.
LOGNAME=myid
HZ=100
TERM=ansi
TZ=CS6CDT
SHELL=/bin/csh
```

```
MAIL=/var/mail/myid
LC_COLLATE=en_US
LC_CTYPE=en_US
LC_MESSAGES=C
LC_MONETARY=en_US
LC_NUMERIC=en_US
LC_TIME=en_US
PWD=/export/home/myid/csh1
USER=myid
myid 11)
[myid@myserver]$
```

LAB 4.3

Run the following command:

```
diff mynewlogin.env mynextlogin.env > mynextlogin.diff
```

c) What are the differences that show up in the `diff` file you just created?

Answer: You must analyze each step of the following to see why it is different. On some of the lines, the differences are due to customization of the `/etc` *files.*

```
myid 15) diff mynewlogin.env mynextlogin.env
1a2
> cdpath          (. /export/home/myid /export/home/myid/
bin /export/home/
myid/etc /export/home/myid/csh1)
3c4
< history        32
---
> history        20
5c6,8
< path   (/bin /usr/bin /usr/ucb /etc .)
---
> ignoreeof
> noclobber
> path   (/bin /usr/bin /etc /usr/ucb /usr/local/bin .)
12c15
< PATH=/bin:/usr/bin:/usr/ucb:/etc:.
---
```

```
> PATH=/bin:/usr/bin:/etc:/usr/ucb:/usr/local/bin:.
16c19
< TZ=PS8PDT
---
> TZ=CS6CDT
myid 16)
```

d) What is the meaning of each of the differences?

Answer:The differences are overviewed as follows:

mynewlogin.env	mynextlogin.env	Explanation
	cdpath (. /export/ home/myid / export/home/ myid/bin / export/home/ myid/etc / export/home/ myid/csh1)	This is the directory path used to search when you enter the cd command.
history 32	history 20	This is the size of the history list. It gives the number of commands to be saved.
path (/bin / usr/bin /usr/ ucb /etc .)	path (/bin / usr/bin /etc / usr/ucb /usr/ local/bin .)	This is the search path searched when a command is given. Notice that the current directory is at the end of the search path. This prevents files, known as Trojan horses (which masquerade as system commands), from being executed before system commands.
	ignoreeof	Ignore any eof command, such as Control-d
	noclobber	Don't clobber or overwrite a file if it currently exists

PATH=/bin:/ usr/bin:/usr/ ucb:/etc:.	PATH=/bin:/usr/ bin:/etc:/usr/ ucb:/usr/local/ bin:.	This is just a repeated version of the search PATH, except it is done by printenv, whereas the above path statement is produced by the set command.
TZ=PS8PDT	TZ=CS6CDT	This is the time zone variable. It obviously was modified between executing the two commands that produced my mynewlogin.env and mynextlogin.env.

LAB 4.3 SELF-REVIEW QUESTIONS

In order to test your progress, you should be able to answer the following questions. Note that one answer may be valid in one version of UNIX and another answer may be valid in another version. It is important that you understand why you got such an error message.

Use the following file as your new /etc/login file called mylogin3:

```
#   my /etc/login file
# This is for the /etc/login file in the C Shell
stty sane
umask 644
set history = 50
# Set environment variables;
echo "This is the /etc/login file"
setenv TERM TERM
# set other variables;
set prompt = "LOGIN \!) "
```

Use the following file as your new /etc/cshrc file, called cshrc3:

```
# This file is /etc/cshrc
# which is to be used for /etc/cshrc
echo "This is the /etc/cshrc file"
set history = 20
set ignoreeof
set noclobber
set prompt = "C Shell \!)) "
set path = ( /bin /usr/bin /etc /usr/ucb /usr/local/
   bin .)
```

Now you should create the following file for your .login file:

```
# my new .login file
```

```
source /etc/login
```
Next, create the following file for your `.cshrc` file:

```
# my new .cshrc file
source /etc/cshrc
```

LAB 4.3

1) When you log in to the C Shell using these files as your `/etc/login` and `/etc/cshrc` files, which of the following prompts do you get?
   a) _____LOGIN 1)
   b) _____C Shell 1))
   c) _____csh))
   d) _____\!))
   e) _____myid@myserver:/home/myid/bin $

2) After doing Question (1), type:

```
csh
```

   What kind of prompt do you get?
   a) _____LOGIN 1)
   b) _____C Shell 1))
   c) _____csh))
   d) _____\!))
   e) _____myid@myserver:/home/myid/bin $

3) Use the following command:

```
set
```

   What is your terminal type?
   a) _____ansi
   b) _____TERM
   c) _____vt100
   d) _____vt220
   e) _____None of the above

4) After first logging in, what is the history list size?
   a) _____10
   b) _____20
   c) _____30
   d) _____40
   e) _____50

5) Enter the command:

```
csh
```

What is the history list size?
a) _____10
b) _____20
c) _____30
d) _____40
e) _____50

Quiz answers appear in Appendix A, Section 4.3.

CHAPTER 4

TEST YOUR THINKING

 The projects in this section are meant to have you utilize all of the skills that you have acquired throughout this chapter. The answers to these projects can be found at the companion Web site to this book, located at:

`http://www.phtpr.com/phptrinteractive`

Visit the Web site periodically to share and discuss your answers.

Note that Projects 1, 2, and 3 are designed to help you understand the regular user environment first, then the root environment, and finally the difference between the two.

1) Log in as a **regular user** in the C Shell. Write a program that sets all your environment variables. You should set all that show up when you type the following commands:

```
set
printenv
```

Save this program, because you can execute it whenever you need to reset your environment.

2) This question is basically the same as question (1), but now you will look at the root environment. Login as **root** in the C Shell. Write a program that sets all your environment variables. You should set all that show up when you type the commands:

```
set
printenv
```

Save this program, because you can execute it whenever you need to reset your environment.

 If you don't have root access, you can still create a file that sets some of the root environment. You can determine much of the root environment by looking at /etc/profile. You might also ask your instructor, if you have one, to provide the environment settings. You could also find a nice, friendly system administrator to see if he or she could provide a copy.

3) Write a program that compares the two programs that resulted from the previous two questions. You might use the command:
    ```
    diff
    ```

    Analyze this program to understand the difference between logging in as a regular user and logging in as root.

4) Write a program that determines whether you are running the program as a regular user or root, and then sets the environment accordingly. Use the programs you created in Projects 1 and 2 to set the proper environments.

 If you don't have root access, you can still change some of your environment variables set in the root environment which do not affect system security. Look at the results of Project 3 for more information. You could start a new shell by executing `sh` if you are concerned about affecting your current environment. When you are finished, you can just type the command `exit`. See the previous bit of Advice as well.

You can change command line prompts and environment variables that are generally used by root. The values can be set even if they make no difference to the user. Again, this is an exercise to get the student thinking.

If you want to be sure you have a clean environment for analysis, be sure that your `.cshrc, login,` and any system default login scripts are not executed. You can do this by renaming the files and then either logging out and in again, or running the command `su - myid -c "/bin/csh"`, where myid is the id you use to login with.

5) Now it's time to be a detective and check out the regular user's environment. Take Project 1 and determine which environmental settings are set up by:

   a) `.login`

   b) `.cshrc`

   c) The C Shell default values

   d) Other sources, such as system-wide user setup files in `/etc`

6) Continuing on as a detective, you need to look at root's environment. Take Project 1 and determine which environmental settings are setup by:

   a) `.login`

   b) `.cshrc`

   c) The C Shell default values

   d) Other Sources, such as system-wide user setup files in `/etc`

7) You have learned about some of the options to the `csh` sh in this chapter. Some that were discussed include -x and -n. Look up the following options for the Korn Shell. Explain what effects they have on executing a shell program. Consider the option as it is used in the following:

   ```
   csh -option myprogram
   ```

8) The options to be considered are as follows:

   a) `-e`

   b) `-i`

   c) `-v`

   d) Look at other options that might be useful.

CHAPTER 5

USER ACCOUNTS

The computer exists for the user. The user can be the programmer, administrator, operator, student, teacher, and anyone that uses the system. It is the job of the system administrator to provide the best possible environment for the user. This implies enforcing rules, developing site standards, and providing a stable system and user environment.—Joe

CHAPTER OBJECTIVES

In this Chapter, you will learn about:

Exercises for the Masses

Administering user accounts is one of the major roles of the system administrator. It is a job that almost every system administrator must do at some time. Adding a user can be done in a very short time, and can be easily delegated to someone else. Yet doing this properly is critical to establishing a stable system. Two of the most common ways for someone to break into a system are to get in by way of a userid that was poorly created, or to create a new id by exploiting some weakness in the program that adds a user to the system. This can be done by creating passwords that can be easily guessed, giving easy access to files and directories, and having lax network security. Addressing these concerns is beyond the reach of this book, and there are already many books on the topic. Later books in this series will address the network issues. This chapter will help you understand a little better some of the steps involved in adding a user, and some of the things you can do as an administrator.

EXERCISES FOR THE MASSES

Various versions of UNIX have tools for changing your user environment. Linux and AIX allow you to change your finger permission, whereas Solaris does not allow you to change the information in your /etc/passwd. You can, however, change the information in files in your home directory.

L A B   5.1

MODIFYING THE USER'S INFORMATION WITH CHFN

LAB OBJECTIVES

After this Lab, you will be able to:

✓ Modify Your finger Information

✓ Understand the Difference Between Using an Interactive Command and a Command Line with Options

---

You should look up the man page references to:

passwd, /etc/passwd, /etc/group, chfn

/ETC/PASSWD

The /etc/passwd file is the primary file containing user information in UNIX, and is readable by all users and writable only by root. This file originally contained the encrypted password information. Ironically, most UNIX manufacturers now have the encrypted password information stored elsewhere in files that are not accessible by the normal user. Thus, the UNIX password file contains most login information about users except the password.

In Linux, there are several files that contain default values used when a user's id is created or accessed. The file /etc/login.defs sets certain default values, such as password expiration times, password length, and various other things. You should examine this file if you want to make any changes to how users are added and maintained on your system.

Solaris uses the files in /etc/default to set user and some system default values.

There are many programs that UNIX vendors have written to add users to a UNIX system. They go by names such as useradd, sysadmin, sysadmsh, SMIT, SAM, and admintool. There are also various programs in the public domain, or that individual administrators have written, which all break down to the same basic thing—creating an entry in the /etc/passwd file that performs the following:

- Gives a name to the /etc/passwd file entry. This is known as the login id, user's id, or user's account, among other things.
- Gives a number to the user's login. This is known as the UID number. It is the only way that the computer really knows a user. The /etc/passwd file is used to convert from the UID number for ownership of a file to the real name. Without the /etc/passwd file, an ls -l would show the owner of a file to be just another number. (Hmm! We're basically numbers to UNIX! Sounds closer to reality then we might think.) It's actually easier for the computer to track and store numbers than to store names for ownership.
- Creates a password entry, either in the /etc/passwd file or in some other file that stores the encrypted password,

depending on the version of UNIX. Many versions of UNIX have either a /etc/shadow password file or a special directory that stores the encrypted password and is not readable by regular users. This prevents someone from reading the password file and trying to determine what your password is.

- Associates the user's login with a group. This is known as the Group ID, which is also just a number.
- Adds information in the comment field, such as the user's name. It can also include other information, such as phone numbers, office numbers, and other information that you will see in this Lab.
- Gives the user a home directory. This is where the user starts out when logging in. If the directory doesn't exist, the user can be assigned to any one of several directories, depending on how your system is set up. Their directories can include the /usr, /home, /ua directories. Normally, you don't put user login directories under root, though some special applications might point to a subdirectory or symbolic link that starts under root.
- Assigns a default startup shell to be used by the user when logging in. If this is left blank, then whatever is used as the default shell on your system will be the user's login shell.

Before you add the user, you must understand the layout of the password file. A typical password file in Linux looks like the following:

```
root:9NrWk7zl1N7I6:0:0:root:/root:/bin/bash
bin:*:1:1:bin:/bin:
daemon:*:2:2:daemon:/sbin:
adm:*:3:4:adm:/var/adm:
lp:*:4:7:lp:/var/spool/lpd:
sync:*:5:0:sync:/sbin:/bin/sync
shutdown:*:6:0:shutdown:/sbin:/sbin/shutdown
halt:*:7:0:halt:/sbin:/sbin/halt
mail:*:8:12:mail:/var/spool/mail:
news:*:9:13:news:/var/spool/news:
uucp:*:10:14:uucp:/var/spool/uucp:
operator:*:11:0:operator:/root:
games:*:12:100:games:/usr/games:
gopher:*:13:30:gopher:/usr/lib/gopher-data:
ftp:*:14:50:FTP User:/home/ftp:
```

```
nobody:*:99:99:Nobody:/:
myid:APrQvjnMcmxq.:1001:1001:My   Name,My   Bldg   rm
   10,354-555-4321,354-555-4321
:/home/myid:/bin/bash
cshid:9TuvQRP0r2d2:601:100:C shell id:/home/cshid:/
   bin/csh
```

Let's examine the last line of the file. The fields are broken down as follows:

`cshid`	The name of the user's account
`9TuvQRP0r2d2`	The encrypted user's password
`601`	The numeric UID number (what the system really knows you by)
`100`	The numeric GID number (the group id)
`C shell id`	The comment field, also called GCOS, GECOS, user's name, etc.
`/home/cshid`	The user's home directory
`/bin/csh`	The user's login shell

CHFN

The `chfn` command changes the user's finger information in the `/etc/passwd` file. It works in Linux, AIX, and other versions of UNIX. However, it does not work in Solaris because it does not allow the user to change any information in the `/etc/passwd` file. (Solaris does, however, allow you to change information in your NIS database if your are running NIS. But this is a topic for another discussion.) The `finger` command displays four things that can be changed by `chfn`. This information is totally under your control. Those things are your:

- Name
- Office Location
- Work Phone
- Home Phone

You can change your information in two ways. One is to enter the following command:

```
chfn
```

With this command, you will be stepped through a number of prompts. This is the interactive version of the chfn command.

You can also use the following command, in the following format:

```
chfn -f "My Name" -o "Bldg 15" -p "123-456-7890"
```

This is the command line version of the chfn command. Instead of having to step through a number of questions, you can execute the command at once. This makes it very useful to include in batch programs which include a number of other UNIX commands, and also reduces the time necessary to execute a command. It can often simplify your work. You can also get the information from another file by simply redirecting it from that file. This way, you can create a single file that has information about a number of users and executes everything at once.

We discuss both versions in this Lab.

LAB 5.1 EXERCISES

5.1.1 THE INTERACTIVE VERSION OF CHFN

Log in as a regular, non-root user and create your working directory for this chapter. Do the following:

```
mkdir user
cd user
```

Now you can save any information related to this chapter in that directory.

First you need to find out what your current user finger information is. Do this with the following command:

```
finger myid      (where myid is your login id)
```

Based on your results, answer Questions (a) through (e):

a) What is your name?

_____

_____

b) What is your office location?

_____

_____

c) What is your office phone number?

_____

_____

d) What is your home phone number?

_____

_____

e) Look up and explain the meaning of the other items that result from the `finger` command.

_____

_____

You can change your user information by using the interactive version of the `chfn` command. Do this by entering the following command:

```
chfn
```

Now you are prompted to enter information as it has been described previously in this Lab.

Answer Questions (f) through (i) based on how you answered the questions from `chfn`.

f) What did you put in as your name?

_____

_____

g) What did you use as your office location?

_____

_____

h) What office phone number did you use?

_____

_____

i) How did you fill in your home phone number?

_____

_____

Now enter the following command:

```
finger myid
```

j) What do you see?

_____

_____

You can verify your information by using the grep command on the /etc/passwd file.

Enter the following command:

```
grep myid /etc/passwd     (where myid is your login id)
```

k) What do you see?

_____

_____

l) Is this the same information that you entered with the chfn command? If not, try to analyze what went wrong. If it was wrong and you fixed it, what did you do?

_____

_____

5.1.2 THE COMMAND LINE VERSION OF CHFN

When you have a command line program that has an option with more than one string (e.g., a name can include first and last name), you should put the information in quotes. You should also not use commas and other special characters, such as the colon, in these strings, because commas and colons are sometimes used as separators. It is best to develop good habits now to prevent problems later.

You can execute the command line version of chfn in Linux by using the following format:

```
chfn  [ -f full-name ]  [ -o office ]  [ -p office-
     phone ] [ -h home-phone ] [ -u ] [ -v ] [ username ]
```

The options are explained as follows:

- **-f full-name**—where you put your name or the user's name (e.g., -f "John Smith")
- **-o office**—your office information (e.g. -o "Bldg 255 rm 211")
- **-p office-phone**—your office phone number (e.g. -p "425-555-1234")
- **-h home-phone**—your home phone number (e.g. -h "425-555-4321")
- **-u**—gives the usage message and then exits

- **-v**—gives the version number of the command and then exits
- **username**—the name of the user whose information is being changed. If you leave this blank, your own information is changed.

The developers of Linux have tried to make options more consistent and a little friendlier. Options in Linux can have a long form as well as the short form. The long form of the option uses two dashes before the option name. This is to prevent any misinterpretation by the command line interpreter. You will see that the man page on chfn *in Linux gives both versions. For example, instead of* -o, *you can use* -office.

Now, try out the following command and substitute your own personal information:

```
chfn -f "My Name" -o "My Bldg rm 10" -p "354-555-4321"
  -h "354-555-4321"
```

a) What kind of results do you get?

_____

_____

Now do the following command, replacing myid with your login id:

```
grep myid /etc/passwd
```

b) Does this agree with the changes you did in Question a?

_____

_____

If not, refer to Exercise 5.1.1 to see what steps you can use to fix it or figure out what is wrong.

LAB 5.1 EXERCISE ANSWERS

 This section gives you some suggested answers to the questions in Lab 5.1, with discussion related to those answers. Your answers may vary, but the most important thing is whether your answer works. Use this discussion to analyze differences between your answers and those presented here.

If you have alternative answers to the questions in this Exercise, you are encouraged to post your answers and discuss them at the companion Web site for this book, located at:

        http://www.phptr.com/phptrinteractive

5.1.1 ANSWERS

First you need to find out what your current user `finger` information is. Do this with the following command:

        finger myid

Sample results are as follows:

```
[myid@myserver user]$ finger myid
Login: myid                          Name: My ID
Directory: /home/myid                Shell: /bin/bash
Office: my office mybldg, 312-555-1212  Home Phone: 312-
555-7890
On since Sun May 10 14:00 (CDT) on ttyp0 from skates
No mail.
On since Thu May  7 21:14 (CDT) on ttyp0 from myo-
therserver (messages off)
Mail last read Wed Dec 31 18:00 1969 (CST)
No Plan.
[myid@myserver user]$
```

Based on your results, answer Questions (a) through (e):

a) What is your name?

Answer: Your name will show up in the finger result following the word Name:

So in the preceding sample output, your name is `My ID`. Your real id will in the same spot in place of it.

b) What is your office location?

Answer: Your office location shows up in the string:

```
Office: my office mybldg, 312-555-1212  Home Phone: 312-
555-7890
```

You see the string `Office` followed by the office location, which is `myoffice mybldg`.

c) What is your office phone number?

Answer: The same string has the `office phone number`, which in this example is `312-555-1212`.

d) What is your home phone number?

Answer: Again, the same string has the `home phone number`, which in this example is `312-555-7890`.

e) Look up and explain the meaning of the other items that result from the finger command.

Answer: Following are explanations of each list of items that result from the `finger` command. Your results will be different, depending on your system. You may even get an access denied message if you are looking at a system that has access restrictions.

Login: myid	The login id that you use when you login
Directory: /home/myid	Your home directory
Shell: /bin/bash	Your default shell
On since Sun May 10 14:00 (CDT) on ttyp0 from myotherserver	How long you have been on, from what terminal, and from what system
(messages off)	You have disabled receiving messages via write or other online messaging (this does not affect mail)

Mail last read Wed Dec 31 18:00 1969 (CST)	The last time you read your mail. (Looks like you have some catching up to do!). If you never had mail, it would say "No Mail".
No Plan.	You have no plan. (This is not a personal thing, you just need to create a file called .plan in your home directory, and voila—life has direction.)

You can change your user information by using the interactive version of the chfn command. Do this by entering the following command:

```
chfn
```

Now you are prompted to enter information as it has been described previously in this Lab.

You should see the following dialogue:

```
[myid@myserver myid]$ chfn myid
Changing finger information for myid.
Password:
Name [My ID]: My New ID
Office [myoffice mybldg]: My Office My Bldg
Office Phone [312-555-1212]: 777-555-4567
Home Phone [312-555-7890]: 777-555-0987
Finger information changed.
[myid@myserver myid]$
```

Notice that the old entries are listed as the default in the square brackets while you were doing the chfn *command.*

Answer Questions (f) through (l) based on how you answered the questions from chfn.

f) What did you put in as your name?

Answer:You should have put in your real name.

g) What did you use as your office location?

Answer: Be sure to put in your real office location.

h) What office phone number did you use?

Answer: Use your office phone number.

i) How did you fill in your home phone number?

Answer: Use your home phone number.

Now enter the command:

```
finger myid
```

j) What do you see?

Answer: You should see something similar to the following: [myid@myserver myid]$ finger myid.

```
Login: myid                         Name: My New Id
Directory: /home/myid               Shell: /bin/bash
Office: My Office My Bldg, 777-555-4567 Home Phone: 777-
555-0987
On since Sun May 10 14:00 (CDT) on ttyp0 from skates
(messages off)
Mail last read Wed Dec 31 18:00 1969 (CST)
No Plan.
[myid@myserver myid]$
```

Enter the following command:

```
grep myid /etc/passwd(where myid is your login id)
```

k) What do you see?

You should see a line similar to the following:

```
myid:*:101:100:My Name, My Bldg rm10, 354-555-4321,
    354-555-4321:/home/myid:/bin/bash
```

The only differences will be that the information you entered will replace the information in the respective fields.

l) Is this the same information that you entered with the chfn command? If not, try to analyze what went wrong. If it was wrong and you fixed it, what did you do?

Answer: Some of the possible steps you could take include:

- Redo the preceding steps to change the information again, and be sure that you complete all the steps.
- If this doesn't work, reexamine the `man chfn` command and make sure the command is valid and that you didn't miss some option.
- Try running the command as root. There may be some requirement that root needs to run the command. There may either be no error message returned, or it will be misdirected.

5.1.2 ANSWERS

Now you can try out the following command and substitute your own personal information:

```
chfn -f "My Name" -o "My Bldg rm 10" -p "354-555-4321"
   -h "354-555-4321"
```

a) What kind of results do you get?

Answer: Look at the following dialogue for a sample result.

```
[myid@myserver myid]$ chfn -f "My Name" -o "My Bldg rm
10" -p "354-555-4321"  -h "354-555-4321"
Changing finger information for myid.
Password:
Finger information changed.
[myid@myserver myid]$
```
Now, do the following command, replacing `myid` with your login id:
```
grep myid /etc/passwd
```

b) Does this agree with the changes you did in Question (a)?

Answer: Look at the following results:

```
[myid@myserver myid]$ grep myid /etc/passwd
myid:APrKvjnLcmxq.:1001:1001:My Name,My Bldg rm 10,354-
555-4321,354-555-4321:/home/myid:/bin/bash
[myid@myserver myid]$
```

LAB 5.1 SELF-REVIEW QUESTIONS

In order to test your progress, you should be able to answer the following questions. Note that one answer may be valid in one version of UNIX and another answer may be valid in another version. It is important that you understand why you got such an error message.

1) Which option to chfn do you need to change the users name in the /etc/passwd comment field?
   a) _____ -f
   b) _____ -o
   c) _____ -p
   d) _____ -h
   e) _____ None of the above

2) Which option to chfn do you need to change the user's home phone number in the /etc/passwd comment field?
   a) _____ -f
   b) _____ -o
   c) _____ -p
   d) _____ -h
   e) _____ None of the above

3) You can use chfn to change the default login shell.
   a) _____ True
   b) _____ False

4) Which command in Linux or AIX would you use to change a user's default login shell?
   a) _____ chfn
   b) _____ passwd
   c) _____ chsh
   d) _____ login
   e) _____ None of the above

5) Which file would you change to modify a No Plan message when you run the finger command?
   a) _____ .profile
   b) _____ .Xinitrc
   c) _____ .cshrc
   d) _____ .plan
   e) _____ login

Quiz answers appear in Appendix A, Section 5.1.

LAB EXERCISES FOR THE GREAT AND SUPER USER

You may have noticed that we have discussed many features of a UNIX user's account. We have examined a user's id from many perspectives. Because we have covered the major features of a user's account, we can now put it into practice.

L A B 5.2

ADDING A USER

LAB OBJECTIVES

After this Lab, you will be able to:

✓ Create a Regular UNIX userid

In UNIX, there are several things that you need to consider when adding a user. The major things to look at are:

- **Policies**—You need to find out what the current policies are. Oftentimes there are restrictions and policies about adding and using accounts on your system.
- **Space**—You must be sure that there is enough space assigned to the user to carry out their responsibilities.
- **Home, sweet home**—On many systems, home directories are scattered in a number of different directory structures. Sometimes this can cause a lot of confusion. Having ids under /usr, /user1, /user2, /home, /ua, and so forth can sometimes cause problems when you are trying to administer the system. You should be aware that, on some systems, you may need to break down a filesystem, because it may

exceed the maximum partition size, or the backup software may not be able to handle or track large filesystems. Other then that, Keep It Simple Sam (KISS).

- **Access rights**—What kinds of access do you give the user's directories? You must decide how much access rights the rest of the users and groups on the system must have to this user's directory.
- **The shell game**—Which shell does the user use? Developers tend to use the C Shell, whereas administrators tend to use the Korn Shell. You will need to ask the user directly.
- **Is the user God or the next best thing?** If the user needs administrative control, the version of UNIX you are using may allow you to setup the id with administrative rights.
- **Well, there goes the neighborhood!** The user may need to belong to a group and may need to have access to the group's files. The group may need access to the user's files. These are all things you must determine ahead of time.
- **To log, to log, to build a big log**. Do you need to document the fact that a user was added?
- **I've got a secret and who do I tell?** When you add a user, who gets informed, and by what means?
- **Etc.**—There are often other site-dependent issues—usually administrative and policy issues. Sometimes you need to notify more than your local staff if you are part of a WAN.

USERADD

Run the UNIX man command and look up the following commands:

`useradd`, `usermod`, `userdel`

The `useradd` command can use a number of options. Some of the options are only used rarely, so we'll discuss the most commonly used options. When you look up the usage of the `useradd` command, you will see the following kinds of options:

```
usage: useradd [-u uid [-o]] [-g group] [-G group,...]
               [-d home] [-s shell] [-c comment]
               [-m [-k template]][-f inactive]
```

```
              [-e expire mm/dd/yy] [-p passwd] [-n]
              [-r] name
    useradd  -D [-g group] [-b base] [-s shell]
              [-f inactive] [-e expire]
```

The first form of useradd is used for adding individual users to the system. The second form is used to change the system default values. The default values are used when you do not specify an actual value for an item when you create the id. A good example is the GID, or group id number. If you do not specify a value for this, the system automatically uses the default value.

Some versions of UNIX have a size limitation of eight characters for the login name. Linux and other versions of UNIX allow names of more than eight characters.

UNIX allows you to have a default directory /etc/skel that stores copies of the default files for user accounts. In the case of Linux, /etc/skel has the default files for:

- .Xdefaults
- .bash_profile
- .bash_logout
- .bashrc

These files are executed when the user logs in or logs out of the bash shell, which is the default in Linux. They are put in the user's home directory. Similar files exist on other UNIX systems and are usually stored in /etc/skel.

In Solaris, you would see the following files in the user's home directory when a userid is created:

- .profile
- local.cshrc
- local.login
- local.profile

The Red Hat Linux useradd *command creates a* /etc/group *file entry for each password file entry, unless you disable it with the* −n *option. This means that, if you create a UID of 5000, there will also be a GID of 5000.*

The most important options needed for adding your first account are outlined as follows:

-u uid [-o]	The numeric UID number. By default, Linux prevents you from creating an id with a currently-existing UID number, unless you use the −o option.
-g group	The numeric GID or group id number found in /etc/group.
-d home	The home directory. By default, the user's login name will be appended to whatever is the default home directory, unless this is specified.
-s shell	The default shell.
-c comment	The comment field. As we saw in the previous exercises in this chapter, you can put a lot of information in this field.
Name	The actual login name used to get into the system with this id. Remember that the system only knows you by your UID number. This is just an alias for the real thing.

USERMOD. USERDEL

There are other commands that can be used by root to modify a user's account information. The command usermod modifies a user's information. You might want to try it when you are done with this chapter. Another command is userdel, which deletes a user's account. This command may or may not delete a user's directory. This is usually dependent on setting an option or answering a prompt.

LAB 5.2 EXERCISES

5.2.1 CREATING A REGULAR *UNIX* USER ACCOUNT

In this Exercise, you will create a regular UNIX user account that you can use. This account will have all the privileges of a regular user, and none of the privileges of root or superuser.

 In some versions of UNIX, a non-root user account can have all the privileges of root or superuser. This can happen even if the id has a non-zero UID and GID number. Usually the system does this by having a certain range of addresses with these privileges. Oftentimes, ids under 100 have special privileges, though in AIX, ids under 200 can sometimes have special privileges.

To start the process, you must log in as root or superuser. Use a particular UID number for this Exercise; choose the UID number 5000. Now, check to make sure that this number is not used (I chose such a high number because it is almost never used). You can do this with the following command:

```
grep 5000 /etc/passwd
```

a) What kind of results do you get?

_____

_____

Analyze your results and see if they are consistent with the UNIX philosophy that "no news is good news."

This step is necessary to make sure that you do not use an id or UID number that is currently in use.

Most programs used to add users to UNIX systems check to see if a UID number is in use. If so, the program either gives you a warning message and allows you to create the id anyway, or it kicks you out of the program. In the latter case, you may need to add an id manually. It is always a good idea to do a manual check first if you are not sure how your program handles duplicate UID numbers.

LAB 5.2

UNIX has several tools, both command line and X-windows based, to add users. This Exercise focuses on the command line version. The program you should use is called `useradd`. To find out what kinds of options you can use, enter the following command:

```
useradd
```

b) Compare the results with the earlier discussion of `useradd`. Is this consistent, and what you would expect?

_____

_____

As mentioned in the earlier discussion, you can find out what the system default values are by using an option to `useradd`. Try the following:

```
useradd -D
```

c) Identify the default values and explain what they mean.

_____

_____

Now you're ready to add a new id. Start by letting the system create the default values for the id. Enter the following command:

```
useradd my1stid
```

You can substitute `my1stid` for an id of your own choosing. Just remember which one it is for the subsequent discussion.

d) What do you see on the screen when you type the following?

```
grep my1stid /etc/passwd
```

_____

_____

e) Is this what you expected?

_____

_____

If you don't see that id, you need to step through the process and make sure you entered all the commands correctly.

f) How does this compare to the default values found earlier?

_____

_____

5.2.2 CREATING A CUSTOMIZED UNIX USER ACCOUNT

Now you're going to create a second id and add to the command some options. Create an id with the following characteristics:

UID:	5000
Home Directory:	/home/seconddir
Group ID:	users or 100
Shell:	/bin/sh
Name:	my2ndid

Now, create the id. Use the following format:

```
useradd  -u 5000 -d /home/seconddir -g 100 -s /bin/sh
    my2ndid
```

a) What do you see on the screen?

_____

_____

Experiment with using the other options for `useradd`*. There are some nice security features for account expiration there. There is a project on this at the end of the chapter to test your skills.*

Now, to verify that you created the id properly, grep the password file with:

```
grep my2ndid /etc/passwd
```

b) What is the result? Is this the result you expected?

_____

_____

You need to first setup a password. Do that with the following command:

```
passwd my2ndid
```

Then follow the prompts.

c) What did you have to do to change the password?

_____

_____

You may find that certain passwords are not acceptable. You may need to change the pattern of the password. Oftentimes it requires one or more numbers as well as letters. There is usually a minimum length also. Be aware that, as root, you can often bypass the rules, so don't get too cozy!

Test the id by logging in with it. You can do this easily as root by typing the following:

```
su - my2ndid
```

d) What did you see change?

_____

_____

You can check that your home directory is current with the following:

```
pwd
```

e) Is this what you expected? If not, why not?

_____

_____

Change the password. Use the following command:

```
passwd
```

This should step you through several prompts.

f) Did you get any errors? If so, how would you explain them?

_____

_____

g) Why did you have to enter the user id when you first changed the password after creating the id, whereas now you only had to enter the string `passwd`?

_____

_____

h) The final test is to log out of the system and log in again. Try that. Are you prompted to change the password?

_____

_____

Sometimes a UNIX system will prompt you to change the password on the first login, even if you have already changed it. This is a security feature. Once you have done a regular login and changed your password, the system won't prompt you to change it again. Of course, if password expiration is in effect, it will prompt you again when the password expires.

Congratulations! If you are a first-time administrator, you have now created a user id in UNIX. If this is old hat to you, then hopefully you will have gained some additional insights into the process.

LAB 5.2 EXERCISE ANSWERS

This section gives you some suggested answers to the questions in Lab 5.2, with discussion related to those answers. Your answers may vary, but the most important thing is whether your answer works. Use this discussion to analyze differences between your answers and those presented here.

If you have alternative answers to the questions in this Exercise, you are encouraged to post your answers and discuss them at the companion Web site for this book, located at:

        http://www.phptr.com/phptrinteractive

5.2.1 ANSWERS

To start the process, you must login as root or superuser. Use a particular UID number for this Exercise; choose the UID number 5000. Now, check to make sure that this number is not used (I chose such a high number because it is almost never used). You can do this with the command:

```
grep 5000 /etc/passwd
```

a)   What kind of results do you get?

```
[root@myserver /root]# grep 5000 /etc/passwd
[root@myserver /root]#
```

Analyze your results and see if they are consistent with the UNIX philosophy that "no news is good news."

Your results should be just a command line prompt, which is usually just the # symbol for root. If you came up with a result that gave you a line from the password file, just choose another number that does not return any results. If you got an error, you need to look at your command and be sure you typed it correctly. If all goes well, you will now have a UID number that is not in use.

To find out what kind of options you can use, enter the following command:

```
useradd
```

b) Compare the results with the earlier discussion of `useradd`. Is this consistent, and what you would expect?

Answer: The following results are from Linux. The results in Linux, Solaris, and other operating systems are similar. You should see something like:

```
[root@myserver /root]# useradd
usage: useradd [-u uid [-o]] [-g group] [-G group,...]
               [-d home] [-s shell] [-c comment]
               [-m [-k template]] [-f inactive]
               [-e expire mm/dd/yy] [-p passwd] [-n]
               [-r] name
       useradd  -D [-g group] [-b base] [-s shell] [-f
inactive] [-e expire]
[root@myserver /root]#
```

As mentioned in the earlier discussion, you can find out what the system default values are by using an option to useradd. Try this:

```
useradd -D
```

c) Identify the default values and explain what they mean.

Answer: You should see results that are similar to the following:

```
[root@myserver /root]# useradd -D
GROUP=100
HOME=/home
INACTIVE=-1
EXPIRE=
```

```
SHELL=/bin/bash
SKEL=/etc/skel
[root@myserver /root]#
```

The results are explained as follows:

GROUP=100	The default group id
HOME=/home	The default directory where the user's home directory is created. By default, the user's home directory has the same name as the login name and is under this directory
INACTIVE=-1	This says that, if the password expires, don't permanently disable the account
EXPIRE=	When the account will expire
SHELL=/bin/ bash	The default login shell for all user accounts
SKEL=/etc/skel	Where the skeleton files are located for the shells. For example, in Solaris, you would have a skeleton file for .profile in this directory. In Linux, you have skeleton files for bash there by default.

Now you're ready to add a new id. Start by letting the system create the default values for the id. Enter the following command:

```
useradd my1stid
```

You can substitute `my1stid` for an id of your own choosing. Just remember which one it is for the subsequent discussion.

d) What do you see on the screen when you type:

```
grep my1stid /etc/passwd
```

Answer:You should see something similar to the following:

```
[root@myserver /root]# grep my1stid /etc/passwd
my1stid:!:1003:1003::/home/my1stid:/bin/bash
[root@myserver /root]#
```

e) Is this what you expected?

Answer:This should be what you would expect.

The UID number may be different, and the shell and login name may be different, but the format should be the same. If you don't see that id, you need to step through the process and make sure you entered all the commands correctly.

f) How does this compare to the default values found earlier?

Answer: It should compare exactly. If not, retrace your steps and try again.

You may need to delete the account and start over again. To delete the account, just type the following command:

```
userdel my1stid
```

The id will be deleted from your system. Then you can start over. (If you didn't use `my1stid` as your id, just substitute the id you did use.)

5.2.2 ANSWERS

Here, you created a second id with given characteristics.

a) What do you see on the screen?

Answer: You should just get the command line prompt back.

Now, to verify that you created the id properly, grep the password file with the following:

```
grep my2ndid /etc/passwd
```

b) What is the result? Is this the result you expected?

Answer: You should see something similar to the following:

```
[root@myserver /root]# grep my2ndid /etc/passwd
my2ndid:!:5000:100::/home/seconddir:/bin/sh
[root@myserver /root]#
```

This should be what you expected.

You now need to set up a password. Do that with the following command:

```
passwd my2ndid
```

Then follow the prompts.

```
[root@myserver /root]# passwd my2ndid
New UNIX password:
Retype new UNIX password:
passwd: all authentication tokens updated successfully
[root@myserver /root]#
```

c)   What did you have to do to change the password?

Answer:You should have seen results similar to the answer to Question (b) of this Exercise.

Test the id by logging in with it.You can do this easily as root by typing the following:

```
su - my2ndid
```

d)   What did you see change?

Answer:You should see the following or similar results:

```
[root@myserver /root]# su - my2ndid
my2ndid@myserver:/home/seconddir$
```

This is a means for you to change your id to any other user's id on the system if you start out as root. This is another reason to protect the root id.

You can check that your home directory is current with the following:

```
pwd
```

e)   Is this what you expected? If not, why not?

Answer:You should have seen the absolute path of your home directory. In this case, you would see the following:

```
my2ndid@myserver:/home/seconddir$ pwd
/home/seconddir
my2ndid@myserver:/home/seconddir$
```

There are other commands you can use in many versions of UNIX to verify who you are. You might try using the commands `id` and `groups`, among others.

Change the password by using the following command:

```
passwd
```

This should step you through several prompts.

f)   Did you get any errors? If so, how would you explain them?

Answer:You may get an error which indicates that you are trying to change the password of the id with which you originally logged in. If you try to change your password with the command `passwd my2ndid`, *you will get a message which says that only root can specify a user to the* `passwd` *command.*

g) Why did you have to enter the user id when you first changed the password after creating the id, whereas now you only had to enter the string `passwd`?

Answer: You changed the password first as root, so it was necessary to specify the user whose password was changed. The second time, you were logged in with `my2ndid`. *By default, the password of the current user is changed by the* `passwd` *command.*

h) The final test is to log out of the system and log in again. Try that. Are you prompted to change the password?

Answer: With Red Hat Linux 5.0, you will not be prompted to change your password at login if you have changed it beforehand. Some versions of UNIX will, however, ask you to change your password at your first login from the login prompt. This is a security feature which helps protect your password and account.

LAB 5.2 SELF-REVIEW QUESTIONS

In order to test your progress, you should be able to answer the following questions. Note that one answer may be valid in one version of UNIX and another answer may be valid in another version. It is important that you understand why you got such an error message.

1) In a system that supports the `useradd` command, which of the following commands would you use to find the default values for setting up login ids?
   a) _____`useradd -D`
   b) _____`useradd -g`
   c) _____`user -default`
   d) _____`skel -d`
   e) _____None of the above

2) Which directory contains the basic user login files that are copied to each user's home directory when the id is created?
   a) _____`/etc/rc/skel`
   b) _____`/usr/lib/skel`
   c) _____`/etc/skel`
   d) _____`/skel`
   e) _____None of the above

3) You can use `chfn` to change the default login shell.
    a) _____True
    b) _____False

4) Which command(s) can be used to create or modify a user's comment field?
    a) _____passwd
    b) _____useradd
    c) _____chfn
    d) _____both (a) and (b)
    e) _____both (b) and (c)

5) In a system that supports `useradd`, this command allows *anyone* to add a user to a UNIX system.
    a) _____True
    b) _____False

Quiz answers appear in Appendix A, Section 5.2.

C H A P T E R   5

TEST YOUR THINKING

The projects in this section are meant to have you utilize all of the skills that you have acquired throughout this chapter. The answers to these projects are found at the companion Web site to this book, located at:

```
http://www.phptr.com/phptrinteractive
```

Visit the Web site periodically to share and discuss your answers.

1) Log in as a **regular user**. Write a batch program that sets your user comment information for the command line version of:

```
chfn
```

Take the input from a separate text file.

2) Log in as a **root**. Write a batch program that sets all the comment information for at least two users. Use the command line version of:

```
chfn
```

Take the input from a separate text file.

3) Go over this chapter using Linux and redo all the steps that use command line options. Wherever the text uses the short form of an option, use the long form instead. For example, the short form of the usage option for `chfn` is `-u`; the long form of the usage option is `-help`. See the man pages for more information on the long options.

4) Create a batch program that takes a file as input and automatically creates user logins on the system. You should include the following characteristics for each user:

   a) login id

b) UID number that will make it a system account (i.e., one with special privileges)

c) password

 Note that you must experiment with the password format. It is not the unencrypted password. Make a standard login password for everyone that can be changed when the user first logs in.

d) home directory

e) expiration date

f) a group membership

g) a second group membership

h) create the home directory if it doesn't exist

5) Log in as **root**. Write a batch program that sets all the comment information for at least two users. Use the command line version of:

```
chfn
```

Take the input from a separate text file.

C H A P T E R 6

STARTUP PROCESSES

When administering a system, it is very important to understand the system throughout its running cycle. So you need to start at the beginning and continue on until you're done. —Joe

This chapter discusses several of the major processes that run when starting up the system. The processes chosen are those that can be configured by the administrator. It is not possible or advisable for an administrator to make many changes to the system configuration without detailed knowledge of the inner workings of UNIX. This chapter is a prelude to the next chapter, in which you will actually shutdown and reboot a system.

It is important for an administrator to understand the chain of events in bringing up a system. Often, things that do not work when a system is brought up can be related to a feature or program that failed to startup. This chapter attempts to clarify and discuss some of the important setup files and startup processes.

You will make some system changes and then study the impact of those changes. Some of these changes can be done by a normal user. Others require root access. If you don't have root access, you can still work along and read some of the later descriptions. If your instructor or administrator has root access, you may still watch the results of the changes in a group setting.

EXERCISES FOR THE MASSES

This Lab gives you some experience in analyzing the /etc/inittab file. Because you need to be root to make any changes to this file, you will simply be asked to analyze the file. There will be no exercise for root only, but if you are root, you might consider some ways in which you can make changes to the file. Some of the later exercises will involve modifying crontab and rc files.

L A B   6.1

SYSTEM CONFIGURATION FILES

LAB OBJECTIVES

After this Lab, you will be able to better understand:

✓ The /etc/inittab File

When UNIX starts up, there are a number of files that are executed to set up the system. Some systems, such as AIX, go through detailed diagnostics and system checks. They then execute a number of the system scripts and go through a detailed execution of information stored in a system database. Other versions of UNIX, such as Linux and Solaris, depend more on any hardware diagnostics built into the box and execute a minimum of software diagnostics before they run the standard scripts.

LAB
6.1

Look in the man pages for the following:

`init inittab rc cron crontab  ps`

While there are a number of UNIX operating system manufacturers, each with their own variations, it is possible to filter out many of the differences and concentrate on the similarities. Linux, in particular, has simplified some of the files, so it is a good tool with which to start the discussion.

The primary files or directories that should be considered if there are system problems after bootup, or if you want to start some special process, are:

- The **rc** files and directories. These are files in the `/etc` directory, and they all begin with the name rc. The common theme among them is that their names usually relate to running certain processes at certain run levels (e.g., run levels 2 or 3 are the normal multiuser run levels). Files relating to that run level are labeled `rc2` and directories are called `rc2.d`. In the man pages and your text, you will find discussions of the `rc` variants.
- `crontabs`—A `cron` process is a periodic process that is scheduled to run from a `crontab` file. Both `cron` and `init` can run scheduled processes, but `crontab` allows the user much finer and clearer control over the scheduling. Regular users can schedule processes as well as root. The `crontab` file is located on various systems as follows:

Linux uses:

- `/var/spool/cron` and creates files in this directory with the user's name, which are then used to execute a scheduled process
- `/etc/crontab` is a directory from which it executes scheduled processes
- `/etc/cron.hourly`, `/etc/cron.daily`, and other `/etc/cron` directories are executed according to the name of the directory

Solaris and AIX use:

- the directory `/var/spool/cron/crontabs` and reads a file there with the user's name

All versions of Unix use:

- /etc/inittab file is used by the init process to run processes at a specific run level. Whenever the system goes from one run level to another, the inittab file is checked, and any processes scheduled to run at the new level are kicked off. Also, any processes that don't run at the new level will die or be killed. Inittab can also have processes setup so that a second process will not run until the first is completed. Because UNIX is a multitasking system, it sometimes happens that, in a sequence, the second process starts before the first is completed.

■ FOR EXAMPLE:

Let's look at the /etc/inittab file from Red Hat Linux:

```
# inittab        This file describes how the INIT pro-
  cess should set up
# the system in a certain run-level.
#
# Author: Miquel van Smoorenburg,
  <miquels@drinkel.nl.mugnet.org>
# Modified for RHS Linux by Marc Ewing and Donnie Barnes
#
# Default runlevel. The runlevels used by RHS are:
#   0 - halt (Do NOT set initdefault to this)
#   1 - Single user mode
#   2 - Multiuser, without NFS (The same as 3, if you
  do not have networking)
#   3 - Full multiuser mode
#   4 - unused
#   5 - X11
#   6 - reboot (Do NOT set initdefault to this)
#
id:3:initdefault:
# System initialization.
si::sysinit:/etc/rc.d/rc.sysinit
10:0:wait:/etc/rc.d/rc 0
```

```
12:2:wait:/etc/rc.d/rc 2
13:3:wait:/etc/rc.d/rc 3
14:4:wait:/etc/rc.d/rc 4
15:5:wait:/etc/rc.d/rc 5
16:6:wait:/etc/rc.d/rc 6
# Things to run in every runlevel.
ud::once:/sbin/update
# Trap CTRL-ALT-DELETE
ca::ctrlaltdel:/sbin/shutdown -t3 -r now
# Things to run in every runlevel.
ud::once:/sbin/update
# Trap CTRL-ALT-DELETE
ca::ctrlaltdel:/sbin/shutdown -t3 -r now
# When our UPS tells us power has failed, assume we
  have a few minutes
# of power left.  Schedule a shutdown for 2 minutes
  from now.
#  This  does,  of  course,  assume  you  have  powder
  installed and your
# UPS connected and working correctly.
pf::powerfail:/sbin/shutdown -f -h +2 "Power Failure;
  System Shutting Down"
# If power was restored before the shutdown kicked in,
  cancel it.
pr:12345:powerokwait:/sbin/shutdown     -c     "Power
  Restored; Shutdown Cancelled"

# If power was restored before the shutdown kicked in,
  cancel it.
pr:12345:powerokwait:/sbin/shutdown     -c     "Power
  Restored; Shutdown Cancelled"
# Run gettys in standard runlevels
1:12345:respawn:/sbin/mingetty tty1
2:2345:respawn:/sbin/mingetty tty2
3:2345:respawn:/sbin/mingetty tty3
4:2345:respawn:/sbin/mingetty tty4
5:2345:respawn:/sbin/mingetty tty5
6:2345:respawn:/sbin/mingetty tty6
# Run xdm in runlevel 5
x:5:respawn:/usr/bin/X11/xdm -nodaemon
```

This file may seem quite overwhelming, but it can be broken down in the following summary:

1. **Heading**—An introduction to the file containing such information as who wrote it and an e-mail address to contact in case of problems. The nice thing about Linux is that you can actually contact the people who wrote it.

2. **Default runlevel discussion**—A description of the various run levels used by RHS Linux (Red Hat); provides an excellent summary of what Linux looks at in /etc/inittab.

3. **System initialization**—This is a connection to the various files that are executed at the various run levels. Let's look at one of them:

```
13:3:wait:/etc/rc.d/rc 3
```

The line is broken down as follows:

```
label:runlevel:action:process
```

> label can be anything; it is just a place holder and something that is unique to that line. It is not used anywhere. In the preceding example, the label is 13.
>
> runlevel is the run level, or run levels, at which the process will run, which is 3 in this example.
>
> action is what to do with the process when it is at the run level. In this example, the run level is wait. This means to start the process when run level 3 is reached, and then to wait until the process is completed before continuing on to process later items in /etc/inittab.
>
> process is the actual process with whatever options are needed. This example says to execute the file /etc/rc.d/rc with the option 3, which in this case is the same as the run level.

4. Things to run in every run level. In this example, you see:

```
ud::once:/sbin/update
```

> Note that the second field, the run level field, is blank. This says to run the /sbin/update process once when entering a new level.

5. The next field is to Trap CTRL-ALT-DELETE. That line:

```
ca::ctrlaltdel:/sbin/shutdown -t3 -r now
```

says that, when you press the keys Ctrl, Alt, and Delete together, the system will do an immediate shutdown and then a reboot.

6. Power failure. There are a number of lines here that tell you what to do in case of a power failure. You can have an attached UPS that sends a signal to your system when there is a power outage. The system will then do a shutdown according to a defined sequence. It also tells you what to do in case the power is restored.

7. The line:

```
1:12345:respawn:/sbin/mingetty tty1
```

says that, for any run levels from 1 to 5, run the process /sbin/mingetty on tty1. The respawn action says that if the process should die or be killed, it should be automatically restarted the next time /etc/inittab is scanned. You can force init to read the file by just typing the following command:

```
kill -HUP 1
```

This sends the init process a HUP signal. When that happens, init will reread /etc/inittab.

8. Xdm. The following line:

```
x:5:respawn:/usr/bin/X11/xdm -nodaemon
```

causes the xdm process to be executed when entering run-level 5. Xdm is an xwindows interface.

LAB 6.1 EXERCISES

6.1.1 THE /ETC/INITTAB FILE

The first thing you need to do for this exercise is create a directory to hold your files. Go to your home directory and make a directory called startup. Do this with your regular login id.

Now, find out what your current run level is. In Linux, you can find your current run level with the following command:

```
/sbin/runlevel
```

If you are running Solaris or another standard UNIX, you can try:

```
who -r
```

a) What kind of results do you get?

_____

_____

b) Take a look at `/etc/inittab`. Which lines will be executing only at your current run level? (Ignore those lines that execute at other run levels also.) Write a little program that can filter this out and save it in the directory you created previously.

_____

_____

c) Take another look at `/etc/inittab`. This time, look for lines that will be executing at your current run level, and also at other run levels. (Don't forget those processes that run at all run levels.) Write a little program that will filter for your information also, and save it in the directory you created in this Lab.

_____

_____

LAB 6.1 EXERCISE ANSWERS

 This section gives you some suggested answers to the questions in Lab 6.1, with discussion related to those answers. Your answers may vary, but the most important thing is whether your answer works. Use this discussion to analyze differences between your answers and those presented here.

If you have alternative answers to the questions in this Exercise, you are encouraged to post your answers and discuss them at the companion Web site for this book, located at:

`http://www.phptr.com/phptrinteractive`

6.1.1 ANSWERS

The first thing you did in this Exercise was create a new directory to hold the files for this Exercise. Then you determined your current run level.

a) What kind of results do you get?

Answer: In Linux, when you execute `/sbin/runlevel`, *you should see:*

N 3

Note that if `/sbin` *is in your search path, you can just type* `runlevel`.

And in Solaris, when you run `who -r`, *you should see:*

```
    .        run-level 3  May 16 03:31       3       0  S
```

b) Take a look at `/etc/inittab`. Which lines will be executing only at your current run level? (Ignore those lines that also execute at other run levels.) Write a little program that can filter this out and save it in the directory you created previously.

Answer:You can use the following program (if you don't have bash use sh):

```
#!/bin/bash
# program: find_one
# this program will find all of the single runlevel
  lines in /etc/inittab
for i in `grep ":[0-9]:" /etc/inittab`
do
            echo $i
done
```

This results in the following output in Linux:

```
[myid@myserver startup]$ find_one
id:3:initdefault
10:0:wait:/etc/rc.d/rc 0
11:1:wait:/etc/rc.d/rc 1
12:2:wait:/etc/rc.d/rc 2
13:3:wait:/etc/rc.d/rc 3
14:4:wait:/etc/rc.d/rc 4
15:5:wait:/etc/rc.d/rc 5
16:6:wait:/etc/rc.d/rc 6
x:5:respawn:/usr/bin/X11/xdm -nodaemon
[myid@myserver startup]$
```

c)   Take another look at `/etc/inittab`. This time, look for lines that will be executing at your current run level, and also at other run levels. (Don't forget those processes that run at all run levels.) Write a little program that will filter for your information also, and save it in the directory you created in this Lab.

Answer:The program to do this will be left as a project for you to do at the end of the chapter. You should have found the following entries in `/etc/inittab`.

```
id:3:initdefault:
l0:0:wait:/etc/rc.d/rc 0
l1:1:wait:/etc/rc.d/rc 1
l2:2:wait:/etc/rc.d/rc 2
l3:3:wait:/etc/rc.d/rc 3
l4:4:wait:/etc/rc.d/rc 4
l5:5:wait:/etc/rc.d/rc 5
l6:6:wait:/etc/rc.d/rc 6
pr:12345:powerokwait:/sbin/shutdown -c "Power
Restored;Shutdown Cancelled"
1:12345:respawn:/sbin/mingetty tty1
2:2345:respawn:/sbin/mingetty tty2
3:2345:respawn:/sbin/mingetty tty3
4:2345:respawn:/sbin/mingetty tty4
5:2345:respawn:/sbin/mingetty tty5
6:2345:respawn:/sbin/mingetty tty6
x:5:respawn:/usr/bin/X11/xdm -nodaemon
si::sysinit:/etc/rc.d/rc.sysinit
ud::once:/sbin/update
ca::ctrlaltdel:/sbin/shutdown -t3 -r now
pf::powerfail:/sbin/shutdown -f -h +2 "Power Failure;
System Shutting Down"
```

LAB 6.1 SELF-REVIEW QUESTIONS

In order to test your progress, you should be able to answer the following questions. Questions 1 to 5 refer to the `/etc/inittab` file mentioned in the text. You need to find the label on the line that answers the question. For example, the line that does system initialization is labeled `si`.

1) How is the line that sets the system default run level labeled?
   - **a)** _____ca
   - **b)** _____13
   - **c)** _____3
   - **d)** _____16
   - **e)** _____id

2) How is the line that executes the `rc` file for the default run level labeled?
   - **a)** _____ca
   - **b)** _____13
   - **c)** _____3
   - **d)** _____16
   - **e)** _____id

3) How is the line that starts up a `getty` process on `tty3` labeled?
   - **a)** _____ca
   - **b)** _____13
   - **c)** _____3
   - **d)** _____16
   - **e)** _____id

4) How is the line that executes the appropriate `rc` option when `init` gets a reboot command labeled?
   - **a)** _____ca
   - **b)** _____13
   - **c)** _____3
   - **d)** _____16
   - **e)** _____id

5) Look in the `/etc/inittab` in the Lab discussion and find the actual line that resets the system when it gets a Ctrl-Alt-Delete. How is that line labeled?
   - **a)** _____ca
   - **b)** _____13
   - **c)** _____3
   - **d)** _____6
   - **e)** _____id

Quiz answers appear in Appendix A, Section 6.1.

L A B   6.2

THE CRONTAB FILES

LAB OBJECTIVES

After this series of Exercises, you will be able to:

✓ Create Your Own `crontab` Entry

✓ Further Customization of Your `crontab` File

In UNIX, it is possible to schedule processes on a periodic basis. You can create many possible time combinations to run processes at times when you need them to run. This Lab will explore the `cron` program and the `crontab` file, and will have you create your own `crontab` file.

It is important to understand `cron` and how it relates to the other files in this chapter, which are the `inittab` files and the `/etc/rc.d` files. Sometimes administrators and even software manufacturers get confused on which file does what and, as a result, put files in the wrong locations.

The important difference between `init` and `cron` are as follows:

- The `init` process and the `/etc/inittab` file monitor the system for changes in run level and will execute programs when the run level changes. The file can also be used to maintain processes that are running, such as terminal and modem logins. If there is a disconnect on the terminal process, UNIX will then reset the process and start the login process over again on the device. Thus, the `/etc/inittab` file is run level-dependent, not time-dependent. Because the `rc` files are executed from the `/etc/inittab`, they are also run level-dependent.

- Cron and the crontab files can be used to run files at a specified time, and are thus time-dependent, not run level-dependent. The cron process is actually started from a file in the rc directories. A good example of a cron process would be running a system backup every night at 2 A.M.

The cron process allows administrators to automate a number of routine processes. You can automate backups, database processing and reports, general filesystem cleanup, and a number of other routine tasks that otherwise would have to be run manually.

The administrator can control who has access to running files from crontab by using the following files:

- /usr/lib/cron/cron.allow is a list of all users that are allowed to use cron
- /usr/lib/cron/cron.deny is a list of all users that are not allowed to use cron

In UNIX, if neither cron.allow nor cron.deny don't exist, then all users are allowed to use the cron process.

A crontab line has the following format:

```
minute hour day-of-month month-of-year day-of-week command
```

where the columns or fields are described as follows:

- **minute**—the minute of the hour; has a value from 0 to 59
- **hour**—the hour of the day; has a value from 0-23
- **day-of-month**—the day of the month; has a value from 1 to 31
- **month-of-year**—the month of the year; has a value from 1 to 12
- **day of the week**—these values follow a pattern in which Sunday is 0, Monday is 1, and so forth
- **command**—the name of the command to be executed

There can also be more than one item in each field. You can add additional entries and separate them by commas with no spaces, or you can use the dash to indicate a range. Also, an asterisk or * in a column indicates that anything is acceptable for that column.

■ *FOR EXAMPLE:*

Let's look at the following lines:

```
30  1   *   *   *   mail myid < `date`
10,30,50 ** *   1-5    run_report
0      8 7  10  *   mail john  <  birthday_greeting
```

- The first line says to send mail to myid every day at 1:30 a.m. with the date. This might be useful if you are concerned about time synchronization, or just want to see if your system is up.
- The second line say to run a report on all days from Monday through Friday at 10, 30, and 50 minutes past the hour.
- The last line says to send a mail to the id john on Oct 7 at 8 A.M. This is a birthday greeting. Use the file birthday_greeting as input into the mail.

When you create your crontab entry, you must use the command:

```
crontab  -e
```

This command will take you into your default editor and allow you to change your cron settings. If you don't have a default editor, Linux will take you into vi. If you want to change your editor, you must set the environment variables EDITOR or VISUAL.

LAB 6.2 EXERCISES

6.2.1 CREATE YOUR OWN CRONTAB ENTRY

You should log in with your regular UNIX user id. The following exercises use bash, but in most cases sh and ksh will also work.

You can determine if you already have a crontab entry by using the following command:

```
crontab -l
```

The `crontab -l` command will display the contents of your crontab file.

> **a)** What do you see on the screen when you run the `crontab -l` command?

_____

_____

Did you get any errors? If you received any errors, you must fix them before going on. You might look at your TERM variable. Look at the description under `crontab -e` for some hints.

Now, you need to actually create your first `crontab` entry. Use the command:

```
crontab -e
```

> **b)** What kind of results did you get?

_____

_____

Now you need to create a file that you can execute from cron. Go into your favorite editor and create the following file:

```
echo "Good Morning"  | mail myid
```

Save this file as `/home/myid/startup/my_greeting`.

Remember from your previous labs that `bash -x` or `ksh -x` will allow you to trace a program while it executes. Test this file by executing it as:

```
bash -x /home/myid/startup/my_greeting
```

> **c)** What kind of results did you get?

_____

_____

Now, wait a few minutes and check your mail. You should see your message. If you don't get your message after a while, check with your administrator to be sure that mail is up. You could also try mailing yourself a message to see if it works.

One other thing you need to do is to make the program my_greeting executable. Use the following:

```
chmod 755 /home/myid/startup/my_greeting
```

This will make the file executable by everyone.

Now create a file called `my_cron` in the `/home/myid/startup` directory. It should contain the following:

```
30  7 ** 1-5 /home/myid/startup/my_greeting
```

 In working with files that are to be executed by `cron`, *you might not want to wait for its regularly scheduled time to execute it. Just modify the time in the* `crontab` *entry so that it executes very soon. That way, you can fix any errors without waiting. Then change it back to the proper time when you are done.*

Now you can take your file and input it into the crontab process by:

```
crontab /home/myid/startup/my_cron
```

This will put the file into the cron process.

 You should never modify a non-root `crontab` *file from root with an editor. The* `cron` *process sometimes gets confused, and programs may not execute from* `cron`. *You can use the command:* `su - that_user`, *where* `that_user` *is the name of the user's account. This will put you into* `that_user`'s *account and you can then make any modifications you like with the* `crontab` *command. When you exit the editor, the changes will be picked up by the* `cron` *process. You can also execute the* `crontab` *command as root with the option* `-u that_user`. *So the command would be* `crontab -u that_user`, *and then any other options you would have used.*

This should now send you greetings at 7:30 A.M. every Monday through Friday. You can check the next day to see if it works.

> **d)** Did you get the mail file when you expected it, and in the format in which you expected it?

_____

_____

> **e)** If you didn't, why not?

_____

_____

When running a program from the `crontab` *file, you must be aware of your login environment. When you run a program manually, after you login your environment is set up by your* `.profile, kshrc,` `.login`, *or* `.cshrc` *files. However, when you execute something from* `cron` *the environment is not necessarily set up. You must modify your* `crontab` *entry or the program so that the proper values are set up. This is particularly a problem in executing database programs by the* `cron` *process. Oftentimes there are a number of variables that need to be set up in order to run those programs.*

6.2.2 FURTHER CUSTOMIZATION OF YOUR CRONTAB FILE

In the previous exercise you created any entry in the `crontab` file that runs the program `my_greeting`. The `crontab` entry looks like this:

```
30   7 ** 1-5 /home/myid/startup/my_greeting
```

What happens if it doesn't run? One problem with running a file from `cron` *is that the standard error and standard output are misdirected. It is often just dumped into the bit bucket. Some versions of UNIX allow messages to be sent to a* `cron` *error file. Others don't have an already built-in feature, but require you to build one.*

**LAB
6.2**

You can just add in a redirect of the standard input and output. Do the following modification:

```
30  7 ** 1-5 /home/myid/startup/my_greeting 2>> /home/
    myid/startup/my_greeting.err  1>>  /home/myid/star-
    tup/my_greeting.out
```

Important note: In some of the examples listed here, there is a line wrap at the right margin. Do not press enter at the end of each line in the crontab *file for these exercises. Otherwise, your programs will not work properly. Let the editor do what it wants to do.*

Now, at 7:30 A.M., you should have an email message. You should also have two files, both `my_greeting.err` and `my_greeting.out`.

a) Look at both files after you know that the `cron` has executed. What do you see?

_____

_____

b) Did you get any errors? If so, recheck your program starting from the beginning to make sure that you have no errors. What were your errors, if any?

_____

_____

LAB 6.2 EXERCISE ANSWERS

This section gives you some suggested answers to the questions in Lab 6.2, with discussion related to those answers. Your answers may vary, but the most important thing is whether your answer works. Use this discussion to analyze differences between your answers and those presented here.

If you have alternative answers to the questions in this Exercise, you are encouraged to post your answers and discuss them at the companion Web site for this book, located at:

```
http://www.phptr.com/phptrinteractive
```

6.2.1 ANSWERS

For this Exercise, you logged in with your regular UNIX user id and entered the following command:

```
crontab -l
```

a) What do you see on the screen?

Answer:You should see the following:

```
[myid@myserver startup]$ crontab -l
no crontab for myid
[myid@myserver startup]$
```

Did you received any errors? If so, you must fix them before going on. You might look at your TERM variable. Look at the description under `crontab -e` for some hints.

Now you need to actually create your first `crontab` entry. Use the following command:

```
crontab -e
```

b) What kind of results do you get?

Answer:You should get a blank screen similar to the following:

```
~
~
~
```

```
~

~

"/tmp/crontab.1675" 0 lines, 0 characters
```

You should notice that the file name being edited is actually the following:

```
/tmp/crontab.1675
```

It is important to note that UNIX uses the `/tmp` directory to hold a copy of the file being edited. That way, the original is not touched until you save it.

You should also note the number at the end of the file. This is the process id of the editing process. That way, the system can distinguish between various people editing files.

If you received any errors, consider the following items as possible causes:

- You don't have access to the directories
- You don't have rights to execute the `crontab` command. See the discussion on `cron.deny` and `cron.allow`. You might ask your system administrator.
- You have an invalid TERM variable. You can verify your term variable with the following command:

```
echo $TERM
```

- You have an invalid EDITOR or VISUAL variable. You can check this with the following command:

```
echo $EDITOR or echo $VISUAL
```

c) What kind of results do you get?

Answer:You should have results similar to the following:

```
[myid@myserver startup]$ bash -x my_greeting
+ [ -f /etc/bashrc ]
+ . /etc/bashrc
++ PS1=[\u@\h \W]\$
++ alias which=type -path
+ echo Good Morning
```

```
+ mail myid
[myid@myserver startup]$.
```

If you saw no errors in the output, your mail should be on its way.

d) Did you get the mail file when you expected it, and in the format in which you expected?

Answer:*The file should have been in the following format:*

```
Message 1:
From myid  Thu May 14 15:45:49 1998
Return-Path: <myid>
Received: (from myid@localhost)
        by myserver (8.8.7/8.8.7) id PAA01007
        for myid; Thu, 14 May 1998 15:45:49 -0500
Date: Thu, 14 May 1998 15:45:49 -0500
From: My Name <myid@myserver>
Message-Id: <199805142045.PAA01007@myserver>
To: myid@myserver
Status: R
Good Morning
&
```

e) If you didn't, why not?

Answer: *Follow some of the troubleshooting ideas discussed elsewhere in this Lab to diagnose any errors.*

6.2.2 ANSWERS

a) Look at both files after you know that the cron has executed. What do you see?

Answer: *Both files should be empty. If not, look at their contents and see if there are any problems you need to deal with.*

Some of the problems you might encounter include the following:

- **Typing errors**—Cron can't find the file and you will see an error stating that the file that you specified does not exist.
- **Scheduling errors**—The time combination you entered might be invalid, or the time might not yet have arrived. In the second case the file would not exist.
- **Execution errors**—You might not be able to execute the program because you do not have execution rights. When you execute a program from the crontab file, it will execute with the rights of the owner.
- **Environment errors**—Your environment is not the same as when you run the program manually. You may need to add additional statements in your program to properly set your environment.

b)   Did you get any errors? If so, recheck your program starting from the beginning to make sure that you have no errors. What were your errors, if any?

Answer: Look at the discussion of the previous Question to see what to do about errors. Then go ahead and fix your problems.

LAB 6.2 SELF-REVIEW QUESTIONS

In order to test your progress, you should be able to answer the following questions.

Questions 1 to 5 refers to changes you can make to the `crontab` file. It is possible to use the `crontab` file so that a process can run on:

1) The second Tuesday of the month
   a) _____True
   b) _____False

2) The 13th day of every month
   a) _____True
   b) _____False

3) Jan 22, 2001 (I assume you have fixed the year 2000 problem)
   a) _____True
   b) _____False

4) Every Monday at 1:20 A.M.
   a) _____True
   b) _____False

5) Every Easter Sunday
   a) _____True
   b) _____False

Examine the following `crontab` file:

```
25        4,8,12 *       *    *    clean_up system
25             6       4,8,12* *   clean_up mail
25            12       *    6  *   clean_up room
25            12-15*   *    6      clean_up car
30            16       *    6,11*  start vacation
```

6) Which of the following events occur three times a month:
   a) _____clean_up system
   b) _____clean_up mail
   c) _____clean_up room
   d) _____clean_up car
   e) _____start vacation

7) Which of the following events occur three times a day:
   a) _____clean_up system
   b) _____clean_up mail
   c) _____clean_up room
   d) _____clean_up car
   e) _____start vacation

8) Which of the following events occur once a week:
   a) _____clean_up system
   b) _____clean_up mail
   c) _____clean_up room
   d) _____clean_up car
   e) _____start vacation

9) Which of the following events occur once a year:
   a) _____clean_up system
   b) _____clean_up mail
   c) _____clean_up room
   d) _____clean_up car
   e) _____start vacation

10) Which of the following events occur twice a year:
   a) _____clean_up system
   b) _____clean_up mail
   c) _____clean_up room
   d) _____clean_up car
   e) _____start vacation

Quiz answers appear in Appendix A, Section 6.2.

LAB EXERCISES FOR THE GREAT AND SUPER USER

You will need to run the Exercises in Lab 6.3 as root. The earlier Labs can be done as a regular user. After completing this Lab, you will learn how to create files that can be executed at certain run levels.

L A B   6.3

RC CONFIGURATION FILES

LAB OBJECTIVES

After this Lab, you will be able to:

✓ Better Understand the rc Files

In UNIX, rc files are very important to starting up system processes. Instead of putting all the startup information in a single file for running the system, it was decided with UNIX System V that there would be a directory structure that would contain files that would be executed on bootup. The only requirement for these files to be executed is that they must be in the directory relevant to the run level. You may have noticed that the rc files are executed from the inittab file in Exercise 6.1.1.

Let's take a look at the Linux directory /etc/rc.d/rc3.d. This is the directory that sets up files for your default run level.

```
[root@myserver rc3.d]# ls
```

```
K20rusersd   S10network   S40atd      S60lpd       S85gpm
K20rwalld     S15nfsfs    S40crond    S60rwhod     S85sound
K55routed    S20random    S45pcmcia   S75keytable  S91smb
S01kerneld   S30syslog    S50inet     S80sendmail  S99local

[root@myserver rc3.d]#
```

**LAB
6.3**

The files in the directory are executed in strict sort order. So files beginning with K are executed before files beginning with S.

Let's say you have a file you want to be executed in Linux when going into runlevel 3. You must first be root to create a file in this directory. Second, it must be in the directory /etc/rc.d/rc3.d. (Be aware that any backup copies of files that you keep there will also be executed!) Then it should be executable.

■ FOR EXAMPLE:

Suppose you have to manually change the hostname on your system because some other process gives it the wrong name. (This can actually happen with dhcp.) All you need to do is create a file that would execute after everything else. The last item in an alphabetical sorting of the directory earlier in this Lab is S99local. So if you created a file called S99localone, it would show up as the last item in an alphabetic sort or listing, and would be executed last.

LAB 6.3 EXERCISES

6.3.1 THE RC FILES

Let's look at a sample file. Because I've already mentioned S99local, let's discuss that file.

Enter the following:

```
ls -l /etc/rc.d/rc3.d/S99local
```

a) What do you see?

_____

_____

UNIX has had a /etc/rc *and a* /etc/rc.local *file from almost the beginning. The* /etc/rc *file was used for things the UNIX manufacturer was to setup. The* /etc/rc.local *file was for any custom parameters an administrator might want to give a system. It was used to start up any local programs. Some of the newer versions of UNIX dropped this file in favor of simply putting program files in the* rc.d *directory structure. Linux has brought back the* rc.local.

Following is the S99local file distributed with Red Hat Linux:

```
#!/bin/sh
# This script will be executed *after* all the other
  init scripts.
# You can put your own initialization stuff in here if
  you don't
# want to do the full Sys V style init stuff.
if [ -f /etc/redhat-release ]; then
        R=$(cat /etc/redhat-release)
else
        R="release 3.0.3"
fi
arch=$(uname -m)
a="a"
case "_$arch" in
        _a*) a="an";;
        _i*) a="an";;
esac
# This will overwrite /etc/issue at every boot.  So,
  make any changes you
# want to make to /etc/issue here or you will lose
  them when you reboot.
echo "" > /etc/issue
echo "Red Hat Linux $R" >> /etc/issue
"S99local" 27 lines, 690 characters
```

As you can see, this file is simply a UNIX shell program. It is executed in the Bourne shell, which just so happens to be linked to the bash shell on Red Hat Linux. So it will work the same in either case. The `S99local` file is also linked to the `/etc/rc.d/rc.local` file.

The problem with having a file for every application in `/etc/rc.d` is that some applications only need a one-line program to execute, and sometimes things can get confusing when you have a lot of one-line files sitting around.

Now it's time to create your own custom `rc` file. Go ahead and do a listing of your `rc3.d` directory so that the files are listed alphabetically.

b) What is the last item on the list?

_____

_____

By default, UNIX sorts items in alphabetical order. Go ahead and test it out with the `ls` command and see if you can figure out the sequence. You might even create a dummy file with the `touch` command and see how everything sorts out.

Let's assume that the last item is `S99local`, as shown in the previous example.

Be sure you are in the chapter working directory called `startup`. If you are not sure, just type `pwd` to see where you are. Go ahead and create a new file with `S99local` as the prefix and your name as the end. So let's say if your name is Joe, create a file called `S99localjoe`.

It is important that any file you create be either the very last one executed before a system comes up, or after all other system files are executed. Unless you do a thorough analysis of your system, you may attempt to run a program that depends on processes that have not yet started and, as a result, you may get an error, or the system may hang on you. While this is still a possibility with this Exercise, the chances of a system hang are very low.

If `S99local` was not the last item on the list, pick the last one that shows up and add your name to end of it. Let's assume your e-mail id is `myid` (substitute your id with the name `myid`). The file you want to create is the following:

```
# This is the file S99localjoe (remember to give it
  your own id and your own email address)
# This will send me an email when the system is
  totally # up.  You can actually use your Internet
  email address # so that you can get email whenever a
  system on your    # network is rebooted sent to a
  single id.

mail myid << EOF
This is my first local rc file.
If I get this it means the system has
been rebooted and all other files
have been executed in /etc/rc.d/rc3.d
My Name
EOF
```

This Exercise can be modified for a regular, non-root user. You can ask your always-friendly, eager-to-serve system administrator to copy any files you create to the appropriate `rc` directory. Multiple users can also do this Exercise; just make sure any files created show up in a file listing after the last normal system file. Be sure to follow the naming convention for the local file. That way, if several people are working on the system, you will each have a unique identifier attached to your file.

Now, test the file to make sure it runs smoothly before installing it in the `/etc/rc.d/rc3.d` directory. A good way to debug your shell programs is by using the -x option. Try it and see what happens. You can test the program with:

```
bash -x S99localjoe
```

c) What kind of results do you get?

_____

_____

d) What is the meaning of each line that resulted?

_____

_____

After a few minutes, the program will send you an e-mail. To receive it, type the following:

LAB
6.3

```
mail(where myid is the id you used)
```

e) Look at the mail. What do you see? Is this consistent with what you expected?

_____

_____

Now whenever the system is rebooted, or enters run level 3, which is practically always after a reboot, you will get an e-mail.

LAB 6.3 EXERCISE DISCUSSION

This section gives you some suggested answers to the questions in Lab 6.3, with discussion related to those answers. Your answers may vary, but the most important thing is whether your answer works. Use this discussion to analyze differences between your answers and those presented here.

If you have alternative answers to the questions in this Exercise, you are encouraged to post your answers and discuss them at the companion Web site for this book, located at:

`http://www.phptr.com/phptrinteractive`

LAB 6.3

6.3.1 ANSWERS

In this Exercise, we discussed the `S99local` sample file. Enter the following:

```
ls -l /etc/rc.d/rc3.d/S99local
```

a) What do you see?

Answer: You should see the following:

```
[myid@myserver startup]$ ls -l /etc/rc.d/rc3.d/S99local
lrwxrwxrwx   1 root root 11 Dec 17  1999 /etc/rc.d/
rc3.d/S99local -> ../rc.local
[myid@myserver startup]$
```

Notice that the file is a symbolic link to the file `/etc/rc.d/rc.local`. This is the file used for standard startup processes.

Next, you looked at the `S99local` file that is distributed with Red Hat Linux, and you did an alphabetical listing of your `rc3.d` directory.

b) What is the last item on the list?

Answer: You should see `S99local` as the last item.

If not, note which one is the last item on the list. Some manufacturers have added their own extra files at the end. As long as your file is the last one on the alphabetical list, you can be sure that all necessary programs have started up first. If you are sharing the system with other users, obviously you can't all be last, so make sure your file is anywhere after the last system file that is executed.

Ensure that your program is well documented. This is important in case someone (most likely your system administrator) can look at it and figure out where the file came from. This program will send out a mail message when it is executed.

In Linux, you can test the program with:

```
bash -x S99localjoe
```

In Solaris, you can test the program with:

```
ksh -x S99localjoe
```

c)   What kind of results do you get?

Answer:You should get the following results:

```
[myid@myserver startup]$ bash -x S99localjoe
+ [ -f /etc/bashrc ]
+ . /etc/bashrc
++ PS1=[\u@\h \W]\$
++ alias which=type -path
+ mail myid@myserver
[myserver@myserver startup]$
```

d)   What is the meaning of each line that resulted?

Answer:Your results are summarized and explained in the following table:

Command	Description
+ [-f /etc/bashrc]	Executes the /etc/bashrc because you are starting a new shell
+ . /etc/bashrc	Executes /etc/bashrc using the dot command, which makes changes to the current environment
++ PS1=[\u@\h \W]\$	Sets the command line prompt

++ alias which=type -path   Creates an alias for which (actually the type command with the -path option)

+ mail myid@myserver   Mails the results

   e)   Look at the mail. What do you see? Is this consistent with what you expected?

         Answer: You should have gone through the following process to check your mail:

LAB 6.3

```
[myid@myserver startup]$ mail
Mail version 5.5-kw 5/30/95.  Type ? for help.
"/var/spool/mail/myid": 1 message 1 new
>N  1 myid@myserver        Sat May 16 02:41  16/473
& 1
Message 1:
From myid  Sat May 16 02:41:50 1998
Return-Path: <myid>
Received: (from myid@localhost)
        by myserver (8.8.7/8.8.7) id CAA01792
        for myid; Sat, 16 May 1998 02:41:50 -0500
Date: Sat, 16 May 1998 02:41:50 -0500
From: My Name <myid@myserver>
Message-Id: <199805160741.CAA01792@myserver>
To: myid@myserver
Status: R

This is my first local rc file.
If I get this it means the system has
been rebooted and all other processes
have been executed in /etc/rc.d/rc3.d
My Name

&
```

LAB 6.3 SELF-REVIEW QUESTIONS

In order to test your progress, you should be able to answer the following questions.

**LAB
6.3**

1) The `rc` files are executed by init and are setup in the `/etc/inittab` file.
   a) _____True
   b) _____False

2) In Linux, the `rc` files for run level 3 are executed from the `/etc/rc.d/rc3.d` directory.
   a) _____True
   b) _____False

3) The command `bash -x S99localjoe` in this chapter does which of the following?
   a) _____Only debugs, but does not execute `S99localjoe`
   b) _____Debugs and shows all variable values, but does not execute `S99localjoe`
   c) _____Executes `S99localjoe` and shows the commands as they are being executed
   d) _____Stops on the first error
   e) _____Gives an error message because -x is not a valid option for bash

4) Adding entries to the `S99local` file allows an administrator to execute certain programs that are local to your site without affecting the standard non-local `rc` startup files.
   a) _____True
   b) _____False

Quiz answers appear in Appendix A, Section 6.3.

CHAPTER 6

TEST YOUR THINKING

The projects in this section are meant to have you utilize all of the skills that you have acquired throughout this chapter. The answers to these projects can be found at the companion Web site to this book, located at:

`http://www.prenhall.com`

Visit the Web site periodically to share and discuss your answers.

1) Take the question in Exercise 6.1.1, which involves finding all entries in `/etc/inittab` that are valid only at your current run level, and modify it to include entries that are valid at both your run level and all entries that are valid at all run levels.

Look at the field in `/etc/inittab` *that shows run level.*

2) As root, create an entry that will go in `/etc/inittab` and send an e-mail out to a user on another machine indicating that the machine is going down. This will be done before any other processes. You must be sure that the mail is sent out before shutting down the system.

You can do this in the same manner as the rc exercise in the text; just look up the run level for shutdown.

3) Write a program that will execute at 2:20 A.M. Use the `last` command and check for all logins that have occurred within the last 24 hours. It will create a summary for each user of:

a) The number of times logged in

b) The times logged in

c) How long the login was

 First read up on the `last` *command; you must be able to parse the line with the tools you learned in introductory UNIX. You might consider writing in the shell, using awk, sed, perl, grep, and other commands.*

The program will send this as a report by e-mail to your id.

C H A P T E R 7

REBOOT

 Rebooting a system can be one of the most risky ventures you'll do as an administrator. You don't know if that change you made since the last reboot is going to take or not, if you even remember what it was. I think most administrators breathe a deep sigh of relief once they see that login prompt and no error messages. After that point, you usually have time to go out, relax, and smell and partake of the coffee. — Joe

---

CHAPTER OBJECTIVES

In this Chapter, you will learn about:

Exercises for the Great and Super User

This chapter discusses bringing down and booting a UNIX system. Because you obviously need to be an administrator to do this, there won't be a separate discussion for the non-root user. So if you can't really reboot your system, just come along for the ride. You might see some interesting sights along the way. You also might find someone who can drive, and then you can just look over their shoulder.

The first critical issue to discuss is the shutdown process. While there are times when you can safely turn off the power on a computer, there are also times when an improper shutdown can cause problems with your system. A good shutdown program will prepare the hardware (primarily the disks and filesystem) for the impending power off. Gone are the good old days, when you could just flip a switch in DOS and Windows to power off your PC, and then almost immediately bring it back up. Even Windows 95 and NT expect you to use shutdown programs.

The last chapter discussed the various startup processes, which was in preparation for this chapter. A system reboot involves a sometimes-delicate interplay between hardware and software. You take a box that is totally hardware, power it on, and watch as the software loads and sets up connections between the operating system and the devices. If a process does not startup, you must wind your way through the various programs and files that are used to bring up the system.

Knowledge of both computer hardware and software is important to understand the bootup process and to fix system problems. A detailed discussion of this topic is beyond the range of this book. However, look for future books in this series in which you can learn some of the deeper concepts necessary to fix problems relating to system shutdown and startup.

L A B   7.1

SYSTEM CONFIGURATION FILES

LAB OBJECTIVES

After this Lab, you will be able to:

✓ Shutdown Files and Directories

✓ Understand the Shutdown Process

You can look at the shutdown process as a series of smaller processes. There are several ways of shutting down the system that generally follow the same sequence of processes as shutdown. Some commands allow you to do a quicker shutdown and bypass some steps. Even holding down the Ctrl, Alt, and Del keys in Linux will initiate a series of steps, instead of just doing an immediate reboot.

The actual process can be shown in the following figure (Figure 7.1).

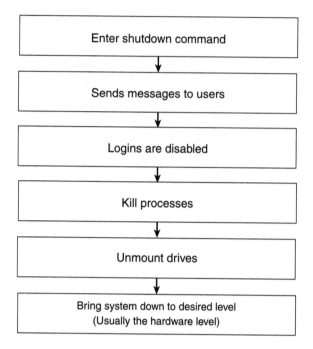

```
┌─────────────────────────────────────────┐
│         Enter shutdown command           │
└─────────────────────────────────────────┘
                    ↓
┌─────────────────────────────────────────┐
│          Sends messages to users         │
└─────────────────────────────────────────┘
                    ↓
┌─────────────────────────────────────────┐
│            Logins are disabled           │
└─────────────────────────────────────────┘
                    ↓
┌─────────────────────────────────────────┐
│              Kill processes              │
└─────────────────────────────────────────┘
                    ↓
┌─────────────────────────────────────────┐
│              Unmount drives              │
└─────────────────────────────────────────┘
                    ↓
┌─────────────────────────────────────────┐
│    Bring system down to desired level    │
│      (Usually the hardware level)        │
└─────────────────────────────────────────┘
```

**Figure 7.1 ■ A summary of the UNIX
shutdown process**

Note that some of the processes occur in parallel, not in series. This diagram shows a summary of the steps that occur when the system is shutdown. There are actually a number of other steps. This summary should help you understand the process a little better.

Look in the man pages for the following:

shutdown

Also look in Appendix B for a discussion of the various forms of the shutdown command.

LAB 7.1 EXERCISES

7.1.1 THE SHUTDOWN FILES AND DIRECTORIES

This Exercise discusses the steps in the shutdown process. This section is based on using Linux, but is similar in other versions of UNIX.

 Note that in several versions of UNIX, such as Solaris, the /etc/rc.d *directory doesn't exist, and the directory* /etc/rc.d/rc0.d *is replaced by the directories* /etc/rc0.d, /etc/rc1.d, *and so forth.*

Input the following command:

```
cd /etc/rc.d/rc0.d
ls -l
```

a) What kind of results do you get? Summarize your findings with the common element among each of the items returned.

_____

_____

Input the following command:

```
cd /etc/rc.d/rc3.d
ls -l
```

b) What kind of results do you get? Summarize your findings with the common element among each of the items returned.

_____

_____

Now, type the following command:

```
cd /etc/rc.d/init.d
ls -l
```

c) What kind of results do you get? Summarize your findings with the common element among each of the items returned.

_____

_____

d) What is the common element among the answers to the preceding three questions?

_____

_____

e) Look at the files in the directory /etc/rc.d/init.d. Which file will unmount the mounted filesystems?

_____

_____

f) Look at the files in the directory /etc/rc.d/init.d. Which file or files will do either the system halt or the reboot?

_____

_____

g) Look at the files in the directory /etc/rc.d/init.d. Which file will disable logins, startup logins, or restart the login process?

_____

_____

7.1.2 THE SHUTDOWN PROCESS

Now is the time to start the actual shutdown process. Let's choose the actual command that you will use. You have seen a number of possible ways of bringing down the system. Let's choose one that is easy to use and will give you what you want.

Remember that in Linux and several other versions of UNIX there may be several commands that do the same thing. The halt command no longer just stops the system. Let's choose the following command:

```
/sbin/shutdown  -t 120 +2 -h
```

a) What do each of these options do?

_____

_____

Now it is time to shutdown the system. Type in the preceding command.

b) What happens?

_____

_____

You are now actually running through the shutdown process.

Eventually the system should come to a halt. At that point, you can turn off the power. You are now ready to go through the next step to bring up the system, which is the purpose of the next Lab.

LAB 7.1 EXERCISE ANSWERS

This section gives you some suggested answers to the questions in Lab 7.1, with discussion related to those answers. Your answers may vary, but the most important thing is whether your answer works. Use this discussion to analyze differences between your answers and those presented here.

If you have alternative answers to the questions in this Exercise, you are encouraged to post your answers and discuss them at the companion Web site for this book, located at:

```
http://www.phptr.com/phptrinteractive
```

7.1.1 ANSWERS

Input the following command:
```
cd /etc/rc.d/rc0.d
ls -l
```

a) What kind of results do you get? Summarize your findings with the common element among each of the items returned.

Answer:You should get results similar to the following:

```
[root@wheels rc0.d]# ls -l
total 0
lrwxrwxrwx   1 root   root    16 Dec 17  1999 K20rwalld ->
../init.d/rwalld
lrwxrwxrwx   1 root root      15 Dec 17  1999 K20rwhod ->
../init.d/rwhod
lrwxrwxrwx   1 root root    18 Dec 17  1999 K30sendmail ->
../init.d/sendmail
lrwxrwxrwx   1 root       root   13 Dec 17  1999 K35smb ->
../init.d/smb
lrwxrwxrwx   1 root       root 14 Dec 17  1999 K50inet ->
../init.d/inet
lrwxrwxrwx   1 root   root   16 Dec 17  1999 K52pcmcia ->
../init.d/pcmcia
```

```
lrwxrwxrwx   1 root root   16 Dec 17   1999 K55routed ->
../init.d/routed
lrwxrwxrwx   1 root  root   13 Dec 17   1999 K60atd ->
../init.d/atd
lrwxrwxrwx   1 root  root  15 Dec 17   1999 K60crond ->
../init.d/crond
lrwxrwxrwx   1 root    root  14 Dec 17   1999 S00halt ->
../init.d/halt
[root@wheels rc0.d]#
```

The common element among all of these items is that they are all linked to the /etc/rc.d/init.d directory.

Input the following command:
```
cd /etc/rc.d/rc3.d
ls -l
```

b) What kind of results do you get? Summarize your findings with the common element among each of the items returned.

Answer: The answer is the same as for Question (a). You should see all the files linked to /etc/rc.d/init.d.

Now, type the following command:
```
cd /etc/rc.d/init.d
ls -l
```

c) What kind of results do you get? Summarize your findings with the common element among each of the items returned.

Answer: You should see results similar to the following:

```
[root@wheels init.d]# ls -l
total 34
-rwxr-xr-x   1 root    root    859 Nov  9  1997 atd
-rwxr-xr-x   1 root    root    809 Nov  9  1997 crond
-rwxr-xr-x   1 root    root   3375 Nov  7  1997 functions
-rwxr-xr-x   1 root    root    981 Nov  3  1997 gpm
-rwxr-xr-x   1 root    root   1351 Nov  7  1997 halt
-rwxr-xr-x   1 root    root   1370 Oct 30  1997 inet
-rwxr-xr-x   1 root    root    780 Nov  9  1997 kerneld
-rwxr-xr-x   1 root    root    851 Nov  5  1997 keytable
```

```
-rwxr-xr-x   1 root    root     446 Nov  7  1997 killall
-rwxr-xr-x   1 root    root    1015 Oct 30  1997 lpd
-rwxr-xr-x   1 root    root    2090 Nov  7  1997 network
-rwxr-xr-x   1 root    root     883 Nov  7  1997 nfsfs
-rwxr-xr-x   1 root    root    2438 Nov  9  1997 pcmcia
-rwxr-xr-x   1 root    root    1168 Nov  7  1997 random
-rwxr-xr-x   1 root    root     859 Oct 28  1997 routed
-rwxr-xr-x   1 root    root     682 Oct 21  1997 rusersd
-rwxr-xr-x   1 root    root     802 Oct 28  1997 rwalld
-rwxr-xr-x   1 root    root     758 Nov  3  1997 rwhod
-rwxr-xr-x   1 root    root     921 Oct 29  1997 sendmail
-rwxr-xr-x   1 root    root     906 Nov  7  1997 single
-rwxr-xr-x   1 root    root     869 Oct 31  1997 smb
-rwxr-xr-x   1 root    root    1320 Nov 11  1997 sound
-rwxr-xr-x   1 root    root     799 Oct 30  1997 syslog
[root@wheels init.d]#
```

Answer: You should notice that there are no links. In fact, many of the rc *files under* /etc/rc.d *directories are linked here. The differences among the calling programs are the options that are used to call them, which in many cases is the run level.*

d)   What is the common element among the answers to the preceding three questions?

Answer: They are basically the same files as explained in the previous answer.

e)   Look at the files in the /etc/rc.d/init.d directory. Which file will unmount the mounted filesystems?

Answer: Here we see a good use of the grep command. The UNIX umount *command will unmount mounted filesystems. So you should do a search for the* umount *command in all files in that directory. Try it from* /etc/rc.d/init.d:

```
[root@wheels init.d]# grep umount *
halt:umount -a
nfsfs:  umount -a -t nfs
[root@wheels init.d]#
```

You will see that there are two files that will unmount filesystems. The first one is the halt file. The command umount -a *will unmount all mounted filesystems, except those critical to system operation, such as the* / *directory. The second file,* nfsfs, *will unmount all remote filesystems on other servers that are mounted using NFS across the network.*

f) Look at the files in the /etc/rc.d/init.d directory. Which file or files will do either the system halt or the reboot?

Answer: Again, using the grep command in the /etc/rc.d/init.d directory in Linux, you see the following:

```
[root@wheels init.d]# grep halt *
halt:# rc.halt       This file is executed by init when
it goes into runlevel
halt:#               0 (halt) or runlevel 6 (reboot). It
kills all processes,
halt:#                  unmounts file systems and then
either halts or reboots.
halt:   *halt)
halt:    message="The system is halted"
halt:    command="halt"
halt:    echo "$0: call me as \"rc.halt\" or
\"rc.reboot\" please!"
halt:halt -w
halt:# Now halt or reboot.
[root@wheels init.d]#
```

If you do a search for the reboot command, you get the same message.

g) Look at the files in the /etc/rc.d/init.d directory. Which file will disable logins, startup logins, or restart the login process?

Answer: The following display shows the results of running the grep command to look for the login command:

```
[root@wheels init.d]# grep login *
inet:# ftp, rsh, and rlogin. Disabling inetd disables all of the \
[root@wheels init.d]#
```

It shows that the file inet contains a line that disables logins. In order to find the actual line, just look at the file and examine the lines that follow the one that showed up. This will show you which line disables logins. If you do not see such a line, it may be located in a different file, or it may be part of /etc/inittab. (You can ignore the \ at the end of the above line, because it is just a continuation marker that says to continue the command on the following line. So this is a comment, and is really unnecessary.)

7.1.2 ANSWERS

In this Exercise, you used the following command to start the shutdown process:

```
/sbin/shutdown  -t 120 +2 -h
```

a) What do each of these options do?

Answer: The `/sbin/shutdown` *command is the actual shutdown command that is used. The options are explained in the following text:*

```
-t 120 +2 -h
```

The +2 says to wait two minutes from the time you first sent users the message that you are shutting down the system, before you start the actual shutdown.

The `-t 120` *tells* `init` *to wait 120 seconds between the time the system starts the actual shutdown when it sends users a warning, and the time the kill signal is sent. Once that time arrives, the system will change to another run level. The* `-h` *option tells you to halt the system after shutdown. A* `-r` *option would reboot the system.*

Now it is time to shutdown the system. Type in the preceding command.

b) What happens?

Answer: The results, with discussion, are as follows:

```
[root@wheels init.d]#  /sbin/shutdown -t120 +2 -h
Broadcast message from root (ttyp0) Fri May 22 10:12:29
1998...The system is going DOWN for system halt in 2
minutes !!
```

This message is being sent to all users with a two-minute warning based on the option to the shutdown command.

```
Broadcast message from root (ttyp0) Fri May 22 10:13:29
1998...
```

This message tells you who is sending the message, and where they are logged in.

```
The system is going DOWN for system halt in 1 minutes
!!Broadcast message from root (ttyp0) Fri May 22
10:14:29 1998...
```

The system will give you a warning periodically. This is the second warning.

```
The system is going down for system halt NOW !!
```

Now the system is actually being shut down. Up to this point, you could have killed the shutdown process without affecting the system. Once you reach this point, the shutdown has begun.

```
INIT: Switching to runlevel 0
```

The system is now at run level 0.

```
INIT: Sending processes the TERM signal
```

Processes are told to terminate what they are doing with the TERM signal. This is done by the `kill` command, which you will want to look up if you are unfamiliar with it.

```
Saving sound configuration: sound
```

This is where Linux will save the sound configuration.

```
Stopping rwho services: rwhod
```

rwhod is the process that allows other users and systems to see who is logged into your system, and also to examine the system `uptime` remotely with the `ruptime` command.

```
Shutting down sendmail: sendmail
```

This is the sendmail daemon, which processes and sends mail remotely.

```
Shutting down SMB services: smbd nmbd
```

The SMB process allows you to use your UNIX file servers from any system running the Microsoft networking protocols. This program on UNIX is called SAMBA.

```
Stopping INET services: inetd
```

inetd is used for Internet and TCP/IP processes for networking. You will see further discussion of this topic in future books in this series on networking.

```
Stopping at daemon: atd
```

This daemon allows you to schedule jobs at a certain time. This is useful in batch processing environments.

```
Stopping cron daemon: crond
```

The cron daemon, which was discussed in Chapter 6, "Startup Processes," is used to run UNIX processes on a regular basis.

```
Shutting down lpd: lpd
```

This is the lpd process that is used for printing.

```
Shutting down system loggers: syslogd klogd
```

The syslogd process keeps track of system errors. The daemon klogd is used to keep track of kernel messages.

```
Saving random seed ...
```

This saves a random number to be used for future processing.

```
Unmounting remote filesystems
```

Now you will unmount any filesystems that you have mounted remotely.

```
Disabling Ipv4 packet forwarding
```

Ipv4 is the standard TCP/IP networking used for the Internet. There is a new version called Ipv6 that is compatible and has just recently been implemented.

```
Stopping kerneld services: kerneld
```

This stops kernel daemon processes.

```
Sending all processes the TERM signal
```

Now all processes are getting the TERM signal. This tells them to terminate what they are doing.

```
INIT: no more processes left in this runlevel
```

There are no more processes at this run level.

```
Sending all processes the KILL signal
```

All processes get the KILL signal.

```
INIT: no more processes left in this runlevel
```

There are no processes left after the KILL signal is sent.

```
Turning off swap
```

The swap process is disabled. You will see more discussion about swapping in Chapters 8 and 10, in which filesystems are discussed.

```
Unmounting filesystems
```

Filesystems are being unmounted.

```
Remounting remaining filesystems (if any) readonly
```

If needed, some filesystems will be remounted, but as readonly.

```
The system is halted
```

The system is halted.

```
System halted
```

This is simply a verification.

LAB 7.1 SELF-REVIEW QUESTIONS

To test your progress, you should be able to answer the following questions. Look in the man pages or the chapter for help on commands. Review your text (if you have an additional textbook), the man pages, and Appendix 2.2 to help you answer these questions. Questions 1 to 5 refer to the following command:

```
/sbin/shutdown -y -g0 -i6
```

 You need to find the best answer to the question. Note that some answers may not be exact replacements. So you will need to think about which one comes closest to the results that you want.

1) To what run level will this command take you?
   a) _____0
   b) _____6
   c) _____y
   d) _____halt
   e) _____none of the above

2) How long will it be before shutdown takes effect?
   a) _____six minutes
   b) _____six seconds
   c) _____immediately
   d) _____whatever the system default is
   e) _____whatever the variable y is set to

3) The command will prompt the user before shutting down.
   a) _____True
   b) _____False

4) In the newer versions of UNIX, this command is most closely equivalent to which other command?
   a) _____halt
   b) _____turning off the power
   c) _____reboot
   d) _____init 0
   e) _____shutdown -h

5) Look in the /etc/inittab in Lab 6.1. What is the label on the line that will be executed when you do the previous command?
   a) _____l0
   b) _____0
   c) _____6
   d) _____l6
   e) _____ca

Quiz answers appear in Appendix A, Section 7.1.

L A B   7.2

SYSTEM STARTUP

LAB OBJECTIVES

After this Lab, you will be able to:

✓ Understand System Hardware and the Bootup Process

There are a number of steps in the computer bootup process. This is true for a number of operating systems. Oftentimes, these steps are hidden from us, but they are nonetheless there. On your Windows PC, you may have noticed that a bootup takes longer once you have added a new piece of software.

You can see a summary of the boot process in Figure 7.2. This does not include all steps that a UNIX system will go through, but it will summarize information that you will find useful.

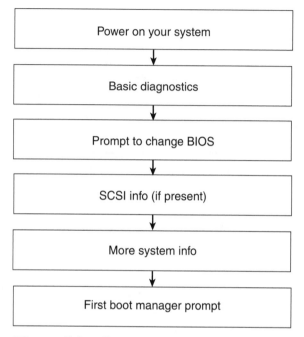

**Figure 7.2 ■ Summary of PC
Hardware Boot Process**

There are boot managers on several computers other than PCs, but they do not have the robustness of the PC boot manager, because a PC an handle many operating systems. Other boot managers usually just allow you to choose the disk, partition or device from which you can boot off, without reference to a different operating system being present.

Running UNIX on a PC gives us some advantage in diagnosing problems. If a system comes up under Windows, but not UNIX, the problem can usually be isolated to the software or some software driver, whereas failure to come up under either operating system usually means that the problem is with the hardware.

When you run multiple operating systems on your PC, you can take advantage of a boot manager. This allows you to manage the boot process into several operating systems. In Appendix G, "Creating a Multiboot PC

Unix/DOS/Linux System," there is a summary discussion of the different boot managers that are available.

THE BOOT PROCESS

While the details of the various stages of the boot process may vary from one version of UNIX to the next, we can summarize much of what happens to certain common steps. These steps are discussed in the following sections.

HARDWARE

The computer is just a piece of hardware; it does not know about operating systems, applications, user needs, or software tools. It just sits there and occupies space. Without power, it becomes the proverbial door stop or boat anchor. The hardware also seems to get outdated faster then the software. It is also usually easier and safer to replace just the hardware on a PC, rather than updating the operating system.

The nice thing about Linux and UNIX, in general, is that these operating systems are relatively independent of the hardware linkage and other software. This is a problem with other PC operating systems, where the operating system and software will sometimes occupy the same or adjacent memory space, causing memory conflicts and system crashes. Hardware and software upgrades in Linux and UNIX are not so dependent on loading a piece of software that will crash your nice, stable system, and cause you headaches while trying to recover—UNIX does a good job of keeping things separate.

However, Linux is fussier about the hardware than other PC operating systems. A piece of hardware will either work well, or it won't work at all, because the fluff can be left out of the code. Because of the free source code, Linux can be written to take advantage of the hardware, and can usually written to tighter specs than commercial software; it can also be changed to support new hardware. This reduces system overhead for the hardware, so Linux will run nicely on a 486. Some adventurous souls are even running it on 386s. All this, of course, depends on the goodwill of hardware manufacturers, who must disclose details that they might not want a competitor to learn.

BIOS

The computer starts out with what is known as the BIOS. This is the built-in operating system. It contains information about the number and type of drives on the computer, amount of memory, type of CPU, and much more. The BIOS is generally configurable on most PCs; some parameters, however, such as CPU type, are automatically determined by the BIOS.

The BIOS is found on all computer systems today. Some of the older mainframe and minicomputer systems had to have the BIOS-type programs manually loaded, but that is no longer the case. Different manufacturers have chosen to implement their BIOS in different ways—such as built-in diagnostics for disks, tapes, memory, and other hardware.

The PC world has been pretty much standardized on a few BIOS configurations, because there are only a few manufacturers who produce the BIOS. This makes it easier for you to setup your PC. PCs generally have many configurable parameters. They also have very few types of diagnostics built-in, which are typically for memory and disks only. Until recently, PC BIOS also prevented the user from booting off an attached CD-ROM, whereas other versions of hardware used for non-PC versions of UNIX allowed a boot off the CD-ROM. This problem has been solved on some of the most recent PC motherboards after an international agreement was reached on this issue.

When you first turn on a PC, it enters the BIOS, and you usually see a message on the screen that tells you how to enter the BIOS configuration. Typically, pressing the Delete key will get you into the BIOS configuration. (You must do this quickly, because after a certain point it ignores the keyboard until the system is up or the system prompts you for a response.) Some manufacturers have chosen different keys to enter the BIOS configuration, so you may have to do some research to find out what exactly your system needs you to do. For example, if you are running Solaris on a Sun box with a standard Sun keyboard, you can press the keys `stop`, which you must hold down while pressing the letter `a`. This will get you into the BIOS configuration mode for the Sun box.

Once you press the actual key that gets you into the BIOS, you can verify and perhaps make some setting changes to have your system recognize hardware changes. Remember that anything you do here will only affect the hardware, not the software. However, the software must eventually recognize whatever hardware you have setup.

Once you get past the BIOS setup, you will continue on with the bootup process and see a screen similar to the following:

```
Processor:     486      Memory: 32 Meg
Speed:      66          Video: VGA
Drive A: 3-1/2" 1.44    Drive C: 1.5 Gig
Drive B:   None         Drive D: 3.5 Gig
```

This confirms that the system took any changes that you may have made. Sometimes additional information is displayed, including the number and addresses of the serial and parallel ports, how memory is broken down, and so forth.

SCSI CARDS

After displaying the previous message on the screen, your system will probe for or become aware of any SCSI cards. With some brands of SCSI cards, you may be able to make changes to the cards' parameters at this point. Your system BIOS may not be aware of your SCSI card on many non-SCSI PC motherboards. Some of the newer motherboards produced since mid-1997 are aware of SCSI cards, and can even boot off the CD-ROMs without a diskette.

BOOT MANAGER

Look in Appendix G for a discussion of the various boot managers available and how they work.

If you have a boot manager, you are prompted to choose an operating system and/or drive from which you would like to boot. The first prompt is from the boot manager in the Master Boot Record. Then, you will be prompted from the boot manager on the partition that contains the operating system you want to run.

LAB 7.2 EXERCISES

7.2.1 SYSTEM HARDWARE AND THE BOOTUP PROCESS

This chapter focuses on PC systems, because that is the type of UNIX system most accessible to students, and because it allows students to actually be root. You may want to compare the descriptions in this text with other non-PC UNIX-based systems.

Start with the power off on your PC. Now turn on your PC. You should see some introductory information and perhaps some basic hardware diagnostics being run. You should also see a message that says something similar to the following:

```
Press the delete key to modify system settings
```

Press the Delete key or the key that your system uses to enter the BIOS configuration. (Note that on some systems, the message is disabled, and you will need to look at your systems hardware manual to determine what to do.)

You should then see a display that gives a basic hardware configuration. Next, you will need to determine the following parameters:

a) What type of processor are you using (i.e., 486, 586, Pentium)?

_____

_____

b) What is your processor's clock speed?

_____

_____

c) How much memory do you have on your system? Be sure to total up any partial listings of memory, such as basic memory, extended memory, and expanded memory, but not video memory.

_____

_____

d) How many disks do you have?

_____

_____

e) How much storage space in megabytes is on each hard drive on your system?

_____

_____

f) Does your BIOS show any CD-ROMs? They usually don't, even if you have one, but sometimes you will be lucky.

_____

_____

Next, follow the directions on the screen to exit the BIOS setup.

You can usually choose to either reboot or continue from this point in the bootup process. It doesn't matter which one you choose.

While watching the bootup or shutdown process, the information often moves to fast on the screen for you to read or write down. Usually, you can simply press the Ctrl and S key together, indicated as <Ctrl-S>, to stop the display. You can also use the Pause key on the PC keyboard. Pressing <Ctrl-Q>, or in some cases anything besides <Ctrl-S>, will start the display again.

One of the next steps you will see is a description of any SCSI controllers on your system.

g) Do you see any SCSI controllers listed?

_____

_____

h) If so, does the SCSI controller message give you any information about configuring the card?

_____

_____

One of the next things the SCSI controller does is test for any devices attached to the SCSI controller, and then list those devices on the screen.

i) If you have a SCSI controller, do you see any devices listed? If so, what are they?

_____

_____

Eventually, you will get some kind of message from your boot manager.

j) What do you see as your boot manager?

_____

_____

When you get to the boot manager, it is often very enlightening to explore how it is set up. Try to get some documentation about your boot manager and see what your configuration possibilities are.

Now just go ahead and choose your operating system from the boot manager and continue on.

LAB 7.2 EXERCISE ANSWERS

This section gives you some suggested answers to the questions in Lab 7.2, with discussion related to those answers. Your answers may vary, but the most important thing is whether your answer works. Use this discussion to analyze differences between your answers and those presented here.

LAB 7.2

If you have alternative answers to the questions in this Exercise, you are encouraged to post your answers and discuss them at the companion Web site for this book, located at:

`http://www.phptr.com/phptrinteractive`

7.2.1 ANSWERS

After starting your PC and viewing the display of your basic hardware configuration, determine the following parameters:

a) What type of processor are you using (i.e., 486, 586, Pentium)?

Answer: You should see a field in the BIOS description that tells you what kind of processor you have. You may have to dig around in several icons or submenus to find the information, but it will be there. It will usually show up on your screen during bootup.

b) What is your processor's clock speed?

Answer: This information will show up in the same area as your processor description. It will often be on your screen when you bootup.

c) How much memory do you have on your system? Be sure to total up any partial listings of memory, such as basic memory, extended memory, and expanded memory, but not video memory.

Answer: This is in the BIOS information and on your screen during bootup.

d) How many disks do you have?

Answer: This will be in the BIOS information and usually in several places on your screen during bootup.

e) How much storage space in megabytes is on each hard drive on your system?

Answer:You will usually see this information in three places:

– When memory testing is done

– In the BIOS

– During bootup when a system summary is displayed

f) Does your BIOS show any CD-ROMs? They usually don't, even if you have one, but sometimes you will be lucky.

Answer: If your BIOS supports CD-ROM, you will usually see it in the BIOS setup. Otherwise, it may show up in several places on bootup. If it is a SCSI CD-ROM, you will see it during the SCSI card configuration part of the bootup.

Now you should follow the directions on the screen to exit the BIOS setup. One of the next steps you will see is a description of any SCSI controllers on your system.

g) Do you see any SCSI controllers listed?

Answer:You will see the term SCSI showing up on the screen, usually when your system detects a SCSI card.

h) If so, does the SCSI controller message give you any information about configuring the card?

Answer: Some manufacturers allow you to configure settings on some of their SCSI cards. This is true of the Adaptec 1542 SCSI controller, but not true of the Adaptec 1520 SCSI controller.

One of the next things the SCSI controller will do is to test for any devices attached to the SCSI controller, and then list those devices on the screen.

i) If you have a SCSI controller, do you see any devices listed? If so, what are they?

Answer:You should see the devices listed after the description of the SCSI controller. You will also see detailed information about things such as the manufacturer, model, and size of disk drives, as well as information about the manufacturer and model of SCSI attached CD-ROMs.

Eventually you will get some kind of message from your boot manager.

j) What do you see as your boot manager?

Answer:You will see one of several possibilities, as follows.

- If you configured your PC with a Master Boot Record (MBR) boot manager such as System Commander, you will see the prompt from its menu. It will allow you to choose your operating system. System Commander will then either boot up your chosen operating system or will give you a prompt from the boot manager on the boot record on the partition used as the first partition for this operating system.
- If you configured your PC with the Solaris X86 boot manager, any choice you make will take you directly to the chosen operating system. However, you will not be able to directly boot to Linux, which you will see later.
- If you chose the Linux LILO as your MBR boot manager, you might be able to choose from several possible operating systems, based on how you configured the system during install or in the `/etc/lilo.conf` file. You won't, however, be able to boot directly to Solaris x86, which is described in the Solaris x86 boot section.

LAB 7.2 SELF-REVIEW QUESTIONS

In order to test your progress, you should be able to answer the following questions. Look in the man pages or the chapter for help on commands. Choose the answer that best fits the question.

1) When starting up some of the newer computers, the system first gets its hardware information loaded from:
   a) ___ punch cards
   b) ___ magnetic tape
   c) ___ hard disk
   d) ___ BIOS
   e) ___ diskette

2) The system performs a minimal hardware check before prompting you about BIOS changes.
   a) ___True
   b) ___False

3) The system first looks for information on what operating system to boot from in the:
   a) ___ Partition Boot Record
   b) ___ BIOS
   c) ___ lilo.conf
   d) ___ Master Boot Record
   e) ___ FAT table

4) After looking in and possibly executing anything that might occur in the location mentioned in question 3, the system will then look for operating system boot information in the:
   a) ___ Partition Boot Record
   b) ___ BIOS
   c) ___ LILO
   d) ___ Master Boot Record
   e) ___ FAT table

5) The boot process will generally recognize a SCSI controller before doing anything related to the operating system.
   a) ___True
   b) ___False

Quiz answers appear in Appendix A, Section 7.2.

L A B 7.3

LINUX STARTUP

LAB OBJECTIVES

After this Lab, you will be able to:

✓ Understand the Linux Boot Manager

✓ Understand the Linux Startup Process

You have the best opportunity to study a PC operating system when you run Linux. The PC hardware boot process is perhaps the most documented boot process of any system, because the PC is the most widely used form of computer. In addition, you have complete access to the source code for Linux, so you can study what is really happening during booting. Linux is widely documented and supported by a large group of users on the Internet.

In this Lab, you will study the Linux boot process where it takes over from the BIOS, and any basic system changes resulting from built-in hardware and peripherals, such as SCSI cards. You will start with the LILO boot manager and continue on.

LAB 7.3 EXERCISES

7.3.1 THE LINUX BOOT MANAGER

 If you haven't already looked at Appendix G on multiple PC boots, go ahead an look at it before continuing on.

If you are running Linux, you have the possibility of booting from two different boot managers.

You can boot off the boot manager on the Master Boot Record. You can also boot off the boot record on the partition where Linux is installed.

Go ahead and boot up until you get to the Linux lilo boot manager prompt.

a) What is your prompt from the lilo boot manager?

_____

_____

b) What happens when you press the Tab key?

_____

_____

 You can configure multiple boot options in Linux by changing the `/etc/LILO.conf` *file.*

You can now choose where you want to bootup to. Just select one of the possible choices to continue booting up your system.

c) What do you see on the screen as your system continues booting up?

_____

_____

You will need the results of this Exercise for the next Exercise.

7.3.2 THE LINUX STARTUP PROCESS

Look at the display given by the startup process. This is the same display you would get from the dmesg command.

Notice in the display that the system detects any attached CD-ROM relatively early and then assigns a device to it.

For more information on assignment of device names to disk drives, see Chapter 8, "Filesystems and Disks."

a) Looking at the output, what would you say is the device assigned to the CD-ROM?

_____

_____

b) How much memory would you say is on the system?

_____

_____

c) What is the email address of the person responsible for this compilation of Linux?

_____

_____

d) What is the size of the drive on this system?

_____

_____

e) Did Linux detect a SCSI card?

_____

_____

f) If so, what are the attached SCSI peripherals?

_____

_____

g) Is there an Ethernet card on the system? (Hint: Look for a device with a name like `eth0`, `elx1`, `enc2`, and so on.)

_____

_____

h) If an Ethernet card is found, what are its characteristics?

_____

_____

i) What kind of error do you see in the display?

_____

_____

Now you should have chosen Linux to boot from on your system. Go ahead and boot if you haven't already. Compare your results with those in the preceding example.

j) What is the email address of the person that compiled your version of Linux?

_____

_____

k) What kind of error do you see in your screen display?

_____

_____

You should now get a system login prompt. From Red Hat Linux, you will see the following prompt:

```
Red Hat LINUX release 5.0 (Hurricane)
Kernel 2.0.31 on an i486
Myserver Login:
```

Now you can log in and work on UNIX.

GUESS WHAT…

After you log in, type the following command:

```
mail
```

l) What do you get? Where does this come from?

_____

_____

LAB 7.3 EXERCISE ANSWERS

 This section gives you some suggested answers to the questions in Lab 7.3, with discussion related to those answers. Your answers may vary, but the most important thing is whether your answer works. Use this discussion to analyze differences between your answers and those presented here.

If you have alternative answers to the questions in this Exercise, you are encouraged to post your answers and discuss them at the companion Web site for this book, located at:

http://www.phptr.com/phptrinteractive

7.3.1 ANSWERS

a) What is your prompt from the lilo boot manager?

   Answer: You should see the following display on the screen:

```
LILO boot:
```

This prompt will allow you to choose from several operating systems up to a total of four primary partitions. If you want to boot from more operating systems, you should look at a boot manager such as System Commander.

You can configure your choices of partitions, operating systems or kernels to boot off with the /etc/LILO.conf file. Whether you are running Linux off the Master Boot Record or the partition boot record, you will see a similar screen, which is displayed by the boot manager when you first start up. If you don't enter anything here, the prompt will time out and the system will automatically start booting.

b) What happens when you press the Tab key?

   Answer: You should see a display of one or several possible operating systems or kernels that you can boot off. You will then see something similar to the following:

```
LILO boot: <tab>
Linux           DOS      Win95
LILO boot: Linux<enter>
```

Here, `<tab>` represents pressing the Tab key and `<enter>` represents pressing the Enter key. These steps represent choosing Linux to boot from.

c) What do you see on the screen as your system continues booting up?

Answer: You should see the following display when you bring up Linux:

```
ide_setup: hdd=cdrom
Console: 16 point font, 400 scans
Console: colour VGA+ 80x25, 1 virtual console (max 63)
pci_init: no BIOS32 detected
Calibrating delay loop.. ok - 39.83 BogoMIPS
Memory: 14672k/16384k available (736k kernel code, 384k
reserved, 592k data)
This processor honours the WP bit even when in supervisor
mode. Good.
Swansea University Computer Society NET3.035 for Linux 2.0
NET3: Unix domain sockets 0.13 for Linux NET3.035.
Swansea University Computer Society TCP/IP for NET3.034
IP Protocols: IGMP, ICMP, UDP, TCP
VFS: Diskquotas version dquot_5.6.0 initialized^M
Checking 386/387 coupling... Ok, fpu using exception 16 error
reporting.
Checking 'hlt' instruction... Ok.
Linux version 2.0.31 (root@porky.redhat.com) (gcc version
2.7.2.3) #1 Sun Nov 9
21:45:23 EST 1997
Starting kswapd v 1.4.2.2
Serial driver version 4.13 with no serial options enabled
tty00 at 0x03f8 (irq = 4) is a 16550A
tty01 at 0x02f8 (irq = 3) is a 16550A
Real Time Clock Driver v1.07
Ramdisk driver initialized : 16 ramdisks of 4096K size
hda: Conner Peripherals 1080MB - CFA1080A, 1032MB w/256kB
Cache, CHS=524/64/63
hdd: CS-R36 1, ATAPI CDROM drive
ide0 at 0x1f0-0x1f7,0x3f6 on irq 14
ide1 at 0x170-0x177,0x376 on irq 15
Floppy drive(s): fd0 is 1.44M
FDC 0 is a post-1991 82077
md driver 0.35 MAX_MD_DEV=4, MAX_REAL=8
scsi : 0 hosts.
```

```
scsi : detected total.
Partition check:
 hda: hda1 hda2 < hda5 hda6 >
VFS: Mounted root (ext2 filesystem) readonly.
hda: irq timeout: status=0x80 { Busy }
ide0: reset: success
Adding Swap: 66492k swap-space (priority -1)
Swansea University Computer Society IPX 0.34 for NET3.035
IPX Portions Copyright (c) 1995 Caldera, Inc.
Appletalk 0.17 for Linux NET3.035
loading device 'eth0'...
ne.c:v1.10 9/23/94 Donald Becker (becker@cesdis.gsfc.nasa.gov)
NE*000 ethercard probe at 0x300: 00 40 05 1a 3c 19
eth0: NE2000 found at 0x300, using IRQ 5.
loading device 'eth1'...
Swansea University Computer Society IPX 0.34 for NET3.035
IPX Portions Copyright (c) 1995 Caldera, Inc.
Appletalk 0.17 for Linux NET3.035
keyboard error
```

Notice that you get information about both hardware that is found and software that is being loaded. You will also get error messages. This is discussed in the first exercise in this Lab.

You can examine this information on your own Linux or UNIX system by executing the command:

```
dmesg
```

This works in most versions of UNIX. This command keeps track of hardware settings, errors, and software that is loaded up until the login prompt. It does not include all the steps, but it includes the major ones that you might be interested in if you have system problems.

7.3.2 ANSWERS

a) Looking at the output given by `dmesg`, what would you say is the device that is assigned to the CD-ROM?

Answer: Looking at the following line, you see the assignment for the CD-ROM:

```
ide_setup: hdd=cdrom
```

You also get this information from the following line:

```
hdd: CS-R36 1, ATAPI CDROM drive
```

So you would see that the CD-ROM is assigned to `/dev/hdd`. *This is discussed further in Chapter 8, "Filesystems and Disks."*

b) How much memory would you say is on the system?

Answer: If you look at the line for memory, you see the following:

```
Memory: 14672k/16384k available (736k kernel code, 384k
reserved, 592k data)
```

From this line, you see that you have 16384k of memory.

LAB
7.3

c) What is the email address of the person responsible for this compilation of Linux?

Answer: You get this information from the following line:

```
Linux version 2.0.31 (root@porky.redhat.com) (gcc ver-
sion 2.7.2.3) #1 Sun Nov 9
```

So the address is `root@porky.redhat.com`.

d) What is the size of the drive on this system?

Answer: Look at the following excerpt from the file:

```
hda: Conner Peripherals 1080MB - CFA1080A, 1032MB w/
256kB Cache, CHS=524/64/63
```

e) Did Linux detect a SCSI card?

Answer: No. It did not determine a SCSI card. You can tell that from the following line:

```
scsi : 0 hosts.
scsi : detected total.
```

f) If so, what are the attached SCSI peripherals?

Answer: The answer to the previous question indicates that Linux did not find any attached SCSI devices.

g)   Is there an Ethernet card on the system?

Answer:*The following lines indicate that there is one Ethernet card.*

```
loading device 'eth0'...
ne.c:v1.10 9/23/94 Donald Becker (becker@cesdis.gsfc.nasa.gov)
NE*000 ethercard probe at 0x300: 00 40 05 1a 3c 19
eth0: NE2000 found at 0x300, using IRQ 5.
loading device 'eth1'...
```

It did not find a second Ethernet card.

h)   If an Ethernet card is found, what are its characteristics?

Answer:*The first Ethernet card is an NE2000. It is found at a base address of 0x300 and has an IRQ of 5.*

i)   What kind of error do you see in the display?

Answer:*You should have seen the following error:*

```
keyboard error
```

j)   What is the email address of the person that compiled your version of Linux?

Answer:*You should look at the answers to Questions (a) through (i) to compare your results.*

k)   What kind of error do you see in your screen display?

Answer:*You may see some errors about devices that Linux cannot find. Also, during the original install process, you will see many errors. However, once the system is installed, any errors should be few and far between. In such cases, you might want to investigate where the errors came from in order to fix any problems that might crop up later. You may also see messages that talk about devices not found, such as SCSI controllers that were not in the original installation. In such cases, you can usually ignore those messages. But examine them anyway and make sure.*

GUESS WHAT...

After you log in, type the following command:

```
mail
```

l) What do you get?

Answer:You should get one email from the file you created in Exercise 6.3.1, /etc/ rc.d/rc3.d. *The mail is sent whenever you bootup.You may also get an email from Exercise 6.2.2, which sends you email every morning.*

LAB 7.3 SELF-REVIEW QUESTIONS

In order to test your progress, you should be able to answer the following questions. Look in the man pages or the chapter for help on commands. Choose the answer that best fits the question.

1) Where is the configuration information for the Linux boot manager located?

    a) _____Linux.tab
    b) _____BIOS
    c) _____/etc/vfstab
    d) _____/etc/lilo.conf
    e) _____/etc/rc.d/rc3.d

2) Which command gives a listing of system information, devices found, and some device drivers that are loaded on UNIX bootup?

    a) _____boot
    b) _____dmesg
    c) _____lilo
    d) _____fsck
    e) _____sysinfo

3) In looking at the results of the dmesg command in Lab 7.3, what is the size of the swap space?

    a) _____128 MB
    b) _____66492k
    c) _____14672k
    d) _____1080 MB
    e) _____None of the above

4) Looking at the results of the dmesg command in the text, what is the filesystem type of root?

    a) _____ext2
    b) _____FAT16
    c) _____FAT32
    d) _____UNIX
    e) _____NTFS

5) dmesg will give you information about programs such as word processors that are on your system.

    a) _____True
    b) _____False

    Quiz answers appear in Appendix A, Section 7.3.

L A B   7.4

SOLARIS X86 STARTUP

LAB OBJECTIVES

After this Lab, you will be able to:

✓ Understand the Solaris x86 Boot Manager

✓ Understand the Solaris x86 Startup Process

Solaris x86 can be used to learn what is considered by many to be the most popular version of UNIX—that is, Solaris on the Sparc processor. The Sparc processor is produced by Sun Microsystems, which was one of the earliest companies to produce UNIX workstations.

Sun started with people that were grounded in Berkeley UNIX (BSD). UNIX by Sun was originally BSD-based. However, with the release of Solaris, they are primarily UNIX System V-based. Sun has produced versions of Solaris for the Sparc processor and for the Intel x86 processor. They have also produced several releases for the Power PC from IBM, but currently do not support that architecture.

This Lab discusses the Solaris Boot Manager, but the principles here can also be applied to other versions of UNIX. If you are running another version of UNIX, you might try stepping through this Lab to see how you can achieve the same results.

Lab 7.4 Exercises

7.4.1 The Solaris x86 Boot Manager

You can visualize the Solaris boot process as a number of steps, just like with Linux. If you look at Figure 7.4, you will see that there are several more interactive steps in booting Solaris x86 than with Linux. Solaris allows you a certain amount of freedom to customize the boot process beyond what you can do with just the boot manager.

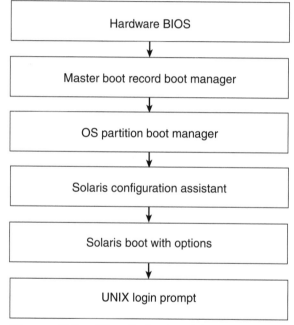

Figure 7.3 ■ The Solaris x86 Boot Process

Solaris has more steps then the Linux boot process.

Now you will step through the boot process and analyze the steps. As you do so, try to visualize some of the details as they occur and why.

If you haven't already looked at Appendix G on Multiboot PC UNIX/DOS/ Linux systems, go ahead and look at it now to see what options you might have in working with and understanding your system.

You should now have now gotten past the BIOS on your system and be in the Boot Manager of your system.

> **a)** What do you see on the screen when your system pauses in the boot process?

_____

_____

**LAB
7.4**

You can now choose the actual partition to boot off. If you do not choose a boot partition, Solaris will choose a partition by default. Go ahead and make your selection.

> **b)** What happens when you choose the partition to boot off?

_____

_____

After choosing the device to boot off, you will see that the Solaris kernel is now being downloaded.

You should try to analyze the messages about the various devices and software as they are loaded. Often you will see messages about device or system errors during this stage.

> **c)** What do you see on the screen as it continues the boot process?

_____

_____

7.4.2 THE SOLARIS X86 STARTUP PROCESS

You can now examine information that the system saves from the bootup process. As mentioned in Exercise 7.4.1, you can get this information any time from the following command:

    dmesg

You should see the same screen output you saw when the system booted up earlier.

For more information on assignment of device names to disk drives, see Chapter 8, "Linux Filesystems and Disks" and Chapter 10, "Solaris Filesystems and Disks."

In the questions that follow, you will be asked to examine the output of the dmesg command. There are a number of concepts that will be explored later. Do your best and things will come together as we continue to explore UNIX.

You will notice that the system detects any attached CD-ROM relatively early and then assigns a device to it.

> **a)** Looking at the previous output, what would you say is the device assigned to the CD-ROM?
>
> _____
>
> _____
>
> **b)** How much memory would you say is on the system?
>
> _____
>
> _____
>
> **c)** What is the version and release number of SunOS that is used?
>
> _____
>
> _____

d) How many drives are on the system?

_____

_____

e) What is the description of each drive?

_____

_____

f) How many Ethernet cards are found?

_____

LAB
7.4

_____

g) What are the descriptions of the Ethernet cards?

_____

_____

h) Which device is used as a dump device?

_____

_____

i) What is the size of the dump device?

_____

_____

Now you should have chosen Solaris x86 to boot from on your system.

Go ahead and boot if you haven't already. Compare your results with those in the previous example.

You should now get a system login prompt. If you are running Solaris x86 in character, you will see the following prompt:

```
SunOS 5.6
login:
```

If you are running openwindows, CDE, or some other X-Windows display software, you will see a similar message, or a location where you can enter your login and password. Once you get to this stage, you can just go ahead and login and work on UNIX.

LAB 7.4 EXERCISE ANSWERS

This section gives you some suggested answers to the questions in Lab 7.4, with discussion related to those answers. Your answers may vary, but the most important thing is whether your answer works. Use this discussion to analyze differences between your answers and those presented here.

If you have alternative answers to the questions in this Exercise, you are encouraged to post your answers and discuss them at the companion Web site for this book, located at:

```
http://www.phptr.com/phptrinteractive
```

7.4.1 ANSWERS

a) What do you see on the screen when your system pauses in the boot process?

Answer: You should see a screen similar to the following display. The actual numbers will vary on your system, but the information will be in the same general format.

If you are booting Solaris x86, you will see a screen similar to the following displayed by the boot record on the Solaris partition:

```
SunOS - Intel Platform Edition Primary Boot Subsystem
vsn 2.0
Current Disk Partition Information
```

```
Part #      Status      Type    Start   Length
              1           ?        63            2056257
              2        ActiveSolaris  2056320    4209030
              3        <unused>
              4        <unused>

24
```

This display shows what you see on the screen when you boot up in Solaris x86. The top line gives the name of the version of UNIX and the platform edition.

The table shows a listing of partitions on the boot drive—both the bootable and non-bootable partitions. The first line of the listing of the four partitions is actually for a partition for Win95 OEM version 2.0 or version B. The partition is actually formatted for FAT32, which is not recognized in this case. The second line of the table shows the current active Solaris partition. It is listed as active in the second column. You can choose the partition you want to boot from by entering the number in the first column. In this example, there are only two partitions to boot from. The third and fourth partitions, though laid out, do not currently have any operating system loaded on them.

The number in the lower left corner indicates how many seconds will elapse before Solaris automatically boots off the active partition. You can then make your choice as to your boot partition. If you are running Windows 95 or NT, you could choose the appropriate partition. Solaris automatically detects the various operating systems on bootup, because it scans all the partitions for their contents.

b) What happens when you choose the partition to boot off?

Answer: Your screen display should stop at a menu called the Hardware Configuration Assistant.

Solaris then prompts you as to whether you want to change the hardware configuration with the Configuration Assistant. This can take you to either the regular boot process or an interactive configuration tool. At this point, you can decide to boot off a CD-ROM, any one of several disks, the network, or another Solaris-recognized device. You can also have Solaris look for new devices, or you can change the hardware device configuration that Solaris looks for. You can also specify a number of different options that can be useful in case of system errors.

c) What do you see on the screen as it continues the boot process?

Answer: The following display will appear when you bring up Solaris x86:

```
May 20 21:50

SunOS Release 5.6 Version Generic [UNIX(R) System V Release
4.0]
Copyright (c) 1983-1997, Sun Microsystems, Inc.
mem = 65148K (0x3f9f000)
avail mem = 56360960
root nexus = i86pc
isa0 at root
ISA-device: ata1
ISA-device: ata0
Disk7:          <Vendor 'MITSUMI ' Product 'CD-ROM FX240S !B'>

cmdk7 at ata1 target 0 lun 0
cmdk7 is /isa/ata@1,170/cmdk@0,0
Disk0:          <Vendor 'Gen-ATA ' Product 'Maxtor 84320A8  '>

cmdk0 at ata0 target 0 lun 0
cmdk0 is /isa/ata@1,1f0/cmdk@0,0
Disk1:          <Vendor 'Gen-ATA ' Product 'Maxtor 88400D8  '>

cmdk1 at ata0 target 1 lun 0
cmdk1 is /isa/ata@1,1f0/cmdk@1,0
ISA-device: aic0
root on /isa/ata@1,1f0/cmdk@0,0:a fstype ufs
ISA-device: asy0
asy0 is /isa/asy@1,3f8
ISA-device: asy1
asy1 is /isa/asy@1,2f8
Number of console virtual screens = 13
cpu 0 initialization complete - online
Ethernet address = 0:20:af:2f:f5:f6
```

```
elx0 (@0x0): 3COM EtherLink III: ether (twpair)
0:20:af:2f:f5:f6
ISA-device: elx1
elx1 is /isa/elx@1,300
elx1 (@0x0): 3COM EtherLink III: ether (twpair)
0:20:af:2f:f6:8b
ISA-device: elx0
elx0 is /isa/elx@1,210
dump on /dev/dsk/c0d0s1 size 112440K
```

You can examine this information on your own Solaris x86 or UNIX system by executing the command:

```
dmesg
```

LAB 7.4

This works in most versions of UNIX. This command keeps track of hardware settings, errors, and software that are loaded up until the login prompt. It does not include all the steps, but it includes the major ones that you might be interested in if you have system problems.

7.4.2 ANSWERS

a) Looking at the output, what would you say is the device assigned to the CD-ROM?

Answer: Look at the following results to determine information about your CD-ROM:

```
Disk7:  <Vendor 'MITSUMI ' Product 'CD-ROM FX240S !B'>
```

This tells you that the CD-ROM is a MITSUMI, and the model number is FX240S IB. It is also described to the system as:

```
cmdk7 at ata1 target 0 lun 0
cmdk7 is /isa/ata@1,170/cmdk@0,0
```

This says that the drive is on the second EIDE controller on the motherboard. You get this from the ata1 device. It is also known as the master drive on the secondary controller. You will see more information about controllers in Chapter 8, "Filesystems and Disks."

b) How much memory would you say is on the system?

Answer: Looking at the dmesg output, you see the following:

```
mem = 65148K (0x3f9f000)
```

This tells you that the system has a total of 65148K of memory. However, the operating system and other software that is loaded when you bootup will take some memory from the system. So you will then see the following message:

```
avail mem = 56360960
```

This is the available memory after the operating system and software have taken their cuts.

c) What is the version and release number of SunOS that is used?

Answer: The following line describes the version of SunOS that is being run on the PC:

```
SunOS Release 5.6 Version Generic [UNIX(R) System V Release 4.0]
```

You should be aware that this release number is actually Solaris 2.6. Because of the numbering system that has the BSD-based Sun OS using 4.x, Sun decided to start numbering the release numbers at 5.x

d) How many drives are on the system?

Answer: There are two drives. They show up as Disk0 and Disk1. Look at the answer to the following question.

e) What is the description of each drive?

Answer: The first drive is described as follows:

```
Disk0:     <Vendor 'Gen-ATA ' Product 'Maxtor 84320A8
'>
cmdk0 at ata0 target 0 lun 0
cmdk0 is /isa/ata@1,1f0/cmdk@0,0
```

This is a Maxtor drive model 84320A8 that is ATA compliant.

Note that this is target 0 on the drive. It so happens to be an EIDE drive, and the first one on the primary EIDE controller. This is also known as the master drive.

The second drive is described as follows:

```
Disk1:    <Vendor 'Gen-ATA ' Product 'Maxtor 88400D8   '>
cmdk1 at ata0 target 1 lun 0
cmdk1 is /isa/ata@1,1f0/cmdk@1,0
```

This is a Maxtor drive model 88400D8 that is ATA compliant.

Note that this is target 1 on the drive. It so happens to be an EIDE drive, and the second one on the primary EIDE controller. This is also known as the slave drive. You will see more discussion on the Solaris EIDE drives in Chapter 10.

f) How many Ethernet cards are found?

Answer:There are two elx0 and elx1.

g) What are the descriptions of the Ethernet cards?

Answer:The description for the first card is as follows (note that I have shifted around the descriptions from dmesg *so that the lines are consistent):*

```
elx0 (@0x0): 3COM EtherLink III: ether (twpair)
0:20:af:2f:f5:f6
ISA-device: elx0
elx0 is /isa/elx@1,210
```

The description for the second card is as follows:

```
elx1 (@0x0): 3COM EtherLink III: ether (twpair)
0:20:af:2f:f6:8b
ISA-device: elx1
elx1 is /isa/elx@1,300
```

The characteristics can be summarized as follows:

device name	elx0	elx1
Ethernet address	0:20:af:2f:f5:f6	0:20:af:2f:f6:8b
card name and manufacturer	3COM EtherLink III	3COM EtherLink III
Ethernet type of connection	twisted pair (twpair)	twisted pair (twpair)
base address	0x210 from /isa/elx@1,210	0x300 from /isa/elx@1,300

h) Which device is used as a dump device?

Answer: The dump device is given by the following line:

```
dump on /dev/dsk/c0d0s1 size 112440K
```

So the actual device is `/dev/dsk/c0d0s1`.

i) What is the size of the dump device?

Answer: The size of the dump device is given by the following line:

```
dump on /dev/dsk/c0d0s1 size 112440K
```

So the actual dump device size is 112440K. The dump device is often used when there is a system crash. UNIX attempts to dump as much information as possible to the dump device. This information is later used to analyze why the system crashed.
Now you should have chosen Solaris x86 to boot from on your system. Go ahead and boot if you haven't already. Compare your results with those in the example above.

j) What is the size of the dump device?

Answer: You should look at the answers to Questions (a) through (i) to compare your results.

LAB 7.4 SELF-REVIEW QUESTIONS

In order to test your progress, you should be able to answer the following questions. Look in the man pages or the chapter for help on commands. Choose the answer that best fits the question.

1) Look at the screen display for the Solaris x86 boot manager and the exercise text. Which of the following operating systems can you boot from?
   a) _____ Solaris x86
   b) _____ Linux
   c) _____ Win95
   d) _____ Solaris x86 and Linux
   e) _____ Solaris x86 and Win95

2) Which command gives a listing of system information, devices found, and some device drivers that are loaded on Solaris x86 bootup?
   a) _____ boot
   b) _____ dmesg
   c) _____ lilo
   d) _____ fsck
   e) _____ sysinfo

3) In looking at the results of the dmesg command in Lab 7.4, what is the size of the available memory?
   a) _____ 65148K
   b) _____ 56360K
   c) _____ 14672k
   d) _____ 1080 MB
   e) _____ None of the above

4) Looking at the results of the dmesg command in the text, this version of UNIX is based on which of the following?
   a) _____ BSD 4.3
   b) _____ ext2
   c) _____ Windows/NT
   d) _____ Linux
   e) _____ System V Release 4.0

5) The Ethernet card on this system uses twisted pair Ethernet.
   a) _____ True
   b) _____ False

Quiz answers appear in Appendix A, Section 7.4.

C H A P T E R   7

TEST YOUR THINKING

 The projects in this section are meant to have you utilize all of the skills that you have acquired throughout this chapter. The answers to these projects can be found at the companion Web site to this book, located at:

`http://www.phptr.com/phptrinteractive`

Visit the Web site periodically to share and discuss your answers.

1) Study your version of UNIX and find all the commands that are executed, and all files that are accessed in shutting down your system.

2) Study your version of UNIX and find all the commands that are executed, and all files that are accessed when the system is brought up.

3) Do some independent research and find four different variants of Linux. Go to their Web site and get information about the packages.

   a) What are the Web sites of each version?

   b) What is the version of the Linux kernel being used by each?

   c) Name one feature that is found in each manufacturer's version of Linux.

   d) Find out whether each of the manufacturers offers commercial, non-public domain software, other than Linux, that runs under Linux, such as office suites, wordprocessors, and so forth.

4) If your version of UNIX has a text file instead of a binary file for `/etc/shutdown`, then examine it for the following:

   a) Compare it to the steps in figure 7.1.1 and see if any of those steps are handled by the `/etc/shutdown` file.

   b) Does your version of UNIX allow for both `/etc/rc0` and `/etc/rc0.d` files? How are the files in question (b) executed during shutdown? Which program executes them, and/or what file lists them so they can be executed by another program?

   c) Does your version of UNIX have a `/etc/rc.local` file? What is the significance of this file? How are its functions replaced in more current versions of UNIX?

CHAPTER 8

DISKS AND FILESYSTEMS

 In learning UNIX, we need to begin our understanding at the very foundation. Like a house, if the foundation is weak, the house will sag and perhaps collapse. It will not weather the storms very well. But if that foundation is solid, the house will withstand some heavy storms. The hardware, and particularly the disks, are the foundation upon which we build our walls and roof. —Joe

This chapter discusses UNIX disks and filesystems. If you have worked with filesystems on other systems, you will find many concepts familiar. There are also some things that are inherent to UNIX, as well as variations among UNIX versions. Many UNIX manufacturers have gone to disk management systems, which are beyond the scope of this text. However, the basic concepts remain the same.

EXERCISES FOR THE GREAT AND SUPER USER

To truly understand UNIX filesystems, you must experience building filesystems, storing data, doing backups, and actually restoring a system. These are things that need to be done by root, so if you do not have root access, just read along in the text or find someone who has root privilege and work with them. Linux is widely available on CD-ROM and free off the Internet, so you might try installing it on your PC and using it to build your own UNIX filesystem.

Building the filesystem is one of the first things you will do when you install any operating system. You must lay out the structure of the filesystem and determine filesystem types and sizes. In addition, filesystems are mounted somewhere under root, so you must determine where and what to mount. This can sometimes be overwhelming to the beginning administrator who has never worked with a live filesystem or done any installs. This is just something that you gain from experience, and trial and error.

Various versions of UNIX have different commands for dividing up the disk. Some use the `fdisk` command, which is a variant carried over from DOS. Others, such as Solaris, have extended the `format` command to include capabilities that we usually associate with `fdisk`. Working with `fdisk` is one of the first things you will do when installing the operating system or adding a new disk.

The system hardware treats SCSI and EIDE drives differently. Fortunately, today's UNIX systems can work with both kind of drives. Some of the issues involved in choosing the drives are discussed in this chapter.

Look in the man pages for the following:

`fdisk, fsck, mount, mkfs, fstab, dump, inodes`

DRIVE TYPES

Several drive types have been used by UNIX over the years. The number of types for PCs has been basically reduced to IDE and SCSI. While there are other types in use, such as optical fiber links, USB, and parallel port, they currently have only a small percentage of the market.

The following sections address each one individually.

IDE/EIDE

IDE has been around since the Intel 286/AT PC. This type of drive connection requires only one controller cable per drive. In addition, you can have two drives per controller cable. IDE CD-ROMS also follow the same convention as hard disks in Linux. You can see the layout in Figure 8.1.

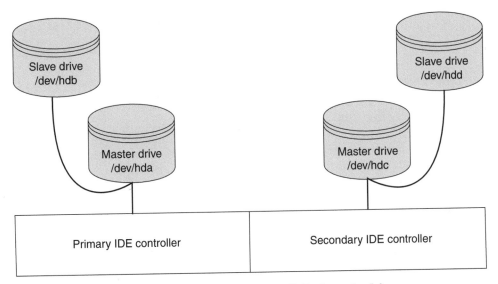

Figure 8.1 ■ Drive Layout for IDE/EIDE Drives in Linux

A computer can usually support both a primary and secondary controller. They differ primarily in the card hardware settings that are used. Each controller can, in turn, have a master and slave drive device on it. The difference between the master and slave device has to do with a jumper, which sets the drive to a master or slave. So by using all the primary, secondary, master, and slave positions, you can run a total of four drive devices off most controllers.

In addition, it is possible to add tertiary, quad, and other controllers on a PC, as long as there are no conflicts with things such as base addresses, IRQs, and DMA channels used. Also, PCI PC controllers can allow for a sharing of IRQs because each slot for a peripheral card is seen separately by the system. Linux currently only recognizes the primary and secondary controllers on bootup and the initial install. Linux can bring the other controllers online once the kernel and drivers for the new devices are loaded.

You will notice in Figure 8.1 that Linux assigns the devices designations in the following sequence:

1. /dev/hda—Master drive on primary IDE controller
2. /dev/hdb—Slave drive on primary IDE controller
3. /dev/hdc—Master drive on secondary IDE controller
4. /dev/hdd—Slave drive on secondary IDE controller

This sequence would be followed by both the hard drives and CD-ROMs which are being used.

There is also a size restriction with IDE devices. The first iteration of IDE devices was restricted to 512 MB per partition, because of the limitation of the addressing that was used. Next came EIDE, which allowed for larger drives by converting the addresses it was given into addresses that could be used by the disk drive. The size limit on EIDE drives is 8 GB. There are, however, new drives that go beyond that size limit, and require special drivers and controller cards to get around the problem.

 If you want to learn more about SCSI interfaces, refer to Appendix H, which discusses SCSI devices.

L A B 8.1

A DISKETTE-BASED LINUX FILESYSTEM

LAB OBJECTIVES

After this Lab, you will be able to:

Create a Linux Diskette Filesystem

Create an MS-DOS Diskette Filesystem

Practically every UNIX system has a diskette. You can use it in the following ways:

- To do backups of files and directories, although it is limited in storage capacity
- To move files from system to system (you can even work with DOS formatted diskettes!)
- As temporary storage
- As the first install media. Until recently, the only way to install a Linux system on a PC was to first boot off the diskette and then either continue the install off the CD-ROM, hard disk, or network. Now, with some of the newer motherboards, it is possible to boot totally off the CD-ROM. But unless you have a system and software that can read and write CD-ROMs, you still need your diskette for the features listed here.

In this Lab, you will learn how to format a floppy diskette, make either a UNIX or DOS format on it, and then mount it under your UNIX system.

8.1.1 CREATE A LINUX DISKETTE FILESYSTEM

In this Exercise, you will create and make accessible a diskette that has the ext2 filesystem on it. This is the default Linux format.

 For this Exercise and any Linux work involving using diskettes, you could use old diskettes that are lying around. Linux supports many different diskette configurations. If you are using a non-standard diskette for these exercises, you may need to adjust some of the commands so you can use that diskette.

This Exercise assumes you are using a 3-1/2" double sided high-density diskette in your Linux system's diskette drive.

Now enter the following command:

```
fdformat /dev/fd0H1440
```

a) What kind of results do you get?

_____

_____

This does a low-level format on the diskette.

Now enter the following command:

```
mkfs -t ext2 /dev/fd0H1440
```

b) What kind of results do you get? Describe the results.

_____

_____

You have made a UNIX ext2 filesystem on a diskette.

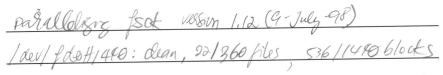

Once you have created a filesystem under UNIX, it is important that you check the filesystem. To do so, just enter the following command:

```
fsck /dev/fd0H1440
```

c) What are your results?

parallelizing fsck version 1.12 (9-July-98)

/dev/fd0H1440: clean, 22/360 files, 536/1440 blocks

Now you can mount the diskette. First you need to have a directory under which to mount it. UNIX usually provides the /mnt/floppy directory to mount diskettes.

You can either mount it here or choose another directory under which to mount it.

In UNIX, you can mount a diskette or drive over a directory that has files or subdirectories. While you do lose access to them, however, they are not lost. When you unmount the diskette or drive, the original files and directories become visible again. Generally, however, any directory used as a mount point should be empty. You might, however, think about some way you can take advantage of this.

You may also need to create the directory where you will mount it. Just use the following command:

```
mkdir /mnt /mnt/floppy
```

This creates the /mnt directory (if it doesn't already exist) and creates the /mnt/floppy mount point.

Now you can enter the following command:

```
mount /dev/fd0H1440 /mnt/floppy
```

d) What kind of results do you get?

This makes your diskette accessible under the `/mnt/floppy` directory.

_____

_____

You can check to see if the drive is mounted by entering the following command:

```
mount
```

e) What kind of description do you see about the diskette?

_____

_____

Next, you will copy a file to the diskette.

Enter the following:

```
cp /etc/passwd /mnt/floppy
```

f) What do you see?

_____

_____

Now enter the following command:

```
ls -l /mnt/floppy
```

g) What do you get?

_____

_____

Now you need to unmount the diskette.

To do so, enter the following command:

```
umount /mnt/floppy
```

Alternatively, you can enter the following:

```
umount /dev/fd0H1440
```

Either one will unmount the diskette.

Now, enter the following command:

```
mount
```

h) What kind of description do you see about the diskette?

_____

_____

It is important to unmount a diskette before removing it. While a PC does not prevent you from unmounting a diskette, the system sometimes gets confused if you do a subsequent mount. Sometimes it lets you do the mount, but remembers the previous mount table on the earlier diskette. Sometimes it causes the system to create an error. I have even seen it copy information from the previous diskette onto the new diskette, without me realizing it. Occasionally, it works OK.

You can now remove the diskette. You have created a UNIX `ext2` formatted diskette, mounted it, copied a file to it, and then unmounted it.

8.1.2 CREATING AN MS-DOS DISKETTE FILESYSTEM

In this Exercise, you will create and make accessible a diskette with an MS-DOS filesystem on it.

The MS-DOS formatted diskette you make will have all the limitations of an MS-DOS filesystem, including names with up to eight characters and extensions of up to three characters, otherwise known as the 8.3 format.

The steps used to create this diskette are similar, but not identical, to the steps used in creating a UNIX formatted diskette under Linux.

For these exercises, you could use some old diskettes that are lying around. Linux supports many different diskette configurations. If you are using a different diskette for these exercises, you may need to adjust some of the commands so you can use that diskette.

This Exercise assumes you are using a 3-1/2" double sided high-density diskette in your Linux systems diskette drive.

Note that some commands, such as `mformat`, *may not be available on a basic install on your version of Linux. A basic install of Red Hat Linux did not have it, but a full install of Caldera Linux did.*

You can use the command `mformat` to create an MS-DOS formatted diskette and create an MS-DOS filesystem on it.

To do that, enter the following command:

```
mformat a:
```

a) What kind of results do you get?

_____

_____

Note that the `fsck` *command in Linux will not work on MS-DOS filesystems, because MS-DOS' filesystem structure is very different UNIXs. Fsck needs to look at an unmounted UNIX filesystem at a very low level.*

Now you can mount the diskette. You must first have a directory under which to mount it. Linux usually provides the `/mnt/floppy` directory to mount diskettes. You can either mount it here or choose another directory under which to mount it.

You may need to create the directory where you will mount it. Just use the following command:

```
mkdir /mnt /mnt/floppy
```

This creates the /mnt directory, if it doesn't already exist, and the /mnt/floppy directory mount point.

Now you can enter the following command:

```
mount -t msdos /dev/fd0H1440 /mnt/floppy
```

b) What kind of results do you get?

_____

_____

You can check to see if the drive is mounted by entering the following command:

```
mount
```

c) What kind of description do you see about the diskette?

_____

_____

This makes files and directories on your diskette accessible in the /mnt/ floppy directory.

Next, copy a file to the diskette. Just enter the following:

```
cp /etc/passwd /mnt/floppy
```

d) What do you see?

_____

_____

Now enter the following command:

```
ls -1 /mnt/floppy
```

e) What do you get?

_____

_____

Now you need to unmount the diskette. Enter the following command:

```
umount /mnt/floppy
```

Alternatively, you can enter the following:

```
umount /dev/fd0H1440
```

f) What do you see?

_____

_____

Either one will unmount the diskette.

Now enter the following command:

```
mount
```

g) What kind of description do you see about the diskette?

_____

_____

It is important to unmount a diskette before removing it. While PCs do not prevent you from unmounting a diskette, the system sometimes gets confused if you do a subsequent mount. Sometimes it lets you do the mount, but remembers the previous mount table on the earlier diskette. Sometimes it causes the system to create an error. I have even seen it copy information from the previous diskette on the new diskette, without me realizing it. Occasionally, it works OK.

You can now remove the diskette. You have created an MS-DOS formatted diskette, mounted it, copied a file to it, and then unmounted it.

LAB 8.1 EXERCISE ANSWERS

This section gives you some suggested answers to the questions in Lab 8.1, with discussion related to those answers. Your answers may vary, but the most important thing is whether your answer works. Use this discussion to analyze differences between your answers and those presented here.

If you have alternative answers to the questions in this Exercise, you are encouraged to post your answers and discuss them at the companion Web site for this book, located at:

```
http://www.phptr.com/phptrinteractive
```

8.1.1 ANSWERS

In the following discussion, you should note that Unix stores information about filesystems, files, and directories in the `superblock`. When you create a file or directory, it is known by a unique number called the `inode number`. It is like an address on the disk. The superblock keeps track of this information. However, the actual name of the file or directory is not stored in the superblock, but is stored in the directory and file information on the disk. This means that a file can have multiple names, because multiple names can point to a single number. Also, a `physical block` has 512 bytes, whereas a `logical block` has 1024 bytes in Linux.

Enter the following command:

```
fdformat /dev/fd0H1440
```

a) What kind of results do you get?

Answer: You should see the following results:

```
[root@myserver /root]# fdformat /dev/fd0H1440
Double-sided, 80 tracks, 18 sec/track. Total capacity 1440 kB.
Formatting ... done
```

```
Verifying ... done
[root@myserver /root]#
```

This does a low-level format of the drive as 1.44 MB, then a verify. It actually gives a display of the cylinder number as it does the format and verify.

Now, enter the following command:

```
mkfs -t ext2 /dev/fd0H1440
```

b) What kind of results do you get? Describe the results.

Answer: You should get the following display on your screen:

```
[root@mohawk /root]# mkfs -t ext2 /dev/fd0H1440
mke2fs 1.10, 24-Apr-97 for EXT2 FS 0.5b, 95/08/09
Linux ext2 filesystem format
Filesystem label=
360 inodes, 1440 blocks
72 blocks (5.00%) reserved for the super user
First data block=1
Block size=1024 (log=0)
Fragment size=1024 (log=0)
1 block group
8192 blocks per group, 8192 fragments per group
360 inodes per group
Writing inode tables: done
Writing superblocks and filesystem accounting information:
done
[root@mohawk /root]#
```

A description of each line in the results follows.

```
mke2fs 1.10, 24-Apr-97 for EXT2 FS 0.5b, 95/08/09
```

You see the version number of the mke2fs, which is the actual command being called by the mkfs command, as follows:

```
Linux ext2 filesystem format
```

Now it makes a filesystem of the ext2 filesystem type:

```
Filesystem label=
```

There is no filesystem label.

```
360 inodes, 1440 blocks
```

It allocates table information for 360 inodes, which is essentially the total number of files and directories. It also allocates 1440 blocks of 1 K each.

```
72 blocks (5.00%) reserved for the super user
```

Here, it reserves 72 blocks (or 5.00%) for the super user.

```
First data block=1
```

The first data block is address number 1.

```
Block size=1024 (log=0)
```

The logical block size is 1024 bytes.

```
Fragment size=1024 (log=0)
```

The disk fragment size is 1024 bytes.

```
1 block group
```

It is creating 1 block group, which is a collection of blocks.

```
8192 blocks per group, 8192 fragments per group
```

There are 8192 blocks per group with 8192 fragments per group. You saw previously that there are 1024 bytes per fragment.

```
360 inodes per group
```

There are 360 inodes per group, which is what you defined at the start.

```
Writing inode tables: done
```

Here, it writes the inode table to the disk.

```
Writing superblocks and filesystem accounting informa-
tion: done
```

It then writes the superblock and filesystem information to the disk.

```
[root@mohawk /root]#
```

You are now returned to the command line prompt.

You have now made a UNIX ext2 filesystem on a diskette.
Once you create a filesystem under UNIX, it is important that you check the filesystem. To do so, just enter the following command:

```
fsck /dev/fd0H1440
```

c) What are your results?

Answer: The results are as follows:

```
[root@mohawk /root]# fsck /dev/fd0H1440
Parallelizing fsck version 1.10 (24-Apr-97)
e2fsck 1.10, 24-Apr-97 for EXT2 FS 0.5b, 95/08/09
/dev/fd0H1440: clean, 11/360 files, 63/1440 blocks
[root@mohawk /root]#
```

Note that if you did not unmount the diskette properly, you will get the following results:

```
[root@mohawk /root]# fsck /dev/fd0H1440
Parallelizing fsck version 1.10 (24-Apr-97)
e2fsck 1.10, 24-Apr-97 for EXT2 FS 0.5b, 95/08/09
/dev/fd0H1440 was not cleanly unmounted, check forced.
Pass 1: Checking inodes, blocks, and sizes
Pass 2: Checking directory structure
Pass 3: Checking directory connectivity
Pass 4: Checking reference counts
Pass 5: Checking group summary information
/dev/fd0H1440: 11/360 files (0.0% non-contiguous), 63/1440
blocks
[root@mohawk /root]#
```

The `fsck` command checks for the integrity of files and directories on a filesystem. If fsck cannot fix the information, it stores files in the lost+found directory.

Next, you created a directory under which to mount the diskette, and you then mounted it by entering the following command:

```
mount /dev/fd0H1440 /mnt/floppy
```

d) What kind of results do you get?

Answer: The results are as follows:

```
[root@mohawk /root]# mount /dev/fd0H1440 /mnt/floppy
[root@mohawk /root]#
```

Answer: You should have gotten just the command line prompt. Another example of the UNIX philosophy of "No news is good news."

You can check to see if the drive is mounted by entering the following command:

```
mount
```

e) What kind of description do you see about the diskette?

Answer: You should have gotten the following results:

```
[root@mohawk /root]# mount
/dev/hda3 on / type ext2 (rw)
/proc on /proc type proc (rw)
/dev/hdb3 on /usr type ext2 (rw)
mohawk:(pid136) on /auto type auto
(intr,rw,port=1023,timeo=8,retrans=110,indire
ct,map=/etc/amd.localdev)
none on /NetWare type nwamd (automounter)
/dev/fd0u1440 on /mnt/floppy type ext2 (rw)
[root@mohawk /root]#
```

The actual line that describes the floppy is the following:

```
/dev/fd0u1440 on /mnt/floppy type ext2 (rw)
```

This makes your diskette accessible under the /mnt directory.

Next, to copy a file to the diskette, just enter the following:
```
cp /etc/passwd /mnt/floppy
```

f) What do you see?

Answer: If the results were successful, you would have just gotten the command line prompt.

Now enter the following command:
```
ls -l /mnt/floppy
```

g) What do you get?

Answer: If your results are successful, you should see the following on the screen:

```
[root@mohawk /root]# ls -l /mnt/floppy
total 13
drwxr-xr-x   2 root   root   12288 May 26 17:29 lost+found
-rw-r--r--   1 root   root     768 May 26 17:59 passwd
[root@mohawk /root ]
```

Note that you have the additional directory called lost+found. This directory was described previously in the discussion about `fsck`.

After unmounting the diskette, you entered the following command:
```
mount
```

h) What kind of description do you see about the diskette?

Answer: You should see something similar to the following on your screen:

```
[root@mohawk /root]# mount
/dev/hda3 on / type ext2 (rw)
/proc on /proc type proc (rw)
/dev/hdb3 on /usr type ext2 (rw)
mohawk:(pid136) on /auto type auto
(intr,rw,port=1023,timeo=8,retrans=110,indire
ct,map=/etc/amd.localdev)
none on /NetWare type nwamd (automounter)
[root@mohawk /root]#
```

Notice that the entry for the diskette is not shown. This is because the diskette has been unmounted.

8.1.2 ANSWERS

You can use the command `mformat` to create an MS-DOS formatted diskette and create an MS-DOS filesystem on it. To do that, enter the following command:

```
mformat a:
```

a) What kind of results do you get?

Answer: You should see the following on your screen. Notice that you just get the command line prompt..

```
[root@mohawk /root]# mformat a:
[root@mohawk /root]#
```
Next, you created a directory under which to mount the diskette, and you then mounted it by entering the following command:

```
mount -t msdos /dev/fd0H1440 /mnt/floppy
```

b) What kind of results do you get?

```
[root@mohawk /root]# mount -t msdos /dev/fd0H1440
/mnt/floppy
[root@mohawk /root]#
```

You can check to see if the drive is mounted by entering the following command:

```
mount
```

c) What kind of description do you see about the diskette?

Answer: You should get the following results:

```
[root@mohawk /root]# mount
/dev/hda3 on / type ext2 (rw)
/proc on /proc type proc (rw)
/dev/hdb3 on /usr type ext2 (rw)
mohawk:(pid136) on /auto type auto
(intr,rw,port=1023,timeo=8,retrans=110,indire
```

```
ct,map=/etc/amd.localdev)
none on /NetWare type nwamd (automounter)
/dev/fd0u1440 on /mnt/floppy type msdos (rw)
[root@mohawk /root]#
```

The actual line you need to look for is:

```
/dev/fd0u1440 on /mnt/floppy type msdos (rw)
```

Note that the filesystem type is listed as msdos and has the characteristics read-write.

Next, copy a file to the diskette. Enter the following:

```
cp /etc/passwd /mnt/floppy
```

d) What do you see?

Answer: You should just get the command line prompt back.
Now enter the following command:

```
ls -l /mnt/floppy
```

e) What do you get?

Answer: You should see the following results:

```
[root@mohawk /root]# ls -l /mnt/floppy
total 1
-rwxr-xr-x   1 root      root       768 May 26 18:17 passwd
[root@mohawk /root]#
```

Note that there is no lost+found directory. This is because lost+found is used to save files that have failed the fsck command. The resulting files are saved there.

Next, you unmounted the diskette.

f) What do you see?

Answer: You should just get the command line prompt back.
Enter the following command:

```
mount
```

g) What kind of description do you see about the diskette?

Answer; You should see the following:

```
[root@mohawk /root]# mount
/dev/hda3 on / type ext2 (rw)
/proc on /proc type proc (rw)
/dev/hdb3 on /usr type ext2 (rw)
mohawk:(pid136) on /auto type auto
(intr,rw,port=1023,timeo=8,retrans=110,indire
ct,map=/etc/amd.localdev)
none on /NetWare type nwamd (automounter)
[root@mohawk /root]#
```

LAB 8.1 SELF-REVIEW QUESTIONS

In order to test your progress, you should be able to answer the following questions.

Look in the man pages or the chapter for help on commands. You need to find the best answer to the question. Note that some answers may not be exact replacements. So you need to think about which one comes closest to the results that you want.

1) If I have an IDE disk that is the slave device on the secondary controller, this will be considered to be the Linux device called which of the following?

    a) _____/dev/had
    b) _____/dev/hdb
    c) _____/dev/hdc
    d) _____/dev/hdd
    e) _____None of the above

2) A CD-ROM that is configured to be the slave device on the primary IDE controller is the Linux device called which of the following?

    a) _____/dev/had
    b) _____/dev/hdb
    c) _____/dev/hdc
    d) _____/dev/hdd
    e) _____None of the above

3) It is possible to use the floppy controller to attach a tape backup device in Linux.

    a) _____True
    b) _____False

4) If the /dev/fd0H1440 is a double high-density 1.440 MB floppy disk, then the device /dev/fd0h720 should be which of the following?

    a) _____single-sided diskette
    b) _____double-sided diskette of density 360 K
    c) _____double-sided high-density diskette of density 720 K
    d) _____double-sided double high-density disk with 1.200 MB density
    e) _____None of the above

5) Which of the following is the command to format a floppy in Linux that will eventually be used for an `ext2` filesystem?

    a) _____`format`

    b) _____`fdisk`

    c) _____`fdformat`

    d) _____`mformat`

    e) _____`mkfs`

6) Which of the following is the command to low-level format a floppy in Linux for a DOS filesystem?

    a) _____`format`

    b) _____`fdisk`

    c) _____`fdformat`

    d) _____`mformat`

    e) _____`mkfs`

Quiz answers appear in Appendix A, Section 8.1.

**LAB
8.1**

L A B   8.2

MAKING A LINUX FILESYSTEM

LAB OBJECTIVES

After this Lab, you will be able to:

Create a Linux Hard Disk Partition

✓ Create a Linux Filesystem

✓ Check the UNIX Filesystem

✓ Mount the UNIX Filesystem

✓ Use /etc/fstab to Mount the Partition

There are a number of steps you need to go through in creating a usable filesystem on a UNIX system. You saw in Lab 8.1 that you can create a UNIX or DOS filesystem on a diskette. In this Lab, you will extend that concept to create a usable filesystem on a hard disk.

In order to do this Lab, you will need some space on a hard disk. Where a particular partition name or device is used in the exercises or examples, you will need to substitute the actual name of the partition or device you are using. You may also need to substitute some size values for those that actually work for you.

Once you master the art of making filesystems under Linux, it is relatively easy to extend it to other versions of UNIX.

You should note that Solaris uses the format command, which also has a menu for fdisk. The Solaris format fdisk command functions differently from the DOS fdisk command and the Linux fdisk command. If you are running Solaris x86 you should research some of the differences. Chapter 10, "Solaris Filesystems," will discuss this further.

LAB 8.2 EXERCISES

8.2.1 CREATE A LINUX HARD DISK PARTITION

You can now setup a Linux Partition. The command you will use is `fdisk`. This works similar to the FDISK command in DOS. However, the Linux `fdisk` command has a lot more options than the DOS version.

The first thing you need to do is determine the current layout of our disks and how much space you have.

A good command to start out with is:

```
fdisk -l
```

This gives the current partition layout of your disk drives.

a) What kind of results do you get?

_____

_____

Now you can actually go into the `fdisk` command and create the partition you want.

You will be adding a new partition to the second IDE hard drive, which on my system is `/dev/hdb`. You will use the remaining space on the disk to create the partition. (You will need to follow along and perform the steps as they apply to your system.)

Enter the following command:

```
fdisk /dev/hdb(Replace the file_system with your own
    device)
```

You should note that if you did not enter the /dev/hdb option, your system would default to /dev/hda as the drive to work with.

b) What do you see when you enter the fdisk command?

_____

_____

Now you want to create a Linux partition. At the prompt from the last command, just enter the letter:

n

This prompts you to create a new partition.

After that, you are prompted for the command action, which will ask you what kind of partition you want to create. You have two options:

e   extended—This creates an extended partition within a currently existing partition. The extended partition must be of the same type as the partition type under which you created it.

p   primary partition (1-4)—This creates a primary partition.

 Note that you can only create four primary partitions, but each one can be a different operating system. In reality, though, root and swap are setup as separate partitions, so you are limited to three operating systems without the help of a boot manager, which you can read about in Appendix G on multi-boot systems.

c) What did you actually choose for the partition type?

_____

_____

From there, you have to choose the actual number of the partition.

```
Partition number (1-4):
```

d) What did you specify for the partition number?

_____

_____

Now you need to specify the cylinder on which to start the partition. The command `fdisk` gives you the actual range of cylinders that are available.

```
First cylinder (751-1021):
```

This prompt says that you can start the partition on cylinder 751, or any number up to 1021.

e) What did you choose for the starting cylinder?

_____

_____

The next prompt you see is the following:

```
Last cylinder or +size or +sizeM or +sizeK ([751]-1021):
```

This means that the last cylinder on this partition can be anywhere from 751 to 1021. You can actually specify a size in Kilobytes or Megabytes.

f) What did you choose for the last cylinder?

_____

_____

You then need to fill in the appropriate values for the system on which you are working.

In the previous Example, a Linux partition was created. You can now verify that you have the new partition. Do this while in `fdisk` with the following letter:

```
p
```

This prints out the partitions on `/dev/hdb`.

g) What kind of results do you get?

_____

_____

If you want to change the partition type, use the following entry to `fdisk`:

```
t
```

This prompts you for the partition number you want to change. You can choose any number from 1 to 4, corresponding to the partition you have chosen.

Now enter the partition number for the type of partition you want to create.

h) What did you choose?

_____

_____

You are now prompted to change the partition's type. It prompts you for a hex code. You can use any number of partition types. If you are making a regular Linux partition, you should choose type 82.

Go ahead and enter your choice.

i) What do you get?

_____

_____

You now need to save the results of creating or modifying the partitions to the partition table. Do so by entering the following command:

```
w
```

j) What do you see?

_____

_____

Note that you will need to reboot Linux for the system to properly reset the partition tables. This is one of the few times in Linux you ever need to reboot.

8.2.2 CREATE A LINUX FILESYSTEM

The command to create a UNIX or Linux filesystem is as follows:

```
mkfs
```

This will **make** a UNIX **file**system; hence the name `mkfs`. The filesystem is made on a partition that has already been created by `fdisk`. There are various versions of `mkfs`. Linux uses the following command:

```
mke2fs
```

This is the same as the following command:

```
mkfs -t ext2
```

This command makes a filesystem of the type `ext2`, which is the most popular version of filesystem for Linux. There are other versions for other filesystem types.

First, find out the current partition layout of the drive by using the following command:

```
fdisk -l
```

This gives all the partitions that have been laid out on the disk.

a) What do you get?

_____

_____

Next, create a filesystem on `/dev/hdb4`. You will want to make the filesystem the same size as the partition you created.

Look at the results of the preceding question. To make a filesystem, use the variation of `mkfs` called `mke2fs`. It has the following format:

```
mke2fs partition_name partition_size
```

A good example is:

```
mke2fs /dev/hdb4 2176807
```

This command says that you will make an `ext2` filesystem on the partition `/dev/hdb4`. The size is 2176807 blocks.

In your case, you should examine the entry for the partition you want to look at. This is the number you will use in making the filesystem.

Look at the following entry. You should consult your results and use the actual size number of your partition.

```
/dev/hdb4        751    751     1021  2176807+  83  Linux native
```

Go ahead and make your filesystem on the partition of your choice; just be sure to replace the partition used in the example with the appropriate partition.

Make your partition.

b) What are your results?

_____

_____

Linux will go through and do a number of checks and then create the filesystem. It wil also do backups of disk information used in creating the filesystem.

8.2.3 CHECK THE UNIX FILESYSTEM

Once you have created the filesystem, you should now check the filesystem to see if there are any problems. In UNIX, the program to do this is as follows:

```
fsck file_system
```

Here, `file_system` is the filesystem you want to check. This will go through and check for inconsistencies in filesystem tables. It can automatically fix some problems. With other problems, you will be prompted as to whether you want to make any changes.

Go ahead and do a filesystem check on the partition you just created.

Run the following command:

```
fsck /dev/hdb4   (Replace hdb4 with the your filesystem)
```

a) What kind of results do you get?

_____

_____

8.2.4 MOUNT THE UNIX FILESYSTEM

This Exercise uses the `mount` command to take a filesystem that you have created in the previous Exercise and mount it under a UNIX directory.

The actual format of the `mount` command is as follows:

```
mount  -t fstype device_name mount_point
```

This command is explained as follows:

`fstype` is the filesystem type used to determine how to mount the filesystem.

`filesystem` is the formatted filesystem in the previous step.

`mount_point` is the mount point, which is a directory where you can mount the filesystem.

Take the filesystem you created in Exercise 8.2.2 and mount it. Let's use the name `/mydir` for the directory mount point. If the mount point, which is a regular UNIX directory, doesn't exist, you can create it with the following command:

```
mkdir /mydir
```

a) What are your results?

_____

_____

Use the following command to mount the filesystem:

```
mount /dev/hdb4 /mydir
```

If you leave out the filesystem type, the system will assume `ext2` as the filesystem.

Go ahead and mount the partition you just created under the directory. Replace `device_name` with the partition name and `directory_name` with the mount point.

b) What kind of results do you get when you mount the filesystem?

_____

_____

Now that you have mounted the filesystem, you can use the `mount` command to verify that the filesystem was actually mounted.

c) What kind of results do you get when you enter the mount command?

_____

_____

8.2.5 USE /ETC/FSTAB TO MOUNT THE PARTITION

As mentioned earlier in this chapter, the `/etc/fstab` is used to mount devices when your system boots up.

Take a look at your `/etc/fstab` file by entering the following command:

```
cat /etc/fstab
```

a) What do you see when you display the `/etc/fstab` file?

_____

_____

You should now go ahead and add an entry for the partition you just created.

When adding an entry to /etc/fstab, you should place it at the end of the file. If the current partition to which you are mounting your new partition has not yet been mounted, you could lose your original mount point. This may happen if that earlier partition is subsequently mounted. It is a good habit to always add things after system-created entries in any file, unless you are sure there will be no problems.

Use the following format for the line you are entering:

```
device_name  mount_point  ext2 defaults 0 2
```

This command is explained as follows:

`device_name` is the `/dev` device name for your partition.

`mount_point` is the UNIX directory where you will be mounting the partition.

`ext2` is the filesystem type you just created, and the default filesystem type for Linux.

`defaults` refers to the mount options you can use to mount the device.

0 is the frequency by which the filesystem should be dumped, and is used by the dump command.

2 refers to the order in which filesystems are checked by `fsck` on bootup. The 3 means that this partition is in the third order for checking.

    b) What is the line you added to `/etc/fstab`?

_____

_____

You can check whether this line works by unmounting the partition, if it is already mounted, by using either of the following commands:

```
umount device_name
umount mount_point
```

    c) What kind of results do you get when you unmount the partition?

_____

_____

Now you can make sure that everything gets mounted by entering the following command:

```
mount -a
```

d) What kind of results do you get from the mount -a command?

_____

_____

Verify the partitions that are mounted with the following command:

```
mount
```

You should see that the partition you created is now mounted.

e) What is displayed when you enter the `mount` command?

_____

_____

The next step is to reboot your Linux box to verify that it is mounted.

While it is rebooting, look at the screen for messages about the partition being mounted. Also look for any error messages.

You have now:

• Made a partition in UNIX

• Created a UNIX filesystem

• Checked it out with `fsck`

• Mounted it under a directory

• Permanently added it to the list of partitions to be mounted on bootup

You can now use the same principles you learned in this Lab to create and mount a filesystem with a different filesystem type.

LAB 8.2 EXERCISE ANSWERS

This section gives you some suggested answers to the questions in Lab 8.2, with discussion related to those answers. Your answers may vary, but the most important thing is whether your answer works. Use this discussion to analyze differences between your answers and those presented here.

If you have alternative answers to the questions in this Exercise, you are encouraged to post your answers and discuss them at the companion Web site for this book, located at:

http://www.phptr.com/phptrinteractive

8.2.1 ANSWERS

The first thing you did was run the following command:
```
fdisk -l
```

a) What kind of results do you get?

Answer: Your results should be similar to the following:

```
[root@mohawk /root]# fdisk -l
Disk /dev/hda: 255 heads, 63 sectors, 527 cylinders
Units = cylinders of 16065 * 512 bytes
Device    Boot Begin Start  End   Blocks    Id  System
/dev/hda1        1     1    128   1028128+  b   Unknown
/dev/hda2      129   129    390   2104515   82  Linux swap
/dev/hda3 *    391   391    499   875542+   83  Linux native
/dev/hda4      500   500    527   224910    82  Linux swap

Disk /dev/hdb: 255 heads, 63 sectors, 1021 cylinders
Units = cylinders of 16065 * 512 bytes

Device  Boot Begin Start End Blocks Id System
/dev/hdb1        1   1   261 2096451   6 DOS 16-bit >=32M
/dev/hdb2      262 262   515 2040255  82 Linux swap
/dev/hdb3      516 516   750 1887637+ 83 Linux native
[root@mohawk /root]#
```

b) What do you see when you enter the `fdisk` command?

> *Answer: You should not see an additional disk drive, but only see the layout for* `/dev/hdb`. *It should look like the following:*

```
wheels:/root #  fdisk
Using /dev/hda as default device!

Command (m for help):
```

This is a default prompt from `fdisk`. In the last question, the results are just a listing of the disk layouts. This question is the start of the interactive process which allows you to build your new disk layouts.

c) What did you actually choose for the partition type?

> *Answer: On the example system, the partition type is primary. Your choice could be different.*

d) What did you specify for the partition number?

> *Answer: On the example system, the partition number is 4. Your choice could be different..*

e) What did you choose for the starting cylinder?

> *Answer: On the example system, the first cylinder chosen was 751. Your choice could be different.*

f) What did you choose for the last cylinder?

> *Answer: On the example system, the last cylinder chosen was 1021. Your choice could be different.*

Next, you printed out the partitions on `/dev/hdb`.

g) What kind of results did you get?

> *Answer: You should have gotten the following results (remember, your settings may be different):*

```
Command (m for help): p
Disk /dev/hdb: 255 heads, 63 sectors, 1021 cylinders
Units = cylinders of 16065 * 512 bytes
Device Boot    Begin    Start      End    Blocks    Id  System
```

```
/dev/hdb1              1         1       261   2096451   6  DOS
16-bit >=32M
/dev/hdb2            262       262       515   2040255   82
Linux swap
/dev/hdb3            516       516       750   1887637+  83
Linux native
/dev/hdb4            751       751      1021   2176807+  83
Linux native
Command (m for help):
```

Enter the partition number now for the type of partition you want to create.

h)   What did you choose?

>   *Answer:You should have seen something similar to the following on your screen:*

```
Command (m for help): t
Partition number (1-4): 4
```

You are now prompted to change the partition's type. It prompts you for a hex code, which is what you saw in Figure 8.1. You can use any number of partition types. If you are making a regular Linux partition, you should choose type 82. Go ahead and enter your choice.

i)   What do you get?

>   *Answer:You should get the following results. If you are not sure which values to choose for the Hex code for the partition, you can just type L to list the codes.*

```
Hex code (type L to list codes): 82
Changed system type of partition 4 to 82 (Linux swap)
Command (m for help):
```

You now need to save the results of creating or modifying the partitions to the partition table. Do so by entering the following command:

```
    w
```

j)   What do you see?

>   *Answer: you should see something similar to the following:*

```
Command (m for help): w
The partition table has been altered!
Calling ioctl() to re-read partition table.
Syncing disks.
```

```
Re-read table failed with error 16: Device or resource
busy.
Reboot your system to ensure the partition table is
updated.

WARNING: If you have created or modified any DOS 6.x
partitions, please see the fdisk manual page for addi-
tional
information.
[root@mohawk man8]#
```

8.2.2 ANSWERS

First, find out the current partition layout of the drive by using the following
command:

```
fdisk -l
```

This gives all the partitions that have been laid out on the disk.

a) What do you get?

Answer:You should have gotten results similar to the following:

```
[root@mohawk filesys]# fdisk -l
Disk /dev/hda: 255 heads, 63 sectors, 527 cylinders
Units = cylinders of 16065 * 512 bytes
    Device Boot   Begin    Start      End    Blocks    Id   System
 /dev/hda1          1        1       128   1028128+   b   Unknown
 /dev/hda2        129      129       390   2104515    82   Linux swap
 /dev/hda3   *    391      391       499   875542+    83   Linux native
 /dev/hda4        500      500       527   224910     82   Linux swap


Disk /dev/hdb: 255 heads, 63 sectors, 1021 cylinders
Units = cylinders of 16065 * 512 bytes
    Device Boot   Begin    Start      End    Blocks    Id   System
 /dev/hdb1          1        1       261   2096451     6   DOS 16-bit
>=32M
 /dev/hdb2        262      262       515   2040255    82   Linux swap
 /dev/hdb3        516      516       750   1887637+   83   Linux native
 /dev/hdb4        751      751      1021   2176807+   83   Linux native
```

Go ahead and make your filesystem on the partition of your choice. Just be sure to replace the partition used in the example with the appropriate partition.

Make your partition.

b) What are your results?

Answer: You should have gotten results similar to the following:

```
[root@mohawk filesys]# mke2fs /dev/hdb4 2176807
mke2fs 1.10, 24-Apr-97 for EXT2 FS 0.5b, 95/08/09
Linux ext2 filesystem format
Filesystem label=
544768 inodes, 2176807 blocks
108840 blocks (5.00%) reserved for the super user
First data block=1
Block size=1024 (log=0)
Fragment size=1024 (log=0)
266 block groups
8192 blocks per group, 8192 fragments per group
2048 inodes per group
Superblock backups stored on blocks:
 8193, 16385, 24577, 32769, 40961, 49153, 57345, 65537,
73729, 811921, 90113, 98305, 106497, 114689, 122881,
131073, 139265, 147457, 155649, 163841, 172033, 180225,
188417, 196609, 204801, 212993, 221185, 229377, 237569,
245761, 253953, 262145, 270337, 278529, 286721, 294913,
303105, 311297, 319489, 327681, 335873, 344065, 352257,
360449, 368641, 376833, 385025, 393217, 401409, 409601,
417793, 425985, 434177, 442369, 450561, 458753, 466945,
475137, 483329, 491521, 499713, 507905, 516097, 524289,
532481, 540673, 548865, 557057, 565249, 573441, 581633,
589825, 598017, 606209, 614401, 622593, 630785, 638977,
647169, 655361, 663553, 671745, 679937, 688129, 696321,
704513, 712705, 720897, 729089, 737281, 745473, 753665,
761857, 770049, 778241, 786433, 794625, 802817, 811009,
819201, 827393, 835585, 843777, 851969, 860161, 868353,
876545, 884737, 892929, 901121, 909313, 917505, 925697,
933889, 942081, 950273, 958465, 966657, 974849, 983041,
```

991233, 999425, 1007617, 1015809, 1024001, 1032193,
1040385, 1048577, 1056769, 1064961, 1073153, 1081345,
1089537, 1097729, 1105921, 1114113, 1122305, 1130497,
1138689, 1146881, 1155073, 1163265, 1171457, 1179649,
1187841, 1196033, 1204225, 1212417, 1220609, 1228801,
1236993, 1245185, 1261569, 1269761, 1277953, 1286145,
1294337, 1302529, 1310721, 1318913, 1327105, 1335297,
1343489, 1351681, 1359873, 1368065, 1376257, 1384449,
1392641, 1400833, 1409025, 1417217, 1425409, 1433601,
1441793, 1449985, 1458177, 1466369, 1474561, 1482753,
1490945, 1499137, 1507329, 1515521, 1523713, 1531905,
1540097, 1548289, 1556481, 1564673, 1572865, 1581057,
1589249, 1597441, 1605633, 1613825, 1622017, 1630209,
1638401, 1646593, 1654785, 1662977, 1671169, 1679361,
1687553, 1695745, 1703937, 1712129, 1720321, 1728513,
1736705, 1744897, 1753089, 1761281, 1769473, 1777665,
1785857, 1794049, 1802241, 1810433, 1818625, 1826817,
1835009, 1843201, 1851393, 1859585, 1867777, 1875969,
1884161, 1892353, 1900545, 1908737, 1916929, 1925121,
1933313, 1941505, 1949697, 1957889, 1966081, 1974273,
1982465, 1990657, 1998849, 2007041, 2015233, 2023425,
2031617, 2039809, 2048001, 2056193, 2072577, 2080769,
2088961, 2097153, 2105345, 2113537, 2121729, 2129921,
2138113, 2146305, 2154497, 2162689, 2170881

```
Writing inode tables:    12/ 266
   26/ 266
   41/ 266
   55/ 266
   69/ 266
   83/ 266
   98/ 266
  112/ 266
  126/ 266
  140/ 266
  154/ 266
  169/ 266
```

**LAB
8.2**

```
183/ 266
197/ 266
211/ 266
226/ 266
240/ 266
done
Writing superblocks and filesystem accounting informa-
tion: done
[root@mohawk filesys]# exit
```

8.2.3 ANSWERS

Go ahead and do a filesystem check on the partition you just created.
Run the following command:

```
fsck /dev/hdb4    (Replace hdb4 with the your filesystem)
```

a)   What kind of results do you get?

Answer: You should get results similar to the following. Just replace /dev/hdb4 *with your own partition.*

```
[root@mohawk filesys]# fsck /dev/hdb4
Parallelizing fsck version 1.10 (24-Apr-97)
e2fsck 1.10, 24-Apr-97 for EXT2 FS 0.5b, 95/08/09
/dev/hdb4: clean, 11/544768 files, 71302/2176807 blocks
[root@mohawk filesys]#
```

Notice that the above command actually calls the program e2fsck. The results indicate that it found 11 out of a maximum of 544768 files. In addition, it found 71302 blocks out of 2176807 maximum blocks in use. This is due to the directory called lost+found, which is used by fsck and other programs when an inconsistency is found in file information. Files that have problems with names, links, or other inconsistencies are stored in lost+found.

8.2.4 ANSWERS

Take the filesystem that you created in Exercise 8.2.2 and mount it. Let's use the name /mydir for the directory mount point. If the mount point, which is a regular UNIX directory, doesn't exist, you can create it with the following command.:

```
mkdir /mydir
```

a) If the directory doesn't exist, go ahead and create it. What are your results?

Answer: You should have just gotten the command line prompt back.

Mount the partition you just created under the directory. Replace `device_name` with the partition name and `directory_name` with the mount point.

b) What kind of results do you get when you mount the filesystem?

Answer: You will just see the command line prompt back.

Now that you've mounted the filesystem, you can use the `mount` command to verify that the filesystem was actually mounted.

c) What kind of results do you get when you enter the `mount` command?

Answer: You should see results similar to the following:

```
[root@mohawk filesys]# mount
/dev/hda3 on / type ext2 (rw)
/proc on /proc type proc (rw)
/dev/hdb3 on /usr type ext2 (rw)
mohawk:(pid136) on /auto type auto
(intr,rw,port=1023,timeo=8,retrans=110,indire
ct,map=/etc/amd.localdev)
none on /NetWare type nwamd (automounter)
/dev/hdb4 on /filesys type ext2 (rw)
```

The actual line that shows the directory we just mounted is:

```
/dev/hdb4 on /mydir type ext2 (rw)
```

8.2.5 ANSWERS

a) a) What do you see when you display the /etc/fstab file?

Answer: You should see a display similar to the following;

```
/dev/hda1          /           ext2       defaults   1   1
/dev/hda2          swap        swap       defaults   0   0
/dev/hda3          /usr        ext2       defaults   1   2
/dev/hda4          /home       ext2       defaults   1   2
/dev/hdd           /cdrom      iso9660    ro,noauto,user 0   0
none               /proc       proc       defaults   0   0
```

**LAB
8.2**

b)   What is the line that you added to `/etc/fstab`?

Answer:That line should look like the following:

```
/dev/hdb4   /mydir  ext2 defaults 0 2
```

This command is the same as explained in the question section, except:

`/dev/hdb4` is the /dev device name for your partition.

`/mydir` is the UNIX directory where you will be mounting the partition.

c)   What kind of results do you get when you unmount the partition?

Answer:You should get the command line prompt back with no other messages.

d)   What kind of results do you get from the mount -a command?

Answer:You will either get the command line prompt back or error messages telling you that the partitions are already mounted or busy. In either case, you can ignore those messages. If you get messages that a mount point or device doesn't exist, then you should reexamine the /etc/fstab file to be sure that you don't have any typos.

e)   What is displayed when you enter the `mount` command?

Answer:You should see the following partition display:

```
/dev/hda1 on / type ext2 (rw)
none on /proc type proc (rw)
/dev/hda3 on /usr type ext2 (rw)
/dev/hda4 on /home type ext2 (rw)
/dev/hdb4 on /mydir type ext2 (rw)
```

You will notice that the partition you added is now at the bottom of the list. The filesystems are usually displayed in the order of mounting, and since our new partition was last in `/etc/fstab`, it also shows up last. It shows the device name, mount point, filesystem type and that it can be read and written to unless otherwise restricted.

L A B   8.3

MAKING A LINUX SWAP FILESYSTEM

LAB OBJECTIVES

After this Lab, you will be able to:

✓ Delete a Partition

✓ Make a Swap Partition

✓ Enable Swapping

✓ Permanently Enable the Swap Partition

The swap filesystem in UNIX is used as an extension of memory. When the system runs out of space in the RAM, it uses a portion of the disk as swap space. Swap space is not absolutely necessary if you have oodles of RAM, but most of us don't. So we use swap space to extend the amount of space we can use for running programs and to store more data.

The general rule of thumb for setting up swap space is that you should have twice the amount of swap space that you have in memory. So if you have 64 MB of RAM, you should setup 128 MB of swap space.

A good indication that you need more memory and swap space is how much you are swapping out to disk. If you hear your hard disk chugging away a lot on big programs that don't do much disk access, it is a good sign that you are hitting swap space. There are also tools that you can use to measure how much you are hitting the memory and swap space, and how heavily they are being used.

In this Lab, you are going to create some swap space on your system. The first thing you need to do is remove the partition you created in Lab 8.2. Then you will reassign the space to be a swap partition, which you will then enable as swap. If you did not do Lab 8.2, you may still need to reassign a partition, so this Lab shows you how to delete, create and reassign a space to swap space. Otherwise, just follow along in the discussion.

LAB 8.3 EXERCISES

8.3.1 DELETE A PARTITION

In order to delete a Linux partition, you must first be sure that it is not mounted. To do this, enter the following command:

```
mount
```

a) What do you see? Is your partition mounted?

_____

_____

If it is mounted, enter either of the following commands:

```
umount mount_directory
umount device_name
```

Here, `mount_directory` is the directory where you mounted the filesystem, and `device_name` is the name you gave it.

You should go ahead and unmount the partition in which you are going to work, if it is already mounted.

b) What kind of results do you get?

_____

_____

The first thing you must do is determine the current layout of your disks and how much space you have.

A good command to start out with is as follows:

```
fdisk -l
```

This gives the current partition layout of your disk drives.

c) What kind of results do you get?

_____

_____

> Note that the commands `mount` and `fdisk` can be easily confused. The `mount` command just gives you a listing of partitions that are mounted. There may be many other partitions that are unmounted. Those can be found by the `fdisk` command. The command `fdisk -l` gives a complete listing of your system disk layout.

Find the partition you created in Lab 8.2.

Look at the results in Question (c) of this Exercise to see if your partition is there. If not, you don't need to remove the partition; otherwise, you must remove it by following the next few steps in this Exercise.

d) Did you find your partition? What is it?

_____

_____

Now, you can actually go into the `fdisk` command and delete the desired partition.

You will be adding the new swap partition to the second IDE hard drive on your system, which is /dev/hdb.

You will use the remaining space on the disk to create the swap partition. (You will need to follow along and do the steps as they apply to your system.)

Enter the following command:

```
fdisk /dev/hdb(Replace  the  /dev/hdb   with your   own
     drive device)
```

You should note that if you did not enter the /dev/hdb option to fdisk, your system will default to /dev/hda as the drive to work with. Also note that the drive is labeled as /dev/hdb, not /dev/hdb4, because /dev/hdb4 is a partition on /dev/hdb.

e) What do you see when you enter the command?

_____

_____

Now you want to delete the Linux partition you created in the previous Lab. We are now going to use that space as swap space.

At the prompt from the last command, enter the following letter:

```
d
```

From there, you have to choose the actual number of the partition, such as the following:

```
Partition number (1-4):
```

f) What are your results?

_____

_____

You can verify that your partition is deleted by entering the following letter:

p

**LAB
8.3**

This prints the partition table.

g) Go ahead and choose this option. Is your partition gone?

_____

_____

8.3.2 MAKE A SWAP PARTITION

You should now be in the `fdisk` command. At the `fdisk` prompt, enter the following letter:

n

a) What do you get?

_____

_____

This asks you what kind of partition you want to create. You have two options:

e extended—This will create an extended partition within a currently existing partition. The extended partition must be of the same type as the partition type under which you created it.

p primary partition (1-4)—This will create a primary partition.

You can only create four primary partitions, but each one can be a different operating system. In reality, though, root and swap are set up as separate partitions, so you are limited to three operating systems without the help of a boot manager, which you can read about in the Appendix G.

You are now asked to choose whether you are creating a primary or extended partition. Linux swap space should be set up as a primary partition.

**LAB
8.3**

    b) What happens when you choose the partition type?

_____

_____

From here, you have to choose the actual number of the partition. You will see the following prompt:

```
Partition number (1-4):
```

    c) What did you specify for the partition number?

_____

_____

Now you need to specify the cylinder on which to start the partition.

Fdisk gives you the actual range of addresses with which you can work. It looks for the first available address range and gives you the starting cylinder address within that range

```
First cylinder (751-1021):
```

This prompt says that you can start the partition on cylinder 751, or any number up to 1021.

Fdisk determines the smallest starting cylinder in the range and gives that as the first number.

d) What did you choose for the starting cylinder?

_____

_____

The next prompt you see is the following:

```
Last cylinder or +size or +sizeM or +sizeK ([751]-1021):
```

Next, you are prompted for the last cylinder, +size, +sizeM, or +sizeK. Fdisk automatically determines the last cylinder in the range that you can use, which is the very last number shown (in this case, 1021).

But it actually says that the partition can start anywhere from cylinder 751 to cylinder 1021.

You can answer the question by providing any of the following pieces of information:

Address of the last cylinder, which is automatically determined.

- +size, which is the size in bytes

- +sizeM, which is the size in Megabytes

- +sizeK, which is the size in Kilobytes

e) What did you choose for the last cylinder?

_____

_____

Then fill in the appropriate values for the system with which you are working.

In the previous example, a Linux partition was created.

You can now verify that you have the new partition. Do this while in fdisk with the following letter:

```
p
```

This prints out the partitions on /dev/hdb.

f) What kind of results do you get from the p option?

_____

_____

In the previous example, a Linux partition was created. Now you must change the partition type to be swap. So you must change the value for the new partition.

To do this, enter the following response to the fdisk prompt:

```
t
```

This prompts you for the number of the partition you want to modify. You should choose a number from 1 to 4, corresponding to the partition number you chose.

g) What partition number did you enter?

_____

_____

Now you are prompted for the partition type. You can look up the value by just entering the letter 1 at this point, to see the choices you have for partition type.

In this particular case, you are creating a swap partition, so you should enter 82. Go ahead and enter this at the prompt:

h) What happens when you enter 82 as the partition type?

_____

_____

As shown previously, you can verify the partition type with the p command.

> **i)** What do you see when you choose p from the menu?

_____

_____

You must now save the results of creating or modifying the partitions to the partition table. Your results are not saved until you actually write them to disk. This is a good safety precaution, in case you change your mind while you are configuring the disk.

LAB 8.3

Enter the following command:

```
w
```

> **j)** What do you see?

_____

_____

This should get you back to the command line prompt.

Note that you need to reboot Linux in order for the system to properly reset the partition tables.

8.3.3 ENABLE SWAPPING

The first thing you must do is set up the swap format on the partition you chose for swapping. To do this, use the following command:

```
mkswap -c device_name size
```

In this command, device_name is the /dev name of the device you are making into a swap partition.

size is the size you get from the fdisk command.

The -c option will actually go through and do a check for bad blocks.

It is always good practice, on either a drive you have never used before or an older drive, to check for bad blocks. If you have any bad blocks, your disk drive utility will mark them as such and will use another block in their place. If you have bad blocks which are not marked as such, you may have some system problems. This is because the system will write good data to a bad disk area, and when the data is read back, it will be corrupted. This can cause all sorts of problems that might show up as symptoms in some other program.

**LAB
8.3**

a) Enter the mkswap command with the options you need for your chosen partition. What is the command line you entered?

_____

_____

b) What kind of results do you get from the mkswap command?

_____

_____

The mkswap command makes the proper filesystem structure on the partition for swapping. Now you need to enable the swap process to recognize the new swap partition.

To do this, use the following command:

```
swapon device_name
```

Here, the device_name is the /dev name of the partition you have chosen for your swap device.

Enter the swapon command with the appropriate device_name for your system.

c) What kind of results do you get?

_____

_____

8.3.4 PERMANENTLY ENABLE THE SWAP PARTITION

You have now enabled the swap process for your chosen device. However, you must now make it a permanent entry. Otherwise, when you reboot, the swap area will not start up.

Do this by modifying the `/etc/fstab` file. This file is discussed at the beginning of this chapter and in Lab 8.2. So the entry we should be entering is similar to the following entry, which should already exist:

```
/dev/hda4 none swap defaults 0 0
```

Go ahead and create your own mount entry for the new swap area. This entry should look like the following:

```
device_name none swap defaults 0 0
```

The device name is the `/dev` name for the device.

a) What does your `/etc/fstab` file look like now?

_____

_____

b) Which line on your system refers to the new swap area?

_____

_____

Now you should go ahead and reboot your system. Pay attention to any references to the swap area and any error messages.

The following command gives a listing of most things that happen on a boot:

```
dmesg
```

You may want to use the `grep` command to search for swap entries in the output of the dmesg command.

> **c)** Run `dmesg`. Look for entries involving swap. What kind of results do you get?

_____

_____

You have now:

• Deleted a partition.

• Created a swap partition.

• Laid it out for swapping.

• Enabled swapping on it.

• Made it a permanent swap area.

You can now use the same principles you learned in this Lab to create and mount a filesystem with a different filesystem type.

LAB 8.3 EXERCISE ANSWERS

This section gives you some suggested answers to the questions in Lab 7.1, with discussion related to those answers. Your answers may vary, but the most important thing is whether your answer works. Use this discussion to analyze differences between your answers and those presented here.

If you have alternative answers to the questions in this Exercise, you are encouraged to post your answers and discuss them at the companion Web site for this book, located at:

http://www.phptr.com/phptrinteractive

8.3.1 ANSWERS

In order to delete a Linux partition, you must first be sure that it is not mounted. To do this, enter the following command:

```
mount
```

a) What do you see? Is your partition mounted?

Answer: You should see the following display when you enter the mount command:

```
[root@mohawk filesys]# mount
/dev/hda3 on / type ext2 (rw)
/proc on /proc type proc (rw)
/dev/hdb3 on /usr type ext2 (rw)
mohawk:(pid136) on /auto type auto
(intr,rw,port=1023,timeo=8,retrans=110,indire
ct,map=/etc/amd.localdev)
none on /NetWare type nwamd (automounter)
/dev/hdb4 on /mnt type ext2 (rw)
[root@mohawk filesys]#
```

Notice that /dev/hdb4 is mounted. This is the partition with which we will be working for this example.

Unmount the partition in which you are going to work, if it is already mounted.

b) What kind of results did you get?

Answer: You should have just gotten the command line prompt back.
The first thing you need to do is determine the current partition layout of your disks and how much space you have. A good command to start out with is as follows:

```
fdisk -l
```

This gives the current partition layout of your disk drives.

c) What kind of results do you get?

Answer: You should get something similar to the following:

```
Disk /dev/hda: 255 heads, 63 sectors, 527 cylinders
Units = cylinders of 16065 * 512 bytes
```

```
      Device Boot      Begin      Start      End    Blocks     Id   System
/dev/hda1                  1          1      128   1028128+     b   Unknown
/dev/hda2                129        129      390   2104515     82   Unknown
/dev/hda3       *        391        391      499    875542+    83   Linux
native
/dev/hda4                500        500      527    224910     82   Linux
swap
```

```
Disk /dev/hdb: 255 heads, 63 sectors, 1021 cylinders
Units = cylinders of 16065 * 512 bytes

      Device Boot   Begin  Start  End   Blocks     Id   System
/dev/hdb1             1      1    261   2096451     6    DOS 16-bit
>=32M
/dev/hdb2           262    262    515   2040255    82    Unknown
/dev/hdb3           516    516    750   1887637+   83    Linux native
/dev/hdb4           751    751   1021   2176807+   83    Linux native
[root@mohawk filesys]#
```

Find the partition that you created in Lab 8.2. Look at the results in Question (c) of this Exercise to see if your partition is there. If not, you don't need to remove the partition; otherwise, you must remove it by following the next few steps in this Exercise.

d) Did you find your partition? What is it?

Answer: Your results should be similar to the following:

```
/dev/hdb4            751       751    1021  2176807+  83   Linux native
```

This is a Linux native partition, just as we created it to be.

        Enter the following command:

```
fdisk /dev/hdb(Replace the /dev/hdb  with your own drive device)
```

e) What do you see when you enter this command?

Answer: You should have seen the following results:

```
[root@mohawk filesys]# fdisk /dev/hdb
Command (m for help):
```

Now you want to delete the Linux partition you created in the previous lab. At the prompt from the last command, enter the following letter:

```
d
```

From there, you must choose the actual number of the partition.

```
Partition number (1-4):
```

f) What are your results?

Answer: Your results should be as follows:

```
fdisk /dev/hdb
Command (m for help): d
Partition number (1-4): 4
Command (m for help):
```
Print the partition table.

g) Is your partition gone?

Answer: You should no longer see an entry for your partition. In the previous example, the following line would be gone:

```
/dev/hdb4          751     751    1021 2176807+  83  Linux native
```

8.3.2 ANSWERS

You should now be in the `fdisk` command. At the `fdisk` prompt, enter the following letter:

```
n
```

a) What do you get?

Answer: Your results should be as follows:

```
Command (m for help): n
Command action
    e   extended
               p   primary partition (1-4)
```

You will now be asked to choose whether you are creating a primary or extended partition. Linux swap space should be set up as a primary partition.

b) What happens when you choose the partition type?

Answer: *It asks you for the partition number.*

From there you must choose the actual number of the partition. You will see the following prompt:

```
Partition number (1-4):
```

c) What did you specify for the partition number?

Answer: *You should have chosen the partition with which you are working. In the example, partition 4 would be chosen, because it is /dev/hdb4.*

d) What did you choose for the starting cylinder?

Answer: *You should choose the first cylinder on the list, unless you have some reason to reserve the space for another application. In the example system, the starting cylinder was chosen to be 751.*

e) What did you choose for the last cylinder?

Answer: *You should choose the size appropriate to your system. In the example system, the cylinder 1021 has been chosen.*

f) What kind of results did you get from the p option?

Answer: *You should have gotten results similar to the following:*

```
Command (m for help): p

Disk /dev/hdb: 255 heads, 63 sectors, 1021 cylinders
Units = cylinders of 16065 * 512 bytes
```

Device Boot	Begin	Start	End	Blocks	Id	System
/dev/hdb1	1	1	261	2096451	6	DOS 16-bit
>=32M						
/dev/hdb2	262	262	515	2040255	82	Linux swap
/dev/hdb3	516	516	750	1887637+	83	Linux native
/dev/hdb4	751	751	1021	2176807+	82	Linux native

```
Command (m for help):
```

You see that the new swap area is being shown by the line:

```
/dev/hdb4         751    751    1021  2176807+   82   Linux native
```

Notice that the partition type is Linux native, which is type 82.

To change the value for the new partition:

g) What partition number did you enter?

Answer: You should have chosen the partition number that you want to change. In the example system, the partition 4 was chosen.

h) What happens when you enter 82 as the partition type?

Answer: You should have seen the following results on your screen:

```
Command (m for help): t
Partition number (1-4): 4
Hex code (type L to list codes): 82

Command (m for help):
```

As shown previously, you can verify the partition type with the p command.

i) What do you see when you choose p from the menu?

Answer: You should see the same results as when you entered p previously, except that the last line would be as follows:

```
/dev/hdb4         751    751    1021  2176807+   82   Linux swap
```

Enter the following command:
```
w
```

j) What do you see?

Answer: You should see the following:

```
Command (m for help): w
The partition table has been altered!

Calling ioctl() to re-read partition table.
Syncing disks.
Re-read table failed with error 16: Device or resource busy.
```

```
Reboot your system to ensure the partition table is updated.

WARNING: If you have created or modified any DOS 6.x parti-
tions, please see the fdisk manual page for additional infor-
mation.
[root@mohawk filesys]#
```

Notice that once you write the new partition table to the disk, `fdisk` automatically exits.

8.3.3 ANSWERS

a) Enter the `mkswap` command with the options you need for your chosen partition. What is the command line you entered?

Answer: The command line is as follows:

```
mkswap -c /dev/hdb4
```

b) What kind of results do you get from the `mkswap` command?

Answer: You should see the following results:

```
[root@mohawk /root]# mkswap -c /dev/hdb4 2176807
mkswap: warning: truncating swap area to 130752kB
Setting up swapspace, size = 133885952 bytes
[root@mohawk /root]#
```

Notice that even though a swap size of 2176807kB was specified, Linux truncated the size specification and set it to 130752kB.

Enter the `swapon` command with the appropriate `device_name` for your system.

c) What kind of results do you get?

Answer: You should have gotten the following results:

```
[root@mohawk /root]# swapon /dev/hdb4
[root@mohawk /root]#
```

Note that you may get a message that the device is busy. This could mean that the system is already trying to swap to the device. You can just enter the command `swapoff /dev/hdb4`, which disables any swap process that uses `/dev/hdb4`. Then reenter the command `swapon /dev/hdb4`. This will startup the swap process

8.3.4 ANSWERS

Create your own mount entry for the new swap area. This entry should look like the following:

```
device_name none swap defaults 0 0
```

LAB 8.3

a) What does your `/etc/fstab` file look like now?

Answer: You should see a file similar to the following:

```
/dev/hda3 / ext2 defaults 0 1
/proc /proc proc defaults 0 0
/dev/hda4 none swap defaults 0 0
/dev/hdb3 /usr ext2 defaults 0 2
/dev/fd0 /mnt/floppy ext2 defaults,noauto 0 0
/dev/hdc /mnt/cdrom iso9660 ro,noauto 0 0
/dev/hdb4 none swap defaults 0 0
```

Note that your device names may be different. The new swap entry you added should be similar to the last line above.

b) Which line on your system refers to the new swap area?

Answer: You should see a line similar to the following:

```
/dev/hdb4 none swap defaults 0 0
```

The following command will give a listing of most things that happen on a boot: `dmesg`

c) Run `dmesg`. Look for entries involving swap. What kind of results do you get?

Answer: You should have seen two lines similar to the following, one for each swap area. Notice that both swap areas are set to the size 130748. This appears to be the maximum in this configuration.

```
Adding Swap: 130748k swap-space (priority -1)
Adding Swap: 130748k swap-space (priority -2)
```

If you used the grep command, you would have used the command:
`dmesg | grep Swap`

This should show the previous output lines.

LAB 8.3 SELF-REVIEW QUESTIONS

In order to test your progress, you should be able to answer the following questions.

Look in the man pages or the chapter for help on commands. You need to find the best answer to the question. Note that some answers may not be exact replacements. So think about which one comes closest to the results you want. Consider the following results from entering the `mount` command:

```
/dev/hda3 on / type ext2 (rw)
/proc on /proc type proc (rw)
/dev/hdb3 on /usr type ext2 (rw)
mohawk:(pid136) on /auto type auto (intr, rw, port=1023,
timeo=8, retrans=110,indirect,map=/etc/amd.localdev)
none on /NetWare type nwamd (automounter)
```

and the results from the `fdisk -1` **command:**

```
Disk /dev/hda: 255 heads, 63 sectors, 527 cylinders
Units = cylinders of 16065 * 512 bytes
```

Device Boot	Begin	Start	End	Blocks	Id	System
/dev/hda1	1	1	128	1028128+	b	Unknown
/dev/hda2	129	129	390	2104515	82	Unknown
/dev/hda3 *	391	391	499	875542+	83	Linux native
/dev/hda4	500	500	527	224910	82	Linux swap

```
Disk /dev/hdb: 255 heads, 63 sectors, 1021 cylinders
Units = cylinders of 16065 * 512 bytes
```

Device Boot	Begin	Start	End	Blocks	Id	System
/dev/hdb1 >=32M	1	1	261	2096451	6	DOS 16-bit
/dev/hdb2	262	262	515	2040255	82	Unknown
/dev/hdb3	516	516	750	1887637+	83	Linux native
/dev/hdb4	751	751	1021	2176807+	82	Linux swap

1) Which of the following are the swap partitions in the previous display?

    a) _____/dev/hda4 and /dev/hda3
    b) _____/dev/hda4 and /dev/hdb4
    c) _____/dev/hda4 and /dev/hdb2
    d) _____/dev/hda4 and /dev/hdb3
    e) _____None of the above

2) The following command:

```
umount /dev/hdb3
```

LAB 8.3

will unmount the filesystem mounted on which of the following directories?

    a) _____/
    b) _____/proc
    c) _____swap
    d) _____/usr
    e) _____/Netware

3) To make a partition on the slave hard drive on the secondary IDE controller, you would first call `fdisk` by which of the following commands?

    a) _____fdisk /dev/hdb4
    b) _____fdisk /dev/hdd4
    c) _____fdisk /dev/hdd
    d) _____format /dev/hdb
    e) _____format /dev/hdd

4) The following command:

```
mkswap -c /dev/hdc2
```

will make a swap partition on which of the following?

a) _____The master drive on the IDE primary controller
b) _____The slave drive on the IDE primary controller
c) _____The master drive on the IDE secondary controller
d) _____The slave drive on the IDE secondary controller
e) _____None of the above

5) Which of the following is the amount of disk space set aside for the
second swap space in the above display?
   a) _____224910 KB
   b) _____2176807 KB
   c) _____751 MB
   d) _____751 KB
   e) _____500 MB

Quiz answers appear in Appendix A, Section 8.3.

CHAPTER 8

TEST YOUR THINKING

 The projects in this section are meant to have you utilize all of the skills that you have acquired throughout this chapter. The answers to these projects can be found at the companion Web site to this book, located at:

`http://www.phptr.com/phptrinteractive`

Visit the Web site periodically to share and discuss your answers.

1) This chapter has discussed disks and filesystems with an emphasis on IDE/ EIDE devices. You have seen how an IDE device can map to a UNIX device. An example is the master drive on the primary IDE controller being mapped to `/dev/hda`. You should research how, or whether, the SCSI Logical Unit Number and SCSI id have a corresponding exact mapping to the UNIX device name. SCSI hard drives usually have a name similar to /dev/sda, /dev/ sdb, and so forth. SCSI CD-ROMs are usually `/dev/sr0`, `/dev/sr1`, and so forth. Refer to Appendix H for further information about SCSI devices.

2) If you have access to a Solaris system or Solaris documentation, take the concepts discussed in this chapter and figure out what you need to do in Solaris to achieve the same results. You should be able to format and mount a diskette in both UNIX and DOS format and create a mounted UNIX filesystem and swap partition. You will see further discussion on Solaris filesystems in Chapter 10.

3) If you have access to an AIX system or AIX documentation, take the concepts discussed in this chapter and figure out what you need to do in AIX to achieve the same results. You should be able to format and mount a diskette in both UNIX and DOS format and create a mounted UNIX filesystem and swap partition.

4) Experiment with various formats for partitions in Linux. You should consider ext, DOS and minix, among others.

    a) Determine which commands you need to prepare and mount these partitions.

    b) Add these partitions to `/etc/fstab`. Then try mounting them with the mount command, using just the mount point or the `/dev` device.

    c) Reboot your system. See if these partitions are properly mounted.

    d) If you are running a dual or multi-boot system with UNIX and DOS/Windows/Win95/NT, see if you can properly mount the DOS partition. You can do this by rebooting into your alternate Microsoft OS and seeing if there are any problems.

CHAPTER 9

BACKUP AND RESTORE

There was a young lady from Dat,
Whose computer suddenly went flat
To the cupboard she went
The backups to get
When she got there, it was for naught.

— Joe

Having dependable backups is essential for protecting your system. There are many things that can go wrong. Files can be accidentally erased. You can have head crashes on your system disk. Someone can pull the plug accidentally. There can be power outages, misbehaving software and a myriad of other possible problems. Without a solid backup, there may be no way of recovering lost data.

This chapter addresses UNIX backups and restores. The basic concepts of backing up data are very standard from one computer type to another, and even from one operating system to another. It is the actual details that will vary. This is often considered the most important part of your job as an administrator.

Check out the Web site for more pointers on doing system backups:

```
http://www.phptr.com/phptrinteractive
```

EXERCISES FOR THE MASSES

Look in the man pages for the following:

`tar, cpio, mt, rmt, tape`

L A B   9.1

A FILE-BASED BACKUP SYSTEM

LAB OBJECTIVES

After this Lab, you will be able to:

✓ Create a File Archive with `tar`

✓ List the Contents of a `tar` File Archive

✓ Restore Data from a `tar` File Archive

The simplest way to backup files is to another file. This can be done by anyone with write access to a directory. You can even use the `/tmp` directory to create your archive if you don't have enough space in your home directory. The directory `/tmp` is writable by everyone. Just be sure to copy your archive to a safe place, because files in `/tmp` have a tendency to disappear when the administrator is looking for space.

In this Lab, you will explore how to use a file as an archive of multiple files. This will give you some backup for situations where you don't have root access. You also do not need to have access to a tape or diskette backup. This is a safe means of backing up. You will see how to backup files using standard UNIX backup commands to a file archive. You will also learn how to read the archive and restore from the archive.

TAR

You can use the tar command to save files. The tar command is short for `tape archive and restore`. You generally have the same type of abilities or options as you would have with `cpio`, which we will be discussing in Labs 9.2 and 9.3.

tar has been around since almost the beginning of time. Back when dinosaurs roamed the earth, the tar fields... (Oops, wrong book! I should say, since almost the beginning of UNIX. Of course, some of you may measure time since the start of UNIX. Back then, the computer dinosaurs really did roam much of the earth.)

The UNIX tar command has gone through a number of migrations. There are various versions out there, some of which are more or less compatible with others, and some of which stand on their own. If you get error messages when working with files or tapes that have been created with tar from other systems, you should go back to the source of the files or tapes and find out their hardware systems, UNIX versions, tar versions, if possible, and the command options they used.

You can consider `tar` to have the following main options, one of which is required to start your list of options:

-c	create—saves the information in your archive
-x	extract—reads the information from your archive
-t	table of contents—lists the contents of your archive

You can add the following additional options to these commands to get more information:

-f {archive}	Saves the information on the specified archive; if you don't specify a default, Linux will use `/dev/rmt0`
-v	Gives a verbose list of the files processed

There are many other options, but these will get you started. You can add others as you need to.

■ *FOR EXAMPLE:*

To backup all the files in your current directory to the default tape device `/dev/rmt0` and do a verbose listing of the files, use the following:

```
tar  -cv *
```

To backup all the files in your bin directory to a `tar` file, you should use:

```
tar -cvf bin.tar bin
```

This creates the file `bin.tar`, which is a single file containing all the files in your bin directory.

To extract a file called `myfile` from the `bin.tar` file, use the following command:

```
tar -xf bin.tar myfile
```

To backup the files in your `bin` directory, but not the directory itself, to the diskette `/dev/fd0H1440` with a verbose listing, use the following:

```
tar -cvf /dev/fd0H1440 bin/*
```

LAB 9.1 EXERCISES

9.1.1 CREATE A FILE ARCHIVE WITH *TAR*

In this Exercise, you will copy files onto a file archive using the UNIX `tar` command.

When you create a file backup, be sure that the file you are creating is not included in the backup. When that file is saved, it is only partially complete. When you recover the files, the partial archive will overwrite your complete archive. You can create it in the /tmp directory and move it back to one of your directories as soon as possible. The directory /tmp may be cleaned up without notice, since it is only temporary storage.

You should first log in with your normal, non-root userid. Then create a directory that you can use for this chapter's exercises. Do the following from your home directory:

```
mkdir backup
```

You should keep any files from this chapter in this directory, except where noted otherwise. Now you can copy some files into this directory. Copy the following files to your backup directory:

```
/etc/passwd
/etc/hosts
/etc/sendmail.cf  ( you might need to use /usr/lib/send-
mail.cf)
/etc/fstab
/etc/inittab
```

On some systems, read access to certain files in /etc *is restricted. In this case, you will get a message that you are denied access because you don't have the proper access rights. Sometimes files are changed by administrators to be accessible by root only. If you get this error, just choose another file to replace each file you can't access.*

a) What command did you use to copy the files?

_____

_____

Now, do a long listing of files in the backup directory.

b) What command did you use to do a long listing of the directory? What do you see?

_____

_____

Now you are ready to create your file archive. You can use the tar command with the appropriate options to create the archive. Enter the following command:

```
tar -cvf backup.tar backup
```

c) What happens when you do this?

_____

_____

d) Explain the meaning of each option and parameter to the previous tar command.

_____

_____

e) Look at your current directory. What new file do you see?

_____

_____

9.1.2 LISTING THE CONTENTS OF A TAR FILE ARCHIVE

In the previous exercise, you created a `tar` file archive. Now you need to verify the contents of the archive. You can do this with the `tar` command also. You need to find your archive file.

a) What is the name of your archive file?

_____

_____

Suppose your archive file is `backup.tar`. You can use the `tar` command to read its contents. First, use the following command:

```
tar -tf backup.tar
```

b) What kind of results do you get?

_____

_____

c) What is the meaning of each option or parameter to the previous `tar` command?

_____

_____

Now, enter the following command:

```
tar -tvf backup.tar
```

d) What kind of results do you get?

_____

_____

e) How does this differ from the previous command in Question (a) of this Exercise?

_____

_____

f) What does the additional option do?

_____

_____

9.1.3 RESTORING DATA FROM A *tar* FILE ARCHIVE

Now you will restore a file from the file archive. The first thing you must do is remove one of the files in the backup directory.

Remove the `passwd` file, because you should not have gotten any errors in copying this file. Do the following from your home directory:

```
rm backup/passwd
```

a) Did you get any errors?

_____

_____

If you did, be sure to fix them before you go on.

You should now verify that the file is gone. Do a listing of the contents of the backup directory.

b) Is the file still there?

_____

_____

Now you need to restore the missing file from the file archive. Assuming you used the filename `backup.tar`, you can enter the following command:

```
tar -xf backup.tar backup/passwd
```

c) What kind of results do you get?

_____

_____

You need to look in the backup directory to see if the file is restored.

d) Is the file `backup/passwd` restored?

_____

_____

Now add the `-v` option to the `tar` command. Enter the following command:

```
tar -xvf backup.tar backup/passwd
```

e) What do you see on the screen that is different?

_____

_____

f) Did you get any errors?

_____

_____

g) If you got any errors, how would you explain them?

_____

_____

h) If you got any errors, how would you prevent them in the future?

_____

_____

Now you need to verify that the file has been restored.

i) Is the `passwd` file restored in the backup directory?

_____

_____

If not, run through the steps in this Exercise again, and see if you can figure out what went wrong.

LAB 9.1 EXERCISE ANSWERS

This section gives you some suggested answers to the questions in Lab 9.1, with discussion related to those answers. Your answers may vary, but the most important thing is whether or not your answer works. Use this discussion to analyze differences between your answers and those presented here.

If you have alternative answers to the questions in this Exercise, you are encouraged to post your answers and discuss them at the companion Web site for this book, located at:

`http://www.phptr.com/phptrinteractive`

9.1.1 ANSWERS

In this Exercise, you will copy files onto a file archive using the UNIX `tar` command.

a) What command did you use to copy the files?

Answer: You should have used the following command:

```
cp /etc/passwd /etc/hosts /etc/sendmail.cf /etc/fstab
   /etc/inittab backup
```

Now, do a long listing of files in the backup directory.

b) What command did you use to see a long listing of the directory? What do you see?

Answer: You should use the following:

```
ls -l backup
```

The display should be similar to the following:

```
[myid@myserver myid]$ ls -l backup
total 36
-rw-r--r--   1 myid myid      380 Jan 13 15:25 fstab
-rw-r--r--   1 myid myid      117 Jan 13 15:25 hosts
-rw-r--r--   1 myid myid     1726 Jan 13 15:25 inittab
-rw-r--r--   1 myid myid      831 Jan 13 15:25 passwd
-rw-r--r--   1 myid myid    30192 Jan 13 15:25 sendmail.cf
[myid@myserver myid]$
```

Now you are ready to create your file archive. You can use the `tar` command with the appropriate options to create the archive. Enter the following command:

```
tar -cvf backup.tar backup
```

c) What happens when you do this?

Answer: You should get the following results:

```
[myid@myserver myid]$ tar -cvf backup.tar backup
backup/
backup/passwd
backup/hosts
```

```
backup/sendmail.cf
backup/fstab
backup/inittab
[myid@myserver myid]$
```

d) Explain the meaning of each of the options and parameters to the previous `tar` command.

Answer: The command `tar -cvf backup.tar backup` *used the following options and parameters:*

-c	This is used in creating the archive
-v	This is for a verbose listing
-f	This is followed by the actual archive device of file name
backup.tar	This is the name of the archive
backup	This is the name of the directory to be archived

e) Look at your current directory. What new file do you see?

Answer: If you do a directory listing, you will see the name of the archive file you just created. In these exercises, it should be called `backup.tar`.

9.1.2 ANSWERS

a) What is the name of your archive file?

Answer: Your archive from the previous exercise should be called `backup.tar`.

Suppose your archive file is `backup.tar`. You can use the `tar` command to read its contents. First, use the following command:

```
tar -tf backup.tar
```

b) What kind of results do you get?

```
[myid@myserver myid]$ tar -tf backup.tar
backup
backup/passwd
backup/hosts
```

```
backup/sendmail.cf
backup/fstab
backup/inittab
[myid@myserver myid]$
```

c) What is the meaning of each option or parameter to the previous `tar` command?

Answer: In the command `tar -tf backup.tar`, *the options and parameters are as follows:*

-t	This says to just do a listing of the archive
-f	This is followed by the archive name
backup.tar	This is the name of the archive

Now, enter the following command:

```
tar -tvf backup.tar
```

d) What kind of results do you get?

Answer: You will get a result similar to the following:

```
[myid@myserver myid]$ tar -tvf backup.tar
drwxrwxr-x myid/myid 0 1980-01-13 15:25 backup/
-rw-r--r-- myid/myid 831 1980-01-13 15:25 backup/passwd
-rw-r--r-- myid/myid 117 1980-01-13 15:25 backup/hosts
-rw-r--r-- myid/myid 30192 1980-01-13 15:25 backup/sendmail.cf
-rw-r--r-- myid/myid   380 1980-01-13 15:25 backup/fstab
-rw-r--r-- myid/myid  1726 1980-01-13 15:25 backup/inittab
[myid@myserver myid]$
```

e) How does this differ from the previous command in Question (a) of this Exercise?

Answer: It has the option `-v`.

f) What does the additional option do?

Answer: The `-v` *option, when combined with the* `-t` *option, gives an* `ls -l` *listing of the contents of a directory.*

9.1.3 ANSWERS

Do the following from your home directory:

```
rm backup/passwd
```

a) Did you get any errors?

Answer: You should only have gotten errors if you mistyped the command, the directory doesn't exist, or you don't have access to the directory.

If you did, be sure to fix them before you go on.
You should now verify that the file is gone. Do a listing of the contents of the backup directory.

b) Is the file still there?

Answer: The file should be gone by now. If not, be sure that the path to the file you entered is correct, and that you made no typos.

Now, you need to restore the missing file from the file archive. Assuming you used the filename `backup.tar`, you can enter the following command:

```
tar -xf backup.tar backup/passwd
```

c) What kind of results did you get?

Answer: You should see results similar to the following:

```
[myid@myserver myid]$ tar -xf backup.tar backup/passwd
[myid@myserver myid]$
```

You need to look in the backup directory to see if the file is restored.

d) Is the file `backup/passwd` restored?

Answer: A directory listing will show that the file is now back.

Now, add the `-v` option to the tar command. Enter the following command:

```
tar -xvf backup.tar backup/passwd
```

e) What do you see on the screen that is different?

Answer: You should see the following on your screen:

```
[myid@myserver myid]$ tar -xvf backup.tar backup/passwd
backup/passwd
[myid@myserver myid]$
```

You should now see the filename backup/passwd. This did not show up when you left off the −v option.

f) Did you get any errors?

Answer: This will actually overwrite the file you extracted earlier. You should be able to overwrite that file without any message or error.

g) If you got any errors, how would you explain them?

Answer: Errors would typically occur if you had noclobber enabled in your environment, whereby you could not overwrite any files. You might also not have write access to your directory. If your umask is incorrectly set, you might be able to create a directory to which you cannot write.

h) If you got any errors, how would you prevent them in the future?

Answer: By making sure that any files or directories you create can be overwritten when you want to.

Now you need to verify that the file has been restored.

i) Is the passwd file restored in the backup directory?

Answer: The file should be in the backup directory.

LAB 9.1 SELF-REVIEW QUESTIONS

In order to test your progress, you should be able to answer the following questions.

Look in the man pages or in this Lab's text for help on commands. You need to find the best answer to the question. Note that some answers may not be exact replacements. So you need to think about which one comes closest to the results you want.

1) In a large site, it is OK to back up only on an as-needed basis, because large systems never go down.
   a) _____True
   b) _____False

2) Which of the following commands may not backup devices and special files?
   a) _____tar
   b) _____cpio
   c) _____dump
   d) _____dd
   e) _____volcopy

3) It is possible to use a writable or rewritable CD-ROM to backup a Linux system.
   a) _____True
   b) _____False

4) Which of the following commands will read from an archive file called `myarch.cpio` and create directories when necessary?
   a) _____cpio -odv < myarch.cpio
   b) _____cpio -odv > myarch.cpio
   c) _____cpio -idv < myarch.cpio
   d) _____cpio -idv > myarch.cpio
   e) _____None of the above

Quiz answers appear in Appendix A, Section 6.1.

EXERCISES FOR THE GREAT AND SUPER USER

L A B   9.2

A DISKETTE-BASED LINUX BACKUP SYSTEM

LAB OBJECTIVES

After this Lab, you will be able to:

✓ Back Up Files on a Diskette with `cpio`

✓ List Data on the Diskette with `cpio`

✓ Restore Data from the Diskette with `cpio`

In the early days of PCs, when networks were rare and expensive, information was often transferred by diskette. You moved information from system to system by copying it to a diskette, carrying it to the new system, and then reading it into the second system. This was the infamous "sneaker net."

The diskette often served as the main disk when there was no hard disk, or was used as a backup device when 10 MB disk drives were considered a luxury. When you look at the size of files, you will notice that many files with which you work will conveniently fit on a diskette. There are programs and various ways to fit a single file on more then one diskette.

In this Lab, you will explore how to use the diskette as a backup device. This will give you some experience with backups in situations where you do not have a tape backup. It will also help you get some experience in performing backups before you actually use tape drives. In the last chapter on filesystems, you learned how to backup files on diskettes formatted in UNIX or DOS formats. In this chapter, you will see how to backup files using standard UNIX backup commands. You will also see how to read the diskettes and then restore from them. You will generally need to be root to do these exercises, unless your administrator has granted you write access to the diskette drive. If you have a tape drive, you might consider modifying this Lab and Lab 9.3 to use a tape drive instead of diskettes.

**LAB
9.2**

BACKUP DEVICES

Sometimes the hardest thing about doing system backups is knowing which devices and device names to use. Because there are so many devices, it is easy to get lost in the names. Fortunately, there are a few simple rules to follow. Once you know them, it will be a lot easier to do your backups and restores.

DISKETTES

You may have noticed that the diskette in Linux is referred to as `/dev/fd0H1440`, and that the diskette just happens to hold 1.440 MB of data. This is no coincidence. In the device name as shown, the following apply:

- `fd` stands for floppy disk
- `0` is the first diskette device. The second diskette would use the number `1`
- `H` stands for high-density, and is often referred to as 2HD on the diskette boxes
- `1440` stands for 1440 Kilobytes. You will see that a standard high-density diskette, which is 720 Kilobytes, is actually referred to as `/dev/fd0h720`. Using this rule, you can figure out how to refer to almost any kind of diskette. See the "Test Your Thinking" section at the end of this chapter for a project on this issue

TAPES

When backing up to a tape archive on your Linux system, there are several ways to designate your device. In Linux, the tape device connected to the floppy controller is called /dev/ftape. So when you backup to a tape using tar on this tape drive, use the following command:

```
tar -cvf /dev/ftape {files_dirs_other}
```

When using Linux to back up to a SCSI device using tar, use the following:

```
tar -cvf /dev/rst0 {files_dirs_other}
```

where files_dir_other is the list of items to backup.

CPIO

The cpio command takes a number of options. The format of the command can be summarized in the following format, where the archive can be a file or files, directory or directories, or backup devices such as tapes or diskettes. The archive_list can contain files, directories, or special devices:

```
cpio -{options} < {archive_list} > {archive}
```

The options list must start with one of the following three options:

- -i   This is for information that you are reading into your system from archive.
- -o   This is for information that you are saving to your archive.
- -p   This is for information that you are copying from one location to another. It is used for what is considered the pass-through mode. This is very useful for copying the contents of one partition to another.

After the initial options, you can use some of the following additional options. (Note that some of the following options don't make sense with some of the initial ones. You can't make a directory when you are sending output to tape.)

- -B   Set the block size to 5120 bytes. By default, it is 512 bytes. This makes more efficient use of the tape, because there are fewer headers for each tape block.
- -c   The old portable ASCII tape format. This is useful for copying files from one UNIX system to another.
- -d   Make directories when necessary
- -l   Link files instead of copying whenever possible
- -m   Retain the previous file modification times when creating files
- -t   Print a table of contents off the archive. This is useful when you want to see what is on the archive before you copy it.
- -u   Replace unconditionally. Doesn't ask whether you want to replace newer files with older files.
- -v   Do a verbose listing of the information processed. When used with -t, this gives an ls -l format to the output.

LAB
9.2

There are other options which you will see when you do a man listing of cpio, but these options are the ones you will use most often when you use the cpio command. Normally, when you create a cpio archive, you will take the output of a command, such as find, pipe it into cpio, and redirect the output to an archive. You would then see something like the following if you were backing up a directory:

```
find  {dir_name} | cpio -ov >  {archive}
```

With most current versions of find, such as in Linux or Solaris x86, you do not need the -print option. It is understood by default. However, some versions, particularly older versions, need it, in which case you would instead use the command:

```
find {dir_name} -print
```

■ FOR EXAMPLE:

To backup all the files in your bin directory to a file called bin.cpio, use the following command:

```
find bin -print | cpio -o >  bin.cpio
```

To backup all the files in your current directory and all subdirectories to a tape device `/dev/rmt0`, and do a verbose listing, use the following command:

```
find . | cpio -ov > /dev/rmt0
```

To read the list of files from the file archive `bin.cpio` without restoring them, and then get a long listing, use the following command:

```
cpio -itv < bin.cpio
```

To restore files from the tape archive `/dev/rmt0`, use:

```
cpio -iv < /dev/rmt0
```

LAB 9.2 EXERCISES

9.2.1 BACKING UP FILES ON A DISKETTE WITH CPIO

In this Exercise, you will backup files onto a diskette using the UNIX cpio command.

You should first log in with your normal, non-root userid.

If you haven't already made the working directory for this chapter, you should create one by doing the following from your home directory:

```
mkdir backup
```

Note that this Lab will recreate a number of steps from Lab 9.1, except you will do some of it as root, use `cpio` instead of `tar`, and save to a diskette instead of a file.

You should keep any files from this chapter in this directory except where noted otherwise.

Now you can copy some files into this directory. If you haven't already done so in the previous Lab, copy the following files to your backup directory:

```
/etc/passwd
/etc/hosts
/etc/sendmail.cf  ( you might need to use /usr/lib/send-
mail.cf)
/etc/fstab
/etc/inittab
```

**LAB
9.2**

On some systems, read access to certain files in /etc is restricted. In this case, you will get a message that you are denied access because you don't have the proper access rights. Sometimes files are changed by administrators to be accessible by root only. Because you are running this chapter as root, you can just change your id by doing a setuserid to root. Just use the su command, or better still, login as root or do an su - root.

a) What command did you use to copy the files?

_____

_____

Now do a long listing of files in the backup directory.

b) What command did you use, and what do you see?

_____

_____

Now you are ready to create your diskette archive. You can use the cpio command with the appropriate options to create the archive.

You now need to become root. At this point, you can just change your id to root. Do the following command:

```
su
```

c) What kind of changes do you see on the screen?

_____

_____

You must verify that you are in your original, regular userid home directory. To do so, enter the following command:

```
pwd
```

d) What is your current directory?

_____

_____

 If you are not in your original home directory, you must change to your regular login id home directory, but stay as root. Often, your home directory is changed because the su *command has been aliased with the command* su -, *which forces you into the root home directory. In the Korn shell or the bash shell, just type* cd ~myid, *where* myid *is replaced by the name of your login id. If you are in the Bourne Shell, either look up your home directory in the* /etc/passwd *file and change to that directory, or go into the Korn or bash shell and type* cd ~myid, *where* myid *is the name of your login id.*

This Exercise assumes that you are using a 3-1/2" diskette in your systems diskette drive.

Now enter the following command:

```
find backup | cpio -o > /dev/fd0H1440
```

e) What happens when you do this?

_____

_____

f) Explain the meaning of each of command, option, and parameter to the preceding `cpio` command.

_____

_____

_____

_____

9.2.2 LIST DATA THAT IS ON THE DISKETTE WITH CPIO

In the previous exercise, you created a `cpio` file archive. Now you must verify the contents of the archive. You can do this with the `cpio` command also.

a) What is the UNIX device name of your archive device from the previous exercise?

_____

_____

In the previous exercise, you should have used /dev/fd0H1440, but you could use any diskette size recognized by Linux. You can use the `cpio` command to read its contents.

First, use the following command:

```
cpio -it < /dev/fd0H1440
```

b) What kind of results do you get?

_____

_____

c) What is the meaning of each of option or parameter to the preceding `cpio` command?

_____

_____

Next, enter the following command:

```
cpio -itv < /dev/fd0H1440
```

d) What kind of results do you get?

_____

_____

e) How does this differ from the command that follows Question (a) in this Exercise?

_____

_____

f) What does the additional option do?

_____

_____

9.2.3 RESTORE DATA FROM THE DISKETTE WITH CPIO

Now you will restore a file from the diskette archive.

The first thing you must do is remove one of the files in the backup directory. Remove the `passwd` file, because you should not have gotten any errors in copying this file.

Do the following from your home directory:

```
rm backup/passwd
```

a) Did you get any errors?

_____

_____

If you did, be sure to fix them before you continue.

You should now verify that the file is gone. Do a listing of the contents of the backup directory.

b) Is the file still there?

_____

_____

Now you need to restore the missing file from the diskette archive.

Assuming you used the diskette device /dev/fd0H1440, you can enter the following command:

```
cpio -i backup/passwd < /dev/fd0H1440
```

c) What kind of results do you get?

_____

_____

Look in the backup directory to see if the file is restored.

d) Is the file backup/passwd restored?

_____

_____

Now, add the -v option to the cpio command by entering the following command:

```
cpio -iv backup/passwd < /dev/fd0H1440
```

e) What do you see on the screen that is different?

_____

_____

f) Do you get any errors or warning messages?

_____

_____

g) If you got any errors or warning messages, how would you explain them?

_____

_____

h) If you got any errors or warning messages, how would you prevent them in the future?

_____

_____

Go ahead and delete the copy of `backup/passwd`. Then repeat the steps starting after Question (d) of this Exercise.

i) What do you see when you restore the file off the diskette?

_____

_____

Now you must verify that the file has been restored.

j) Is the `passwd` file restored in the backup directory?

_____

_____

If not, review the steps in this Exercise to see if you can figure out what went wrong.

LAB 9.2 EXERCISE ANSWERS

This section gives you some suggested answers to the questions in Lab 9.2, with discussion related to those answers. Your answers may vary, but the most important thing is whether or not your answer works. Use this discussion to analyze differences between your answers and those presented here.

If you have alternative answers to the questions in this Exercise, you are encouraged to post your answers and discuss them at the companion Web site for this book, located at:

```
http://www.phptr.com/phptrinteractive
```

9.2.1 ANSWERS

a) What command did you use to copy the files?

Answer: You should have used the command:

```
cp /etc/passwd /etc/hosts /etc/sendmail.cf /etc/fstab
   /etc/inittab backup
```

Now, do a long listing of files in the backup directory.

b) What command did you use, and what do you see?

Answer: By doing the command:

```
ls -l backup
```

you should see the following:

```
[myid@myserver myid]$ ls -l backup
total 36
-rw-r--r--  1 myid myid     380 Jan 13 15:25 fstab
-rw-r--r--  1 myid myid     117 Jan 13 15:25 hosts
-rw-r--r--  1 myid myid    1726 Jan 13 15:25 inittab
-rw-r--r--  1 myid myid     831 Jan 13 15:25 passwd
```

```
-rw-r--r--  1 myid myid   30192 Jan 13 15:25 sendmail.cf
[myid@myserver myid]$
```
Do the following command:
```
su
```

c) What kind of changes do you see on the screen?

Answer: You will be changing your id to root, so your prompt should change. If you are displaying your userid, that will be the biggest change. You should have seen something similar to the following:

```
[myid@myserver myid]$ su
Password:
[root@myserver myid]#
```
Enter the following command:
```
pwd
```

d) What is your current directory?

Answer: You should be in your home directory for your regular userid. It is usually of the form /home/myid.

Insert a diskette in your system's diskette drive.
Now enter the following command:

```
find backup | cpio -o > /dev/fd0H1440
```

e) What happens when you do this?

Answer: You should have seen results similar to the following:

```
[root@mohawk book]# find backup | cpio -o > /dev/fd0H1440
cpio: backup: truncating inode number
cpio: backup/passwd: truncating inode number
cpio: backup/hosts: truncating inode number
cpio: backup/sendmail.cf: truncating inode number
cpio: backup/fstab: truncating inode number
cpio: backup/inittab: truncating inode number
70 blocks
[root@mohawk book]#
```

This display shows the list of files being added to the cpio diskette archive. The -o option says to send the files out to the backup device. You can ignore the message that says `truncating inode number`. This is just an informational message. The important thing is whether the diskette can be read or not, which you'll see how to do shortly.

f) Explain the meaning of each command, option, and parameter to the preceding `cpio` command.

Answer:The command can be broken down as follows:

LAB
9.2

`find`	This says to find all files, directories, and subdirectories beginning with the specified starting search directory.
`backup`	This says to start with the directory named `backup`.
`cpio`	This says to back up the files with `cpio`.
`-o`	This says to send the files as output to the archive.
`/dev/fd0H1440`	This says that the archive is a 1.44 MB diskette.

9.2.2 ANSWERS

a) What is the UNIX device name of your archive device from the previous exercise?

Answer:The archive device is `/dev/fd0H1440`, which is the 1.44 MB diskette.
First, use the command:

```
cpio -it < /dev/fd0H1440
```

b) What kind of results do you get?

Answer:You should have gotten the following results:

```
[root@mohawk book]# cpio -it < /dev/fd0H1440
backup
backup/passwd
backup/hosts
backup/sendmail.cf
backup/fstab
backup/inittab
70 blocks
[root@mohawk book]#
```

c) What is the meaning of each option or parameter to the preceding cpio command?

Answer: The options or parameters are as follows:

-i	Input from the archive device
-t	Table of contents is listed; don't do an actual restore
/dev/fd0H1440	The diskette

Next, enter the following command:

```
cpio -itv < /dev/fd0H1440
```

d) What kind of results do you get?

Answer: You should see the following results:

```
[root@mohawk book]# cpio -itv < /dev/fd0H1440
drwxr-xr-x 2 root root      0   Jun 6 14:27 backup
-rw-r--r-- 1 root root    768   Jun 6 14:27 backup/passwd
-rw-r--r-- 1 root root   1263   Jun 6 14:09 backup/hosts
-rw-r--r-- 1 root root  30579   Jun 6 14:09 backup/sendmail.cf
-rw-r--r-- 1 root root    251   Jun 6 14:09 backup/fstab
-rw-r--r-- 1 root root   2409   Jun 6 14:09 backup/inittab
70 blocks
[root@mohawk book]#
```

e) How does this differ from the previous command in Question (a) of this Exercise?

Answer: The command you used is:

```
cpio -itv < /dev/fd0H1440
```

The difference is the use of the - v option, which is the verbose option.

f) What does the additional option do?

Answer: It will make an output listing that is the same as the command ls -l.

9.2.3 ANSWERS

Do the following from your home directory:

```
rm backup/passwd
```

a) Do you get any errors?

Answer: You should not have gotten any errors. You may get a message if the file has already been deleted, or if you suddenly lost rights to delete the file. These are minor errors. You should just figure out if the errors are OK. If not, figure out how to get around the problem to delete the file.

Do a listing of the contents of the backup directory.

b) Is the file still there?

Answer: If not, be sure to delete it.

Enter the following command:

```
cpio -i backup/passwd < /dev/fd0H1440
```

c) What kind of results do you get?

Answer: You should just have gotten the command line prompt back. Any errors will be displayed; otherwise, no news is good news.

You need to look in the backup directory to see if the file is restored.

d) Is the file `backup/passwd` restored?

Answer: You should see the file back again. This was recovered from the backup.

Enter the following command:

```
cpio -iv backup/passwd < /dev/fd0H1440
```

e) What do you see on the screen that is different?

Answer: You should see the following on your screen:

```
[root@mohawk book]# cpio -iv backup/passwd < /dev/fd0H1440
cpio: backup/passwd not created: newer or same age version exists
70 blocks
[root@mohawk book]#
```

This command will restore files that are backed up in `backup/passwd` to their original location. Any errors are discussed in the next question.

f) Do you get any errors or warning messages?

Answer: You should have gotten the message about the file not being created, because a file that is newer or of the same age exists.

You can override this with an option -u to replace unconditionally.

g) If you got any errors or warning messages, how would you explain them?

Answer: The `backup/passwd` *file is the same file that was restored in an earlier exercise off the same archive. So* `cpio`, *by default, will not replace the same file with an identical file.*

h) If you got any errors or warning messages, how would you prevent them in the future?

Answer: You should use the `-u` *option to unconditionally overwrite all files.*

i) What do you see when you restore the file off the diskette?

Answer: You should see something similar to the following:

```
[root@mohawk book]# cpio -iv backup/passwd <
/dev/fd0H1440
backup/passwd
70 blocks
[root@mohawk book]#
```

j) Is the passwd file restored in the backup directory?

Answer: The file should now have been restored.

LAB 9.2 SELF-REVIEW QUESTIONS

In order to test your progress, you should be able to answer the following questions.

Look in the man pages or the chapter text for help on commands. You need to find the best answer to the question. Note that some answers may not be exact replacements. So you need to think about which one comes closest to the results you want.

I) Consider the following command:

```
find backup | cpio -ov > /dev/fd1H1440
```

What will this command do?

a) _____Save a file on the second diskette on a system and do a verbose listing

b) _____Save a file on the second diskette on a system and do a verify

c) _____Save a file on the first diskette on a system and do a verbose listing

d) _____Save a file on the first diskette on a system and do a verify

e) _____None of the above

2) Consider the following command:

```
cpio -itv < /dev/fd0H1440
```

What will this command do?

a) _____Read the diskette archive and do a verify of its contents

b) _____Read a file archive and do a short listing of its contents

c) _____Read the diskette archive and do an `ls -l` listing of its contents

d) _____It will read a file archive and do an `ls -l` listing of its contents

e) _____None of the above

3) The `find` command can be used with `cpio` to backup all files and directories under a particular directory.

a) _____True

b) _____False

4) Which of the following commands will read from an archive file called `/dev/fd0H1440` and create directories when necessary?

a) _____`cpio -odv <  /dev/fd0H1440`

b) _____`cpio -odv  > /dev/fd0H1440`

c) _____`cpio -idv < /dev/fd0H1440`

d) _____`cpio -idv > /dev/fd0H1440`

e) _____None of the above

Quiz answers appear in Appendix A, Section 9.2.

L A B   9.3

A DISKETTE-BASED SOLARIS BACKUP SYSTEM

LAB OBJECTIVES

After this Lab, you will be able to:

✓ Backup Files on a Diskette with `cpio`

✓ List Data on the Diskette with `cpio`

✓ Restore Data from the Diskette with `cpio`

This Lab will explore using the diskette as a backup device in Solaris. Lab 9.2 discussed using the diskette as a backup device in Linux. The concepts discussed here are the same as in that lab, but the names have been changed to the real thing for Solaris. These names and concepts can actually be used on other versions of UNIX that are based on UNIX System V release 4. Feel free to modify this lab if you have a tape backup device available.

BACKUP DEVICES

Sometimes the hardest thing about doing system backups is knowing which devices and device names to use. Because there are so many devices, it is easy to get lost in the names. Fortunately, there are a few simple rules to follow. Once you know them, it will be a lot easier to do your backups and restores.

DISKETTES

In Solaris, the diskette drive is called /dev/diskette. Any commands that you would use with a tape drive can also be used with a diskette. One problem you may encounter is that the volume manager may be running. If so, you must disable it. To disable the volume manager, do the following:

LAB 9.3

```
/etc/init.d/volmgt stop
```

When you are ready to start up the volume manager, just enter the following command:

```
/etc/init.d/volmgt start
```

This is actually the command that is executed when you boot up the system. It is executed as /etc/rc2.d/S92volmgt.

TAPES

In Solaris, you are generally restricted to only SCSI tape devices. There is no support for floppy controller-based tape drives or IDE controller-based tape drives. The naming scheme used by Solaris is derived from UNIX System V, and is used on a number of computers by various manufacturers.

When you backup to a SCSI tape drive using tar, use the following designation:

```
tar -cvf /dev/rmt/0m
```

This device name can be broken down as follows:

- /dev stands for a device. All devices are either located or linked into the /dev directory.
- rmt is for a **r**aw **m**agnetic **t**ape device, hence the tape drive name
- 0 is for the first tape drive

- m is for medium-density on the tape drive. The relationship between the letter m and the actual tape density actually varies from one manufacturer to another. As tape densities get higher, a high-density on one tape drive will be a low-density on another. So when you read tapes from another machine and you get I/O errors, differences in tape densities is one of the first things to look for.

LAB 9.3 BACKUP COMMAND

In this Lab, you will use the cpio command. The concepts will be the same as in Lab 9.2, but some of the options and device names will change. You should read the introduction to Lab 9.2 for further details on cpio.

LAB 9.3 EXERCISES

9.3.1 BACKING UP FILES ON A DISKETTE WITH CPIO

In this Exercise, you will back up files onto a diskette using the UNIX cpio command.

You should first log in with your normal, non-root userid.

If you haven't already made the working directory for this chapter, you should create one by doing the following from your home directory:

```
mkdir backup
```

Note that this Lab will recreate a number of steps from Lab 9.1, except you will do some of it as root. Use cpio instead of tar, and save to a diskette instead of a file.

You should keep any files from this chapter in this directory except where noted otherwise.

Now you can copy some files into this directory. If you haven't already done so in the previous Lab, copy the following files to your backup directory:

```
/etc/passwd
/etc/hosts
/etc/mail/sendmail.cf   ( you might need to use /usr/lib/
sendmail.cf)
/etc/vfstab
/etc/inittab
```

On some systems, read access to certain files in /etc is restricted. In this case, you will get a message that you are denied access because you don't have the proper access rights. Sometimes files are changed by administrators to be accessible by root only. Because you are running the Exercises in this chapter as root, you can just change your id by doing a setuserid to root. Just type the su command.

a) What command did you use to copy the files?

_____

_____

Now do long listing of files in the backup directory.

b) What command did you use, and what do you see?

_____

_____

Now you are ready to create your diskette archive. You can use the cpio command with the appropriate options to create the archive.

You now need to become root. At this point, you can just change your id to root. Do the following command:

```
su
```

c) What kind of changes do you see on the screen?

_____

_____

You must verify that you are in your original, regular userid home directory.

Enter the following command:

```
pwd
```

d) What is your current directory?

_____

_____

 Note: If you are not in your original home directory, you must change to your regular login id home directory, but stay as root. Oftentimes your home directory is changed because the su *command has been aliased with the command* su -, *which forces you into the root home directory. In the Korn Shell or the bash shell, just type* cd ~myid, *where* myid *is replaced with the name of your login id. If you are in the Bourne Shell, either look up your home directory in the* /etc/passwd *file and change to that directory, or go into the Korn or bash shell and type* cd ~myid, *where* myid *is the name of your login id.*

This Exercise assumes you are using a 3-1/2" diskette in your system's diskette drive.

Now enter the following command:

```
find backup | cpio -o > /dev/diskette
```

e) What happens when you do this?

_____

_____

If you get the following error when you try to write to the diskette, it means that the volume manager is running and has locked access to the diskette from other programs:

```
ksh: /dev/rdiskette: cannot create
```

Normally you would then access the diskette in volume manager. In order to get around this, just enter the following command:

```
/etc/init.d/volmgt stop
```

This disables the volume manager and allows you to access the diskette. You must be sure that disabling the volume manager does not affect other services and disk access on your system. In order to reenable the volume manager when you are done with this Exercise, use the following command:

```
/etc/init.d/volmgt start
```

f) Explain the meaning of each command, option, and parameter to the `cpio` command.

_____

_____

9.3.2 LIST DATA THAT IS ON THE DISKETTE WITH CPIO

In the previous exercise, we created a `cpio` file archive. Now we need to verify the contents of the archive. Again, we can do this with the `cpio` command.

a) What is the UNIX device name of your archive device from the previous exercise?

_____

_____

In the previous exercise, you should have used /dev/diskette, but you could use any diskette size that is recognized by Solaris.

We can use the cpio command to read its contents. First, let's use the following command:

```
cpio -it < /dev/diskette
```

b) What kind of results do you get?

_____

_____

c) What is the meaning of each option or parameter to the cpio command you entered?

_____

_____

Now enter the following command:

```
cpio -itv < /dev/diskette
```

d) What kind of results do you get?

_____

_____

e) How does this differ from the command that follows Question (a) of this Exercise?

_____

_____

f) What does the additional option do?

_____

_____

9.3.3 RESTORE DATA FROM THE DISKETTE WITH CPIO

Now we will restore a file from the diskette archive. The first thing we need to do is remove one of the files in the backup directory.

**LAB
9.3**

Let's remove the `passwd` file, because you should not have gotten any errors in copying this file.

Do the following from your home directory:

```
rm backup/passwd
```

a) Did you get any errors?

_____

_____

If you did, be sure to fix them before you go on.

You should now verify that the file is gone. Do a listing of the contents of the backup directory.

b) Is the file still there?

_____

_____

Now you need to restore the missing file from the diskette archive.

Assuming you used the diskette device `/dev/diskette`, you can enter the following command:

```
cpio -i backup/passwd < /dev/diskette
```

c) What kind of results do you get?

_____

_____

You need to look in the backup directory to see if the file is restored.

d) Is the file backup/passwd restored?

_____

_____

Now add the -v option to the cpio command. Enter the following command:

```
cpio -iv backup/passwd < /dev/diskette
```

e) What do you see on the screen that is different?

_____

_____

f) Do you get any errors or warning messages?

_____

_____

g) If you got any errors or warning messages, how would you explain them?

_____

_____

h) If you got any errors or warning messages, how would you prevent them in the future?

_____

_____

Now you should go ahead and delete the copy of `backup/passwd`. Then repeat the steps starting after Question (d).

i) What do you see when you restored the file off the diskette?

_____

_____

Now you need to verify that the file has been restored.

j) Is the passwd file restored in the backup directory?

_____

_____

LAB 9.3 EXERCISE ANSWERS

This section gives you some suggested answers to the questions in Lab 9.3, with discussion related to those answers. Your answers may vary, but the most important thing is whether or not your answer works. Use this discussion to analyze differences between your answers and those presented here.

If you have alternative answers to the questions in this Exercise, you are encouraged to post your answers and discuss them at the companion Web site for this book, located at:

`http://www.phptr.com/phptrinteractive`

9.3.1 ANSWERS

You should keep any files from this chapter in the working directory you created, except where noted otherwise.

Now you can copy some files into this directory. If you haven't already done so in the previous lab, copy the following files to your backup directory:

```
/etc/passwd
/etc/hosts
/etc/mail/sendmail.cf (you might need to use /usr/lib/sendmail.cf)
/etc/vfstab
/etc/inittab
```

a) What command did you use to copy the files?

Answer: You should have used the following command:

```
cp /etc/passwd /etc/hosts /etc/mail/sendmail.cf /etc/vfstab /etc/inittab backup
```

Now do a long listing of files in the backup directory.

b) What command did you use, and what do you see?

Answer: You should see the following:

```
$ ls -l backup
total 28
-rw-r--r-- 1 myid staff  157 Jun  6 22:11 hosts
-rw-r--r-- 1 myid staff 1030 Jun  6 22:11 inittab
-r--r--r-- 1 myid staff  668 Jun  6 22:11 passwd
-r--r--r-- 1 myid staff 9197 Jun 6 22:11 sendmail.cf
-rw-r--r-- 1 myid staff  627 Jun  6 22:11 vfstab
$
```

Now you are ready to create your diskette archive. You can use the `cpio` command with the appropriate options to create the archive.

You now need to become root. At this point, you can just change your id to root. Do the following command:

```
su
```

c) What kind of changes did you see on the screen?

Answer: You should have seen something similar to the following:

```
$ su
```

```
Password:
#
```

You must verify that you are in your original, regular userid home directory. Enter the following command:

```
pwd
```

d) What is your current directory?

>*Answer: You should be in your home directory for your regular userid. It is usually of the form* `/home/myid`.

>This Exercise assumes you are using a 3-1/2" diskette in your system's diskette drive.

>Now enter the following command:
>```
>find backup | cpio -o > /dev/diskette
>```

LAB 9.3

e) What happens when you did this?

>*Answer: You should have seen results similar to the following:*

```
# find backup | cpio -o > /dev/diskette
24 blocks
#
```

f) Explain the meaning of each command, option, and parameter to the `cpio` command.

>*Answer: The command is broken up in the following table:*

```
find backup | cpio -o > /dev/diskette
```

`find-`	This command will try to find all files, directories, and sub-directories, beginning with the specified starting search directory
`backup`	This says to start with the directory named `backup`
`cpio`	This is the command to back up the files
`-o`	This says to send the files as output to the archive
`/dev/diskette`	This is the archive (a 1.44 MB diskette)

9.3.2 ANSWERS

a) What is the UNIX device name of your archive device from the previous exercise?

Answer:The archive device is `/dev/diskette`, *which is the 1.44 MB diskette.* Use the following command:

```
cpio -it < /dev/diskette
```

b) What kind of results do you get?

Answer:You should have gotten the following results:

```
# cpio -it < /dev/diskette
backup
backup/passwd
backup/hosts
backup/sendmail.cf
backup/vfstab
backup/inittab
24 blocks
#
```

c) What is the meaning of each option or parameter to the `cpio` command you entered?

Answer:The options or parameters are as follows:

```
cpio -it < /dev/diskette
```

`-i`   Read in from the archive device

`-t`   Do a table of contents, not an actual restore

`/dev/diskette` The diskette

Now enter the following command:

```
cpio -itv < /dev/diskette
```

d) What kind of results do you get?

Answer: You should see the following results:

```
# cpio -itv < /dev/diskette
drwxr-xr-x    2 myid staff    0    Jun  6 22:11 1998, backup
-r--r--r--    1 myid staff   668  Jun  6 22:11 1998, backup/passwd
-rw-r--r--    1 myid staff   157  Jun  6 22:11 1998, backup/hosts
-r--r--r--    1 myid staff  9197 Jun  6 22:11 1998, backup/send-
mail.cf
-rw-r--r--    1 myid staff   627  Jun  6 22:11 1998, backup/vfstab
-rw-r--r--    1 myid staff  1030 Jun  6 22:11 1998, backup/init-
tab
24 blocks
#
```

e) How does this differ from the command that follows Question (a) of this Exercise?

Answer: The command you used is:

```
cpio -itv < /dev/diskette
```

The difference is the use of the t *option.*

f) What does the additional option do?

Answer: This will make an output listing that is the same as the command ls -l.

9.3.3 ANSWERS

Do the following from your home directory:

```
rm backup/passwd
```

a) Did you get any errors?

Answer: You should not have gotten any errors. You may get a message if the file has been already been deleted, or if you suddenly lost rights to delete the file. These are minor errors. You should figure out if the errors are OK. If not, figure out how to get around the problem to delete the file.

Do a listing of the contents of the backup directory.

b) Is the file still there?

Answer: If not, be sure to delete it.

Assuming you used the diskette device /dev/diskette, you can enter the following command:

```
cpio -i backup/passwd < /dev/diskette
```

c) What kind of results do you get?

Answer: You should get the following:

```
# cpio -i backup/passwd < /dev/diskette
24 blocks
#
```

You need to look in the backup directory to see if the file is restored.

d) Is the file backup/passwd restored?

Answer: You should see the file back again.

Enter the following command:

```
cpio -iv backup/passwd < /dev/diskette
```

e) What do you see on the screen that is different?

Answer: You should see the following on your screen:

```
# cpio -iv backup/passwd < /dev/diskette
cpio: Existing "backup/passwd" same age or newer
24 blocks
1 error(s)
#
```

f) Did you get any errors or warning messages?

Answer: You should have gotten an error message about the file not being created because a file that is newer or of the same age exists. You can override this with the option -u to replace unconditionally.

g) If you got any errors or warning messages, how would you explain them?

Answer: The backup/passwd file is the same file that was restored in an earlier exercise off the same archive. So cpio, by default, will not replace the same file with an identical file.

h) If you got any errors or warning messages, how would you prevent them in the future?

Answer:You should use the −u *option to unconditionally overwrite all files.*
Now you should go ahead and delete the copy of `backup/passwd`. Then repeat the steps starting after Question (d).

i) What do you see when you restored the file off the diskette?

Answer:You should see something similar to the following:

```
# cpio -iv backup/passwd < /dev/diskette
backup/passwd
24 blocks
#
```

j) Is the `passwd` file restored in the backup directory?

Answer:The file should now have been restored.

LAB 9.3 SELF-REVIEW QUESTIONS

In order to test your progress, you should be able to answer the following questions. Look in the man pages or the chapter for help on commands. You need to find the best answer to the question. Note that some answers may not be exact replacements. So you need to think about which one comes closest to the results you want.

1) Consider the following command:

```
find backup | cpio -ov > /dev/diskette
```

Which of the following will this do:
a) _____Save a file on the second diskette on a system and do a verbose listing
b) _____Save a file on the second diskette on a system and do a verify
c) _____Save a file on the first diskette on a system and do a verbose listing
d) _____Save a file on the first diskette on a system and do a verify
e) _____None of the above

2) Consider the following command:

```
cpio -itv < /dev/diskette
```

Which of the following will this do:
a) _____Read the diskette archive and do a verify of its contents
b) _____Read a file archive and do a short listing of its contents
c) _____Read the diskette archive and do an `ls -l` listing of its contents
d) _____Read a file archive and do an `ls -l` listing of its contents
e) _____None of the above

3) The find command can be used with cpio to backup all files and directories under a particular directory.
a) _____True
b) _____False

4) Which of the following commands will read from an archive file called `/dev/diskette` and create directories when necessary:
a) _____`cpio -odv <  /dev/diskette`
b) _____`cpio -odv  > /dev/diskette`
c) _____`cpio -idv < /dev/diskette`
d) _____`cpio -idv > /dev/diskette`
e) _____None of the above

Quiz answers appear in Appendix A, Section 6.1.

CHAPTER 9

TEST YOUR THINKING

 The projects in this section are meant to have you utilize all of the skills that you have acquired throughout this chapter. The answers to these projects can be found at the companion Web site to this book, located at:

`http://www.phptr.com/phptrinteractive`

Visit the Web site periodically to share and discuss your answers.

1) In Linux, look in the `/dev` directory for definitions for diskette devices. See if you can correlate the device names with floppy sizes you are used to or can buy off the shelf. You can focus on the definitions for diskettes with capacities of 360, 720, 1200, 1440, 2880 Kilobytes. Try to figure out as many of the remaining floppy definitions as possible. (This may require some extensive research into the history of PCs and Linux, so be prepared.)

2) Repeat the backup exercise that uses `tar` to a file, but this time use the `cpio` command. Name the file with the extension `cpio` (for example `myfile.cpio`.) Get a listing of what is in the archive file. Then restore one of the files in the archive. What happens if you try to restore this file and it currently exists?

3) In Linux, repeat Lab 9.2, but this time use the `tar` command. Try it first with a filesystem that will fit on one floppy. Then try it with a filesystem that is bigger than one floppy. (Usually `/etc` will do.) What do you get? Why does this happen? How can you work around it and still use `tar` to back up filesystems bigger than one diskette?

4) In Solaris, repeat Lab 9.2, but this time use the `tar` command. Try it first with a filesystem that will fit on one floppy. Then try it with a filesystem that is bigger than one floppy. (Usually `/etc` will do.) What do you get? Why does this happen? How can you work around it and still use tar to backup filesystems bigger than one diskette?

5) If you have access to an AIX system or AIX documentation, explain what it would take to use `tar` and `cpio` to copy files to a diskette.

6) In Linux, experiment with various options or combinations of UNIX commands so you can use `cpio` and `tar` to store more data than 1.440 MB on a diskette. Explain at least two of the different commands you came up with.

7) In Solaris, experiment with various options or combinations of UNIX commands so you can use `cpio` and `tar` to store more data than 1.440 MB on a diskette. Explain at least two of the different commands you came up with.

8) If you have access to an AIX system, experiment with various options or combinations of UNIX commands so you can use `cpio` and `tar` to store more data than 1.440 MB on a diskette.

9) Repeat Lab 9.2 in Linux and `cpio`, but this time use a tape drive instead of a diskette drive. At a minimum, show all the commands you would have to modify to use the tape drive. Answer all questions based on using the tape drive. If you don't have a tape drive, just write out your answers.

10) Repeat Lab 9.3 in Solaris and `cpio`, but this time use a tape drive instead of a diskette drive. At a minimum, show all the commands you would have to modify to use the tape drive. Answer all questions based on using the tape drive. If you don't have a tape drive, just write out your answers.

11) Repeat Lab 9.2 in Linux, but this time use a tape drive instead of a diskette drive. Also, use `tar` instead of `cpio`. At a minimum, show all the commands you would have to modify to use the tape drive. Answer all questions based on using the tape drive. If you don't have a tape drive, just write out your answers.

12) Repeat Lab 9.3 in Solaris, but this time use a tape drive instead of a diskette drive. Also, use `tar` instead of `cpio`. At a minimum, show all the commands you would have to modify to use the tape drive. Answer all questions based on using the tape drive. If you don't have a tape drive, just write out your answers.

C H A P T E R 10

SOLARIS FILESYSTEMS

Understanding your hard disk layout can make life as an administrator less hectic. When you are in a time crunch, you don't want to think about how to rebuild the system and where to put things. Also, a well-organized hard disk can be an asset in accessing your data. If the disk is poorly organized, it can lead to a much less efficient and more time-consuming system.   *— Joe*

CHAPTER OBJECTIVES

In this Chapter, you will learn about:

Exercises for the Great and Super User

This chapter addresses Solaris disks and filesystems. The concepts you learned in the chapter on Linux can be applied to Solaris. The difference is how you implement them. Solaris has some features that are unique to Solaris. Solaris x86 also adds the ability to do `fdisk` type commands similar to the DOS version, only not as extensive. However, when you add the Solaris `format` command to the Solaris `fdisk` command, you can end up with the same result.

You should review the discussion at the start of Chapter 8, "Disks and Filesystems." Most of the basic concepts discussed there will apply to Solaris as well. This chapter will emphasize areas that are unique to Solaris.

You still need to be root to work with the Solaris filesystems. Solaris, if anything, is a little more restrictive than Linux.

EXERCISES FOR THE GREAT AND SUPER USER

Look in the Solaris man pages for the following:

```
fdisk, fsck, mount, mkfs, format, newfs, fdformat,
vfstab, mount_ufs, mount_pcfs, rmt
```

SOLARIS DISK NAMING CONVENTION

Solaris recognizes several types of hard disk hardware. Because PC hardware has become the predominant computer hardware format, Solaris has been adapted to recognize these new versions. Solaris supports at least three different CPU hardware versions: Sparc, Intel, and PowerPC (though the PowerPC is not currently supported with new versions). Conversely, Linux will work with Sparc, as well as Intel and PowerPC architectures. Solaris is generally more restrictive in terms of the devices it will handle than Linux, but it supports IDE/EIDE, SCSI, and more advanced current drive types that work with PCs.

You should review the basic EIDE/IDE disk concepts. Solaris uses the naming convention that was developed with UNIX System V Release 4, whereas Linux uses a naming convention derived from BSD UNIX and other older versions of UNIX.

Solaris uses the /dev directory location that is standard to all versions of UNIX. However, all the devices there are linked to the /devices directory, where the naming scheme more closely reflects the lower-level hardware architecture on the computer. That naming scheme is very complicated and is not discussed here. We will look at the standard `/dev` directory scheme.

IDE/EIDE

The naming schemes for EIDE/IDE and SCSI are different in Solaris. In Solaris, you will follow this naming scheme for IDE:

```
cXdYsZ
```

The following explains this further:

- X represents the controller number. The computer can handle multiple EIDE/IDE controllers. Each one is assigned a number, starting at 0. The primary disk controller on the PC is considered to be c0, whereas the secondary disk controller is considered to be c1.
- Y is the drive number. The master drive is called d0, whereas the slave drive is d1.
- Z is the slice number, which is usually called the partition number. Partition 0 is called s0, partition 1 is s1, and so on.

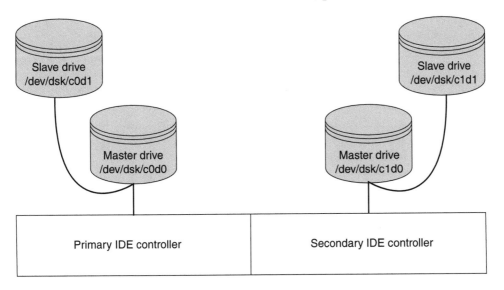

Figure 10.1 ■ Drive Layout for IDE/EIDE Drives in Solaris

You will notice that Solaris assigns the devices' designations in the following sequence:

- `/dev/dsk/c0d0`—Master drive on primary IDE controller
- `/dev/dsk/c0d1`—Slave drive on primary IDE controller
- `/dev/dsk/c1d0`—Master drive on secondary IDE controller
- `/dev/dsk/c1d1`—Slave drive on secondary IDE controller

SCSI

In Solaris, the SCSI naming scheme is as follows:

```
cWtXdYsZ
```

The following explains this further:

- W represents the controller number. The computer can handle multiple SCSI controllers. Each one is assigned a number, starting at 0. The first disk controller on the PC is considered to be c0, the second disk controller is considered to be c1, and so forth.
- X is the physical bus target number; on SCSI controllers this is set by the switch on the back of the unit. This is generally called the SCSI id.
- Y is the drive number. The master drive is called d0, whereas the slave drive is d1. Note: one SCSI ID can handle multiple drives.
- Z is the slice number, which is usually called the partition number. Partition 0 is called s0, partition 1 is s1, and so on.

The following points must be considered when working with systems.

1. If the volume manager is running, you may have a problem in so some of the exercises in this chapter. You will get a message that the diskette drive is busy. As root, you can enter the command `/etc/init.d/volmgt stop`. *This will disable the volume manager. When you want to start it up again, just enter the* `command /etc/init.d/volmgt start`.

2. If you want to permanently disable the volume manager, you can disable this by first moving the file `/etc/rc2.2/S92volmgt` *and any links to it out of the* `/etc/rc*`, *or* `/etc/init.d` *directories. Remember that any files in the* `rc` *or* `init` *directories will be started in the appropriate run levels, so don't keep your backups there.*

3. Occasionally you will get a message that you cannot format the diskette because it is busy. You can often get rid of this message and format the diskette by entering the command `eject floppy`. *You will get a message that it is OK to eject the floppy. At this point, just enter* `<ctrl-c>`, *which will give you back the # prompt. You do not need to actually eject the diskette.*

REBOOT

Once any changes are made to the system involving disks and filesystem, you might want to reboot the system. In UNIX, reboots are usually not required, but if you want to be sure that everything mounts and checks out, you should do a reboot after everything is done.

L A B   10.1

MAKING A DISKETTE-BASED SOLARIS FILESYSTEM

LAB OBJECTIVES

After this Lab, you will be able to:

✓ Create and Mount a UFS Filesystem Diskette

✓ Create and Mount an MS-DOS Filesystem Diskette

In this Lab, you will learn how to format a floppy diskette, make either a UNIX or DOS format on it and then mount it under your Solaris system. You will then copy a file to the diskette mounted filesystem.

MAKE A USABLE DISKETTE

It is easier in Solaris to understand filesystems if you start by working on and practicing with the diskette. You can mess up a diskette without fear of harming the rest of your system. Once you understand the diskette, you will feel more confident about working with the filesystems on the hard disk. To make a filesystem on a diskette, you must do the following:

1. Insert the diskette into the diskette drive.
2. Create a directory mount-point from which you are going to mount the diskette. This can be a directory anywhere

you want, but is typically a directory under root, or one level down. You can name the directory something like / floppy, /mnt/floppy, or whatever is convenient for you. Just don't use an existing mount point.

3. Format the diskette with the fdformat command. Do this as follows:

```
fdformat
```

This will default to the first diskette drive on your system. This is the one known as drive a: in DOS. If the diskette is mounted either automatically by the file manager or manually, you will need to unmount it first. You can unmount and format in one step with the fdformat -U command. If you want to format the diskette with another filesystem type, you can specify several options, which you can look up in the man pages. If you want to create a DOS filesystem on the diskette, use the command:

```
fdformat -d
```

4. Create a filesystem on the diskette. Do this with the newfs command. Enter it as follows:

```
newfs /dev/rdiskette
```

This will make a ufs filesystem on the diskette. If you are going to mount a DOS diskette, you can skip this step.

5. Next, the diskette must be mounted on some mount point. If you are using the ufs-created diskette, just enter the following command:

```
mount /dev/diskette mount-point
```

Here, mount-point is the directory mount point that you created to mount the diskette.
If the diskette is a DOS format, otherwise known in Solaris as pcfs, you can use the following command

```
mount -F pcfs /dev/diskette mount-point
```

Here, mount-point is the directory mount point that you created to mount the diskette.

When you unmount the diskette, you can use either the directory name or the mount point, so both of the following commands work:

```
umount /dev/diskette
umount mount-point
```

LAB 10.1 EXERCISES

10.1.1 CREATE AND MOUNT A UFS FILESYSTEM DISKETTE

This Exercise will create and make accessible to you a diskette with the `ufs` filesystem on it. This is the default Solaris format.

 This exercise assumes you are using a 3-1/2" 1.44 MB diskette.

Insert a diskette into your Solaris systems diskette drive. Now, enter the following command:

```
fdformat
```

a) What kind of results do you get? How did you handle any errors?

_____

_____

This does a low-level format on the diskette.

You can now create a filesystem with the `newfs` command by entering the following:

```
newfs /dev/rdiskette
```

b) What kind of results do you get? Describe them.

_____

_____

Now you have made a UNIX `ufs` filesystem on a diskette.

Once you create a filesystem under UNIX, it is important that you check it. To do so, enter the following command:

```
fsck /dev/rdiskette
```

c) What are your results?

_____

_____

Now you can mount the diskette. You first must have a directory to mount it under.

For the purposes of this Exercise, you can create the `/floppy` directory to mount diskettes. Just use the following command:

```
mkdir /floppy
```

This makes the `/floppy` directory if it doesn't exist, and creates the `/floppy` mount point.

d) What kind of results do you get?

_____

_____

Now you can enter the following command:

```
mount /dev/diskette /floppy
```

e) What kind of results do you get?

_____

_____

f) Why did you use the /dev/diskette device to mount the floppy, whereas you used the /dev/rdiskette device for fdformat and fsck?

_____

_____

You can check to see if the diskette is mounted by entering the following command:

```
mount
```

g) What kind of description do you see about the diskette?

_____

_____

This makes your diskette accessible under the /floppy directory.

Now just copy a file to the diskette by typing the following:

```
cp /etc/passwd /floppy
```

h) What do you see?

_____

_____

Now do the following command:

```
ls -l /floppy
```

i) What do you get?

_____

_____

Now you must unmount the diskette.

Type the following command:

```
umount /floppy
```

Alternatively, the following will work:

```
umount /dev/diskette
```

Now type the following command:

```
mount
```

j) What kind of description do you see about the diskette?

_____

_____

It is important to unmount a diskette before removing it. While PCs do not prevent you from unmounting a diskette, the system sometimes gets confused if you do a subsequent mount. Sometimes it lets you do the mount, but remembers the previous mount table on the earlier diskette, so it causes the system to create an error. I have even seen it copy directory information from the previous diskette on the new diskette, without it being obvious. Occasionally, it works OK.

With Solaris, you can use the command `eject floppy` *to unmount and eject the floppy. If you have a diskette drive that does not automatically eject, you must manually eject the floppy. The program may sit there and wait for a response. You may also need to enter* `<ctrl-c>` *to kill the process, so you can get your command line prompt back.*

You can now remove the diskette.

You have created a Solaris ufs formatted diskette, mounted it, copied a file to it, and then unmounted it.

10.1.2 CREATE AND MOUNT AN MS-DOS FILESYSTEM DISKETTE

This Exercise will create and make accessible to you a diskette that has an MS-DOS filesystem on it.

Making an MS-DOS formatted diskette will have all the limitations of an MS-DOS filesystem, including names with up to eight characters and extensions of up to three characters, otherwise known as the 8.3 format.

The steps used to create this diskette are similar, but not identical to the steps used in creating a UFS formatted diskette under Solaris.

Solaris will detect whether you are using a 1.44 MB 3-1/2" diskette. If you are using a higher or lower density diskette, you must use the appropriate option. You can find the various options by doing a man fdformat. *This Exercise assumes you are using a 3-1/2" 1.44 MB diskette.*

Insert a diskette in your Solaris system's diskette drive.

You can use the command fdformat to create an MS-DOS formatted diskette and create an MS-DOS filesystem on it. To do that, enter the following command:

```
fdformat -d
```

Alternatively, the following command will work:

```
fdformat -t dos
```

a) What kind of results do you get?

_____

_____

Note that the fsck *command in Solaris will not work on MS-DOS filesystems, because MS-DOS has a very different filesystem structure than UNIX. The command* fsck *needs to look at an unmounted filesystem at a very low level.*

Now you can mount the diskette.

First you need a directory under which to mount it. For this Exercise, you can just create a directory called /dos.

You may also need to create the directory where you will mount it. Just use the following command:

```
mkdir /dos
```

b) What kind of results do you get?

_____

_____

This makes the /dos directory, if it doesn't already exist, and the /dos directory mount point.

Now you can enter the following command:

```
mount -F pcfs /dev/diskette /dos
```

c) What kind of results do you get?

_____

_____

You can check to see if the drive is mounted by entering the following command:

```
mount
```

d) What kind of description do you see about the diskette?

_____

_____

This makes your diskette accessible under the /dos directory.

Now just copy a file to the diskette by typing the following:

```
cp /etc/passwd /dos
```

e) What do you see?

_____

_____

Now do the command:

```
ls -l /dos
```

f) What do you get?

_____

_____

Now you must unmount the diskette.

Type the following command:

```
umount /dos
```

Alternatively, the following command will work:

```
umount /dev/diskette
```

g) What do you see?

_____

_____

Now type the following command:

```
mount
```

h) What kind of description do you see about the diskette?

You can now remove the diskette.

You have created an MS-DOS formatted diskette, mounted it, copied a file to it, and then unmounted it

LAB 10.1 EXERCISE ANSWERS

This section gives you some suggested answers to the questions in Lab 10.1, with discussion related to those answers. Your answers may vary, but the most important thing is whether or not your answer works. Use this discussion to analyze differences between your answers and those presented here.

If you have alternative answers to the questions in this Exercise, you are encouraged to post your answers and discuss them at the companion Web site for this book, located at:

```
http://www.phptr.com/phptrinteractive
```

10.1.1 ANSWERS

Insert a diskette into your Solaris system's diskette drive and enter the following command:
    fdformat

a) What kind of results do you get? How did you handle any errors?

Answer: You should see the following results:

```
# fdformat
fdformat: /dev/rdiskette is mounted (use -U flag)
# fdformat -U
Formatting 1.44 MB in /dev/rdiskette
Press return to start formatting floppy.
```

. . . .
. . . .
#

The `fdformat` first tells you that this diskette is mounted. It cannot format a diskette that is mounted, so the `fdformat` `-U` command will unmount the diskette while it is being formatted. It then tells you the size of the diskette.

Enter the following:

```
newfs /dev/rdiskette
```

b) What kind of results do you get? Describe them.

Answer:You should get the following display on your screen:

```
# newfs /dev/rdiskette
newfs: construct a new file system /dev/rdiskette: (y/n)? y
/dev/rdiskette: 2880 sectors in 80 cylinders of 2 tracks, 18
  sectors
        1.4MB in 5 cyl groups (16 c/g, 0.28MB/g, 128 i/g)
super-block backups (for fsck -F ufs -o b=#) at:
 32, 640, 1184, 1792, 2336,
#
```

First you are asked whether you want to create a new filesystem. Then it returns the device name with the diskette characteristics—2880 sectors, which result from 80 cylinders of two tracks with 18 sectors each.

In UNIX, a filesystem is referred to by a number known as the `inode number`. Each disk slice has its own set of inode numbers. The inode number and file information are stored in a part of the disk called the `super-block`. Every piece of information about a file is stored there, except the file name, which is stored on the disk in the filesystem. Thus you can have hard links, because several names can point to a single inode number. You can find the inode number by doing the command `ls` `-i`. The data is stored on the disk in blocks. The disk is formatted in `physical blocks` which are generally 512 bytes in size. `Physical` `blocks` are then grouped into `logical` blocks, which are generally 1024 bytes. Oftentimes `logical blocks` are part of larger groups. In AIX, these are called `physical` and `logical` `partitions`, which are separate concepts from partitions in AIX. Other versions of UNIX may call them `cyl-`

`inder groups`. You may have seen this concept in DOS and Windows, which divide the disk into `clusters`.

Enter the following command:

```
fsck /dev/rdiskette
```

c) What are your results?

Answer:You should see the following:

```
# fsck /dev/rdiskette
** /dev/rdiskette
** Last Mounted on
** Phase 1 - Check Blocks and Sizes
** Phase 2 - Check Pathnames
** Phase 3 - Check Connectivity
** Phase 4 - Check Reference Counts
** Phase 5 - Check Cyl groups
2 files, 9 used, 1254 free (14 frags, 155 blocks,  1.1%
fragmentation)
#
```

It first tells you the name of the raw device you are checking. If it has been previously mounted, it will give you the mount point following the "`** Last Mounted on`" line. Then it checks for filesystem consistency and reconciles differences in the inode tables. The final messages tell you how many files exist. Note that there are some hidden directories counted in the total.

The `fsck` command is very important to the administrator. It is one of those tools you should learn to use early in the game. It allows you to check your newly created or existing filesystem for inconsistencies. It works like `chkdsk` in DOS/Windows. It can check for things such as inodes that have no names associated with them. It can check whether an inode is listed in the table of free inodes, and check for inodes that are in use. It checks for an actual file's size and the reported size of the file in the superblock. It reports inconsistencies in those numbers.

Enter the following command:

```
mkdir /floppy
```

d)   What kind of results did you get?

Answer: You should not get any errors. Two possible causes are:
- You are not root
- The directory exists

Now you can enter the following command:

```
mount /dev/diskette /floppy
```

e)   What kind of results did you get?

Answer: You should not get any messages, and should only get the # prompt back. Check the possible errors in the answer to Question (c) to see what the causes might be.

f)   Why did you use the /dev/diskette device to mount the floppy, whereas you used the /dev/rdiskette device for `fdformat` and `fsck`?

Answer: /dev/rdiskette is the raw partition and is character- and byte-based, whereas /dev/diskette is based on physical blocks.

You cannot mount a disk until it has a blocked structure and filesystem. That is the purpose of `fdformat`, which will lay out a block structure on the diskette. The layout will be 512 bytes per physical block. The command `newfs` will create logical blocks consisting of several physical blocks. It will also add operating system-specific information on the partition, which will then allow you to mount it. The `fsck` command works on both raw and blocked disks.

You can check to see if the diskette is mounted by entering the command:

```
mount
```

g)   What kind of description do you see about the diskette?

Answer: You should see a line similar to the following when you enter the `mount` command:

```
/floppy on /dev/diskette setuid/read/write/largefiles on Mon Jul
6 20:45:29 1998
```

Note that several options are listed. They are: `setuid`, `read`, `write` and `largefiles`. You can look up the meaning of these by doing the man page on `mount_ufs`.

Now just copy a file to the diskette by typing the following:

```
cp /etc/passwd /floppy
```

h) What do you see?

Answer: You should not see anything on your screen other then the prompt.
Now do the following command:

```
ls -l /floppy
```

i) What do you get?

Answer: You should see the following:

```
# ls -l /floppy
total 18
drwx------   2 root      root        8192 Jul  6 20:24 lost+found
-r--r--r--   1 root      other        668 Jul  6 21:10 passwd
#
```

Type the following command:

```
umount /floppy
```

Now type the following command:

```
mount
```

j) What kind of description do you see about the diskette?

Answer: You should not see any description for the floppy if you have properly unmounted it. If you do, just retrace the steps above and see if you skipped a step or missed an error message.

10.1.2 ANSWERS

Enter the following command:

```
fdformat -d
```

a) What kind of results do you get?

Answer: You should see the following:

```
# fdformat -d -U
Formatting 1.44 MB in /dev/rdiskette
Press return to start formatting floppy.
```

. . . .

Note that the `fdformat` used the `-U` option to unmount the diskette before it was formatted.

Next, you created a directory called /dos using the following command:

```
mkdir /dos
```

b) What kind of results do you get?

Answer: You should just get your command line prompt back.
Now you can enter the following command:

```
mount -F pcfs /dev/diskette /dos
```

c) What kind of results did you get?

Answer: You should just get the command line prompt back.

Note that the option `-F pcfs` says that the diskette should be mounted as a `pcfs` filesystem. This is a DOS disk format.

You can check to see if the drive is mounted by entering the following command:

```
mount
```

d) What kind of description do you see about the diskette?

Answer: You should see the following:

```
/dos on /dev/diskette read/write/nohidden/nofoldcase on Mon Jul  6
21:26:34 1998
```

Note that the diskette now has the options: `read, write, nohidden, nofoldcase.` *You can find the meaning of these options by running* `man mount_pcfs.`

Now just copy a file to the diskette by typing the following:

```
cp /etc/passwd /dos
```

e) What do you see?

Answer: You should only get the command prompt back. If you get any errors, you should look at access and file rights, and determine whether the file already exists.

Now do the following command:

```
ls -l /dos
```

f) What do you get?

Answer: You should get a listing of the files in the /dos *directory as follows:*

```
total 2
-r-xr-xr-x   1 root      other          668 Jul  6 21:47
passwd
#
```

Note that you have the access rights of read and execute/access for the owner, all users and the group; however, the diskette is DOS-formatted. When you mount this diskette under DOS/Windows, these rights are not necessarily the same as in DOS.

Type the following command:

```
umount /dos
```

g) What do you see?

Answer: You will just get command line prompt back.

Now type the following command:

```
mount
```

h) What kind of description do you see about the diskette?

Answer: You will not get any description for the diskette, because it is now unmounted. If you do, retrace your steps.

LAB 10.1 SELF-REVIEW QUESTIONS

In order to test your progress, you should be able to answer the following questions. Look in the man pages or the chapter for help on commands. You need to find the best answer to the question. Note that some answers may not be exact replacements. Think about which comes closest to the results you want.

1) Solaris will only work with SCSI devices.
   a) _____True
   b) _____False

2) If you have an IDE disk that is the slave device on the secondary controller, this will be considered to be the Solaris device called:
   a) _____/dev/dsk/c0d0
   b) _____/dev/dsk/c0d1
   c) _____/dev/dsk/c1d0
   d) _____/dev/dsk/c1d1
   e) _____None of the above

3) A hard disk that is configured to be the slave device on the primary IDE controller is which of the following Linux devices?
   a) _____/dev/dsk/c0d0
   b) _____/dev/dsk/c0d1
   c) _____/dev/dsk/c1d0
   d) _____/dev/dsk/c1d1
   e) _____None of the above

4) It is possible to use the floppy controller to attach a tape backup in Solaris.
   a) _____True
   b) _____False

5) The command `fdformat -D` means you are working with a:
   a) _____single-sided diskette
   b) _____double-sided diskette of density 360 K
   c) _____double-sided high-density diskette of density 720 K
   d) _____double-sided double high-density disk with 1.200 MB density
   e) _____None of the above

6) Which command to format a 3-1/2" diskette used for a UFS filesystem?
   a) _____fdformat -D
   b) _____fdformat -U
   c) _____fdformat -d
   d) _____newfs
   e) _____mkfs

7) Which command would you use to format a 3-1/2"diskette for a DOS filesystem?

   a) _____fdformat -D

   b) _____fdformat -U

   c) _____fdformat -d

   d) _____newfs

   e) _____mkfs

Quiz answers appear in Appendix A, Section 10.1.

**LAB
10.1**

L A B   10.2

MAKING A SOLARIS FILESYSTEM

LAB OBJECTIVES

After this Lab, you will be able to:

✓ Partition a Hard Drive in Solaris x86

✓ Create Disk Slices

✓ Make and Check a Filesystem

✓ Mount the New Filesystem

✓ Permanently Mount the Filesystem

You saw in Lab 10.1 that you can create a UNIX or DOS filesystem on a diskette. You also saw, in Chapter 8, how to create a filesystem on a diskette and multiple filesystems on a hard disk in Linux. We are now going to discuss creating multiple filesystems on a hard disk in Solaris.

In order to do this Lab, you should have an additional hard disk that is unused or that you can overwrite. This is not an absolute requirement to add a Solaris partition. However, there may be some additional things you may need to do, particularly if you have Linux on the second disk. This chapter assumes that you have a free second hard disk.

Where a particular partition name or device is used in the exercises or examples, substitute the actual name of the partition or device you are using. You may also need to substitute some size values for those that actually work for you.

 You should look at Appendix G on Multi-Boot PC UNIX/DOS/Linux Systems for information on creating multiple boot partitions on a hard disk.

FDISK

You have seen that you can use the DOS and Linux `fdisk` command to make partitions on a hard disk. This command allows you to put multiple operating systems on a drive.

 The `fdisk` command is only available in Solaris x86, and not in the Solaris Sparc version, which is the standard version. If you are using the later version, you should still read the text references to `fdisk` in order to understand some of Solaris x86's capabilities.

The Solaris version of `fdisk` is different from the DOS or Linux version with which you are familiar. This version is called the Solaris `format` command.

 You should read comparable information in Chapter 8 concerning hard disks in Linux.

MAKE A HARD DISK USABLE IN SOLARIS

When you install Solaris on a disk drive, or add one to an existing system, you must prepare it first. Solaris has support for a number of different types of filesystems, including DOS FAT 16. If you do the man pages on the various commands discussed here, you can get a better idea of what is available to you. Solaris does not have the wide variety of filesystem support that Linux does; however, for most people, the additional filesystems will never be needed.

While you can create hard disk partitions of various types in Solaris, you should not use Solaris to create anything other than Solaris partitions. Sometimes incompatibilities can arise if you do this. For example, you should not use Solaris to create a DOS partition unless you are sure there will be no problems later. The best thing to do is experiment.

LAB 10.2

The command steps in Solaris to create a working filesystem on a hard disk can be summarized as follows:

1. Format. If you do not specify an initial startup drive, you will see a list of drives available for you to work with.
2. A list of various options are available to you. Solaris x86 v2.6 will show them to you as follows:

FORMAT MENU:

- disk   select a disk
- type   select (define) a disk type
- partition   select (define) a partition table
- current   describe the current disk
- format   format and analyze the disk
- fdisk   run the fdisk program
- repair   repair a defective sector
- show   translate a disk address
- label   write label to the disk
- analyze   surface analysis
- defect   defect list management
- backup   search for backup labels
- verify   read and display labels
- save   save new disk/partition definitions
- volname   set eight-character volume name
- !<cmd>   execute <cmd>, then return
- quit   exit the format menu

These features will be discussed as needed in the exercises. One very important one is fdisk. A discussion about this feature follows.

3. fdisk—In the previous steps, you will see the fdisk command. This will work similar to the fdisk command in DOS, and will allow you to create partitions on the drive for multiple operating systems. Solaris will allow you to

further break the partition you choose for Solaris into slices or extended partitions for use by Solaris.

4. `newfs`—This command will create the ufs filesystem on the disk drive, just like we discussed earlier for the diskette.

5. `mount`—Once you have created a working filesystem, you can use the mount command to mount it.

FILESYSTEM TABLE /ETC/VFSTAB

The filesystem table in Solaris, otherwise known as /etc/vfstab, is a listing of all the filesystems mounted on bootup. It is similar to the /etc/fstab in Linux and other versions of UNIX. You can be permanently mount a device by adding it to the file /etc/vfstab. It will also set the mount characteristics of the filesystem. You can mount filesystems with characteristics such as read-only, no setuid to root, and various other features. You can also tell Solaris to check the filesystem on bootup. It can be useful for the dump backup command because it can set the dump level at which you should backup the partition. Your /etc/vfstab should look like the following:

```
#device          device     mount FS   fsck mount   mount
#to mount   to fsck      point type pass at boot options
#
fd                     -                       /dev/fd fd      -     no     -
/proc                -                       /proc   proc   -     no     -
/dev/dsk/c0d0s1  -                       -            swap   -     no     -
/dev/dsk/c0d0s0 /dev/rdsk/c0d0s0 /          ufs    1     no     -
/dev/dsk/c0d0s6 /dev/rdsk/c0d0s6 /usr       ufs    1     no     -
/dev/dsk/c0d0s3 /dev/rdsk/c0d0s3 /export ufs    2     yes    -
/dev/dsk/c0d0s7 /dev/rdsk/c0d0s7 /export/home ufs 2 yes  -
/dev/dsk/c0d0s4 /dev/rdsk/c0d0s4 /export/swap ufs 2 yes  -
/dev/dsk/c0d0s5 /dev/rdsk/c0d0s5 /opt       ufs    2     yes    -
/dev/dsk/c0d1s2 /dev/rdsk/c0d1s2 /usr/local ufs 2 yes    -
  swap                 -                       /tmp    tmpfs  -     yes    -
/dev/dsk/c1d1s0 /dev/rdsk/c1d1s0 /mnt       ufs    2     yes    -
/mnt/swap       -                       -            swap   -     no     -
```

Let's analyze one of the lines from this file:

```
/dev/dsk/c1d0s2 /dev/rdsk/c1d0s2 /usr ufs  1 yes -
```

This line can be described as follows:

- **/dev/dsk/c1d0s2** is the /dev name for the partition that contains the actual filesystem. This is the block device name. This handled data is a block generally of 512 bytes.
- **/dev/rdsk/c1d0s2** is the /dev name to be used when running fsck. It is also the character device name. It is used for accessing a device on a byte-by-byte basis.
- **/usr** is the mount point in UNIX where the filesystem is mounted. This is a directory. (If there are items in the current directory, they will become unavailable until the filesystem is unmounted, but will not be lost by a simple mount.)
- **ufs** is the filesystem type. We will be creating this filesystem in this Lab. There are many filesystem types, but Solaris generally uses ufs. Others will generally work. You will also sometimes see proc listed. This is actually a pointer to device and software drivers used by the system. Also, fd is used by the diskette, but the actual mount point is /dev/diskette. The swap area can be a reference to a file, disk slice, or remote NFS filesystem.
- **1**, the fifth field, is used by fsck on bootup to determine the order in which the filesystem are checked. Root and /usr usually get 1 and all other filesystems usually get 2. The - means that fsck will not check the filesystem on bootup.
- **yes** says to mount at bootup.
- **-** are options to be set on mount.

Note that Solaris uses a file similar to /etc/fstab *called* /etc/vfstab. *It contains much of the same information in* /etc/fstab. *It includes some things that are not in* /etc/fstab, *and adds others. If you are running Solaris, you should look up its characteristics and compare them to* /etc/fstab.

LAB 10.2 EXERCISES

10.2.1 PARTITION A HARD DRIVE IN SOLARIS X86

 If you are running Solaris Sparc, you will not be able to do this Exercise. This is because Solaris Sparc doesn't allow for multiple partitions on a disk, other then disk slices, which are discussed later. However, you can still read this lab and continue on with Exercise 10.2.2.

The first thing you need to do is determine the current layout of your disks and how much space you have.

This Exercise assumes that your hard disk has no partitions on it. If you have partitions on it and you are using your whole drive for these exercises, you should delete those partitions.

Let's begin with the `format` command.

Enter the following:

```
format
```

a) What do you see when you type the `format` command? What is your prompt?

_____

_____

This will give you several drives from which to choose. You should choose the hard drive with which you will be working.

Enter that choice now.

b) What happens when you select your hard drive?

_____

_____

At this point, you will be prompted for available drive types. Just choose the second default for now.

      c) What happens when you choose the second default drive type?

_____

_____

You should see the prompts for various choices you can make from the format command.

Now choose the `fdisk` command. Do the following from the `format` prompt:

      `fdisk`

      d) What happens when you choose the `fdisk` option?

_____

_____

You will now be given a choice as to whether you want to use the whole disk for Solaris or not. For the purposes of this Exercise, choose no (or n).

      e) What happens when you answer n to use the whole disk?

_____

_____

You will now be prompted with several actions you can take from the `fdisk` option.

At this point, you will want to create a partition, so choose the appropriate option.

f) What happens when you choose to create a partition?

_____

_____

Now you can choose of the type of partition you wish to create. You should choose Solaris.

g) What happens when you choose Solaris?

_____

_____

You should be prompted for the percentage of the disk to use for Solaris. For the purposes of this Exercise, choose 50%.

h) When you enter 50, what happens?

_____

_____

You will now be asked whether you want to make this the active partition. Choose yes.

An active partition is the partition from which you boot. In DOS, this is on the C: drive and is the partition to which you default when you bootup. You can have multiple C: drives in DOS, but only one at a time is bootable and visible from DOS. Hence, it is sometimes used to determine which drives are visible from an operating system. In Solaris x86, there is only one active partition per drive.

i) What happens when you answer yes to making the partition the active partition?

_____

_____

You should now get back the main `fdisk` menu.

Solaris will have a problem with multiple Solaris type partitions on the same disk. The naming convention allows for only one Solaris partition on the disk. All slices (which we'll discuss later) must be in the same partition. Strange results, including disappearing partitions and even the inability to boot Solaris, can result if this rule is not adhered to.

Next you will create an additional partition.

> **j)** What happens when you choose to create a partition?

> _____

> _____

Now we will create an additional partition.

Choose DOSBIG.

> **k)** What happens when you choose DOSBIG for the additional partition?

> _____

> _____

You can now choose the percentage of the disk to use for DOS.

For this Exercise, choose 25%.

> **l)** When you choose 25% for the DOS partition, what happens?

> _____

> _____

You will again be prompted as to whether you want to make this your active partition. It doesn't matter here whether you choose yes or no.

For this Exercise, choose yes.

m) What happens when you enter yes (or y)?

_____

_____

Now change your active partition back to the Solaris partition. Choose the menu option to change your active partition.

n) What did you choose? What happens when you select this menu option?

_____

_____

Now choose to make the Solaris partition the active partition.

o) What was your choice? What happened?

_____

_____

Now you can exit the `fdisk` utility. From the screen, choose the option:

```
Exit (Update disk configuration and exit)
```

p) What do you see when you exit the `fdisk` program?

_____

_____

Note that you may need to save your configuration and/or relabel the disk. Just go ahead and follow the prompts.

You should now go ahead and save the disk layout to a file.

Just choose the save option from the format menu and use the default values.

q) What happens when you choose the `save` option in the format menu?

_____

_____

You should now be back to the format menu.

Now go ahead and quit the format program. Use the `quit` option.

r) What happens when you choose the `quit` option in `format`?

_____

_____

10.2.2 CREATE DISK SLICES

You are now ready to make disk slices on the Solaris partition you created. These steps are generally usable in both Solaris x86 and Solaris Sparc.

You should start from the command line prompt for root, which is normally #.

Now enter the following command:

```
format
```

a) What happens when you run the `format` command?

_____

_____

Choose label option. This will put a label (and other information) onto the disk.

b) What happens when you write the label to the disk?

_____

_____

Go ahead and label the disk.

Now you should just save the new disk and partition definitions to a file.

c) What happens when you save the disk format?

_____

_____

Now you will create your slices or extended partitions on the Solaris partition.

Solaris x86 uses the term partition in two different ways. You can create a partition when you run the `fdisk` *command. But you can also create a partition when you are in the partition option of format. In this case, you can think of the second type of partition as being an extended partition. This is not a confusing issue in Solaris Sparc, because* `fdisk` *is not available in that version.*

Choose a partition from the format prompt.

d) What shows up on the screen?

_____

_____

You will see a number of choices on the screen. Your prompt will be as follows:

```
partition >
```

You will now want to display the current Solaris partition layout. You can do this with the `print` option from the `partition` prompt.

e) What happens when you choose the `print` option to partition?

_____

_____

You will see a number of choices on the screen.

Look for any slices from 0 to 7, other than 2, with a size other than 0. If you find any, you should go ahead and set the starting point, ending, point and size to 0. The purpose of this is to ensure that there are no conflicts when you setup your slices. You can make the changes by choosing the slice number. Solaris will prompt you for the new values.

 In Solaris Sparc you will have slices from 0 to 7, whereas in Solaris x86, you will have slices 0 to 9. The slice 8 contains the boot slice information that allows Solaris x86 to boot from this partition and hard disk. Slice 9 is an area reserved for alternate disk blocks in Solaris x86. Slice 2 is for the whole partition in Solaris.

f) What kind of prompts did you get when you changed the values for your slice? What were your answers?

_____

_____

Now you need to look at the results of your changes.

g) How did you display the new Solaris partition layout?

_____

_____

 The discussion that follows will be based on a 4 GB drive that is split into a 1.98 MB Solaris partition. Select sizes that reflect your own hard disk.

Now select the 0 partition and create a partition that starts on cylinder 0 and has a size of 1 GB.

h) What are the steps involved in creating the new partition from the partition prompt?

_____

_____

Now you can reexamine the disk layout to see what the changes are like that you made.

i) What characteristics do you see for partition 0 when you print out the partition layout?

_____

_____

You should pay attention to the ending cylinder for the new partition. The partition will be displayed in a range format, such as 0 -130 in this example. So the last cylinder is 130. The next partition, which is partition 1, cannot overlap any other cylinder in use. You will then need to add one to the last cylinder of the previous partition in order to create the new partition. In this example, you would choose 131 as the starting point.

Now go ahead and create a second partition bigger than the space available in the Solaris partition. In the example, choosing 1 GB would be bigger than the .98 available.

j) What happens when you try to create a second slice on the Solaris partition of 1 GB?

_____

_____

Now reduce the size so that it will fit into the space available. In this case, that would be .97 GB, because some space is needed by the OS and because of rounding errors.

k) What happens when you create a properly-sized slice on the disk?

_____

_____

l) What are your steps, and what do you notice about the new partition table when you display it?

_____

_____

Now you are ready to label the disk.

Use the `label` command from the partition prompt.

m) What happens when you label the disk?

_____

_____

Now quit this with the `quit` command.

n) What do you see?

_____

_____

Save the disk layout with the `save` command.

o) What happens when you save the partition layout?

_____

_____

Now you can quit this with the `quit` command.

p) What is your prompt when you enter the quit command this time?

_____

_____

You have now created extended partitions, or slices, in Solaris that you can use for additional file systems, swap space, or raw space for databases.

10.2.3 MAKE AND CHECK A FILESYSTEM

Now you can use the `newfs` command to create a filesystem. This Exercise assumes that you are using the `/dev/dsk/c1d1` disk. You should replace this name with the drive with which you are working.

Now you can create the filesystem with the following command:

```
newfs raw-diskname
```

or, in this Exercise:

```
newfs /dev/rdsk/c1d1s0
```

a) What is the command line you used with `newfs`? What kind of results did you get? Explain those results.

_____

_____

This will make a new fileSystem, hence the name `newfs`. This command will make a Solaris filesystem on a partition that has already been created by `fdisk` and `format`.

Once you have created the filesystem, you should now check the filesystem to see if there are any problems.

In UNIX, the program to do this is as follows:

```
fsck file_system
```

This will go through and check for inconsistencies in filesystem tables. It can automatically fix some problems. With other problems, you will get prompted as to whether you want to make any changes.

Go ahead and do a filesystem check on the partition you just created.

The actual format of the `fsck` is shown as follows:

```
fsck /dev/rdsk/c1d1s0   (Replace c1d1s0 with the name of your working file-
                     system)
```

You can use either the raw or block device.

    b) What happens when you run the `fsck` command?

    _____

    _____

    c) What kind of results do you get?

    _____

    _____

10.2.4 MOUNT THE NEW FILESYSTEM

This Exercise will use the `mount` command to take a filesystem that you have created in the previous exercises and mount it under a UNIX directory. If the mount point, which is a regular UNIX directory, doesn't exist, you can create it with the following:

```
mkdir directory_name
```

The actual format of the `mount` command is:

```
mount  -F fstype device_name mount_point
```

The `-F` options indicates the filesystem type you are mounting. This is a standard System V format. Linux will use a `-t` option. Here, `fstype` is the filesystem type used to determine how to mount the filesystem. If you are using the default filesystem in Solaris, which is `ufs`, you can leave out this option. `file-system` is the formatted filesystem in the previous step. `mount_point` is the mount point, which is a directory where you can mount the filesystem.

So now you can take the filesystem you created previously and mount it. Let's assume that you are using the `/mnt` directory as your mount point.

**LAB
10.2**

> **a)** If your mount point directory doesn't exist, go ahead and create it. What are your results?

_____

_____

The actual format of the mount command would be:

```
mount device_name directory_name
```

In this Exercise, use the following:

```
mount /dev/dsk/c1d1s0 /mnt
```

If you leave out the filesystem type, the system assumes `ufs` as the filesystem. You can determine the actual default filesystem type for your system by looking at the file /etc/default/fs.

Go ahead and mount the partition you just created under the directory. Just replace `device_name` with the partition name, and `directory_name` with the mount point.

In this example, you can use the following:

```
mount /dev/dsk/c1d1s0 /mnt
```

> **b)** What kind of results do you get when you mount the filesystem?

_____

_____

These are the steps used to mount the filesystem. Now you can use the `mount` command to verify that the filesystem was actually mounted.

A good way to find the amount of space used by a slice is to use the following command:

```
df -tk
```

This gives the disk free space. The option `-t`, which stands for totals, gives the total space allocated, disk space used and similar information about the inodes. The `-k` gives the results in terms of `kilobytes`, which in this case is actually 1024 bytes.

> **c)** What kind of results do you get when you enter the `mount` command?

10.2.5 PERMANENTLY MOUNT THE FILESYSTEM

As mentioned earlier in this lab, the `/etc/vfstab` is used to mount devices when your system boots up. Take a look at your `/etc/vfstab` file by entering the following command:

```
cat /etc/vfstab
```

> **a)** What kind of results do you get?

You should now go ahead and add an entry for the partition you just created. Add your entry at the end of the file, in case your mount point is dependent on one of the previous partitions already being mounted (i.e., you can't properly or safely mount `/usr/local` if `/usr` isn't mounted yet).

Use the following format for the line you are entering:

```
block_device raw_device mount_point  ufs 1 yes -
```

In this example, you can use:

```
/dev/dsk/c1d1s0 /dev/rdsk/c1d1s0 /mnt  ufs defaults 0 2
```

    b) What is the line that you added to `/etc/vfstab`?

_____

_____

You can check whether this line works by unmounting the partition if it is already mounted, by using the command:

```
umount device_name
```

or

```
umount mount_point
```

    c) What kind of results do you get?

_____

_____

Before doing the following steps, you need to make sure that everything in `/etc/vfstab` is currently mounted except for your new partition. If not, check to see why.

You should also be sure that the directory you are mounting over is empty, or has files that you don't want to access when the new filesystem is mounted. If you mount over a directory with files or subdirectories, there will be no permanent damage. However, you will not be able to access that data during the new mount.

Make sure that everything gets mounted by entering the following command:

```
mount -a
```

This will give you some error messages about devices already being mounted or busy. You can ignore those messages if the filesystems they name are already mounted.

Go ahead and enter the above command.

    d) What kind of results do you get?

_____

_____

Now verify the partitions that are mounted with the following command:

```
mount
```

You should see that the partition you created is now mounted

    e) What happens when you enter the `mount` command?

_____

_____

The next step is to reboot your Solaris box to verify that it is mounted. While it is rebooting, look at the screen for messages about the partition being mounted. Also look for any error messages.

You have now:

- Made a partition in Solaris
- Created a Solaris filesystem
- Checked it out with `fsck`
- Mounted it under a directory
- Permanently added it to the list of partitions to be mounted on bootup

You can now use these principles to create and mount a filesystem with a different filesystem type.

LAB 10.2 EXERCISE ANSWERS

This section gives you some suggested answers to the questions in Lab 10.2, with discussion related to those answers. Your answers may vary, but the most important thing is whether or not your answer works. Use this discussion to analyze differences between your answers and those presented here.

If you have alternative answers to the questions in this Exercise, you are encouraged to post your answers and discuss them at the companion Web site for this book, located at:

```
http://www.phptr.com/phptrinteractive
```

10.2.1 ANSWERS

a) What do you see when you type the `format` command? What is your prompt?

Answer: You will see the available disks, similar to the following:

```
# format
Searching for disks...done

AVAILABLE DISK SELECTIONS:
       0. c0d0 <DEFAULT cyl 260 alt 2 hd 255 sec 63>
          /isa/ata@1,1f0/cmdk@0,0
       1. c0d1 <DEFAULT cyl 252 alt 2 hd 255 sec 63>  local
          /isa/ata@1,1f0/cmdk@1,0
       2. c1d1 <drive type unknown>
          /isa/ata@1,170/cmdk@1,0
Specify disk (enter its number): 2
```

Notice that the format command will search for all the drives that the system can see. The drive we are working with as an example is the one labeled drive 2. Notice that the drive type comes up as unknown. That is because it has not yet been defined to Solaris. Drive 2 has been chosen; you should choose the drive appropriate to your system.

b) What happens when you select your hard drive?

Answer:*You are given several choices for drive types.*

You will see the following display on your screen:

```
AVAILABLE DRIVE TYPES:
        0. DEFAULT
        1. DEFAULT
        2. other
Specify disk type (enter its number): 1
```

The above choices are only displayed if your chosen drive does not have a current disk layout. Once your chosen disk is laid out, you won't see the above choices. They will, however, show up in the future when you first go into the format command as being assigned to drives. Unfortunately, you do not have enough information from the above display to decide which drive type to choose for a new drive. Fortunately, it doesn't really matter. You can go back and choose a different drive type, or you can create your own in the format command.

The original choice for disks when you first setup your system is the DEFAULT value, which is 0 above and other, which would be listed as 1. Since we have added a new filesystem layout and saved it, the original DEFAULT stays as choice 0, the new DEFAULT now becomes choice 1, and other becomes choice 2. As a result, the drive type you should choose is 1. This is not critical, because once you save your new drive setup, a new DEFAULT drive will be defined as option 2, and the other choice will become 3. You can always read your current disk layout on bootup from the disk once you are in the format command, and then save that as a new disk format. You can also use the DEFAULT option as the basis for creating a new disk layout, and then save it as a new DEFAULT. If you have a number of drives with the same characteristics and you choose the same option above, layout your new drives the same way.

c) What happens when you choose the second default drive type?

Answer:You now have several choices in the format menu.

```
selecting c1d1
No current partition list
No defect list found
[disk formatted, no defect list found]


FORMAT MENU:
        disk       - select a disk
        type       - select (define) a disk type
        partition  - select (define) a partition table
        current    - describe the current disk
        format     - format and analyze the disk
        fdisk      - run the fdisk program
        repair     - repair a defective sector
        show       - translate a disk address
        label      - write label to the disk
        analyze    - surface analysis
        defect     - defect list management
        backup     - search for backup labels
        verify     - read and display labels
        save       - save new disk/partition definitions
        volname    - set eight-character volume name
        !<cmd>     - execute <cmd>, then return
        quit
format>
```

Notice that you are shown a number of possible choices for working with the drive. Some of these choices are non-destructive, whereas others will wipe out data that you may have on your disk. A good reading of the man pages should clarify most of this. If you are still unclear, setup a test system if you can, and try out the various options.

d) What happens when you choose the `fdisk` option?

Answer:You have possible choices, much like `fdisk` on Linux and DOS.

The fdisk option will allow you to partition your hard drive into multiple partitions, each of which can have a different operating system. The default response by the system is to make the whole drive a single Solaris partition. In this case, we are only using half of it, so the answer is no (or n).

```
format> fdisk
The recommended default partitioning for your disk is:

   a 100% "SOLARIS System" partition.

To select this, please type "y".  To partition your disk
differently, type "n" and the "fdisk" program will let you
select other partitions. n
```

e) What happens when you answer n to use the whole disk?

Answer: It is not necessary in Solaris to use the whole disk.

At this point, you will want to create a partition, so choose the appropriate option. This will give the current partition layout of your disk drives. If you have no partitions, the breakdown will be blank.

You will also be given a choice of several options for the fdisk command. If you have used the fdisk command in DOS or Linux, these options should be familiar to you.

In this example, the following results are obtained. Your system may show things differently.

```
Total disk size is 520 cylinders
Cylinder size is 16065 (512 byte) blocks
Cylinders
Partition    Status    Type      Start    End    Length     %
=========    ======    =====     =====    ===    ======    ===




SELECT ONE OF THE FOLLOWING:
```

```
1.    Create a partition
2.    Change Active (Boot from) partition
3.    Delete a partition
4.    Exit (Update disk configuration and exit)
Enter Selection:
```

You have several possible selections here. You want to create a partition, but notice that you can change the Active partition or delete a partition. Notice also that choosing the Exit option will automatically update the disk configuration. This may or may not be destructive, depending on whether you decide to save it to disk later and label the disk.

f) What happens when you choose to create a partition?

Answer:You will be given a choice of several types.

You will get a prompt indicating several types of partitions you can create. Notice that this does not create the filesystem itself. It only creates the basic format or framework upon which you can put the operating system.

```
Indicate the type of partition you want to create
    (1=SOLARIS, 2=UNIX, 3=PCIXOS, 4=Other, 5=DOS12)
    (6=DOS16, 7=DOSEXT, 8=DOSBIG, 9=PowerPC Boot)
    (A=x86 Boot, 0=Exit) ?
```

As mentioned in the text, do not rely on Solaris to produce the proper format for DOS or any other operating system listed. The formatting should be done by the actual operating system for which the partition is intended. Also be aware that you should never make the Master Boot Record bootable from DOS. This may cause Solaris to not work. See Appendix G for a multi-boot discussion.

Now you have a choice of the type of partition to create. You should choose Solaris.

g) What happens when you choose Solaris?

Answer: Solaris is the type with which we will start.You will be given an opportunity to specify the percentage to be used.

```
Indicate the percentage of the disk you want this partition
to use (or enter "c" to specify in cylinders).
```

You should be prompted for the percentage of the disk to use for Solaris. For the purposes of this exercise, you should choose 50%.

You can choose up to 100% of the disk, or any number down to zero. Just remember that you can only create one Solaris partition per disk with `fdisk`. You can, however, create multiple extended partitions within this partition.

h) When you enter 50, what happens?

Answer: You are asked if you want to make this your active partition. In this example, we will choose yes.

```
Do you want this to become the Active partition? If so, it will be activated
each time you reset your computer or when you turn it on again.
Please type "y" or "n".
```

i) What happens when you answer yes to making the partition the active partition?

Answer: You will see the following display showing the disk layout:

```
Total disk size is 520 cylinders
Cylinder size is 16065 (512 byte) blocks
```

			Cylinders			
Partition	Status	Type	Start	End	Length	%
=========	======	=======	=====	===	======	===
1	Active	Solaris	1	260	260	50

```
SELECT ONE OF THE FOLLOWING:

    1.    Create a partition
    2.    Change Active (Boot from) partition
    3.    Delete a partition
    4.    Exit (Update disk configuration and exit)
Enter Selection:
```

You will see the same choices you saw when you first got into fdisk, except now you have a partition showing up.

Note that the display above shows that 50% of the disk is used by Solaris. It also shows the starting and ending cylinders. It is important to keep track of this information, because the next partition you add cannot overlap another partition. So the next starting cylinder would be 261. The active partition is not relevant except on the boot drive, because it specifies the boot partition. But you can go ahead and choose it to be the active partition anyway.

You should now get back the main `fdisk` menu.
Now, create an additional partition.

j)   What happens when you choose to create a partition?

Answer: You should see a prompt for the type of partition you want to create.

```
Indicate the type of partition you want to create
  (1=SOLARIS, 2=UNIX, 3=PCIXOS, 4=Other, 5=DOS12)
  (6=DOS16, 7=DOSEXT, 8=DOSBIG, 9=PowerPC Boot)
  (A=x86 Boot, 0=Exit) ?
```

Notice that there are several versions of DOS partitions. Be sure to choose DOSBIG, which is choice 8, unless you are using a small hard disk. The other choices will only work on smaller disks and are older versions of the DOS format.

You should see several choices on the screen.
Let's choose DOSBIG.

k)   What happens when you choose DOSBIG for the additional partition?

Answer: You will get the following. Notice that you have seen this screen earlier.

```
Indicate the percentage of the disk you want this partition
to use (or enter "c" to specify in cylinders).
```
You can now choose the percentage of the disk to use for DOS. Let's choose 25%.

l)   When you choose 25% for the DOS partition, what happens?

Answer: You will see the following:

```
Do you want this to become the Active partition? If so, it will be activated
each time you reset your computer or when you turn it on again.
Please type "y" or "n".
```
You will again be prompted as to whether you want to make this your active partition. It doesn't matter here whether you choose yes or no. This is only

valid on the boot drive. (However, some versions of UNIX, such as SCO, require that all partitions in use must be labelled as active.) Choose yes.

m) What happens when you enter yes (or y)?

Answer:You will see the following display:

```
Total disk size is 520 cylinders
Cylinder size is 16065 (512 byte) blocks
                                  Cylinders
Partition  Status    Type      Start   End    Length    %
=========  ======    ========  =====   ===    ======   ===
    1                Solaris     1     260      260      50
    2      Active    DOS-BIG    261    390      130      25


SELECT ONE OF THE FOLLOWING:

    1.    Create a partition
    2.    Change Active (Boot from) partition
    3.    Delete a partition
    4.    Exit (Update disk configuration and exit)
Enter Selection:
```

Notice that the DOS-BIG partition starts at 261, just as we discussed earlier.

Now change your active partition back to the Solaris partition.
Choose the menu option to change your active partition.

n) What did you choose? What happens when you select this menu option?

Answer:You should have made choice 2, which is:

```
Change Active (Boot from) partition
```
Now choose to make the Solaris partition the active partition.

o) What was your choice? What happened?

Answer:You should have made choice I.Your screen will show:

```
Enter the number of the partition you want to boot from
(or enter 0 for none): 1
```

```
Partition 1 is now Active.  The system will start up
from this
Total disk size is 520 cylinders
Cylinder size is 16065 (512 byte) blocks
                                    Cylinders
Partition  Status   Type      Start   End   Length    %
=========  ======   ========  =====   ===   ======   ===
    1      Active   Solaris     1     260     260     50
    2               DOS-BIG    261    390     130     25


SELECT ONE OF THE FOLLOWING:

    1.    Create a partition
    2.    Change Active (Boot from) partition
    3.    Delete a partition
    4.    Exit (Update disk configuration and exit)
Enter Selection:
```

Now partition 1 is active. We have changed it from partition 2 being active.

p) What do you see when you exit the `fdisk` program?

Answer:You are told that the fdisk partition layout has changed, and that you need to relabel the disk with the new information. You should answer yes to the prompt. You will see:

```
WARNING: Solaris fdisk partition changed - Please relabel the disk
```

If you are not sure about the selections, you can enter the question mark, as shown below, which will show you the various options available.

```
format> ?
Expecting one of the following: (abbreviations ok):
        disk       - select a disk
        type       - select (define) a disk type
        partition  - select (define) a partition table
        current    - describe the current disk
        format     - format and analyze the disk
        fdisk      - run the fdisk program
        repair     - repair a defective sector
        show       - translate a disk address
```

```
            label       - write label to the disk
            analyze     - surface analysis
            defect      - defect list management
            backup      - search for backup labels
            verify      - read and display labels
            save        - save new disk/partition definitions
            volname     - set eight-character volume name
            !<cmd>      - execute <cmd>, then return
            quit

format> label

Ready to label disk, continue? yes

format> current
Current Disk = c1d1
<DEFAULT cyl 258 alt 2 hd 255 sec 63>
/isa/ata@1,170/cmdk@1,0
```

q) What happens when you choose the save option in the format menu?

Answer: You will see that the format is saved to the file `/format.dat` *by default. You can choose another file elsewhere if you wish.*

r) What happens when you choose the quit option in format?

Answer: You should now get back the command line prompt, which is normally the # prompt.

10.2.2 ANSWERS

a) What happens when you run the format command?

Answer: Look at the display in Exercise 10.2.1, Question (a), and relevant discussion.

If you did the previous exercise, you may be prompted with an additional disk layout. This was created by Exercise 10.2.1. Just go ahead and choose the new DEFAULT disk layout.

b) What happens when you write the label to the disk?

Answer: Again refer to Exercise 10.2.1, Question (p), to see what happens when you label the disk.

c) What happens when you save the disk format?

Answer: Refer to Exercise 10.2.1, Question (q).

Choose partition from the format prompt.

**LAB
10.2**

d) What shows up on the screen?

Answer: You will see a display of a number of things you can do to the partition.

```
format> partition


PARTITION MENU:
        0          - change `0' partition
        1          - change `1' partition
        2          - change `2' partition
        3          - change `3' partition
        4          - change `4' partition
        5          - change `5' partition
        6          - change `6' partition
        7          - change `7' partition
        select  - select a predefined table
        modify  - modify a predefined partition table
        name    - name the current table
        print   - display the current table
        label   - write partition map and label to the disk
        !<cmd>  - execute <cmd>, then return
        quit
partition>
```

Note that there are a number of things you can do to the partition, or slice, as Solaris calls it. The term slice and extended partition can be considered interchangeable for the purpose of this discussion.

Notice that you are given a number of choices to modify partitions. Again, it is very important that any changes you make to a partition should not overlap another partition. The one exception to this rule is that UNIX considers partition 2 as being the whole disk, or the full partition, in the case of a partition created by fdisk. This should not be set to 0 size; any other partition from 0 to 7 can (and should) be set to 0 size, and starting at cylinder 0.

e) What happens when you choose the print option to partition?

Answer: You will see a display of the current default partition table.

```
partition> p
Current partition table (original):
Total disk cylinders available: 258 + 2 (reserved cylinders)
```

Part	Tag	Flag	Cylinders	Size	Blocks	
0	root	wm	0	0	(0/0/0)	0
1	swap	wu	0	0	(0/0/0)	0
2	backup	wu	0 - 257	1.98GB	(258/0/0)	4144770
3	unassigned	wm	40 - 83	345.15MB	(44/0/0)	706860
4	unassigned	wm	84 - 160	604.01MB	(77/0/0)	1237005
5	unassigned	wm	0	0	(0/0/0)	0
6	usr	wm	0	0	(0/0/0)	0
7	unassigned	wm	0	0	(0/0/0)	0
8	boot	wu	0- 0	7.84MB	(1/0/0)	16065
9	alternates	wu	1- 2	15.69MB	(2/0/0)	32130

```
partition> ?
```

Notice that partition 2 is labeled as backup, but is really the full disk. The size that shows up is 1.98 GB. Remember that when we first setup the Solaris partition with fdisk in the previous exercise, the partition range was 1-261, with a length of 260. The difference is due to overhead that is necessary for Solaris when a format is put down on the disk. This includes space for the superblock, backup labels and other things. A detailed discussion of the details is beyond the scope of this book, but you might want to look at a good book on UNIX operating system design for more details.

f) What kind of prompts did you get when you changed the values for your partition? What were your answers?

Answer: You should see the following display on the screen. The example is for partition 0. You can apply this to other partitions and disks.

```
partition> 0
Part          Tag Flag  Cylinders   Size            Blocks
  0          root  wm   0            0       (0/0/0)          0

Enter partition id tag[root]:
Enter partition permission flags[wm]:
Enter new starting cyl[0]: 0
Enter partition size[0b, 0c, 0.00mb, 0.00gb]: 0
partition>
```

You are prompted for a label for the partition. This is just a label, and is not required. The partition permission flags refer to characteristics of the partition. By default, Solaris partitions are set to be writable and modifiable. You should have done this for all partitions from 0 to 7, except for 2.

g) How did you display the new Solaris partition layout.

Answer: By using the print option as discussed earlier, you can display the new partition layout. You should see the following:

```
partition> p
Current partition table (original):
Total disk cylinders available: 258 + 2 (reserved cylinders)

Part       Tag Flag  Cylinders    Size            Blocks
0 unassigned  wm   0             0       (131/0/0) 0
1 unassigned  wu   0             0       (127/0/0) 0
2 backup      wu   0 - 257       1.98GB  (258/0/0) 4144770
3 unassigned  wm   0             0       (0/0/0)   0
4 unassigned  wm   0             0       (0/0/0)   0
5 unassigned  wm   0             0       (0/0/0)   0
6        usr  wm   0             0       (0/0/0)   0
7 unassigned  wm   0             0       (0/0/0)   0
8       boot  wu   0 - 0         7.84MB  (1/0/0)   16065
9 alternates  wu   1 - 2         15.69MB (2/0/0)   32130

partition>
```

h) Which steps are involved in creating the new partition from the partition prompt?

Answer: You will go through the following steps:

```
Partition> 0
Part       Tag Flag  Cylinders    Size         Blocks
0 unassigned   wm    0            0        (131/0/0) 0

Enter partition id tag[root]:
Enter partition permission flags[wm]:
Enter new starting cyl[0]:
Enter partition size[0b, 0c, 0.00mb, 0.00gb]: 1.00gb
partition>
```

Now you have created a new slice on the Solaris partition by entering a partition size. Otherwise, you would stick with the default values for everything else. The starting point is not critical for slice 0, but it usually starts at 0. However, some applications, such as certain database applications, may want you to start at 1 or some other number.

Now you can reexamine the disk layout to see what your changes are like.

i) What characteristics do you see for partition 0 when you print out the partition layout?

```
partition> p
Current partition table (original):
Total disk cylinders available: 258 + 2 (reserved cylinders)

Part       Tag Flag  Cylinders    Size          Blocks
0 unassigned   wm    0 - 130    1.00 GB (131/0/0) 2104515
1 unassigned   wu    0            0      (127/0/0) 0
2 backup       wu    0 - 257    1.98GB  (258/0/0) 4144770
3 unassigned   wm    0            0      (0/0/0)   0
4 unassigned   wm    0            0      (0/0/0)   0
5 unassigned   wm    0            0      (0/0/0)   0
6        usr   wm    0            0      (0/0/0)   0
7 unassigned   wm    0            0      (0/0/0)   0
8        boot  wu    0 - 0      7.84MB  (1/0/0)   16065
```

```
9 alternates   wu    1 -  2         15.69MB   (2/0/0)    32130

partition>
```

You see above that the new slice 0 runs from cylinders 0 to 130, with a size of 1.00 GB. None of the other slices have changed.

j) What happens when you try to create a second slice on the Solaris partition of 1 GB?

Answer: You will get a message that there is no space left.

Since you already created a slice of 1 GB on the Solaris partition of 1.98 GB, you only have .98 GB left. However, because of round-off errors and overhead, you can really only create a slice of .97 GB.

Now reduce the size so that it fits into the space available. In this case, that would be .97 GB, because some space is needed by the OS and because of rounding errors.

k) What happens when you create a properly-sized slice on the disk?

Answer: You will get messages similar to the ones you got when you created the first slice on the disk.

l) What are your steps and what do you notice about the new partition table when you display it?

Answer: Your steps and the new partition table will look like the following:

```
partition> p
Current partition table (original):
Total disk cylinders available: 258 + 2 (reserved cylinders)
Part          Tag Flag  Cylinders      Size            Blocks
0 unassigned  wm    0 - 130      1.00 GB (131/0/0) 2104515
1 unassigned  wu  131 - 257    996.22MB  (127/0/0) 2040255
2 backup      wu    0 - 257      1.98GB  (258/0/0) 4144770
3 unassigned  wm    0              0       (0/0/0)    0
4 unassigned  wm    0              0       (0/0/0)    0
5 unassigned  wm    0              0       (0/0/0)    0
6        usr  wm    0              0       (0/0/0)    0
7 unassigned  wm    0              0       (0/0/0)    0
```

```
8         boot   wu    0 - 0           7.84MB   (1/0/0)    16065
9 alternates   wu    1 - 2          15.69MB   (2/0/0)    32130
```

```
partition>
```

Now you are ready to label the disk. Just use the label command from the partition prompt.

m)   What happens when you label the disk?

   Answer: You should just see the following:

```
partition> label
Ready to label disk, continue? yes
```

```
partition>
```
Now quit this with the `quit` command.

n)   What do you see?

   Answer: You should see the format> prompt.
Now save the disk layout with the `save` command.

o)   What happens when you save the partition layout?

   Answer: You will see the same display as before. You can choose to use the same file, /
   format.dat, or you can choose a different file.

```
format> save
Saving new disk and partition definitions
Enter file name["./format.dat"]:
format> partition
```
Now you can quit this with the quit command.

p)   What is your prompt when you enter the quit command this time?

   Answer: You are now returned to the command line prompt for root.

10.2.3 ANSWERS

a) What command line did you use with `newfs`? What kind of results did you get? Explain those results.

Answer: Let's assume you are making a ufs filesystem on the first slice on the example hard disk. So in this case, we would use /dev/rdsk/c1d1s0. Remember from the above exercise that it was created to be 1 Gig in size. You will see the following results:

```
# newfs /dev/rdsk/c1d1s0
newfs: construct a new file system /dev/rdsk/c1d1s0: (y/n)? y
Warning: 12286 sector(s) in last cylinder unallocated
/dev/rdsk/c1d1s0:        2104514 sectors in 140 cylinders of 240
tracks, 63 sectors
        1027.6MB in 24 cyl groups (6 c/g, 44.30MB/g, 10688 i/g)
super-block backups (for fsck -F ufs -o b=#) at:
 32, 90816, 181600, 272384, 363168, 453952, 544736, 635520,
726304, 817088, 907872, 998656, 1089440, 1180224, 1271008,
1361792, 1452576, 1543360, 1634144, 1724928, 1815712, 1906496,
1997280, 2088064,
```

When you enter the `newfs` command, you are prompted as to whether you want to create the filesystem. You should go ahead and create it. You are given a warning that 6 MB (12286 sectors) in the last cylinder are unallocated. This is because of the size that has been chosen. You can ignore this unless you are really planning your space tightly. Notice that the size is given as 1027.6 MB. This is because a 1 GB of space is actually 1024 MB. Only Western Digital counts 1 GB as 1000 MB. The superblock is backed up on several addresses, in case the main superblock is corrupted. You can restore the superblock with `fsck` and the proper options.

b) What happens when you run the fsck command?

Answer: You will see the fsck command line, followed by results from a number of steps that fsck goes through:

```
# fsck /dev/rdsk/c1d1s0
** /dev/rdsk/c1d1s0
** Last Mounted on /mnt
** Phase 1 - Check Blocks and Sizes
** Phase 2 - Check Pathnames
```

```
** Phase 3 - Check Connectivity
** Phase 4 - Check Reference Counts
** Phase 5 - Check Cyl groups
2 files, 9 used, 1019783 free (15 frags, 127471 blocks,
0.0% fragmentation)
#
```

Notice that you get back the name of the device, and then each of the phases that fsck goes through. If you had any problems, they would be displayed on the screen. In some cases, you may be asked to respond to a prompt. The final result is the number of files, disk space used and disk space free. It is faster to use the raw device for fsck than the block device, because there is less overhead for fsck to go through.

10.2.4 ANSWERS

a) If your mount point directory doesn't exist, go ahead and create it. What are your results?

Answer: If you needed to create the directory, you should get just the command line prompt back, unless there are errors.

b) What kind of results do you get when you mount the filesystem?

Answer: Again, you should only get the command line prompt back.

c) What kind of results do you get when you enter the mount command?

Answer: Your results should be similar to the following:

```
# df -tk
Filesystem          kbytes   used     avail capacity   Mounted on
/dev/dsk/c0d0s0     105814   29133    76576    28%      /
/dev/dsk/c0d0s6     534962   414387   120041   78%      /usr
/proc                    0        0        0    0%      /proc
fd                       0        0        0    0%      /dev/fd
/dev/dsk/c0d0s3     179515       11   179325    1%      /export
/dev/dsk/c0d0s7     309443    48072   261062   16%      /export/home
/dev/dsk/c0d0s4     195580        9   195376    1%      /export/swap
/dev/dsk/c0d0s5     505040   375594   128941   75%      /opt
```

```
/dev/dsk/c0d1s2 1963333 457900 1498889    24%    /usr/local
swap              120988     12 120976     1%    /tmp
/dev/dsk/c1d1s0 1019792      9 1018084     1%    /mnt
#
```

Notice that the amount of disk space for the slice we chose is 1019792 KB. Again, we see that there are some differences between UNIX commands, depending on what is read on the disk and what is counted. You should use the df -tk option often as an administrator so that you can be sure you don't run out of space. You don't need to worry about running out of inodes, because that almost never happens in today's computer systems.

10.2.5 ANSWERS

Take a look at your /etc/vfstab file by entering the command:

```
cat /etc/vfstab
```

a) What kind of results do you get?

Answer: You should see something similar to the following:

```
#_cat /etc/vfstab
```

#device #to mount #	device to fsck	mount point	FS type	fsck pass	mount at boot	mount options
fd	-	/dev/fd	fd	-	no	-
/proc	-	/proc	proc	-	no	-
/dev/dsk/c0d0s1	-	-	swap	-	no	-
/dev/dsk/c0d0s0	/dev/rdsk/c0d0s0	/	ufs	1	no	-
/dev/dsk/c0d0s6	/dev/rdsk/c0d0s6	/usr	ufs	1	no	-
/dev/dsk/c0d0s3	/dev/rdsk/c0d0s3	/export	ufs	2	yes	-
/dev/dsk/c0d0s7	/dev/rdsk/c0d0s7	/export/home	ufs	2	yes	-
/dev/dsk/c0d0s4	/dev/rdsk/c0d0s4	/export/swap	ufs	2	yes	-
/dev/dsk/c0d0s5	/dev/rdsk/c0d0s5	/opt	ufs	2	yes	-
/dev/dsk/c0d1s2	/dev/rdsk/c0d1s2	/usr/local	ufs	2	yes	-
swap	-	/tmp	tmpfs	-	yes	-

b)   What line did you add to `/etc/vfstab`?

Answer: You should see a line similar to the following:

```
/dev/dsk/c1d1s0 /dev/rdsk/c1d1s0      /mnt    ufs    2      yes
```

You should review the descriptions at the start of this chapter to understand each item. Look them up in the man pages as well.

You can check whether this line works by unmounting the partition, if it is already mounted, by using the command:

```
umount device_name
```

c)   What kind of results did you get?

Answer: You will just get the command line prompt back.

Now you can make sure that everything gets mounted by entering the following command:

```
mount -a
```

d)   What kind of results did you get?

Answer: You will see the following display. Notice that the messages are not errors, but only warnings. If the `mount` *command sees that something is already mounted it just continues on to the next item.*

```
# mount -a
mount: /dev/dsk/c0d0s5 is already mounted, /opt is busy,
or the allowable number of mount points has been exceeded
mount: /dev/dsk/c0d0s3 is already mounted, /export is
busy,       or the allowable number of mount points has been
exceeded
mount: /tmp already mounted
mount: /dev/dsk/c0d1s2 is already mounted, /usr/local is busy,
or the allowable number of mount points has been exceeded
mount: /dev/dsk/c0d0s4 is already mounted, /export/swap is
busy, or the allowable number of mount points has been
exceeded
mount: /dev/dsk/c0d0s7 is already mounted, /export/home is
busy, or the allowable number of mount points has been
exceeded
#
```

Now you can verify the partitions that are mounted with the command:

```
mount
```

e) What happens when you enter the `mount` command?

Answer: You should see results similar to the following:

```
# mount
/ on /dev/dsk/c0d0s0 read/write/setuid/largefiles on
Wed Jul  8 19:29:00 1998
/usr on /dev/dsk/c0d0s6 read/write/setuid/largefiles on
Wed Jul  8 19:29:00 1998
/proc on /proc read/write/setuid on Wed Jul  8 19:29:00
1998
/dev/fd on fd read/write/setuid on Wed Jul  8 19:29:00
1998
/export on /dev/dsk/c0d0s3 setuid/read/write/largefiles
on Wed Jul  8 19:29:03 1998
/export/home on /dev/dsk/c0d0s7 setuid/read/write/
largefiles on Wed Jul  8 19:29:04 1998
/export/swap on /dev/dsk/c0d0s4 setuid/read/write/
largefiles on Wed Jul  8 19:29:04 1998
/opt on /dev/dsk/c0d0s5 setuid/read/write/largefiles on
Wed Jul  8 19:29:03 1998
/usr/local on /dev/dsk/c0d1s2 setuid/read/write/large-
files on Wed Jul  8 19:29:03 1998
/tmp on swap read/write on Wed Jul  8 19:29:03 1998
/mnt on /dev/dsk/c1d1s0 setuid/read/write/largefiles on
Thu Jul  9 21:44:08 1998
#
```

LAB 10.2 SELF-REVIEW QUESTIONS

In order to test your progress, you should be able to answer the following questions.

Look in the man pages or the chapter for help on commands. You need to find the best answer to the question. Note that some answers may not be exact replacements. So you need to think about which one comes closest to the results you want.

1) In Solaris x86 you are at the format> prompt. What is the command to create a Solaris partition on a blank hard disk?
   a) _____fdisk
   b) _____format
   c) _____fsck
   d) _____mformat
   e) _____newfs

2) Which of the following command will create a filesystem on a Solaris partition that already exists on a hard disk?
   a) _____fdisk
   b) _____format
   c) _____fsck
   d) _____mformat
   e) _____newfs

3) In Solaris x86, you want to make a Solaris partition active and bootable on the master disk on the primary IDE controller. Which of the following would you use?
   a) _____the -b option to newfs
   b) _____the flag /s to the format command
   c) _____the boot option to mkfs
   d) _____a menu choice in fdisk in the format menu
   e) _____None of the above

4) It is possible to have two Solaris x86 partitions active on the same drive at the same time.
   a) _____True
   b) _____False

Quiz answers appear in Appendix A, Section 10.2.

L A B 10.3

MAKING A SOLARIS SWAP SPACE

LAB OBJECTIVES

After this Lab, you will be able to:

✓ Create a Swap Space

✓ Delete a Swap Space

✓ Permanently Mounting the Swap

UNIX and many other operating systems use disk space as an extension of memory. Some processes take more space than you have memory available to run in. The alternatives for the process include:

- Don't run at all.
- Load and run only small portions of the program into memory at a time. When they are completed, unload their information and then load in new information. This is how a computer used to run when memory was scarce and disk space was either nonexistent or at a premium.
- Use part of the disk as an extension of memory. When you run out of disk space, swap pages of memory out to disk and either swap back others or make memory available for new processes. This is the most common way of running large or multiple programs that go beyond the memory available.

Solaris allows you to use swap space on either a raw disk slice, a UNIX file or a remote filesystem mounted via NFS. You may have noticed that when you did a `mount` or `df` in Solaris in previous exercises, the `/tmp` space was also known as `swap`. You will find out that this is not the swap space. We will discuss how to find the current swap space, make new space, delete a swap space and permanently add a swap space.

MAKING AN ADDITIONAL SWAP SPACE IN SOLARIS

Solaris can use a regular file, unused disk partition, or even a file accessed remotely via NFS as the **swap** space. This is similar to DOS/Windows, which also uses just a swap file. By default, the system uses part of the /tmp directory for swap space. If you want to create additional swap space, you can summarize the steps as:

1.   `mkfile` -- where `mkfile` has the following format:

    mkfile size{k|b|n} file-name

Here, `size` is the size in kilobytes, blocks, or megabytes, followed by the appropriate single letter to create the Solaris partition, and file-name is the name of the file to be used for swapping.

2.   `swap -a` -- You can enable swapping with the following:

    swap -a path-name

Here, `path-name` is the absolute path-name of the file created previously by the `mkfile` command.

This is similar to the `swapon` command in Linux.

You should review the swap space discussion in the Linux chapter. Also look in the man pages for:

swap

LAB 10.3 EXERCISES

10.3.1 CREATE A SWAP SPACE

You can determine what your current swap space by using the command:

```
swap -l
```

a) What do you see when you type the `swap -l` command? What is your prompt?

LAB 10.3

_____

_____

This will give you a listing of all the current swap space you have in use.

Now take the disk space you created in Lab 10.2, which is now mounted as `/mnt`, and create a swap file. You are going to use a regular file for swap instead of creating another partition, though you could certainly create your own partition.

On our example system, we will create a 100 MB swap file. To do this, we use the command in the following format:

```
mkswap nnn{k|b|m} file-name
```

Here, k, b, or m stand for kilobytes, blocks, or megabytes. On our example system, we will use the following command:

```
mkswap 100m /mnt/swap
```

Now go ahead and create the swap file on your system.

b) What happens when you create the swap file?

_____

_____

You must now activate the swap space. Use the following command:

```
swap -a file-name
```

The -a stands for add. In our example system, we will use:

```
swap -a /mnt/swap
```

Now you can go ahead and activate the swap space. You should notice that swap -a is basically the same command as swapon in Linux.

**LAB
10.3**

c) What happens when you run the swap -a command?

_____

_____

You must verify that the swap space is now active. Do this with the following command:

```
swap -l
```

d) What happens when you enter the swap -l command?

_____

_____

10.3.2 DELETE A SWAP SPACE

This exercise will show you how to delete a swap space.

You should not delete a swap space unless you are sure that it is OK to do so. On a live multiuser system, your system may panic if there is not enough swap space to handle all the swap data. When you delete a swap space, newer versions of Solaris will just move the data off the swap space to be deleted to another swap space that is still active. This assumes that there is enough swap space. Solaris may also give you a message that there is not enough swap space in which the data can be

moved. If you are running some other version of UNIX, such as AIX, just deleting a swap space may not take effect until the system is rebooted.

Enter the following command:

```
swap -l
```

a) What do you see when you run the swap -l command?

_____

_____

**LAB
10.3**

To delete the swap space, just use the following:

```
swap -d path-name
```

In our example system, we would use:

```
swap -d /mnt/swap
```

b) What happens when you execute swap -d path-name?

_____

_____

Now list the swap spaces like you did in Question a of this Exercise.

c) What command did you use to list the swap spaces? What were your results?

_____

_____

You should just see the original swap space or spaces that you started out with. You will note that we have only disabled the swap file. If you want to permanently remove the swap space, just use the command, as in our example system:

```
rm /mnt/swap
```

This will remove it permanently.

10.3.3 PERMANENTLY MOUNT THE SWAP SPACE

If you deleted the swap space in the previous exercise, just go ahead and create the swap space as described in Exercise 10.3.1.

If you have disabled the swap space in the previous exercise, you can just start it up again with the following command:

```
swap -a path-name
```

or you can use:

```
swap -a /mnt/swap
```

In order to permanently mount the swap space you just created, you must add it to `/etc/vfstab`. The line will have the following format:

```
path-name -- swap- no-
```

So, for our example system, we would use:

```
/mnt/swap -- swap- no-
```

Now you should go ahead and edit your `/etc/vfstab` and add this line to the bottom of the file. Just replace the path-name with the name of the file you are using.

a) What do you see when you add the line to `/etc/vfstab`?

_____

_____

You want to reboot the system now to be sure that the swap space comes up automatically.

Once you have logged back in, do a listing of the swap space in use.

b) What command did you use to determine the swap space in use? What are your results?

_____

_____

LAB 10.3 EXERCISE DISCUSSION

This section gives you some suggested answers to the questions in Lab 10.3, with discussion related to those answers. Your answers may vary, but the most important thing is whether or not your answer works. Use this discussion to analyze differences between your answers and those presented here.

If you have alternative answers to the questions in this Exercise, you are encouraged to post your answers and discuss them at the companion Web site for this book, located at:

```
http://www.phptr.com/phptrinteractive
```

10.3.1 ANSWERS

a) What do you see when you type the `swap -l` command? What is your prompt?

Answer: Your results should look like:

```
# swap -l
swapfile            dev  swaplo blocks    free
/dev/dsk/c0d0s1     102,1    8 224896 224896
#
```

The first column gives the block device name that is currently used for swap space. The numbers 102,1 refer to the major and minor numbers of the device. This is followed by the swaplo, which is the swaplow value. Blocks refers to the number of blocks assigned to the swap space, and free is the number of swap blocks that are free. You will notice that the two are the same on this system, because this system is not currently using any swap space. If you were monitoring your swapping, you might want to look at this and see if your swap space is sufficient. If you are running out of swap space, you may want to consider increasing the swap space, or better still, increasing the available memory, since the system will swap when it needs more memory. Decreasing the swapping will increase your system performance.

b) What happens when you create the swap file?

Answer: You will see the following:

```
# mkfile 100m /mnt/swap
#
```

If everything works OK, you will just get the command line prompt.

c) What happens when you run the swap -a command?

Answer: You will see the following:

```
# swap -a /mnt/swap
#
```

If there are no errors, you will just get the command line prompt back.

d) What happens when you enter the swap -l command?

Answer: You will see the following:

```
# swap -l
swapfile              dev   swaplo blocks    free
/dev/dsk/c0d0s1      102,1      8 224896 224896
/mnt/swap                -      8 204792 204792
#
```

Notice that we have added the /mnt/swap partition to the list of current swap spaces.

10.3.2 ANSWERS

Enter the following command:

```
swap -l
```

a) What do you see when you run the swap -l command?

Answer: You should see something similar to the following:

```
# swap -1
swapfile                dev  swaplo blocks   free
/dev/dsk/c0d0s1        102,1      8 224896 224896
/mnt/swap                -        8 204792 204792
#
```

LAB
10.3

If you just completed the previous exercise, the results will be the same as those at the end of the previous exercise.

b) What happens when you execute swap -d path-name?

Answer: You should just get back the command line prompt.

c) What command did you use to list the swap spaces? What were your results?

Answer: You would use the swap -1, and you should no longer see the swap file you created.

d) What happens when you try to list the /mnt/swap file?

Answer: If you do the command ls -1 /mnt/swap, you will get a message that there is no such file or directory. An ls -1 /mnt will just give a listing of the directory without the swap file.

10.3.3 ANSWERS

a) What do you see when you add the line to /etc/vfstab?

Answer: Your file should look like the following:

#device #to mount	device to fsck	mount point	FS type	fsck pass	mount at boot	mount options
#						
fd	-	/dev/fd	fd	-	no	-
/proc	-	/proc	proc	-	no	-
/dev/dsk/c0d0s1	-	-	swap	-	no	-
/dev/dsk/c0d0s0	/dev/rdsk/c0d0s0	/	ufs	1	no	-

```
/dev/dsk/c0d0s6 /dev/rdsk/c0d0s6 /usr           ufs    1    no    -
/dev/dsk/c0d0s3 /dev/rdsk/c0d0s3 /export        ufs    2    yes   -
/dev/dsk/c0d0s7 /dev/rdsk/c0d0s7 /export/home   ufs    2    yes   -
/dev/dsk/c0d0s4 /dev/rdsk/c0d0s4 /export/swap   ufs    2    yes   -
/dev/dsk/c0d0s5 /dev/rdsk/c0d0s5 /opt           ufs    2    yes   -
/dev/dsk/c0d1s2 /dev/rdsk/c0d1s2 /usr/local     ufs    2    yes   -
swap             -                /tmp          tmpfs  -    yes   -
/dev/dsk/c1d1s0 /dev/rdsk/c1d1s0 /mnt           ufs    2    yes   -
/mnt/swap        -                -             swap   -    no    -
```

Notice that the swap space is the last line in the file. It is important that, in general, anything you add should be at the end of the file. In the previous example, /mnt/swap is part of /mnt, which is also mounted from the file. If you put the mounted filesystem ahead of the filesystem where it will be mounted, you will minimally not be able to use the mounted filesystem. Your mileage may vary.

b) What command did you use to determine the swap space in use? What are your results?

Answer: Again, you can use the swap -1 command.

LAB 10.3 SELF-REVIEW QUESTIONS

In order to test your progress, you should be able to answer the following questions.

Look in the man pages or the chapter for help on commands. You need to find the best answer to the question. Note that some answers may not be exact replacements. So you need to think about which one comes closest to the results that you want.

Consider the following results from entering the `swap -l` command:

```
# swap -l
swapfile            dev   swaplo  blocks    free
/dev/dsk/c0t0d0s1   102,1   8     224896    222320
/mnt/swap           -       8     204792    200792
#
```

1) The first swap device is actually a full disk slice.
   a) _____ True
   b) _____ False

2) The swap space in the above display is (are) which of the following?
   a) _____ /dev/dsk/c0t0d0s1
   b) _____ /mnt/swap
   c) _____ /dev/dsk/c0t0d0s1 and /mnt/swap
   d) _____ /dev/dsk/c0t0d0s1, /mnt/swap, /tmp
   e) _____ None of the above

3) The numbers 102,1 actually refer to the inode number of the first swap space.
   a) _____ True
   b) _____ False

4) To determine the amount of swap space that is actually in use, you can use the following formula:

   Swap_Used = Total_Swap - Swap_Free
   - Swap_Used is the amount of swap space that is in use
   - Total_Swap is the total amount set aside for swap and is under the column heading blocks
   - Swap_Free is the amount of free swap space and is under the column heading free

Which of the following is the amount of swap space used in the first swap space in this section?

a) _____224896

b) _____222320

c) _____8

d) _____102

e) _____2576

5) The first swap space is on a SCSI device.

a) _____True

b) _____False

6) Which of the following is the command to only disable the above Solaris swap space /mnt/swap?

a) _____rm /mnt/swap

b) _____del /mnt/swap

c) _____swap -d /mnt/swap

d) _____swapoff /mnt/swap

e) _____swap -ad /mnt/swap

7) Which of the following is the command to delete the above disabled Solaris swap space /mnt/swap?

a) _____rm /mnt/swap

b) _____del /mnt/swap

c) _____swap -d /mnt/swap

d) _____swapoff /mnt/swap

e) _____swap -ad /mnt/swap

8) If you look in /etc/vfstab and see the following entry:

```
/home/swap -    - swap -no -
```

it means that the swap device is which of the following?

a) _____/home

b) _____/home/swap/swap

c) _____/home/swap

d) _____/mnt/swap

e) _____None of the above

9) The command to enable a swap partition in Solaris is which of the following?

a) _____swapon
b) _____swap -a
c) _____swap -on
d) _____swapit
e) _____swap -e

10) The command:

```
mkfile 5b /home/swap
```

**LAB
10.3**

will make a file whose size is which of the following?

a) _____5.12 MB
b) _____2.56 MB
c) _____5.12 K
d) _____2.56 K
e) _____None of the above

If you are not sure about the last question, try it, even as a regular user, by running `/usr/sbin/mkfile` *with the above options and checking the results.*

Quiz answers appear in Appendix A, Section 10.3.

CHAPTER 10

TEST YOUR THINKING

The projects in this section are meant to have you utilize all of the skills that you have acquired throughout this chapter. The answers to these projects can be found at the companion Web site to this book, located at:

`http://www.phptr.com/phptrinteractive`

Visit the Web site periodically to share and discuss your answers.

1) Format a diskette in Solaris with a DOS format. Look at the diskette in a DOS/Windows system. What are the necessary steps to read and properly mount this diskette?

    Save a file to the diskette. Go back to Solaris and see if you can read the diskette. Congratulations—you have just created your own sneaker-net!

2) This chapter has discussed disks and filesystems with an emphasis on IDE/ EIDE devices. You have seen how an IDE device can map to a Solaris device. An example is the master drive on the primary IDE controller being mapped to `/dev/rdsk/c0d1`.

    Research how, or whether, the SCSI Logical Unit Number and SCSI id have a corresponding exact mapping to the Solaris device name. Remember that the SCSI names are similar to the IDE names, except that they have an additional component with a t. SCSI CD-ROMs are usually `/dev/cd0`, `/dev/cd1`, and the like.

3) Experiment with various formats for partitions in Solaris. Consider `ufs`, and various DOS formats.

    a) Try formatting the partitions with Solaris. What happens?

    b) If you are running a multi-boot Solaris x86 system, boot to DOS/Windows and try formatting the DOS partition you created in Solaris. Determine which commands you must prepare.

c) Go back to Solaris and mount these partitions.

d) Add these partitions to `/etc/fstab`. Then try mounting them with the `mount` command, using just the mount point or the `/dev` device.

e) Reboot your system. See if these partitions are properly mounted.

4) This Project will give you an understanding of swap space usage.

a) Do the command `swap -l` on your Solaris system to determine the current swap space usage. What are your results?

b) Create an additional swap space as a file on the same Solaris partition. How did you do it, and what happens?

c) Create an additional swap slice on the same Solaris partition. How did you do it, and what happens?

d) Add the new swap spaces to your `/etc/vfstab` tab. What does your new file look like?

e) Reboot your system and enter the `swap -l` command again. What do you see?

f) What is the difference between Steps (a) and (e) of this Project?

APPENDIX A

ANSWERS TO SELF-REVIEW QUESTIONS

CHAPTER 1

Lab 1.1 ■ Self-Review Answers

Question	Answer	Comments
1)	a	
2)	a	
3)	b	
4)	b	
5)	c	
6)	b	
7)	c	
8)	c	
9)	c	

Lab 1.2 ■ Self-Review Answers

Question	Answer	Comments
1)	e	
2)	d	
3)	a	
4)	c	

Lab 1.2 ■ Self-Review Answers

Question	Answer	Comments
5)	c	
6)	d	
7)	b	
8)	c	
9)	d	
10)	d	
11)	e	

CHAPTER 2

Lab 2.1 ■ Self-Review Answers

1)	c
2)	c
3)	e

Lab 2.2 ■ Self-Review Answers

1)	b
2)	c
3)	b
4)	a
5)	d
6)	c

Lab 2.3 ■ Self-Review Answers

1)	c
2)	d
3)	b
4)	b
5)	d
6)	b

Lab 2.3 ■ Self-Review Answers (Continued)

7)   a

8)   c

CHAPTER 3
Lab 3.1 ■ Self-Review Answers

1)   b

2)   a

3)   d

4)   d

5)   c

6)   c

7)   d

8)   d

Lab 3.2 ■ Self-Review Answers

1)   a

2)   b

3)   b

4)   b

5)   b

6)   d

CHAPTER 4
Lab 4.1 ■ Self-Review Answers

1)   a

2)   c

3)   b

4)   c

5)   d

Lab 4.2 ■ Self-Review Answers

1)	a	The .login file is executed last and overwrites other values.
2)	b	Only the .cshrc file is executed, not .login.
3)	c	The C Shell will check for a valid terminal type.
4)	e	Again, .login is executed last.
5)	b	

Lab 4.3 ■ Self-Review Answers

1)	a
2)	b
3)	b
4)	e
5)	b

CHAPTER 5

Lab 5.1 ■ Self-Review Answers

1)	a
2)	d
3)	a
4)	c
5)	d

Lab 5.2 ■ Self-Review Answers

1)	a
2)	c
3)	b
4)	e
5)	b

CHAPTER 6

Lab 6.1 ■ Self-Review Answers

1)   a
2)   b
3)   c
4)   d
5)   d

Lab 6.2 ■ Self-Review Answers

1)   b
2)   a
3)   b
4)   a
5)   b
6)   b
7)   a
8)   d
9)   c
10)   e

Lab 6.3 ■ Self-Review Answers

1)   a
2)   a
3)   c
4)   a

CHAPTER 7

Lab 7.1 ■ Self-Review Answers

1)   b
2)   c
3)   b
4)   c
5)   d

Lab 7.2 ■ Self-Review Answers

1)   d
2)   a
3)   d
4)   a

Lab 7.3 ■ Self-Review Answers

1)   d
2)   b
3)   b
4)   a
5)   b

Lab 7.4 ■ Self-Review Answers

1)   e
2)   b
3)   b
4)   e
5)   a

CHAPTER 8

Lab 8.1 ■ Self-Review Answers

1)   b
2)   d
3)   a
4)   c
5)   c
6)   d

Lab 8.2 ■ Self-Review Answers

1)   a
2)   e
3)   a
4)   a   This is type 83. The type 82 is linux swap.
5)   a

Lab 8.3 ■ Self-Review Answers

1)   b
2)   d
3)   c
4)   c
5)   b

CHAPTER 9

Lab 9.1 ■ Self-Review Answers

1)   b
2)   a
3)   b
4)   c

Lab 9.2 ■ Self-Review Answers

1)   a
2)   c
3)   a
4)   c

Lab 9.3 ■ Self-Review Answers

1)   c
2)   c
3)   a
4)   c

CHAPTER 10

Lab 10.1 ■ Self-Review Answers

1)   a
2)   d
3)   b
4)   b
5)   c
6)   a
7)   c

Lab 10.2 ■ Self-Review Answers

1)   a
2)   e
3)   d
4)   d
5)   b

Lab 10.3 ■ Self-Review Answers

1)	a	
2)	c	
3)	b	
4)	e	
5)	a	You can tell by the extra t0, which is only found on SCSI
6)	c	
7)	a	
8)	c	
9)	b	
10)	d	The b stands for physical, not logical blocks.

IMPORTANT UNIX COMMANDS

In an age where information and knowledge is growing at a fantastic rate, it is impossible to know all the information we need to advance in our career. The important thing is to know where and how to find the information. —Joe

THE FIND COMMAND

Look at your UNIX text (if you have one) and the man pages for the `find` *command for more information.*

The `find` command is a very useful command. You can use it to check on the security of your system, backup the system, and many other everyday things you will do as a system administrator.

When trying to understand the `find` command, it can be useful to understand the properties of a file and what is stored concerning the file. A file's inode contains (or is referred to by) the following information:

- inode number—Used by the partition to reference the file
- mode—Permission mask and type of file
- link count—Number of directories that contain an entry with this inode number
- user ID—ID of the file's owner
- group ID—ID of the file's group
- size—Number of bytes in this file
- access time—Time at which the file was last accessed

- mod time—Time at which the file was last modified
- inode time—Time at which this inode structure was last modified

Other information that is stored about a file and not in the inode is as follows:

- name

The find command can examine this and other information about a file. There are often numeric arguments to a command to look for time that is greater than, equal to, or less than a certain amount. The numeric arguments can be specified as follows:

- +n—for greater than n
- --n—for less than n
- n—for exactly n

Basically, you use the command in the format find -options. There are many options to the find command. The following options are valid and probably the most useful in Linux when using find:

You will use the find *command with several labs in this workbook and will use it often as an administrator.*

-mount   Don't descend directories on other filesystems. An alternate name for -xdev, for compatibility with some other versions of find. A good example of its use is:
find /usr -mount -print | cpio -oBcv > /dev/rmt/0m
This is the same as:
find /usr -xdev -print | cpio -oBcv > /dev/rmt/0m
This will find all the files on the /usr partition and will save them to the tape drive using cpio. It will not backup any filesystems that are mounted under /usr.

`-depth`	Process each directory's contents before the directory itself. This is sometimes necessary when an operation must be performed on the contents of a directory before the directory itself. Sometimes this is used on `cpio`, because otherwise the modification dates on copied directories would not match the originals. find /usr mount -print | cpio -oBcv > /dev/rmt/0m
`-xdev`	Don't descend directories on other filesystems. This is also equivalent to `-mount`. See the example for `-mount`.
`-amin n`	File was last accessed **n** minutes ago. Used to find all files that have been accessed more or less than a certain time. It looks at the inode information for access time. find /-amin -10 -print | cpio -oBcv > /dev/rmt/0m This finds all files that have been accessed less than 10 minutes ago and backs them up.
`-atime n`	File was last accessed **n***24 hours ago. It looks at the inode access time information. find /usr -atime -10 -print This displays finds all files under /usr that have been accessed less than 10 days ago.
`-cmin n`	File's status was last changed **n** minutes ago. find /usr -cmin -10 -print This will find all files that have been changed within the last 10 minutes.
`-cnewer file`	File's status was last changed more recently than file was modified. `-cnewer` is affected by `-follow` only if `-follow` comes before `-cnewer` on the command line. find /etc -cnewer /etc/passwd This will find all files under /etc that are newer then /etc/passwd.
`-ctime n`	File's status was last changed **n***24 hours ago. find /etc -ctime -10 /etc/passwd This will find all files under /etc where the file's status was changed less than 10 days ago.
`-gid n`	File's numeric group ID is **n**. Will find files whose group id is **n**. An example is: find /home -gid 15 This will find files that have the group id 15 under the /home directory.
`-mmin n`	Will find files whose data was last modified **n** minutes ago.

`-mtime n`	Will find files whose data was last modified **n***24 hours ago.
`-name pattern`	Base of file name (the path with the leading directories removed) matches shell pattern. The metacharacters ("*", "?", and "[]") do not match a `.' at the start of the base name.  To ignore a directory and the files under it, use prune; see an example in the description of -path. Another example is: find /usr -name \*user\* -print This will find files that have the string "user" as part of their name. Some examples include `moduser, adduser, useradd`.
`-perm mode`	File's permission bits are exactly mode (octal or symbolic). Symbolic modes use mode 0 as a point of departure.

■ AS AN EXAMPLE

Consider the following command:

```
find . -perm 700
```

This returns the following results:

```
./junk
./security
./security/file_list
```

When you do an `ls -l` on the files, you will see the following:

```
-rwx------ 1 myid mygroup    0 Mar 5 21:07 junk
drwx------ 2 myid mygroup 1024 Mar 6 14:51 security
-rwx------ 1 myid mygroup 1268 Mar 614:51 file_list
```

`-perm -mode`	All of the permission bits mode are set for the file.

■ AS AN EXAMPLE

Consider the following command:

```
find . -perm -700
```

This returns the following results:

```
./junk
./security
```

```
        ./security/file_list
```
When you do an `ls -l` on the files, you will see the following:

```
        -rwxr-x-- 1 myid mygroup    0 Mar 5 21:07 junk
        drwx-w---x 2 myid mygroup 1024 Mar 6 14:51 security
        -rwxr-xr-x 1 myid mygroup 1268 Mar 614:51 file_list
```
But it will not return the file that has the following attributes for `ls -l`:

```
        -rw-r-x-- 1 myid mygroup    0 Mar 5 21:07 myfile
```

    `-perm    +mode`   Any of the permission bits mode are set for the file.

■ AS AN EXAMPLE

Consider the following command:

```
        find . -perm +700
```
This returns the following results:

```
        ./junk
        ./security
        ./security/file_list
```
When you do an `ls -l` on the files, you will see the following:

```
        -rwxr-x-- 1 myid mygroup    0 Mar 5 21:07 junk
        drwx-w---x 2 myid mygroup 1024 Mar 6 14:51 security
        -rwxr-xr-x 1 myid mygroup 1268 Mar 614:51 file_list
```
But it will not return the file that has the following attributes for `ls -l`:

```
        d---r-x-- 1 myid mygroup    0 Mar 5 21:07 mydir
```

        `-type c`   File is of type **c**:

Where the type c is:

b   block (buffered) special

c   character (unbuffered) special

d   directory

p   named pipe (FIFO)

f   regular file

l   symbolic link

s   socket

Consider the following command:

find . -type d

This returns all directories and subdirectories under your current directory.

-uid n   File's numeric user ID is **n**.

The following command:

find . -uid 100

returns all files and directories under your current directory that are owned by the **uid** 100.

-exec command   Execute command; true if 0 status is returned. All following arguments to find are taken to be arguments to the command until an argument consisting of ";" is encountered. The string "{}" is replaced by the current file name being processed everywhere it occurs in the arguments to the command, not just in arguments where it is alone, as in some versions of find. Both of these constructions might need to be escaped (with a "\") or quoted to protect them from expansion by the shell. The command is executed in the starting directory. A good example is:
find . -exec ls -l {} \;
This will find all files and subdirectories under the current directories and do a long listing (-ls) of the files.

-print   Print the full file name on the standard output, followed by a newline. Note that this is required for find on some versions of UNIX to get any output. Current versions of Linux and UNIX generally do not require the use of the print option.
find /home -type d -print
This will print out all the directories under the /home directory.

-ls   True; list current file in "ls -dils" format on standard output. The block counts are of 1K blocks, unless the environment variable POSIXLY_CORRECT is set, in which case 512-byte blocks are used. The command:
find $HOME -ls
will find all the files under your home directory and do a listing in the following format: 10362 0 -rwx------1 root myid 0 Mar 21 16:02 ./myprog.

VARIOUS SHUTDOWN COMMANDS

You have seen, in the chapter on rebooting the system, there are various ways to do so. The discussion that follows examines the various ways of shutting down the system.

Look in the man pages for:

`shutdown halt reboot sync init`

FLIP THE SWITCH

There are a number of ways to bring down a UNIX system. The quickest way is to flip the switch. This should only be done in the most drastic of situations. The computer keeps track of what it is doing in memory, because this approach is faster than storing the information on disk. However, when you shutdown your system, there is often information in memory that must be written to disk. If the information on the disk is incomplete, the system may have errors when it comes back up.

SYNC AND HALT

The `sync` command synchronizes the memory and disk information. The operating system process `/etc/update` will run the sync command every 30 seconds. The `halt` command just stops the system in the quickest possible way, bypassing any system cleanup procedures. The quickest way to bring down the system and save the memory information is to do the following:

`sync; sync; halt`

You should note that with the current versions of Linux and some other versions of UNIX, the halt command actually calls the shutdown command if it is in run level 1 - 5. In this case, it is the same as doing the following:

`shutdown -h`

The halt process does more than backup memory information. Otherwise, that would be all we need. There are other programs that are more complete and carry out the shutdown process.

REBOOT

The reboot process does a system halt and then a reboot. This is typically an init with run level 6. There are a number of options to the reboot command. Usually, all you must do to cause a reboot is type:

```
reboot
```

In the newer versions of UNIX, this is the same as the command:

```
shutdown -r
```

INIT

`Init` can be used with the run level to change the level of the system. `Init` looks up information in the `/etc/inittab` table. It then processes whichever programs are needed to change to the new level. If a reboot is called for, then looks for all entries with 6 in the `/etc/inittab` table, because run level 6 is a reboot. So you could enter the command:

```
init 6
```

This is similar to the reboot command, and in fact, may even be the same, depending on how the reboot command is defined.

/SBIN/SHUTDOWN

`/sbin/shutdown` is a binary executable file and is the standard shutdown command in current versions of UNIX. There are various options to the shutdown command. You saw previously the use of `-r` and `-h`. When `shutdown` is called with one of those options, along with possibly some others, the `init` process will reread the `/etc/inittab` table and then execute the processes appropriate to the run level. In the case of `halt`, it is run level 0, and in the case of reboot, it is run level 6.

There are oftentimes `rc` directories or files relating to the halt and reboot. Just look for files or directories of the name `rc0`, `rc0.d`, `rc6`, and `rc6.d`. Those files or directories contain programs that can be executed when shutting down or rebooting the system. Linux uses the directory `/etc/rc.d` to hold those directories. Solaris and other versions of UNIX based on System V use `/etc/rc0.d`, `/etc/rc1.d`, and so forth.

There are other useful options to shutdown, such as -f . This option causes a fast reboot, and may bypass some things on the startup, such as running hardware and software diagnostics, removing old tmp files, and other kinds of housekeeping chores. The command would then be:

```
shutdown -f
```

This would cause the system to do a fast reboot.

/ETC/SHUTDOWN

This is often just a link to /sbin/shutdown, as in Solaris 2.6. Other times it is actually a separate program. The program /etc/shutdown is practically always a shell program. Its main function is to bring down the system cleanly.

The usage of /etc/shutdown and, by extension, /sbin/shutdown is as follows:

```
Usage: /etc/shutdown [ -y ] [ -g<grace> ] [ -i<initstate> ] [
message ]
```

/USR/UCB/SHUTDOWN

This is a carryover from Berkeley UNIX. The actual format is as follows:

```
Usage: shutdown [ -krhfn ] shutdowntime [ message ]
```

Many things are carried over from Berkeley UNIX. There are some really nice programs, such as whereis, *that can help you work with UNIX. There are also many commands that you are familiar with, but are just written differently and may have some different options. You should look in* /usr/ucb *to see what is available there.*

APPENDIX C

RUNNING YGGDRASIL LINUX

 Our ability to learn is dependent upon the tools we have. All the systems in the world would mean nothing to us if we couldn't use them to meet our needs. Being a system administrator means that you have learned how to administer a system. We need to practice what we preach. We also need to be able to totally mess up a system and then recover from our mistakes. —Joe

The challenge of learning to be an administrator in UNIX is that you need to administer the system to learn. Oftentimes there are issues that keep the beginning administrator from getting the control necessary. In many environments, security concerns prevent the student from exercising full administrative control. This is particularly true in academic environments, where the training can be spread over many weeks and many people have access to a system. For the classes I have taught, I have chosen Yggdrasil Linux, because it gives the student the ability to administer a system without damaging the network or computer infrastructure.

WHY LINUX?

There are several manufacturers that have UNIX or UNIX-like operating system (OS) for the PC. They include SCO UNIX, Solaris x86, and several others. However, none of them have the wealth of free software or source code that Linux has. In addition, there is no licensing or distribution restrictions on Linux, other than the GNU-type copyrights. It is supported by a wealth of USENET newsgroups and there are many people on the Internet who are very helpful.

WHY YGGDRASIL LINUX?

To use Linux in the class I teach, I needed a version that is easy to run, does not require configuration by the students, and runs right out of the box. I experimented with a number of versions of Linux. Except for Yggdrasil, all the versions either used the CD-ROM for install only, or if they had a live file system, required some knowledge of Linux in order to run and required a hard disk partition to be setup first (which was not possible in the academic environment). I wanted running Linux to be easy.

For my classes, I chose Yggdrasil Linux. Yggdrasil Linux will run on most PC-based computers. It can also be run entirely from CD-ROM. You need a boot disk to boot Linux. (A boot diskette is included with the software.) All further discussions here will be based on the Fall 1995 revision B of Yggdrasil Linux. This is the most current version as of Winter 1998. You will see "revision B" on the boot diskette and CD-ROM. There is a second CD-ROM that is included that contains source code to many of the programs used by Linux, as well as many other additional free programs.

Because Yggdrasil Linux uses the CD-ROM, I decided to take advantage of this feature to teach UNIX. This was used in addition to using AIX for exercises that did not require administrative access. It was an overwhelming success, and in fact, most students welcomed running Linux at home, because it allowed them to do assignments without having to come into the college except for class. Every student but one had a PC at home that included a CD-ROM. The PCs at the college all had CD-ROMs installed (after much encouragement from me and other instructors). Therefore, using Linux did not handicap any students in doing their assignments.

HARDWARE REQUIREMENTS

The essential hardware ingredients are:

1. RAM. The kernel and other files are loaded into RAM from the boot diskette. This is mounted as the filesystem /ram-disk.
2. Boot Diskette. This contains the basic Linux kernel and basic Linux system files. Once the software is loaded into RAM, the boot diskette is no longer needed. This frees the diskette drive to be used for loading in customized files or backup.

3. CD-ROM. Loads more advanced files into /ramdisk and contains the remainder of the live filesystem to run Linux. This is then mounted as /.

You may think that the missing ingredient is the hard disk. That's because you don't need it. Yggdrasil Linux runs entirely off the listed hardware. This means that you don't have to mess with any hard disk setup.

STARTING LINUX

You start Linux by putting the boot diskette and Linux CD-ROM into the proper drives and then powering on or rebooting the PC. You can reboot your PC by pressing the key combination Ctrl-Alt-Del. This causes your PC to reboot. If your PC does not respond, just power off the PC for about 10 seconds and power it up again.

The PC then loads in the basic Linux kernel and checks for various hardware devices, resulting in many messages on the screen while it is booting. The program is checking to see if various kinds of hardware are there by probing various base addresses and seeing what kind of response is given. Sometimes this probing process causes the PC to hang, in which case it may be necessary to modify the boot parameters.

THE BOOT PROMPT

You have the opportunity to change the boot parameters when you see a screen with YGI in big letters and the following prompt:

```
boot:
```

In some versions of Linux, you will only see the boot prompt with no YGI or other graphics on the screen. I have found that, with many of the PCs I have worked with, it has been necessary or advisable to use additional parameters at the boot prompt. If you wish to continue with no changes, just press Enter at this point.

You usually do not need additional boot parameters when running Linux on a SCSI-based system. However, colleges and computer training facilities usually use EIDE hard drives and IDE/ATAPI CD-ROMS on their PCs. SCSI devices tend to be used only on servers, because they are more expensive. Therefore, the discussion in this chapter will focus on IDE/EIDE devices.

Using an IDE or EIDE hard disk and CD-ROM presents some configuration challenges. Most current EIDE controller cards allow for primary and secondary IDE controllers. In addition, two devices, known as master and slave drives, can be attached to each channel. IDE CD-ROMS follow the same hardware and Linux conventions as hard disks. You can see, in Figure C.1, the actual layout of the hard drives on the system and the naming convention used by Linux.

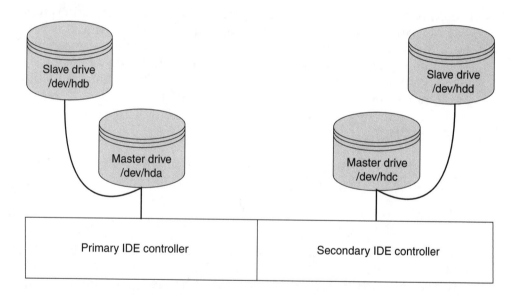

Figure C.1 ■ **Layout of Master and Slave Primary and Secondary Controllers**

It is important that students understand the hardware configuration in case there are any errors. The students may need to set up the boot parameters based on the hardware. Over half of my students in one class had problems that were eliminated once they understood the IDE configuration issues.

If your PC configuration is not recognized by the boot diskette, you may need to boot with some options. This discussion will only cover running Linux on an IDE or EIDE based PC, using only an IDE CD-ROM.

SOME PROBLEMS TO BE AWARE OF

Experience teaches that it is better to have a motherboard with integrated, rather than separate, IDE controllers. Separate IDE controllers sometimes have timing problems with some motherboards. If you should later decide to add a better IDE controller than the motherboard has, you can always disable the onboard controller.

Some motherboards look at an IDE controller as the primary controller and ignore a secondary controller on the controller card. This has been seen on some older motherboards, but it may affect how you set up your PC. In this case, you may want to make sure your CD-ROM is on the primary controller as the slave device.

HARD DISK AND CD-ROM PARAMETERS

Some students have had to add several common boot parameters in order to get Linux working on both the school's system and their home systems. If you are using an IDE CD-ROM that is not recognized right away, you may need to enter an option similar to the following:

```
linux hdc=cdrom
```

Here, /dev/hdc is a UNIX device reference to the CD-ROM. Looking at Figure C.1, you can see that this is the master drive on the secondary controller. You may need to replace hdc with hdb or hdd, depending on where the CD-ROM is connected to the controller and its jumper settings. The same convention is used for hard disks and CD-ROMs.

The references are as follows:

- **hda** is the master drive on the primary IDE controller
- **hdb** is the slave drive on the primary IDE controller
- **hdc** is the master drive on the secondary IDE controller
- **hdd** is the slave drive on the secondary IDE controller

RAMDISK PARAMETERS

When the system boots up, it allocates a certain amount of memory as ramdisk. This ramdisk acts like a regular disk and allows you to copy and work with files without affecting or needing a hard disk. Further, the ramdisk is mounted and loaded just like a regular hard disk. The /var, /etc, and other filesystems are copied to /ramdisk and are modified as needed. By default, Linux uses 512 K of memory for ramdisk. This is sufficient for some things done in a class environment.

Because most of the file system is stored in RAM, you may need to increase the size of the RAM disk. On a system with 16 MB of RAM, a RAM disk of 8 MB is sufficient for classwork, leaving 8 MB for the OS. You can adjust the size upward as memory size increases. You can also add an entry to set the size of the ramdisk. To set the RAM disk size of 8 MB, use the following command:

```
ramdisk=8000
```

This would create a ramdisk whose size is 8 MB (8000 blocks of 1024 bytes). This assumes you have at least 8 MB of additional memory available. However, if you allocate too much memory for the ramdisk, Linux is smart enough to allocate a minimum amount of memory for the OS and applications, and then leave the rest for the ramdisk. It won't give an error message, and the only indications of the reduced size appear on the bootup messages for size and when you use the UNIX mount command. This will show the memory allocated to the ramdisk, which will make it easier to run Linux and other operations later.

An actual boot entry for a CD-ROM, as on the secondary controller with the CD-ROM as the master drive, would then be as follows:

```
linux hdc=CD-ROM ramdisk=8000.
```

ADDITIONAL USEFUL PARAMETERS

SERIALIZE

Sometimes there appears to be a problem with the IDE controller that prevents it from handling both the primary and secondary controllers at the same time. In this case, a very useful option is `hda=serialize`, a parameter that forces Linux to handle one controller at a time. This may, however, slow down the response of your system. A complete command line in this case may now look like:

```
linux ramdisk=8000 hda=serialize hdc=cdrom
```

OTHERS

There are other useful options that can speed things up, such as disabling the check for a Sound Blaster Pro CD-ROM controller.

BEYOND THE BOOT PROMPT

When you are done entering the Linux command line options, just press the Enter key. This will then to bootup the Linux OS. You will get many error messages, because Linux will try to guess how your PC is set up and will test certain things to see if there is a response. This may cause some PCs to hang if something responds in an unexpected manner. You will also notice that Linux will find certain devices, and will give messages about any devices it finds. You may want to keep track of all the devices found. Once you have figured out how to run Linux properly, it will be possible to make a customized boot disk that will not do all the probing done here, and will boot up a lot quicker. After many messages concerning various hardware devices, the system eventually gives you a login prompt.

GETTING TO LOGIN

Once the system has stopped booting, you will see a menu with the YGI on it. There are four different login options with Yggdrasil Linux, as follows:

1. **demo**—This gives an X-windows demo program that runs very slowly from the CD-ROM on the first use, but runs much quicker once it is in memory.
2. **guest**—This sets up a guest login with normal user rights. This is useful in teaching labs in which students must determine access rights for certain files and directories by trying to access them as guest.

3. **install**—This allows you to install Linux and gives several further installation menus.

4. **root**—This gives you all rights to files and commands.

At the bottom of the menu will be the following prompt:

```
login:
```

If you are running Linux off the CD-ROM, just enter the `root` id. You will have complete administrative control of your PC. For the purposes of this discussion, a root login is assumed.

 DO NOT enter the install id unless you are running on your own PC and plan on installing Linux on your hard disk. Entering the install id will not allow you to run commands as root. It will only install Linux on the PC.

You will now have the following prompt:

```
#
```

This is the standard UNIX command line prompt for root.

FILE SYSTEM STRUCTURE

Yggdrasil Linux uses memory for the file system area that is changeable. Figure C.2 shows the Linux file system structure that you will eventually end up with. You should refer to this diagram as you read through the rest of this discussion.

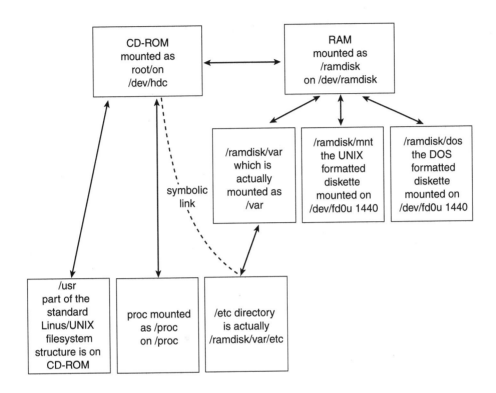

Figure C.2 ■ Linux File System Structure

Type the following command:

```
mount
```

When you type the `mount` command without arguments, the screen output will look similar to the following:

```
/dev/hdc on / type iso9660 (ro)
/dev/ramdisk on /ramdisk type ext2 (rw)
/proc on on type /proc (type)
```

- **/dev/hdc** refers to the CD-ROM, which is mounted as root.

- **/dev/ramdisk** refers to the filesystem named /ramdisk, which is using internal RAM. This filesystem contains files that can be changed.
- **/proc** is the standard UNIX pointer location for devices.

The structure is shown in Figure C.3.

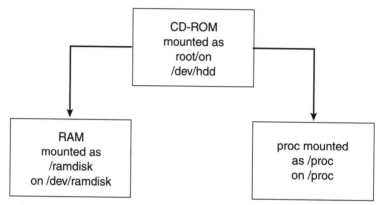

Figure C.3 ■ The Initial Layout of the Linux File Structure

At this point, you can create some working directories to be used as mount points for the diskette. This will allow you to save any work you do. You can make the directories as follows:

```
mkdir /ramdisk/mnt /ramdisk/dos
```

This command will create two directories on /ramdisk to be used as follows:

- /ramdisk/mnt is used to mount a UNIX-formatted diskette.
- /ramdisk/dos is used to mount a DOS-formatted diskette.

Note that unless you have two diskette drives, you can only use one mount point at a time. The purpose of two mount points is to help you keep track of which diskette type is mounted at which time, to allow you to create scripts to automatically mount and unmount the diskettes.

USING DISKS AND DISKETTES

There are several steps in making a disk available to UNIX. The steps can be summarized as follows:

1. Create partitions using `fdisk`. This is the same procedure as in DOS. You can make the whole drive a single partition, or you can have up to four primary partitions and a number of extended ones within each of the primary partitions.
2. Format the diskette or disk partition. Linux uses two major disk and diskette formats, UNIX and DOS. The UNIX format is called `ext2fs` for the extended filesystem. There are, however, a number of other formats that can be used by Linux.
3. Make a filesystem on the diskette or disk. The disk must be formatted to the filesystem type used by the OS. For UNIX, this includes establishing free inode tables, lists of free and used blocks, and OS-specific information on the disk.
4. Mount the disk as part of the UNIX filesystem.

CREATING A LINUX FILE SYSTEM ON THE DISKETTE

You can format a 1.44 MB diskette in Linux with the standard Linux file format, which is `ext2fs`, by typing the following command:

```
fdformat /dev/fd0h1440
```

The following will appear on the screen:

```
Double sided, 80 tracks, 19s sec/track. Total capac-
ity is 1440 KB
formatting...done
verifying... done
```

Note that formatting the diskette will destroy any files already on the diskette you insert.

You must now create a UNIX filesystem on the diskette. Type the following command:

```
mkfs /dev/fd0H1440
```

You can then mount the diskette as follows:

```
mount /dev/fd0H1440 /ramdisk/mnt
```

Now when you type mount alone you will see the following:

```
/dev/hdc on / type iso9660 (ro)
/dev/ramdisk on /ramdisk type ext2 (rw)
/proc on on type /proc (type)
/dev/fd0u1440 on /ramdisk/mnt type ext2 (rw)
```

In this example, /dev/fd0H1440 actually was mounted as /dev/fd0u1440. This is just another name for the same Linux device. Linux files can now be saved to /ramdisk/mnt.

So you can now look at the filesystem by visualizing the structure in Figure C.4.

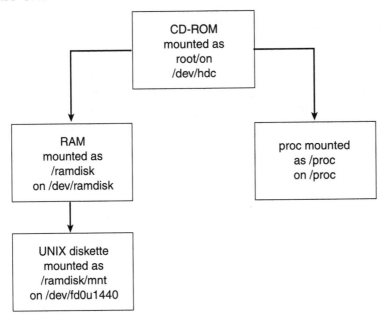

Figure C.4 ■ Drawing of File System Showing UNIX-Formatted Diskette

To unmount the diskette, use the following command:

```
umount /ramdisk/mnt
```

Alternatively, the following will also work:

```
umount /dev/fd0H1440
```

USING AN MS-DOS-BASED DISKETTE AND FILES

It is sometimes necessary to transfer student assignments from Linux to other UNIX systems or MS-DOS-based systems. Because networking is not enabled by default with Yggdrasil Linux, you must look at alternative ways of moving data. This brings us to what used to be known as "sneaker-net." If there is no printer attached to the PC, it is necessary to save the file to an MS-DOS diskette so it can be read and printed from DOS. In order to do that, you must first setup the diskette as an MS-DOS filesystem under Linux. You can also create or mount an MS-DOS filesystem and reboot under DOS/WINDOWS.

Start with a diskette that is already formatted for DOS, or format one under DOS or Windows. Linux can also be used to format the diskette. Before formatting a diskette under Linux, you should be sure that the diskette from the previous exercises are unmounted. Otherwise, you may get an error message; in some cases, other unpredictable things could happen.

If you have a diskette that you want to DOS format, first verify that you can overwrite the diskette. Once you overwrite it, all the information is lost. You can format a diskette in Linux with a DOS format by doing the following:

```
mformat a:
```

Mount the DOS diskette with the following command:

```
mount -t msdos /dev/fd0H1440 /ramdisk/dos
```

Notice that you are now using the option `-t msdos` for `mount`. This option is derived from UNIX System V release 4 and allows you to mount a number of filesystems of various types on the fly.

Typing `mount` alone produces the following output:

```
/dev/hdc on / type iso9660 (ro)
/dev/ramdisk on /ramdisk type ext2 (rw)
/proc on on type /proc (type)
/dev/fd0u1440 on /ramdisk/dos type msdos (rw)
```

You can now save files in DOS format to `/ramdisk/dos`. Note that you must use the standard DOS file naming convention of up to eight characters for the prefix, then a period, then up to three characters for the extension.

Once the diskette is mounted, you can work with it by doing the following:

- Save the file to the directory `/ramdisk/dos`.

- See what is saved on the diskette by using the command:

```
ls /ramdisk/dos
```

- Unmount it by typing the following command:

```
umount /ramdisk/dos
```

- Put the diskette in your DOS-based PC.
- Use any text-based viewer or editor to look at the file or files on the A: drive.

Be sure that when you are done using the diskette under Linux, you always unmount the diskette with the following command:

```
umount /ramdisk/dos
```

If you fail to unmount the diskette, you can sometimes get system errors or a later mount will fail.

See Figure C.5 for the new layout of the Linux filesystem showing the DOS diskette mounted under Linux.

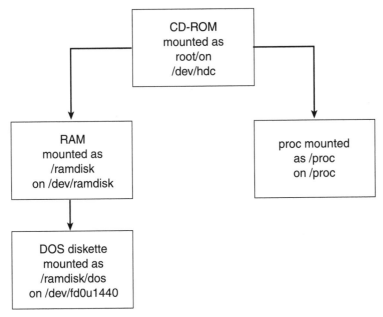

Figure C.5 ■ Layout of the File System Showing the DOS-Formatted Diskette

PRINTING FROM YGGDRASIL LINUX

Printing is one of the biggest problems I have encountered while running the Yggdrasil Linux. Because the Linux is not networked by default, a printer must be directly attached to the PC in order to print. Otherwise, any files must be saved to a DOS-formatted diskette and then printed from DOS/Windows. In addition, setting up the print spooler requires modifying configuration files and running daemons, which in turn requires some configuration on the part of the student.

Until you have more experience with Linux, one quick and dirty way to print is to print the output directly to the hardware device and bypass the print spooler. Generally, Yggdrasil Linux sets up the PC printer port as /dev/lp1. (This requires an attached printer.) For some unknown reason, it sometimes establishes /dev/lp0 as the printer port. Keep this in mind throughout the following discussion.

Files can be printed by using the following command:

```
cat filename > /dev/lp1 (This will send the raw file
   to the device port)
echo ^v^l > /dev/lp1 (use the sequence <ctrl-v><ctrl-
   l>) (
```

The second step is necessary because the first step will not completely print out the file. This will send a form feed to the printer to eject the last page of your printout. Otherwise, your last page will just sit in the printer until the next print job. If you are logged in as guest, make sure you have read/write permissions on the printer port by typing:

```
chmod 666 /dev/lp1
```

or:

```
chmod 666 /dev/lp0
```

Some printers, like the IBM Proprinter, have a problem with UNIX files and do not put out a carriage return when they receive a line feed. So the file output will look like steps going across and down the page. This problem has not been seen with the Canon inkjet printer. Some printers allow you to customize this setting. This problem is caused by the fact that UNIX ends a line with a line-feed, whereas DOS ends a line with a carriage-return and line-feed.

Some versions of Linux and UNIX have a DOS-to-UNIX and UNIX-to-DOS conversion utility. If you have a stepping problem when you print, you might try converting your file first. If you try printing a DOS file in UNIX, you may end up with a double-spaced file. If you have an `lpr` print spooler running, you might try the following command:

```
cat filename | todos | lpr
```

Here `todos` is a program to convert Linux files to DOS-formatted files so they can print on a DOS-type printer. You can also try the following command when the print spooler is not running:

```
cat filename | todos > /dev/lp1
echo ^v^l > /dev/lp1
```

The `todos` command is not available in some versions of UNIX. It is also known by other names in other versions of UNIX. You will need to research the appropriate command on your version of UNIX.

The ultimate solution to the printing problem is, of course, to run the print spooler. However, if the configuration is not done just right, the spooler doesn't work; thus, using the quick and dirty way makes it easier to get started using Linux. It also helps students understand the printing process and provides a way of debugging printer problems. You can eventually set up the printer system by establishing the `/etc/printcap` file. Save the file to diskette and then copy it back the next time you use Yggdrasil Linux.

MODIFYING SYSTEM FILES

The `/etc` directory is symbolically linked to the `/ramdisk/var/etc` directory; therefore, students have write access to most files needed to administer the system. The files are saved on the diskette in Linux format, and the next time the student reboots the system, the changed files can be copied back in once the system is running again. It is even possible to modify the boot diskette; just be sure to back it up. However, modifying the boot diskette requires some knowledge of how the boot diskette is laid out, so be prepared for a lot of work if you don't understand it. You should look at Figure C.6 to get an idea of how the filesystem is linked and how to use /etc.

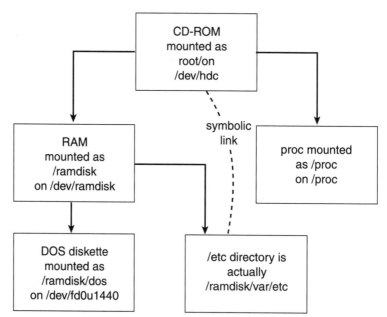

Figure C.6 ■ Layout of the Linux File System Showing /etc Linkage

SUMMARY

After the preceding steps are completed and understood, you can have full control of the Linux system. There is no need to network or save files to a hard disk. This gets you up to speed very quickly in learning administration. By using Linux without the hard disk, there is no way you can cause permanent damage to the UNIX. If the system hangs, a simple reboot will restore the previous values, and you can start over again in administering your system.

However, because networking is a possibility with Linux, it should be entirely possible to network Yggdrasil Linux to print remotely across the network. Once the hardware is in place and network security issues are addressed, I am sure it will be an effective tool to teach networking concepts as well. This is a matter for further research.

Yggdrasil Linux can therefore be set up quite effectively to teach UNIX administration. It is inexpensive, relatively secure, and students can use it at home, work, or school without modifying their PCs. It helps solve the biggest problems I have experienced as an instructor of UNIX.

CLOSING POINTS TO BE AWARE OF

- When formatting the diskette, because the information is stored in RAM, the file system and mount information is lost on reboot. Of course, any information that is saved to diskette will be there, unless you reformat the diskette or overwrite the files.
- With MS-DOS, you are restricted to a file name with eight characters before the period and three characters after the period. If you were to save a file in Linux with a longer file name and read it in MS-DOS, you may see unpredictable things.
- All MS-DOS files end with both a line feed and carriage return, symbolized by `<lf><cr>`, whereas UNIX files end with only a line feed, `<lf>`. So when you look at UNIX files in MS-DOS, they will seem to hop across the screen, whereas if you look at MS-DOS single-spaced files, they will look double-spaced.
- You cannot use any DOS files modified or created with a word processor in UNIX unless you have saved them totally as text files. You cannot use WRITE or any word processor in

its native format. This is because these programs will add extra control characters that cannot be recognized by the UNIX OS. They will cause the system to give error messages or to crash. You can only use files accessed by

- EDIT
- NOTEPAD
- Any other text-only based editor
- Processed and saved by a word processor as text files

- Some Windows 95 programs will incorrectly read the file even if they recognize it as a text file and try to read it without formatting. You can run EDIT from the RUN option for WIN95 to look at and change your files.

- If you get an error about being unable to mount the diskette because of the existence of /etc/mtab~, or when you try to save a file to /etc, it means that the link from /etc to /ramdisk/etc is not or cannot be made. You should then create a separate link for /etc:

```
mkdir /ramdisk/etc
cd /etc
find . -print | cpio -pdmuv /ramdisk/etc
ln -s /etc /ramdisk/etc
```

- **/ramdisk/etc** will be used to hold a copy of the /etc directory, and its contents will be used instead of the contents on the CD-ROM. Otherwise, you could not do any programs that involve changing /etc, such as mounting files. You cannot access the diskette until you have /etc on the ramdisk area. Once you are pointing to /ramdisk/etc, you can create additional links to /ramdisk/mnt/etc if you want to use the /etc directory on the diskette.

- You must umount any diskette before you eject it. If you add any files to the diskette and reinsert it in the disk drive, the new files will not be recognized until you remount it.

APPENDIX D

LINUX INFORMATION SHEET

Major computer advances have generally been made in two ways. The first is to throw a lot of money at solving a problem without a definite expectation of a return on the investment. The second way is to throw a lot of time at solving a problem without a definite expectation of a return on the investment.
                                                                    —Joe

This article was written by Michael K. Johnson <johnsonm@redhat.com> v4.13, 24 October 1997, and is available at many Linux sites on the Internet, including `http://sunsite.unc.edu` *as the Linux HOW-TO. It is reprinted based on the GNU GPL (Gnu General Public License), which that allows free copying as long as proper attribution is given and the copying is done in its entirety, which it is.*

This document provides basic information about the Linux operating system, including an explanation of Linux, a list of features, some requirements, and some resources.

1. INTRODUCTION TO LINUX

Linux is a completely free reimplementation of the POSIX specification, with SYSV and BSD extensions (which means it looks like UNIX, but does not come from the same source code base), which is available in both source code and binary form. Its copyright is owned by Linus Torvalds

<torvalds@transmeta.com> and other contributors, and is freely redistributable under the terms of the GNU General Public License (GPL). A copy of the GPL is included with the Linux source; you can also get a copy from <ftp://prep.ai.mit.edu/pub/gnu/COPYING>.

Linux is not public domain, nor is it "shareware." It is "free" software, commonly called freeware, and you may give away or sell copies, but you must include the source code or make it available in the same way as any binaries you give or sell. If you distribute any modifications, you are legally bound to distribute the source for those modifications. See the GNU General Public License for details.

 Linux is still free as of version 2.0, and will continue to be free. Because of the nature of the GPL to which Linux is subject, it would be illegal for it to be made not free. Note carefully: the "free" part involves access to the source code rather than money; it is perfectly legal to charge money for distributing Linux, so long as you also distribute the source code. This is a generalization; if you want the fine points, read the GPL.

Linux runs on 386/486/Pentium machines with ISA, EISA, PCI and VLB busses. MCA (IBM's proprietary bus) is not well-supported in 2.0.x and earlier versions, but support has been added to the current development tree, 2.1.x. If you are interested, see <http://glycerine.itsmm.uni.edu/mca>. There is a port to multiple Motorola 680x0 platforms (currently running on some Amigas, Ataris, and VME machines), which now works quite well. It requires a 68020 with an MMU, a 68030, 68040, or a 68060, and also requires an FPU. Networking and X now work. See <news:comp.os.linux.m68k>.

Linux runs well on DEC's Alpha CPU, currently supporting the "Jensen", "NoName", "Cabriolet", "Universal Desktop Box" (better known as the Multia), and many other platforms. For more information, see <http://www.azstarnet.com/~axplinux/FAQ.html>.

Linux runs well on Sun SPARCs; most sun4c and sun4m machines now run Linux, with support for sun4 and sun4u in active development. Red Hat Linux is (as of this writing) the only Linux distribution available for SPARCs; see <http://www.redhat.com/support/docs/rhl-sparc/>.

Linux is being actively ported to the PowerPC architecture, including PowerMac (Nubus and PCI), Motorola, IBM, and Be machines. See

`<http://www.cs.nmt.edu/~linuxppc/>` and `<http://www.linux-ppc.org/>`

Ports to other machines, including MIPS and ARM, are under way and showing various amounts of progress. Don't hold your breath, but if you are interested and able to contribute, you may well find other developers who wish to work with you.

Linux is no longer considered to be in beta testing, as version 1.0 was released on March 14, 1994. There are still bugs in the system, and new bugs will creep up and be fixed as time goes on. Because Linux follows the "open development model," all new versions will be released to the public, whether or not they are considered "production quality." However, in order to help people tell whether they are getting a stable version or not, the following scheme has been implemented: Versions 1.x.y, where x is an even number, are stable versions, and only bug fixes will be applied as y is incremented. So from version 1.2.2 to 1.2.3, there were only bug fixes, and no new features. Versions 1.x.y, where x is an odd number, are beta-quality releases for developers only, and may be unstable and may crash, and are having new features added to them all the time. From time to time, as the correct development kernel stabilizes, it will be frozen as the new "stable" kernel, and development will continue on a new development version of the kernel.

The current stable version is 2.0.31 (this will continue to change as new device drivers get added and bugs fixed), and development has also started on the experimental 2.1.x kernels. If 2.0.x is too new for you, you may want to stick with 1.2.13 for the time being. However, the latest releases of 2.0 have proved quite stable. Do note that in order to upgrade from 1.2 to 2.0, you need to upgrade some utilities as well; you may wish to upgrade to the latest version of your Linux distribution in order to obtain those utilities. The Linux kernel source code also contains a file, Documentation/Changes, which explains these changes and more.

Most versions of Linux, beta or not, are quite stable, and you can keep using those if they do what you need and you don't want to be on the bleeding edge. One site had a computer running version 0.97p1 (dating from the summer of 1992) for over 136 days without an error or crash. (It would have been longer if the backhoe operator hadn't mistaken a main power transformer for a dumpster...) Others have posted uptimes in excess of a year. One site still had a computer running Linux 0.99p15s over 600 days at last report.

One thing to be aware of is that Linux is developed using an open and distributed model, instead of a closed and centralized model like much other software. This means that the current development version is always public (with up to a week or two of delay) so that anybody can use it. The result is that whenever a version with new functionality is released, it almost always contains bugs, but it also results in a very rapid development so that the bugs are found and corrected quickly, often in hours, as many people work to fix them.

In contrast, the closed and centralized model means that there is only one person or team working on the project, and they only release software that they think is working well. Often this leads to long intervals between releases, long waiting for bug fixes, and slower development. The latest release of such software to the public is sometimes of higher quality, but the development speed is generally much slower.

As of October 24, 1997, the current stable version of Linux is 2.0.31, and the latest development version is 2.1.59.

2. LINUX FEATURES

- multitasking: several programs running at once.

- multiuser: several users on the same machine at once (and no two-user licenses!)

- multiplatform: runs on many different CPUs, not just Intel.

- multiprocessor: SMP support is available on the Intel and SPARC

- platforms (with work currently in progress on other platforms), and Linux is used in several loosely-coupled MP applications, including Beowulf systems (see <http://cesdis.gsfc.nasa.gov/linux-web/beowulf/beowulf.html>) and the Fujitsu AP1000+ SPARC-based supercomputer.

- runs in protected mode on the 386.

- has memory protection between processes, so that one program can't bring the whole system down.

- demand loads executables: Linux only reads from disk those parts of a program that are actually used.

- shared copy-on-write pages among executables. This means that multiple process can use the same memory to run in. When one tries to write to that memory, that page (4KB piece of memory) is copied somewhere else. Copy-on-write has two benefits: increasing speed and decreasing memory use.

- virtual memory using paging (not swapping whole processes) to disk: to a separate partition or a file in the filesystem, or both, with the possibility of adding more swapping areas during runtime (yes, they're still called swapping areas). A total of 16 of these 128 MB swapping areas can be used at once, for a theoretical total of 2 GB of useable swap space. It is simple to increase this if necessary, by changing a few lines of source code.

- a unified memory pool for user programs and disk cache, so that all free memory can be used for caching, and the cache can be reduced when running large programs.

- dynamically linked shared libraries (DLL's), and static libraries too, of course.

- does core dumps for post-mortem analysis, allowing the use of a debugger on a program not only while it is running but also after it has crashed.

- mostly compatible with POSIX, System V, and BSD at the source level.

- through an iBCS2-compliant emulation module, mostly compatible with SCO, SVR3, and SVR4 at the binary level.

- all source code is available, including the whole kernel and all drivers, the development tools and all user programs; also, all of it is freely distributable. Plenty of commercial programs are being provided for Linux without source, but everything that has been free, including the entire base operating system, is still free.

- POSIX job control.

- pseudoterminals (pty's).

- 387-emulation in the kernel so that programs don't need to do their own math emulation. Every computer running Linux appears to have a math coprocessor. Of course, if your computer already contains an FPU, it will be used instead of the emulation, and you can even compile your own kernel with math emulation removed, for a small memory gain.

- support for many national or customized keyboards, and it is fairly easy to add new ones dynamically.

- multiple virtual consoles: several independent login sessions through the console, you switch by pressing a hot-key combination (not dependent on video hardware). These are dynamically allocated; you can use up to 64.

- Supports several common filesystems, including minix, Xenix, and all the common system V filesystems, and has an advanced filesystem of its own, which offers filesystems of up to 4 TB, and names up to 255 characters long.

- transparent access to MS-DOS partitions (or OS/2 FAT partitions) via a special filesystem: you don't need any special commands to use the MS-DOS partition, it looks just like a normal Unix filesystem (except for funny restrictions on filenames, permissions, and so on). MS-DOS 6 compressed partitions do not work at this time without a patch (dmsdosfs). VFAT (WNT, Windows 95) support is available in Linux 2.0.

- special filesystem called UMSDOS which allows Linux to be installed on a DOS filesystem.

- read-only HPFS-2 support for OS/2 2.1

- HFS (Macintosh) file system support is available separately as a module.

- CD-ROM filesystem which reads all standard formats of CD-ROMs.

- TCP/IP networking, including ftp, telnet, NFS, etc.

- Appletalk server

- Netware client and server

- Lan Manager (SMB) client and server

- Many networking protocols: the base protocols available in the latest development kernels include TCP, IPv4, IPv6, AX.25, X.25, IPX, DDP (Appletalk), NetBEUI, Netrom, and others. Stable network protocols included in the stable kernels currently include TCP, IPv4, IPX, DDP, and AX.25.

3. HARDWARE ISSUES

3.1 MINIMAL CONFIGURATION

The following is probably the smallest possible configuration that Linux will work on: 386SX/16, 1 MB RAM, 1.44 MB or 1.2 MB floppy, any supported video card (+ keyboards, monitors, and so on of course). This should allow you to boot and test whether it works at all on the machine, but you won't be able to do anything useful. See <http://rsphy1.anu.edu.au/~gpg109/mem.html> for minimal Linux configurations.

In order to do something, you will want some hard disk space as well, 5 to 10 MB should suffice for a very minimal setup (with only the most important commands and perhaps one or two small applications installed, like, say, a terminal program). This is still very, very limited, and very uncomfortable, as it doesn't leave enough room to do just about anything, unless your applications are quite limited. It's generally not recommended for anything but testing if things work, and of course to be able to brag about small resource requirements.

3.2 USABLE CONFIGURATION

If you are going to run computationally intensive programs, such as gcc, X, and TeX, you will probably want a faster processor than a 386SX/16, but even that should suffice if you are patient.In practice, you will want at least 4 MB of RAM if you don't use X, and 8 MB if you do. Also, if you want to have several users at a time, or run several large programs (compilations for example) at a time, you may want more than 4 MB of memory. It will still work with a smaller amount of memory (should work even with 2 MB), but it will use virtual memory (using the hard drive as slow memory) and that will be so slow as to be unusable. If you use many programs at once, 16 MB will reduce swapping considerably. If you don't want to swap appreciably under any normal load, 32 MB will probably suffice. Of course, if you run memory-hungry applications, you may want more.

The amount of hard disk you need depends on what software you want to install. The normal basic set of Unix utilities, shells, and administrative programs should be comfortable in less than 10 MB, with a bit of room to spare for user files. For a more complete system, get Red Hat, Debian, or another distribution, and assume that you will need 60 to 300 MB, depending on what you choose to install and what distribution you get. Add whatever space you want to reserve for user files to these totals. With today's prices on hard drives, if you are buying a new system, it makes no sense to buy a drive that is too small. Get at least 500 MB, preferably 1GB or more, and you will not regret it.

Add more memory, more hard disk, a faster processor and other stuff depending on your needs, wishes and budget to go beyond the merely usable. In general, one big difference from DOS is that with Linux, adding memory makes a large difference, whereas with DOS, extra memory doesn't make that much difference. This of course has something to do with DOS's 640KB limit, which is completely nonexistent under Linux.

3.3 SUPPORTED HARDWARE

CPU:

Anything that runs 386 protected mode programs (all models of 386's 486's, 586's, and 686's should work. 286s and below may someday be supported on a smaller kernel called ELKS (Embeddable Linux Kernel Subset), but don't expect the same capabilities). A version for the 680x0 CPU (for x = 2 with external MMU, 3, 4, and 6) which runs on Amigas and Ataris can be found at tsx-11.mit.edu in the 680x0 directory. Many DEC Alphas, SPARCs, and PowerPC machines are supported. Ports are also being done to the ARM, StrongARM, and MIPS architectures. More details are available elsewhere.

ARCHITECTURE:

ISA or EISA bus. MCA (mostly true blue PS/2's) support is incomplete but improving (see above). Local busses (VLB and PCI) work. Linux puts higher demands on hardware than DOS, Windows, and in fact most operating systems. This means that some marginal hardware that doesn't fail when running less demanding operating system may fail when running Linux. Linux is an excellent memory tester...

RAM:

Up to 1 GB on Intel; more on 64-bit platforms. Some people (including Linux) have noted that adding ram without adding more cache at the same time has slowed down their machine extremely,so if you add memory and find your machine slower, try adding more cache. Some machines can only cache certain amounts of memory regardless of how much RAM is installed (64 MB is the most one popular chipset can cache). Over 64 MB of memory will require a boot-time parameter, as the BIOS cannot report more than 64MB, because it is "broken as designed."

DATA STORAGE:

Generic AT drives (EIDE, IDE, 16 bit HD controllers with MFM or RLL, or ESDI) are supported, as are SCSI hard disks and CD-ROMs, with a supported SCSI adaptor. Generic XT controllers (8 bit controllers with MFM or RLL) are also supported. Supported SCSI adaptors: Advansys, Adaptec

1542, 1522, 1740, 27xx, and 29xx (with some exceptions) series, Buslogic MultiMaster and Flashpoint, NCR53c8xx-based controllers, DPT controllers, Qlogic ISP and FAS controllers, Seagate ST-01 and ST-02, Future Domain TMC-88x series (or any board based on the TMC950 chip) and TMC1660/1680, Ultrastor 14F, 24F and 34F, Western Digital wd7000, and others. SCSI, QIC-02, and some QIC-80 tapes are also supported. Several CD-ROM devices are also supported, including Matsushita/Panasonic, Mitsumi, Sony, Soundblaster, Toshiba, ATAPI (EIDE), SCSI, and others. For exact models, check the hardware compatibility HOWTO.

VIDEO:

VGA, EGA, CGA, or Hercules (and compatibles) work in text mode. For graphics and X, there is support for (at least) normal VGA, some super-VGA cards (most of the cards based on ET3000, ET4000, Paradise, and some Trident chipsets), S3, 8514/A, ATI, MACH8/32/64, and hercules. (Linux uses the Xfree86 X server, so that determines what cards are supported. A full list of supported chipsets alone takes over a page.)

NETWORKING:

- Ethernet support includes 3COM 503/509/579/589/595/905 (501/505/507 are supported but not recomended), AT&T GIS (neé NCR) WaveLAN, most WD8390-based cards, most WD80x3-based cards, NE1000/2000 and most clones, AC3200, Apricot 82596, AT1700, ATP, DE425/434/435/500, D-Link DE-600/620, DEPCA, DE100/101, DE200/201/202 Turbo, DE210, DE422, Cabletron E2100 (not recommended), Intel EtherExpress (not recommended), DEC EtherWORKS 3, HP LAN, HP PCLAN/plus, most AMD LANCE-based cards, NI5210, ni6510, SMC Ultra, DEC 21040 (tulip), Zenith Z-Note Ethernet. All Zircom cards and all Cabletron cards other than the E2100 are unsupported, due to the manufacturers' unwillingness to release programming information freely.
- FDDI support currently includes the DEFxx cards from DEC.
- Point-to-Point networking support includes PPP, SLIP, CSLIP, and PLIP.
- Limited Token Ring support is available.

SERIAL:

Most 16450 and 16550 UART-based boards, including AST Fourport, the Usenet Serial Card II, and others. Intelligent boards supported include Cyclades Cyclom series (supported by the manufacturer), Comtrol Rocketport series (supported by the manufacturer), Stallion (most boards; supported by the manufacturer), and Digi (some boards; supported by the manufacturer). Some ISDN, frame relay, and leased line hardware is supported.

OTHER HARDWARE:

SoundBlaster, ProAudio Spectrum 16, Gravis Ultrasound, most other sound cards, most (all?) flavours of bus mice (Microsoft, Logitech, PS/2), etc.

4. AN INCOMPLETE LIST OF PORTED PROGRAMS AND OTHER SOFTWARE

Most of the common UNIX tools and programs have been ported to Linux, including almost all of the GNU stuff and many X clients from various sources. Actually, ported is often too strong a word, since many programs compile out of the box without modifications, or only small modifications, because Linux tracks POSIX quite closely. Unfortunately, there are not as many end-user applications yet as we would like, but this is changing rapidly. Contact the vendor of your favorite commercial UNIX application and ask if they have ported it to Linux.

Here is an incomplete list of software that is known to work under Linux:

Basic Unix commands:

ls, tr, sed, awk and so on (you name it, Linux probably has it).

Development tools:

gcc, gdb, make, bison, flex, perl, rcs, cvs, prof.

Languages and Environments:

C, C++, Objective C, Java, Modula-3, Modula-2, Oberon, Ada95, Pascal, Fortran, ML, scheme, Tcl/tk, Perl, Python, Common Lisp, and many others.

Graphical environments:

X11R5 (XFree86 2.x), X11R6 (XFree86 3.x), MGR.

Editors:

GNU Emacs, XEmacs, MicroEmacs, jove, ez, epoch, elvis (GNU vi), vim, vile, joe, pico, jed, and others.

Shells:

bash (POSIX sh-compatible), zsh (includes ksh compatiblity mode), pdksh, tcsh, csh, rc, es, ash (mostly sh-compatible shell used as /bin/sh by BSD), and many more.

Telecommunication:

Taylor (BNU-compatible) UUCP, SLIP, CSLIP, PPP, kermit, szrz, minicom, pcomm, xcomm, term (runs multiple shells, redirects network activity, and allows remote X, all over one modem line), Seyon (popular X-windows communications program), and several fax and voice-mail (using ZyXEL and other modems) packages are available. Of course, remote serial logins are supported.

News and mail:

C-news, innd, trn, nn, tin, smail, elm, mh, pine, etc.

Textprocessing:

TeX, groff, doc, ez, LyX, Lout, Linuxdoc-SGML, and others.

Games:

Nethack, several Muds and X games, and lots of others. One of those games is looking through all the games available at tsx-11 and sunsite.

Suites:

AUIS, the Andrew User Interface System. ez is part of this suite.

All of these programs (and this isn't even a hundredth of what is available) are freely available. Commercial software is becoming widely available; ask the vendor of your favorite commercial software if they support Linux.

5. WHO USES LINUX?

Linux is freely available, and no one is required to register their copies with any central authority, so it is difficult to know how many people use Linux. Several businesses now survive solely on selling and supporting Linux (and relatively few Linux users purchase products from those businesses), and the Linux newsgroups are some of the most heavily read on the Internet, so the number is likely in the millions, but firm numbers are hard to come by.

However, one brave soul, Harald T. Alvestrand <Harald.T.Alvestrand@uninett.no>, has decided to try. If you are willing to be counted as a Linux user, please use the web forms available at <http://counter.li.org/> Alternatively, you can send a message to linux-counter@uninett.no with one of the following subjects: "I use Linux at home," "I use Linux at work," or "I use Linux at home and at work." He will also accept "third-party" registrations; ask him for details.

He posts his counts to <news:comp.os.linux.misc> each month; they are also available from <http://counter.li.org/>.

6. GETTING LINUX

6.1 ANONYMOUS FTP

For freely-redistributable Linux documentation, see the Linux Documentation Project sites at

`<ftp://sunsite.unc.edu/pub/Linux/docs/LDP/>` and `<http://sunsite.unc.edu/LDP/>`

Stay tuned to the `<news:comp.os.linux.announce>` newsgroup for further developments.

At least the following anonymous FTP sites carry Linux.

Textual name	Numeric address	Linux directory
tsx-11.mit.edu	18.172.1.2	/pub/linux
sunsite.unc.edu	152.2.22.81	/pub/Linux
ftp.funet.fi	128.214.248.6	/pub/Linux
net.tamu.edu	128.194.177.1	/pub/linux
ftp.mcc.ac.uk	130.88.203.12	/pub/linux
src.doc.ic.ac.uk	146.169.2.1	/packages/linux
fgb1.fgb.mw.tu-muenchen.de	129.187.200.1	/pub/linux
ftp.informatik.tu-muenchen.de	131.159.0.110	/pub/comp/os/linux
ftp.dfv.rwth-aachen.de	137.226.4.111	/pub/linux
ftp.informatik.rwth-aachen.de	137.226.225.3	/pub/Linux
ftp.Germany.EU.net	192.76.144.75	/pub/os/Linux
ftp.ibp.fr	132.227.60.2	/pub/linux
ftp.uu.net	137.39.1.9	/systems/unix/linux
wuarchive.wustl.edu	128.252.135.4	/mirrors/linux
ftp.win.tue.nl	131.155.70.100	/pub/linux
ftp.stack.urc.tue.nl	131.155.2.71	/pub/linux
srawgw.sra.co.jp	133.137.4.3	/pub/os/linux

cair.kaist.ac.kr/pub/Linux

ftp.denet.dk	129.142.6.74	/pub/OS/linux
NCTUCCCA.edu.tw	140.111.1.10	/Operating-Systems/Linux
nic.switch.ch	130.59.1.40	/mirror/linux
sunsite.cnlab-switch.ch	193.5.24.1	/mirror/linux
cnuce_arch.cnr.it	131.114.1.10	/pub/Linux
ftp.monash.edu.au	130.194.11.8	/pub/linux
ftp.dstc.edu.au	30.102.181.31	/pub/linux
ftp.sydutech.usyd.edu.au	129.78.192.2	/pub/linux

tsx-11.mit.edu and fgb1.fgb.mw.tu-muenchen.de are the official sites for Linux's GCC. Some sites mirror other sites. Please use the site closest (network-wise) to you whenever possible.

At least `sunsite.unc.edu` and `ftp.informatik.tu-muenchen.de` offer ftpmail services. Mail `ftpmail@sunsite.unc.edu` or `ftp@informatik.tu-muenchen.de` for help.

If you are lost, try looking at `<ftp://sunsite.unc.edu/pub/Linux/distributions/>`, where several distributions are offered. Red Hat Linux and Debian appear to be the most popular distributions at the moment, at least in the U.S.

6.2 CD-ROM

Many people now install Linux from CD-ROM's. The distributions have grown to hundreds of MBs of Linux software, and downloading that over even a 28.8 modem takes a long time.

There are essentially two ways to purchase a Linux distribution on CD-ROM: as part of an archive of FTP sites, or directly from the manufacturer. If you purchase an archive, you will almost always get several different distributions to choose from, but usually support is not included. When you purchase a distribution directly from the vendor, you usually only get one distribution, but you usually get some form of support (mostly installation support).

6.3 OTHER METHODS OF OBTAINING LINUX

There are many BBSs that have Linux files. A list of them is occasionally posted to `comp.os.linux.announce`. Ask friends and user groups, or order one of the commercial distributions. A list of these is contained in the Linux distribution HOWTO, available as `<ftp://sun-site.unc.edu/pub/Linux/docs/HOWTO/distribution-HOWTO>`, and posted regularly to the `<news:comp.os.linux.announce>` newsgroup.

7. GETTING STARTED

As mentioned at the beginning, Linux is not centrally administered. Because of this, there is no "official" release that one could point at, and say "That's Linux." Instead, there are various "distributions," which are more or less complete collections of software configured and packaged so that they can be used to install a Linux system.

The first thing you should do is to get and read the list of Frequently Asked Questions (FAQ) from one of the FTP sites, or by using the normal Usenet FAQ archives (e.g. `rtfm.mit.edu`). This document has plenty of instructions on what to do to get started, what files you need, and how to solve most of the common problems (during installation or otherwise).

8. LEGAL STATUS OF LINUX

Although Linux is supplied with the complete source code, it is copyrighted software, not public domain. However, it is available for free under the GNU General Public License, sometimes referred to as the "copyleft." See the GPL for more information. The programs that run under Linux each have their own copyrights, although many of them use the GPL as well. X uses the MIT X copyright, and some utilities are under the BSD copyright. In any case, all of the software on the FTP site is freely distributable (or else it shouldn't be there).

9. NEWS ABOUT LINUX

A monthly magazine, called *Linux Journal*, was launched over three years ago. It includes articles intended for almost all skill levels, and is intended to be helpful to all Linux users. One-year subscriptions are $22 in the U.S., $27 in Canada and Mexico, and $32 elsewhere, payable in U.S. currency. Subscription inquiries can be sent via email to subs@ssc.com, or faxed to +1-206-782-7191, or phoned to +1-206-782-7733, or mailed to *Linux Journal*, PO Box 85867, Seattle, WA 98145-1867 USA. SSC has a PGP public key available for encrypting your mail to protect your credit card number; finger info@ssc.com to get the key.

There are several Usenet newsgroups for Linux discussion, and also several mailing lists. See the Linux FAQ for more information about the mailing lists (you should be able to find the FAQ either in the newsgroup or on the FTP sites).

The newsgroup `<news:comp.os.linux.announce>` is a moderated newsgroup for announcements about Linux (new programs, bug fixes, etc).

The newsgroup `<news:comp.os.linux.answers>` is a moderated newsgroup to which the Linux FAQ, HOWTO documents, and other documentation postings are made.

The newsgroup `<news:comp.os.linux.admin>` is an unmoderated newsgroup for discussion of administration of Linux systems.

The newsgroup `<news:comp.os.linux.development.system>` is an unmoderated newsgroup specifically for discussion of Linux kernel development. The only application development questions that should be discussed here are those that are intimately associated with the kernel. All other development questions are probably generic UNIX development questions and should be directed to a comp.unix group instead, unless they are very Linux-specific applications questions, in which case they should be directed at `comp.os.linux.development.apps`.

The newsgroup `<news:comp.os.linux.development.apps>` is an unmoderated newsgroup specifically for discussion of Linux-related applications development. It is not for discussion of where to get applications for Linux, nor a discussion forum for those who would like to see applications for Linux.

The newsgroup <news:comp.os.linux.hardware> is for Linux-specific hardware questions.

The newsgroup <news:comp.os.linux.networking> is for Linux-specific networking development and setup questions.

The newsgroup <news:comp.os.linux.x> is for Linux-specific X Windows questions.

The newsgroup <news:comp.os.linux.misc> is the replacement for comp.os.linux, and is meant for any discussion that doesn't belong elsewhere.

In general, do not crosspost between the Linux newsgroups. The only crossposting that is appropriate is an occasional posting between one unmoderated group and <news:comp.os.linux.announce>. The whole point of splitting the old comp.os.linux group into many groups is to reduce traffic in each group. Those that do not follow this rule will be flamed without mercy...

Linux is on the web at the URL <http://sunsite.unc.edu/LDP/>.

10. THE FUTURE

After Linux 1.0 was released, work was done on several enhancements. Linux 1.2 included disk access speedups, TTY improvements, virtual memory enhancements, multiple platform support, quotas, and more. Linux 2.0, the current stable version, has even more enhancements, including many performance improvements, several new networking protocols, one of the fastest TCP/IP implementations in the world, and far, far more. Even higher performance, more networking protocols, and more device drivers will be available in Linux 2.2.

Even with over 3/4 million lines of code in the kernel, there is plenty of code left to write, and even more documentation. Please join the linux-doc@vger.rutgers.edu mailing list if you would like to contribute to the documentation. Send mail to majordomo@vger.rutgers.edu with a single line containing the word "help" in the body (NOT the subject) of the message.

II. THIS DOCUMENT

This document is maintained by Michael K. Johnson `<johnsonm@redhat.com>`. Please mail me with any comments, no matter how small. I can't do a good job of maintaining this document without your help. A more-or-less current copy of this document can always be found at `<http://sunsite.unc.edu/LDP/>`.

12. LEGALESE

Trademarks are owned by their owners. There is no warranty about the information in this document. Use and distribute at your own risk. The content of this document is in the public domain, but please be polite and attribute any quotes.

APPENDIX E

LINUX INSTALLATION AND USAGE TIPS

When learning to administer an operating system, you should start with the very beginning. This means installing the software on a new system or a system on which you can wipe the disks clean. You should be able to remove and overwrite whatever was there before and start from the beginning. You should also be willing to reinstall the software a number of times while you learn and optimize it. Unfortunately, this is not always possible, but it should be considered whenever possible. —Joe

This Appendix provides some tips on installing and using Linux. Note that you *cannot install* Linux on many college computers. Some versions of Linux, in particular Yggdrasil, can be run from the CD-ROM, RAM, and diskette on these PCs. This discussion will not cover all the issues concerning Linux installation and usage.

There are no guarantees in life as far as computer installations are concerned. Your mileage may vary.

BOOTING

Linux will attempt to determine your hardware configuration when you boot off the diskette and CD-ROM. However, it will not work with all PC hardware configurations. There are several basically compatible versions of Linux. Versions of Linux, other than Yggdrasil, require at least a minimal amount of hard disk space to be used. Some versions of Linux give the user more flexibility, but require more knowledge of the software and hardware configurations you want to use. They may also require you to install Linux on your hard disk, and cannot be run totally from CD-ROM.

SCSI AND IDE

You should be able to run Linux from a PC that supports EIDE disks with an IDE/ATAPI CD-ROM. This will also work from a system that has entirely SCSI disk, CD-ROM, and tape drives. Mixing IDE or EIDE and SCSI complicates Linux installation and is not recommended for a first installation.

It is better to have a motherboard with a built-in hard disk, floppy disk, serial, and printer ports. This is because there are often timing issues between controller cards, video cards, and the motherboard that seem to be exaggerated in Linux and other versions of UNIX for PCs. There are many hardware devices supported by Linux, but your first system should have as simple a combination of devices as possible.

Some SCSI UNIX systems expect devices to be set up in a certain way. When starting up a system, the SCSI controller will probe SCSI IDs starting at 0. So your boot disk should be 0. The following is a listing of recommended SCSI ID Numbers:

- ID 0 First Boot Disk
- ID 1 Second Disk
- ID 2 Third Disk
- ID 4 Fourth Disk or Second Tape Backup Unit
- ID 5 First Tape Backup Unit
- ID 6 CD-ROM
- ID 7 SCSI Controller Card

There is sometimes a heavy power drain on the system's power supply to bring up a hard disk. Typically, the current draw is double when a drive is being brought up, compared to the current draw when the drive is running stable. Bringing up all the drives at once can be a big drain on the power supply and can sometimes be so heavy that the system will not come up. There are special jumpers on many SCSI drives to enable power up only when accessed. The drives are accessed and probed sequentially when the system is booted up. So by accessing the drives one at a time, the power drain is lessened. You should see the disk drive manufacturer instructions to determine which jumpers need to be set.

BACKUP

The three most important points to consider when installing and administering a PC or any operating system are:

1. Backup!
2. Backup!
3. Backup!

This cannot be overemphasized. If you have any information you think is worth saving, you should backup your system before installing Linux. Linux can and will modify your disk partition layout and master book tracks. It can modify FAT tables and partition information. By backing up your system before installation, you can safeguard your data. It is possible to run DOS once Linux is installed if you have not overwritten any DOS partitions, or if you reinstall your DOS and Windows software.

Tape backup units can be purchased for somewhere between $100 to $150 for 1600 MB floppy controller-based storage. Linux will recognize the 250/350 MB QIC-80 tape drives, as well as many of the higher capacity drives that run off the PC diskette drive cable. Some of the older versions of Linux may not recognize some of the larger capacity drives that use this cable, or they may recognize these tape drives as 250/350 MB tape drives. Linux will also recognize QC02 and many SCSI tape drives that will require additional software to be loaded or configured.

You must have a free partition on your hard disk to install Linux. It uses a filesystem different from DOS. To install and run Linux on your PC and continue to have access to your other software, you cannot have a total of more than four partitions, including Linux. (There are some tricks and special software that can be used to access more than this, but Linux just can't do it easily by itself.) You can use either the DOS or Linux FDISK command to modify or view your partition layout.

By taking these precautions, you can use Linux to learn UNIX at home or with a spare PC at work. You can administer systems on your own without causing problems on production systems. By creating a multi-boot option either within Linux, or some other software package, you can continue to use DOS, Windows, and most other PC-based operating systems.

PC-BASED UNIX SYSTEMS

A COMPARISON

The PC is the ideal tool to learn UNIX. Most of us have at least one. All that is required is a little hard disk space and some software, which can often be obtained for free or for a minimal price. The hardest decision is which version to get.   —Joe

PCs have become the most dominant form of computers in the world. The power of today's PCs equals that of the mainframes of 10 years ago. The computing power of the PC at least doubles every year. The PC is becoming the most dominant system running UNIX or UNIX-like operating systems (OSs).

The Intel microprocessors form the heart of the PC. This architecture is not the most ideal for running UNIX. It requires more complicated programming than other processors, such as the Motorola processors that have been used in the Apple PCs, or the PowerPC used in the newer Apples and IBM RS60000s. Because it has become popular by running PC-DOS, we are finding that we have to work with it to run inexpensive versions of UNIX.

A number of PC-based UNIX systems or UNIX emulators have been produced over the years. Some of the software packages just allowed you to run UNIX-like commands on a PC. Earlier PCs were handicapped by their slow speed and the limited architecture of the Intel 8088/86 processors used in the first IBM-compatible PCs.

XENIX

Several of the packages were notable in what they were able to accomplish. Xenix was originally marketed by Microsoft and even had a version that ran on the Digital Equipment Corporation PDP/11, as well as the PC. This product was eventually sold to Santa Cruz Operations (SCO), which has merged Xenix into its other PC-based product lines.

MINIX

The first commercial public domain UNIX for PCs was Minix. This was produced with much public help, though it was also sold commercially and parts of it were copyrighted.

LINUX

Eventually Minix was replaced by Linux, which was initially developed by a graduate student, Linus Torvalds, who developed it as a project to replace Minix. Its goal was to totally rewrite UNIX so that it contained no copyrighted code, which would reduce the cost to users and developers that used it.

A number of companies have packaged Linux and sold it commercially. The prices they charge are usually very low, because they do not have the development costs of a commercial package. Sometimes these companies also add value to Linux by creating installation programs and various graphical user interfaces (GUIs). However, any changes they make to publicly-available code also must be made publicly available.

Some of the commercial versions of Linux are described next.

RED HAT

This product can be purchased in several computer stores, such as CompUSA, or at computer shows. The installation program in this version is very easy to use, and the software is usually installed without a problem.

SLACKWARE

This is the official release by Linus Torvalds, and is the standard by which others are compared. The installation program is more complex and not for the beginning user. For the experienced user, though, Slackware offers a lot of control over the various packages that are installed.

CALDERA

This company has been at the forefront of producing a commercially-viable package of Linux. It was funded by Ray Norda, who was one of the founders of Novell. It can be compared in many ways to the commercialization of SCO UNIX. Caldera has added many additional features to Linux. They also sell various commercial software packages and an Office Suite that can be used with Linux.

YGGDRASIL

This was one of the first commercial packages of Linux. They also produce the Linux Bible and several other packages for Linux. They produce the only version of Linux that can be used without a hard disk. It can boot directly off the diskette, CD-ROM, and memory.

OTHER VERSIONS OF LINUX

Other versions include Debian, SuSe, and several other smaller packages of Linux. Some have features specialized for certain applications, such as real-time processing. Some book publishers include limited versions of the various versions of Linux as part of their publications.

There are now a number of companies that make commercial software packages for Linux, including word processors, office suites, firewalls—even WordPerfect is available for Linux. While there are number of people developing Linux, there has been an informal grouping of developers and sharing of ideas that has kept much of the Linux code uniform. Part of the uniformity is due to ELF (Extended Library Format), which allows developers to develop software with different specifications and table sizes and still be compatible. This was actually introduced with UNIX System V release 4, and has been adopted by a number of UNIX manufacturers to make software development easier across various product lines.

SOLARIS X86

Sun Microsystems Corporation (SMC) has developed and modified its version of Solaris so that it is source-code compatible across three microprocessor architectures: SUN Sparc, x86 and the PowerPC. This means that a developer can write code for multiple architectures and, with a simple recompile and perhaps a few hardware-specific libraries, quickly come out with a new version of a software product. Many manufacturers are writing programs for the x86 Solaris. It is possible to get an education or personal version of Solaris x86 for free except for shipping and handling. An annual service contract for Solaris with full 7x24 hr. software support can cost about the price of an Windows NT server software package.

OTHERS

Other manufacturers have also developed versions of UNIX. But the products outlined here are considered the most popular or most useful. They also probably have the best future for users running x86. The market does, however, change very quickly. So stay tuned.

APPENDIX G

MULTI-BOOT PC UNIX/DOS/LINUX SYSTEMS

 When installing a PC-based OS, one of the toughest decisions to make is whether to spend the money on a separate box or expand the current PC to handle both the current and the new OS. Fortunately, or unfortunately, we have many choices in how to do it.   *—Joe*

One of the advantages of running UNIX on a PC is that you have the ability to run multiple operating systems (OSs). Sometimes you need to reboot between the various OSs, whereas some of them run together with others. The software that controls the choice of OSs from which to boot is called the `boot manager`.

If you are going to install a boot manager, it is best to understand how it works. There are several How-Tos on the Internet and Linux documentation which discuss the boot manager, LILO, and other relevant concepts. As with any adventure you take with the PC, you must be sure to back up everything before you install any boot manager. Some boot managers do unpredictable things to your PC.

 Microsoft OSs want to be the only OSs on your PC. They can often wipe out other boot managers or boot sectors unless you take special precautions. The best precaution is to install any Microsoft OS first. Then you can install other OSs or boot managers and configure the boot manager accordingly to handle all the various OSs.

The basic idea of a boot manager is that, on your boot disk, you have a Master Boot Record. In addition, each partition on your disk can have its own boot record. Therefore, you can have a boot manager on your disk that can point to multiple boot records, each of which can boot a different OS. Look at Figure G.1 to get a simplified idea of how the disks can be laid out.

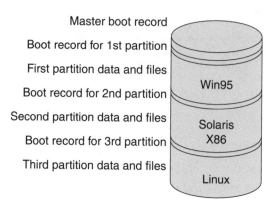

Master boot record
Boot record for 1st partition
First partition data and files
Boot record for 2nd partition
Second partition data and files
Boot record for 3rd partition
Third partition data and files

Win95

Solaris
X86

Linux

Figure G.1 ■ A Simplified View of a Boot Disk Layout for Booting Multiple OSs

Some boot managers on the master boot record on your disk can coexist with other boot managers. Some of your boot manager choices are listed in the following sections.

OS/2

OS/2 is sold by IBM, and was actually the first version of Windows/NT. Microsoft and IBM had a parting of ways in the early 1990s, but there are still some applications that will run both in NT and OS/2 mode. The OS/2 boot manager has been highly rated by many users, because it does not interfere with other OSs that might be installed on the PC. It has a very configurable user interface and supports Linux, NT, Win95, OS/2, Windows and DOS. You should install OS/2 after Microsoft products. Fortunately, the OS/2 boot manager sometimes just requires a simple reconfiguration if you install it first.

NT

NT has a multiple boot capability. Again, it wants to be the primary OS, so you must adhere to some precautions. It is not totally destructive if you are careful.

WIN95/98

Win95 is the worst culprit of all the Microsoft products. It will wipe out other boot managers and is totally destructive. It will work if you reinstall the boot manager after installing Win95, but an OS install may sometimes be necessary. Win95 does have a boot manager, but it is not easy to set up and is not multi-OS friendly.

SOLARIS X86

Solaris x86 will install nicely on a PC that already has an OS on it. It automatically detects the other OS and builds a table with all the OSs on your PC into a menu. It couldn't be easier.

LINUX

Linux has a boot manager called LILO, which will detect other OSs on your PC. The newer releases of Linux support the NT file system, NTFS, the OS2 file system, HPFS, and the FAT 32 filesystem used in the OEM version of Win95, which supports filesystems greater than 2 GB.

 Note that it is not currently possible to run both Solaris x86 and Linux using LILO alone. This is because the Solaris x86 filesystem partition type and the Linux swap partition file type use the same filesystem type number. Both Solaris and Linux can get confused by this.

SYSTEM COMMANDER

This is a commercial boot manager that can support many OSs on the same PC. It is easy to reinstall if the boot manager should get corrupted. It is perhaps the most robust of the boot managers, because much research time and expense has been spent on making it work on multiple OSs. The cost of the software is almost the same as buying a full-blown PC OS, but if you experiment with PCs a lot, it could pay for itself by reducing your level of frustration. There are currently two versions of System Commander. The standard version will allow you to set up over 100 OSs on your PC and boot from any one of them.

The Deluxe version also has the ability to resize partitions on your PC. You can reduce or increase the amount of disk space used by your system. If you reduce the size of a partition, you can then add additional partitions. If you increase the size of a partition, you can then store more information on the disk. This can be done without copying the files to another disk or tape.

OTHERS

There are other multi-boot software packages. The market moves quickly, so you may know of others that will work well.

APPENDIX H

SCSI INTERFACES

SCSI stands for Small Computer System Interface. It has been very popular with UNIX systems since the early 80s. SCSI devices and controllers are more expensive than IDE/EIDE devices, because the SCSI devices have more intelligence built into their hard drives. SCSI devices also handle data on a block-by-block basis, whereas IDE devices handle data on a byte-by-byte basis. IDE controllers must also keep track of addresses where data is stored, whereas the SCSI drives keep much more of the information on board. SCSI drives usually cost at least $75 more then IDE drives. In addition, good SCSI controllers cost at least $100 more than IDE controllers. However, if you are concerned about performance, you need to use SCSI devices.

There have been a number of variations and extensions of SCSI, most of which are compatible with each other. Some of them are:

- SCSI I
- SCSI II
- Fast SCSI II
- Fast-Wide SCSI II
- Ultra SCSI
- SCSI III

As you move down this list, the drives and the bus because faster and more expensive. There are other variants of SCSI that are compatible with those on this list. In addition, there is differential SCSI, which allows two computers to share a SCSI bus. There are also variations that manufacturers such as Seagate did with the ST01 and ST02 drives, which are not standard SCSI. Some CD-ROM manufacturers have modified SCSI controllers to run only their own design of CD-ROM devices. You must realize this when installing SCSI devices that you may have found lying around. If they are older devices, they might need a special controller card.

SCSI uses at least two numbering schemes to identify different cards and devices. The first numbering scheme involves the SCSI id. This number runs from 0 to 7. The controller card should always be set to SCSI id 7. Any other SCSI devices will be assigned numbers 0 through 6. The second numbering scheme is Logical Unit Number (LUN). Each SCSI controller card is assigned a LUN so that it can be distinguished from another SCSI card. The first SCSI card is LUN 0, the second is LUN 1, and so forth. In addition, there are sometimes additional numbering schemes that are used with the SCSI addressing to distinguish multiple devices attached to a single SCSI controller.

The SCSI controller will scan one SCSI id at a time on bootup to determine the device's characteristics. It will start probing ids at SCSI id 0 and go up the sequence to SCSI id 6. (It already knows that SCSI id 7 works). It is sometimes possible, and often recommended, that your SCSI devices be set to startup only when probed. This prevents a power shock to the system of all the SCSI devices starting up at once. Your disk drive documentation can tell you whether this is possible, and how to do it.

Some versions of UNIX like particular devices at certain SCSI id numbers. Solaris likes the CD-ROM at SCSI id 6. When doing an install, the system often tries to install the OS on the disk drive with SCSI id 0. It is usually better to have the faster devices at the lower SCSI id numbers because of the way id numbers are scanned. While these are not hard and fast requirements, it is generally a good practice to set up devices at certain addresses. (During that 3:00 a.m. system rebuild, you really don't want to think about where your devices are.)

The following is a suggested rule of thumb for assigning SCSI ids.

SCSI ID	Device
0	Boot Hard Disk
1	Hard Disk
2	Hard Disk
3	Hard Disk
4	Hard Disk or Tape Drive
5	Hard Disk, Tape Drive, or Secondary CD-ROM
6	Primary CD-ROM
7	SCSI controller—default value which is automatically set

While most of the manufacturers follow the same convention as to the order of the SCSI id probing, some manufacturers, such as Future Domain, will start probing with SCSI id 7, then 6, 5 … You may have to rethink your ordering of devices. In this case, if you are interested in the best performance, you should contact the manufacturer of the SCSI controller and device for more details.

INDEX

Learn Through Doing! It's Fast, Fun, and Easy!

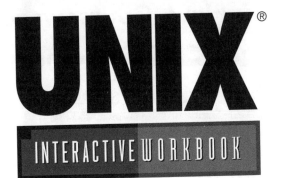

UNIX®

INTERACTIVE WORKBOOK

S E R I E S

Each title includes a FREE web-based companion training module that features:

▶ A home page that contains links to all of the other training modules in the series.

▶ A *Message Board* where authors and students can interact informally.

▶ Interactive questions and answers available.

▶ *Author's Corner* for updates, new information, etc.

▶ A feedback section for students to help shape the future of the series.

UNIX User's Interactive Workbook

JOHN McMULLEN

1999, 624PP, PAPER, 0-13-099820-6

A quick, friendly, hands-on tutorial on using UNIX. This interactive workbook covers everything UNIX users need to know to get productive fast! For everyone who needs to learn the basics of using UNIX.

UNIX Awk And Sed Programmer's Interactive Workbook

PETER PATSIS

1999, 500PP, PAPER, 0-13-082675-8

Learn how to solve practical problems with awk, sed and grep. Begin with a hands-on introduction to regular expressions and grep. Through interactive Labs, learn the fundamentals of sed, including addressing, commands, scripting and much more.

UNIX System Administrator's Interactive Workbook

JOSEPH KAPLENK

1999, 640PP, PAPER, 0-13-081308-7

BOOK WITH CD-ROM

This interactive workbook focuses on helping users develop the "thinking skills" and understanding that UNIX system administrators need. Includes CBT Systems UNIX System Administration training module on CD-ROM!

UNIX Shell Programmer's Interactive Workbook

CHRISTOPHER VICKERY

1999, 496PP, PAPER, 0-13-020064-6

BOOK WITH CD-ROM

Includes CBT Systems UNIX training module on CD-ROM! This interactive workbook is for UNIX and NT users and sysadmins who are new to UNIX shell programming and looking for ways to automate as many tasks as possible. Learn how to customize the command line; build basic scripts; execute internal and external commands; use token splitting and much more.

UNIX Web Server Administrator's Interactive Workbook

JIM MOHR

1999, 624PP, PAPER, 0-13-020065-4

BOOK WITH CD-ROM

This is soup-to-nuts Apache coverage — all of it hands-on and interactive! Learn how to compile, modify, install and configure Apache. Discover how to develop and organize a site, implement searching and indexing, extend HTML with graphics, image maps, frames and tables; and secure a system with firewalls. Includes OpenLinux™ Lite with Apache on CD-ROM.

VISIT US TODAY AT:

PRENTICE HALL PTR ™

interactive

We make it click.

www.phptr.com/phptrinteractive

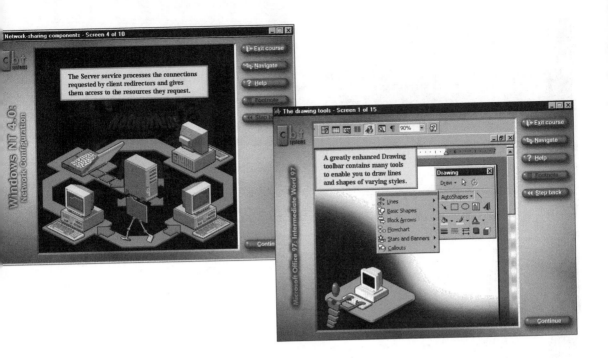

Other curricula available from CBT Systems:

- Cisco
- Informix
- Java
- Marimba
- Microsoft
- Netscape
- Novell

- Oracle
- SAP
- Sybase
- C/C++
- Centura
- Information Technology/
  Core Concepts

- Internet and Intranet
  Skills
- Internetworking
- UNIX

CBT SOFTWARE LICENSE AGREEMENT

IF YOU DO NOT AGREE WITH THESE TERMS AND CONDITIONS, DO NOT INSTALL THE SOFTWARE.

This is a legal agreement between you and CBT Systems Ltd. ("Licensor"), the licensor ("Licensor") from whom you have licensed the CBT Group PLC courseware (the "Software"). By installing, copying or otherwise using the Software, you agree to be bound by the terms of this License Agreement (the "License"). If you do not agree to the terms of this License, the Licensor is unwilling to license the Software to you. In such event, you may not use or copy the Software, and you should promptly contact the Licensor for instructions on the return of the unused Software.

1. **Use.** Licensor grants to you a non-exclusive, nontransferable license to use Licensor's software product (the "Software") and accompanying documentation in accordance with the terms and conditions of this license agreement ("License") License and as specified in your agreement with Licensor (the "Governing Agreement"). In the event of any conflict between this License and the Governing Agreement, the Governing Agreement shall control.

You may:

a. (if specified as a "personal use" version) install the Software on a single stand-alone computer or a single network node from which node the Software cannot be accessed by another computer, provided that such Software shall be used by only one individual; or

b. (if specified as a "workstation" version) install the Software on a single stand-alone computer or network node from which node the Software cannot be accessed by another computer, provided that such Software shall be used only by employees of your organization; or

c. (if specified as a "LAN" version) install the Software on a local area network server that provides access to multiple computers, up to the maximum number of computers or users specified in your Governing Agreement, provided that such Software shall be used only by employees of your organization; or

d. (if specified as an "enterprise" version) install the Software or copies of the Software on multiple local or wide area network servers, intranet servers, stand-alone computers and network nodes (and to make copies of the Software for such purpose) at one or more sites, which servers provide access to a multiple number of users, up to the maximum number of users specified in your Governing Agreement, provided that such Software shall be used only by employees of your organization.

This License is not a sale. Title and copyrights to the Software, accompanying documentation and any copy made by you remain with Licensor or its suppliers or licensors.

2. **Intellectual Property**. The Software is owned by Licensor or its licensors and is protected by United States and other jurisdictions' copyright laws and international treaty provisions. Therefore, you may not use, copy, or distribute the Software without the express written authorization of CBT Group PLC. This License authorizes you to use the Software for the internal training needs of your employees only, and to make one copy of the Software solely for backup or archival purposes. You may not print copies of any user documentation provided in "online" or electronic form. Licensor retains all rights not expressly granted.

3. **Restrictions**. You may not transfer, rent, lease, loan or time-share the Software or accompanying documentation. You may not reverse engineer, decompile, or disassemble the Software, except to the extent the foregoing restriction is expressly prohibited by applicable law. You may not modify, or create derivative works based upon the Software in whole or in part.

1. **Confidentiality**. The Software contains confidential trade secret information belonging to Licensor, and you may use the software only pursuant to the terms of your Governing Agreement, if any, and the license set forth herein. In addition, you may not disclose the Software to any third party.

2. **Limited Liability**. IN NO EVENT WILL THE LICENSOR'S LIABILITY UNDER, ARISING OUT OF OR RELATING TO THIS AGREEMENT EXCEED THE AMOUNT PAID TO LICENSOR FOR THE SOFTWARE. LICENSOR SHALL NOT BE LIABLE FOR ANY SPECIAL, INCIDENTAL, INDIRECT OR CONSEQUENTIAL DAMAGES, HOWEVER CAUSED AND ON ANY THEORY OF LIABILITY, REGARDLESS OF WHETHER LICENSOR HAS BEEN ADVISED OF THE POSSIBILITY OF SUCH DAMAGES. WITHOUT LIMITING THE FOREGOING, LICENSOR WILL NOT BE LIABLE FOR LOST PROFITS, LOSS OF DATA, OR COSTS OF COVER.

3. **Limited Warranty**. LICENSOR WARRANTS THAT SOFTWARE WILL BE FREE FROM DEFECTS IN MATERIALS AND WORKMANSHIP UNDER NORMAL USE FOR A PERIOD OF THIRTY (30) DAYS FROM THE DATE OF RECEIPT. THIS LIMITED WARRANTY IS VOID IF FAILURE OF THE SOFTWARE HAS RESULTED FROM ABUSE OR MISAPPLICATION. ANY REPLACEMENT SOFTWARE WILL BE WARRANTED FOR A PERIOD OF THIRTY (30) DAYS FROM THE DATE OF RECEIPT OF SUCH REPLACEMENT SOFTWARE. THE SOFTWARE AND DOCUMENTATION ARE PROVIDED "AS IS". LICENSOR HEREBY DISCLAIMS ALL OTHER WARRANTIES, EXPRESS, IMPLIED, OR STATUTORY, INCLUDING WITHOUT LIMITATION, THE IMPLIED WARRANTIES OF MERCHANTABILITY AND FITNESS FOR A PARTICULAR PURPOSE.

4. **Exceptions**. SOME STATES DO NOT ALLOW THE LIMITATION OF INCIDENTAL DAMAGES OR LIMITATIONS ON HOW LONG AN IMPLIED WARRANTY LASTS, SO THE ABOVE LIMITATIONS OR EXCLUSIONS MAY NOT APPLY TO YOU. This agreement gives you specific legal rights, and you may also have other rights which vary from state to state.

5. **U.S. Government-Restricted Rights**. The Software and accompanying documentation are deemed to be "commercial computer Software" and "commercial computer Software documentation," respectively, pursuant to DFAR Section 227.7202 and FAR Section 12.212, as applicable. Any use, modification, reproduction release, performance, display or disclosure of the Software and accompanying documentation by the U.S. Government shall be governed solely by the terms of this Agreement and shall be prohibited except to the extent expressly permitted by the terms of this Agreement.

6. **Export Restrictions**. You may not download, export, or re-export the Software (a) into, or to a national or resident of, Cuba, Iraq, Libya, Yugoslavia, North Korea, Iran, Syria or any other country to which the United States has embargoed goods, or (b) to anyone on the United States Treasury Department's list of Specially Designated Nationals or the U.S. Commerce Department's Table of Deny Orders. By installing or using the Software, you are representing and warranting that you are not located in, under the control of, or a national or resident of any such country or on any such list.

7. **General**. This License is governed by the laws of the United States and the State of California, without reference to conflict of laws principles. The parties agree that the United Nations Convention on Contracts for the International Sale of Goods shall not apply to this License. If any provision of this Agreement is held invalid, the remainder of this License shall continue in full force and effect.

8. **More Information**. Should you have any questions concerning this Agreement, or if you desire to contact Licensor for any reason, please contact: CBT Systems USA Ltd., 1005 Hamilton Court, Menlo Park, California 94025, Attn: Chief Legal Officer.

IF YOU DO NOT AGREE WITH THE ABOVE TERMS AND CONDITIONS, DO NOT INSTALL THE SOFTWARE AND RETURN IT TO THE LICENSOR.

ABOUT THE CD

The CD enclosed contains the following computer-based training (CBT) course module:

Solaris 2.5.1 System Administration: System Configuration

For information on installing, at the Start menu select Run... and type in D:/readme.txt.

If you have a problem with the CBT software, please contact CBT Technical Support. In the US call 1 (800) 938-3247. If you are outside the US call 3531-283-0380.

This CD will run on Windows NT/95 (Windows 98 is currently not supported).

Technical Support

Prentice Hall does not offer technical support for this software. However, if there is a problem with the media, you may obtain a replacement copy by e-mailing us with your problem at: disc_exchange@prenhall.com